IDEAS, INSTITUTIONS, AND INTERESTS

The Drivers of Canadian Provincial Science, Technology, and Innovation Policy

Edited by Peter W.B. Phillips and David Castle

Canada's thirteen provinces and territories are significant actors in Canadian society, directly shaping cultural, political, and economic domains. Regions also play a key role in creating diversity within innovative activity. The role of provinces and territories in setting science, technology, and innovation policy is, however, notably underexplored.

Ideas, Institutions, and Interests examines each province and territory to offer real-world insights into the complexity and opportunities of regionally differentiated innovation policy in a pan-continental system. Contributing scholars detail the distinctive ways in which provinces and territories articulate ideas and interests through their institutions, programs, and policies. Many of the contributing authors have engaged first-hand with either micro- or macro-level policy innovation and are innovation leaders in their own right, providing invaluable perspectives on the topic. Exploring the vital role of provinces in the last thirty years of science, technology, and innovation policy development and implementation, *Ideas, Institutions, and Interests* is an insightful book that places innovation policy in the context of multilevel governance.

PETER W.B. PHILLIPS is a distinguished professor at the Johnson Shoyama Graduate School of Public Policy at the University of Saskatchewan.

DAVID CASTLE is a professor in the School of Public Administration and Gustavson School of Business at the University of Victoria.

Ideas, Institutions, and Interests

The Drivers of Canadian Provincial Science, Technology, and Innovation Policy

EDITED BY PETER W.B. PHILLIPS
AND DAVID CASTLE

UNIVERSITY OF TORONTO PRESS
Toronto Buffalo London

© University of Toronto Press 2022
Toronto Buffalo London
utorontopress.com
Printed and bound by CPI Group (UK) Ltd, Croydon, CR0 4YY

ISBN 978-1-4875-0676-6 (cloth)   ISBN 978-1-4875-3481-3 (EPUB)
ISBN 978-1-4875-2454-8 (paper)   ISBN 978-1-4875-3480-6 (PDF)

Library and Archives Canada Cataloguing in Publication

Title: Ideas, institutions, and interests : the drivers of Canadian provincial
    science, technology, and innovation policy / edited by Peter W.B. Phillips
    and David Castle.
Names: Phillips, Peter W. B., editor. | Castle, David, 1967– editor.
Description: Includes bibliographical references and index.
Identifiers: Canadiana (print) 20210379227 | Canadiana (ebook) 20210379332 |
    ISBN 9781487506766 (cloth) | ISBN 9781487524548 (paper) |
    ISBN 9781487534813 (EPUB) | ISBN 9781487534806 (PDF)
Subjects: LCSH: Technological innovations – Government policy – Canada –
    Provinces. | LCSH: Technology and state – Canada – Provinces. |
    LCSH: Science and state – Canada – Provinces.
Classification: LCC HC120.T4 I34 2022 | DDC 338.971/06 – dc23

We wish to acknowledge the land on which the University of Toronto Press
operates. This land is the traditional territory of the Wendat, the Anishnaabeg,
the Haudenosaunee, the Métis, and the Mississaugas of the Credit First
Nation.

University of Toronto Press acknowledges the financial support of the
Government of Canada, the Canada Council for the Arts, and the Ontario Arts
Council, an agency of the Government of Ontario, for its publishing activities.

Canada Council   Conseil des Arts
for the Arts   du Canada

ONTARIO ARTS COUNCIL
CONSEIL DES ARTS DE L'ONTARIO
an Ontario government agency
un organisme du gouvernement de l'Ontario

Funded by the   Financé par le
Government   gouvernement | Canada
of Canada   du Canada

Contents

Acknowledgments

This book is a passion project that allowed us to merge our deep interest in innovation and policy to produce a work that we believe fills an important gap in our policy literature – namely, the role of provinces and territories in motivating and delivering science, technology, and innovation policy in Canada.

We would like to thank all of our co-authors for joining us in this venture. Their enthusiastic engagement with this project was critical. The diversity and insights from this work are due in large measure to their support and guidance.

The three anonymous peer reviewers organized by the University of Toronto Press provided excellent and detailed suggestions on how we could improve our work. We took all their advice that fit within the intent of this work.

We would also like to thank the University of Toronto Press, especially Stephen Jones, acquisitions editor for science and technology, and Barry Norris, our freelance copy editor. They both made this book possible and ensured it was a strong contribution to the field.

We would like to acknowledge a range of funders. Much of the primary research that grounds this work was financed by a host of funders, including the Social Sciences and Humanities Research Council, Genome Canada, and the Global Institute for Food Security. We would especially like to acknowledge and thank the Bev Robertson family and its generous financial support of the Johnson Shoyama Graduate School of Public Policy. The Robertson Endowment Fund provided assistance for our workshop in Banff, Alberta, in August 2019. Bev, who died in 2018, would have enjoyed the conversation at that meeting.

Aaron Hertes and Canute Rosaasen provided essential support as data collectors and scribes at our Banff workshop and as assistants in gathering the evidence we used to support the introductory chapters.

Canute was instrumental in pulling the final draft together in a consistent format.

Finally, we need to recognize Bethany Penn, Strategic Research Officer with the Centre for the Study of Science and Innovation Policy, who kept this project on the move when our energies lagged and attention wandered.

Peter W.B. Phillips
Saskatoon

David Castle
Victoria

IDEAS, INSTITUTIONS, AND INTERESTS

IDEAS, INSTITUTIONS, AND INTERESTS

PART I

The Policy Challenge

1 Introduction to Innovation Policy in Canada

PETER W.B. PHILLIPS AND DAVID CASTLE

Why This Book?

Science, technology, and innovation have been drivers of development and growth around the world for much of the post-war era. Despite impressive outcomes in terms of growth and development (Gordon 2017; Radelet 2015), there is extensive debate everywhere about the best way to encourage and manage the processes of change, and reminders that the "idea of material progress is a very recent one" (Wright 2004).

Canada is part of the global movement that seeks wealth and prosperity from science-, technology-, and innovation-driven economic growth. Although Canada is now among the top rich industrial democracies, its roots as a colony of the British Empire resonate through its history. Aspects of the scientific revolution, the development of constitutional governance, and the first and second industrial revolutions in Britain between the late 1600s through the mid-1800s worked to transform the economic and social condition of Britain and its imperial subjects. This set of ideas and practices diffused widely within and beyond the Empire, at various times and speeds. Canada came relatively late to the party, having pursued, since first European contact, a strategy of nation building (Savoie 1987, 2003). While this effort involved developing and adapting both local and global innovations, the focus was primarily on exploiting the vast natural resources of British North America through the application of immigrant labour and foreign capital. In a quintessential Canadian way, we landed on the notion of "innovation if necessary, but not necessarily innovation."

Nevertheless, Canada is now fully on the global innovation bandwagon. One benchmark of this transition is tracking the number of citations and references to "innovation," in all its guises, on the World Wide Web. A Web search in late 2019 showed that the discussion about innovation that was launched in early writings by Adam Smith, Alfred Marshall, and Joseph Schumpeter entered common parlance only after 1970, and since its use has grown logarithmically to the point that, in the past decade, most governments, the business press, and many firms now define themselves in the context of this term, albeit in widely diverse and not always compatible ways. An unsophisticated search of the Web shows that Canada was there at the beginning in the 1970s, contributing moderately to early global usage, but then interest fell off to the point that Canada's engagement with the concept was little more than a rounding error in global terms between 1990 and the late 2000s; the concept regained traction during the 2010s, with Canadian-based references to innovation representing more than three times the country's share of the global economy or society. This tells us two things about Canada's place in the world: it does not always follow global trends, and, even when it is engaged, it is a small part of a much bigger story.

This book offers a scan of the uptake and use of the innovation narrative in Canadian policy, particularly at the provincial and territorial levels. This is not the first treatment of Canada's engagement with innovation, but it differs materially from all the other work we can find. The bulk of the existing work focuses on state-level, macro innovation policy in Canada. Many authors of chapters in this book have contributed elsewhere to that macro effort, with a generous nod to the enduring notion of nation building and Canada's place among global innovation leaders. The other dominant perspective is micro-level examinations of the sectors and communities where specific waves of innovation emerge, mostly within sectors or in major cities (Bradford and Bramwell 2014; Grant 2014). Both are important perspectives, but in almost every case the existing literature ignores the role of provinces and territories. This book is designed to fill that gap and bridge the macro and micro perspectives. While we anchor on existing literature on the national and local innovation effort, we have designed this work to explore explicitly the role that provincial and territorial governments play in defining and motivating innovation.

The role of provinces and territories in setting science, technology, and innovation policy is notably underexplored in the literature, even though their vital role and proximity to the impact of their policies are widely recognized. This is a widespread issue: there are twenty-seven federal states in the world, including Canada. Although the academic and policy literature acknowledges the role of regional innovation systems, and recognizes the presence of subnational governments in this policy area, there is little detailed work on their role and impact on the development and use of science, technology, and innovation (e.g. Australia 2017; CCA 2017; Shapira and Youtie 2010; Wessner and Wolff 2012). Why this should be is up for speculation; our task is to document the underlying dynamics of the role and impact of provinces and territories in Canada's innovation system. The basic contours of this analysis are well known: constitutionally and practically, provinces and territories have broad authority in Canadian Confederation. As with most things in the Constitution, however, there are limits to the so-called watertight compartments implied by the division of powers. For example, the general assignment of "peace, order and good government" to the federal government, section 121 establishing the free movement of goods within and between provinces, and the informal spending power have all worked to lever some of what look like provincial powers into federal hands.

Nevertheless, provinces and territories do have important powers. By constitutional authority, provinces define and motivate the municipalities where firms and the primary, secondary, and higher education sectors operate. Place matters a lot for innovation. Municipalities are where the bulk of the effort happens, both in Canada and in most advanced industrial economies. Also by constitutional design, the provinces control all Crown lands and all matters of a local or private nature, which embraces most private law related to transactions and virtually all commercial transactions. A number of key foundational powers that affect private matters remain with the federal government: bankruptcy and insolvency, weights and measures, intellectual property rights, and privacy legislation, among others. Land, labour, and capital are essentially the domain of provinces to manage. Provinces and territories also work with Innovation, Science and Economic Development Canada and various line departments and agencies to define, target, implement, and evaluate federal-provincial programming aligned with provincial interests. While much of the Canadian effort supporting science, technology, and innovation is grounded on federal granting programs and tax incentives, most provinces and territories have a distinct and sometimes discrete layer of inwardly focused research efforts, delivered through special provincial research organizations, universities, provincial intramural research, or contracts with industry.

Provinces and territories are indisputable actors in Canadian society, shaping regional cultural, political, and economic domains. They play a key role in creating diversity in Canadian innovation policy, the types of innovative activity present or planned, and the nature and distribution of the effort and effects of innovation policy. It is inconceivable that one could hope to understand the design, structure, and performance

of Canada's science and innovation system without appreciation for
the role of provinces and territories.

Previous Work

So numerous are the studies of Canada's national innovation performance that the nationally prominent journalist Jeffrey Simpson wryly
observed that, in Canada, rather than getting on with the business of
innovation with urgency, "we write reports" (Simpson 2009). He had
a point: there is a multidecadal surfeit of work on Canada's national
policy context and economic performance. Much of the output from the
federal government and, as we will show, from the provinces and territories has been more aspirational than analytical, as various configu-
rations of economic ministries and related agencies issue assessments
and plans for action. Evaluation of the measures undertaken is seldom
done, and any results have had limited impact on program management. Beyond executive government, a number of especially empowered, generally arm's-length entities have been commissioned to review
the economy and advise on remedial action. Early foundational work
was done by the Economic Council of Canada (ECC) and the Science
Council of Canada (SCC), created in 1963 and 1966, respectively. Most
important, the Senate Special Committee on Science Policy chaired by
Senator Maurice Lamontagne (1967–70) helped define the structure of
the policy debate and the management of the policy file in Canada,
dividing it between executive government and the advisory sector. One
possible reason for Canada's somewhat delayed uptake of the innovation agenda was that both the ECC and SCC were disbanded by the
Mulroney government in the early 1990s just as innovation policy was
starting to gain traction globally (Kinder and Dufour 2018).

Beginning in the late 1980s, the federal government used a cascading
set of more narrowly mandated advisory groups, such as the National
Biotechnology Advisory Council (1983–98), the National Round Table
on the Environment and the Economy (1987–2013), the Council of
Science and Technology Advisors (1998–2007), the Canadian Biotechnology Advisory Council (1999–2007), the Science, Technology and
Innovation Council (2007–15), and a range of time-limited expert pan-
els, such as the Independent Panel on Federal Support to Research and
Development (the "Jenkins Report") and the National Advisory Council
on Research and Innovation (the "Naylor Report"). In 2005, the federal
government created the Canadian Council of the Academies (CCA),
which has produced more than fifty assessments, many of which consider aspects of the federal science, technology, and innovation system,

and six provide assessments of Canada's performance (see especially CCA 2006, 2009, 2013a, 2013b, 2013c, 2015, 2017, 2018, 2019). Almost all of these efforts acknowledge that provinces and territories exist and are part of the system, but few see provinces and territories as instigators in their own right of science, technology, and innovation policy; most see them simply as silent (sometimes not so silent) partners. The exception was the Council of Canadian Academies report on *Science Policy: Considerations for Subnational Governments* (CCA 2017), commissioned by the Alberta government, which directly investigated the role of provinces in the national science system. Even this report tended to focus on the fit between provincial efforts and national objectives, rather than explore the heterogeneity of objectives, structures, practices, and performance in the provinces themselves.

Outside government, scholars and policy think tanks have also focused mostly on the national level. The series of reports on science, technology, and innovation policy in the annual book series *How Ottawa Spends* are by design focused on federal outlays (e.g. Castle and Phillips 2011; de la Mothe 2000, 2003; Phillips and Castle 2010, 2012, 2013, 2016; Phillips et al. 2017), while a range of discrete works have explored the structure, function, and performance of the system as a whole (e.g. Britton and Gilmour 1978; Brassard 1996; Doern, Phillips, and Castle 2016; Dufour and Gingras 1988; Hawkins 2012; Niosi 2000). As for output and outcome evaluations, there has been a range of reports from the auditor general, while organizations such as the Conference Board of Canada produce evaluation scorecards that rank provinces, albeit using relatively simple proxies for what are undoubtedly complex features of the innovation system.

A second stream of literature looks at the science, technology, and innovation activities of certain federal institutions such as the National Research Council (NRC) (Doern and Levesque 2002), regulatory science and scientists (Doern and Reed 2001; Leiss 2000), federal labs (Kinder 2010), granting agencies and programs such as the National Centres of Excellence (Atkinson-Grosjean 2006; Salazar and Holbrook 2007; Veletanlić and Sá 2020), big science projects (Fortin and Currie 2013), and special operating agencies such as Genome Canada (Lemay 2020; Sharma 2013; Zhang 2014); and AECL (Bothwell 1988).

A third stream, which gets closest to the provincial area, is the focus on higher education. Given that Canada relies on the higher education sector to perform research and development more than do most other member countries of the Organisation for Economic Co-operation and Development, there has been significant effort to explore the sector and its impact (e.g. Beach, Boadway, and McInnis 2005; MacKinnon 2014).

One aspect that has garnered specific attention is the effort of universities to translate their advances and inventions into use, specifically through technology transfer offices (Bubela and Caulfield 2010; Doern and Stoney 2009; Madgett and Stoney 2009).

A complementary literature explores sectoral strategies and efforts, focusing less on government and more on the vertical and horizontal relationships that drive innovation within a specific technology (e.g. agricultural biotechnology, such as in Phillips and Khatchatourians 2001), sector (e.g. Hayter and Clapp 2020), or innovation ecosystem (e.g. Milley, Szijarto, and Bennett 2020; Tamtik 2018a, 2018b; Wolfe 2018). Much of this work has been done by social scientists and humanists in collaboration with or embedded in specific scientific or technical projects. This approach was required as 3–5 per cent of the budget of the Human Genome Project was directed to the study of Ethical, Legal and Social Aspects or Issues (ELSA, ESLI) of science, sponsored by the US Department of Energy. Canada has its own special take on this. Since its beginning in February 2000, Genome Canada has mandated that all programs and, increasingly, all projects include a Genomics, Ethics, Environmental, Economic, Legal or Social (GE³LS) investigation (Doern and Prince 2012; Migone and Howlett 2009; Phillips et al. 2012). At times this work narrows down to exploring efforts within and around a single innovative firm, such as Bombardier (MacDonald 2001).

Last, but far from least, a wide-ranging effort, at times supported by various federal departments and granting agencies, has looked at cities and other localized innovation spaces. A series of grants from NRC and the Social Sciences and Humanities Research Council (SSHRC) has supported more than twenty years of exploration by a large national team, led from the University of Toronto, that has explored clusters, innovation systems, creative communities, and the impact of digital technologies on the innovation and industrial architecture of Canada's many subprovincial regions (Bradford and Bramwell 2014; Grant 2014; Holbrook and Wolfe 2003, 2002; Wolfe 2014; Wolfe and Gertler 2016; Wolfe and Lucas 2004, 2005). Other scholars have taken up the challenge to explore local and regional dynamics in Canada (de la Mothe and Paquet 1998; Niosi 2005). Even though these explorations have all been embedded directly in provinces, they seldom have done much to assess the impact of the government of the host province. There has also been some work on the role of cities in the multilevel governance of innovation policy, but once again with provinces in the shadows (Galvin 2019).

While others have acknowledged that provinces and territories have important powers and are critical actors, the literature generally has circled around the roles of provinces and territories but failed to land on them as influential. It would be unfair to say that no one has thought about provinces and territories in this context. Conteh (2019) offers an exploration of the multilevel governance challenges in the context of Ontario's innovation process. Phillips and Khatchatourians (2001), Bouchard (2013), and Chiappetta (2020) instead focus explicitly on the provincial level, exploring Saskatchewan's bioscience cluster, Quebec's emerging social economy, and Ontario's pharmaceutical innovation ecosystem, respectively. Hall and Vodden (2019) explore learning, knowledge flows, and innovation ecosystems in British Columbia, Ontario, Quebec, and Newfoundland and Labrador. For the most part, however, the topic is underexplored, especially in any comprehensive way that allows for comparisons about the respective roles and contributions of provincial and territorial governments. In effect, the field of Canadian science, technology, and innovation policy is theory rich, informed with a range of methodological applications (see Phillips et al. 2012), and provides contextualized analyses of the national system and its component parts and local and regional adaptations, but not much at all specifically on the role and impact of provinces and territories. Our coast-to-coast-to-coast effort is designed to fill that gap.

Our Approach

This book is a work of political economy. In contrast to the economics of innovation, where incentives drive outcomes, with ideas and institutions often assumed away or held constant, we believe the only way to understand fully the broad and diffuse policy effort in the science, technology, and innovation space is to engage with all the fundamental drivers of the political economy. By that we mean that this book and each chapter in it explores the interplay and balance of ideas, institutions, and interests on the resulting economic and policy systems. To avoid giving one of these three factors primacy over the others or becoming subsumed under another, our approach in this book is to create equipoise between them. The final chapter explores this idea further, probing for insights about how provinces and territories are held back from benefiting from innovation, finding the balance and fruitful interactions between ideas, institutions, and interests difficult to achieve. The winning solution, we suggest, is to land the "trifecta" in which the three factors work synergistically as contextual determinants of innovation.

Quite a few scholars and analysts have landed on the triad of ideas, interests (sometimes labelled actors), and institutions as the drivers and

determinants of policy. Peter Hall offers one of the more cogent expla-
nations of the roots and range of implications of the three approaches,
situating them in the history of policy studies (Hall 1997). Interests are
"the real, material interests of the principal actors, whether conceived
as individuals or as groups." Institutions "are usually organizations
representing key collectives in the economy," including firms, unions,
and the state itself. Ideas are "ideological or cultural factors" that defining meaning. Each of these implies that different variables are part of
the analysis. Depending on the variable given primacy, one can discern
"differing causal propositions."

For our purposes, we take and apply this framing, but with one mod-
ification concerning the order. Most political economists would start
with interests, move to institutions, and then deal with ideas last, as
does Hall. The underlying logic is that self-interested actors will work
to exploit any power system and that institutions are simply the mirror
image of power (Milward 1981). That approach leads to a conclusion
that might is right and ideas are simply *post facto* rationalizations of the
existing distribution of power. Majone (2001) appears mostly to agree,
asserting that ideas do not drive policy, but, rather, are a by-product
and handmaiden of policy. In his take, ideas rationalize activity by providing a conceptual foundation for otherwise discrete and disjointed
decisions, which transforms discrete changes into a sequential game
by making communication among the players possible. By contrast, we
think that order of analysis is inappropriate for policy efforts in science,
technology, and innovation policy. Here, ideas and institutions are less
a reflection of overt interests and power, and more a reflection of the
uncertain paths to gain power and influence. We think John Maynard
Keynes's admonishment at the end of his great masterpiece, *The General
Theory* ([1936] 1973, 383), is absolutely correct:

> The ideas of economists and political philosophers, both when they are
> right and when they are wrong, are more powerful than is commonly
> understood. Indeed the world is ruled by little else. Practical men, who
> believe themselves to be quite exempt from any intellectual influence, are
> usually the slaves of some defunct economist. Madmen in authority, who
> hear voices in the air, are distilling their frenzy from some academic scrib-
> bler of a few years back…the power of vested interests is vastly exaggera-
> ted compared with the gradual encroachment of ideas.

The entirety of this volume explores the development and interplay of
ideas, institutions, and interests as three key contributors to the policy
system.

Rodrik (2014) is a strong advocate for the role of ideas in policy. His take is more transactional than some, but still useful. He asserts our preferences, both private and collective, are formed by ideas about who we are, which determines what we value and want, and about how the world works, which together shape our view about the tools we have at our disposal. In effect, he believes that ideas in the market and in society help the existing order "sidestep constraints." In that sense, policy ideas that work to relax political, social, and economic constraints "can be thought of as the consequence of both idiosyncratic processes and purposive behavior" (Rodrik 2014, 202). One might infer that ideas lubricate action.

Ideas can be either foundational or instrumental. At our core, our worldviews anchor our expectations and focus attention on different units of analysis, different motivations, different problems, and different solutions. Gilpin (1975) suggested three dominant worldviews drive the framing of policy, each of which can be seen in science, technology, and innovation policy somewhere in the world. He posited that realists see the world as a zero-sum competition of states and actors seeking to amass and project their power, such that conflict dominates unless order is secured by some balance of power – imposed by a hegemonic state such as the United States through a duopoly as in the Cold War or via a concert of powers as in Europe in the eighteenth and nineteenth centuries. Mercantilism and beggar-thy-neighbour tactics are go-to measures for those seeing the world this way. The liberal regime (Gilpin's sovereignty-at-bay model) assumes that self-optimizing individuals engage competitively to generate positive-sum outcomes, with the state being more of a problem than a solution. Here we tend to develop rules and processes to narrow the power of the state to intervene – for example, using the logic of public choice theory domestically or human rights and international treaties internationally. Most of the firm-specific strategies for innovation implicitly assume this is the best framing. Gilpin's dystopian model (he called it "dependencia") assumes that either multinational corporations or social groups in society (for example, workers, women, environmentalists) are mobilized to collectively counter imbalances of power that generate negative-sum outcomes; conflict, rebellion, and revolution are the pathways to change. This model is advocated and pursued by many who want to rebalance power to advance new socio-economic priorities. Against this background of diverging worldviews, there is a range of what Stone (1989) calls causal stories that struggle to define the policy agenda. Fischer (2003) asserts politics is simply "a struggle for power played out in significant part through arguments about the 'best story.'"

Moving to institutions, Nobel Prize–winning economist Douglass North provides the classical economically grounded definition. Institutions are

> the humanly devised constraints that structure political, economic and social interaction. They consist of both informal constraints (sanctions, taboos, customs, traditions, and codes of conduct) and formal rules (constitutions, laws, property rights). Throughout history, institutions have been devised by human beings to create order and reduce uncertainty in exchange...they define the choice set and therefore determine transaction and production costs and hence the profitability and feasibility of engaging in economic activity. They evolve incrementally, connecting the past with the present and the future; history in consequence is largely a story of institutional evolution in which the historical performance of economies can only be understood as a part of a sequential story. Institutions provide the incentive structure of an economy; as that structure evolves, it shapes the direction of economic change towards growth, stagnation, or decline. (North 1991, 97)

In our study, we are particularly concerned about exploring the multilevel challenges of governing science, technology, and innovation. As we have already argued, provinces and territories are an integral but far from independent part of the policy system. There are many ways they operate alone or in partnership with cities, with the federal government and its agencies, with other provinces and territories, with industry and universities, and with the international marketplace.

Last, but not least, we are interested in how actors and agents work to optimize their own self-interest. Blyth (2002) asserts that material interests are both rationally grounded and relatively stable over time, such that they are "knowable." Actors and agents are important at two levels. In the first instance, they proactively engage in trying to set the rules of the game in support of their interests. In that sense, they are important drivers of the system. At the same time, actors and agents are influenced and affected by operation of the institutional architecture – they react to the pressures and opportunities of the day.

Effective and enduring policy emerges from some balance and constructive interaction among ideas, institutions, and interests. For government to work effectively, there needs to be some tacit, or preferably explicit, agreement on how the stable allocation of power and authority across institutions will deliver some mix of outcomes that satisfies competing interests in the economy and society.

Our Method

By comparison with other countries around the world, Canada is frequently associated with diversity – from its founding peoples to contemporary multiculturalism, language, culture, geography, economics, and politics. Diversity within the country is also remarkable: the differences between the provinces and territories are what make Canada such an interesting country for study of subnational innovation policy. Perhaps internal borders look like arbitrary lines on a map, but anyone familiar with Confederation knows that each province and territory has a character of its own. There might be institutional and high-level socio-economic unity in the land, but it is manifested through local dynamics that differentially affect subnational science, technology, and innovation policy.

If unity and difference are the hallmarks of the interaction between national and subnational innovation policy in Canada, we needed an approach that would document this richness. Early on, we simply sought to fill a major gap in the literature about subnational innovation policy, but quickly realized that the task felt as vast as the country. More importantly, given our base in two Western provinces, we could not credibly give an on-the-ground account of provincial and territorial innovation coast to coast to coast. Our response was to create the overall structure of the book, to write about the provinces in which we reside and work, and to recruit colleagues from other provinces and territories to contribute their expertise and insight and complete the work.

We also were aware of limits in our analytical approaches. We note that, while there has been an effort to create a discrete field of science and technology studies (STS), innovation policy studies are differentially undertaken by economists, business analysts, and scientists cum policy entrepreneurs. We took to heart advice from the European Union Shape-ID Project (Baptista et al. 2020) to engage a wider array of interdisciplinary researchers. Our team has a mix of social scientists and applied humanists (for example, management and business, economics, geography, history, law, philosophy, political science, sociology, and STS), with backgrounds in science and technology (for example, biology, chemistry, engineering, and information technology) and extensive experience in industry, university management, and federal, provincial, and community governance.

The contributors were asked to set the current context of the economy and relative rates of growth, describe the overall innovation architecture of the province or territory, assess the innovation policy effort, and draw some conclusions about what can or should be done to improve innovation policy. A stipulation was made that the modern era of Canadian federal science, technology, and innovation policy commenced in 1990 with the creation of the federal Ministry of Industry, Science and Technology, renamed since then Industry Canada and now Innovation, Science and Economic Development. References to events and activities prior to 1990 were deemed acceptable if crucial to the narrative, but the intent of the book is to reflect recent provincial and territorial activity.

With those instructions, and a request for an extended outline, a workshop was convened in Banff, Alberta, in August 2019. At the workshop, the plan for the book was discussed, as was an early draft of the chapters setting out the framework of ideas, institutions, and interests. Each provincial and territorial chapter outline was discussed by the group in detail, including options for how best to organize the narrative and what evidence would be most appropriate. After the workshop, everyone commenced working on their drafts over the next six months. When the chapter drafts were completed, we sent each chapter for review to another contributor, but without revealing who was doing the review. That review was consolidated with our own input and returned to the contributor for final editing. At that point, we were in a position to finalize the first three and the final chapters of the book.

With this approach, we have striven to generate a sense of unity in the book, all the while respecting the fundamental diversity that exists across the country.

Structure of the Book

Part I of this book explores the common ideas, institutions, and interests that bind and drive the science, technology, and innovation system nationally and across the provinces and territories. Part II then applies this approach to each province and territory to expose the similarities and differences that coexist in Canada. In some ways this offers a rich set of natural experiments in policy design and delivery; in a perfect world, we would want a control group and extensive evaluations of comparative impacts, but this set of limited reviews still offers insights into how different ideas, institutions, and interests drive the policy agenda. Part III examines commonalities and differences across the country, and draws conclusions and lessons for those who need to work with provinces and territories to achieve their science, technology, or innovation goals.

References

Atkinson-Grosjean, J. 2006. *Public Science, Private Interests: Culture and Commerce in Canada's Networks of Centres of Excellence.* Toronto: University of Toronto Press.
Australia. 2017. Innovation and Science Australia. "Performance Review of the Australian Innovation, Science and Research System, 2016." Canberra: Commonwealth of Australia. Online at https://www.industry.gov.au /sites/g/files/net3906/f/2018-10/performance-review-of-the-australian -innovation-science-and-research-system-isa.pdf, accessed 9 November 2020.
Baptista, B., C. Lyall, J. Ohlmeyer, J. Spaapen, D. Wallace, and C. Pohl. 2020. "Improving Pathways to Interdisciplinary and Transdisciplinary Research for the Arts, Humanities, and Social Sciences: First Lesson from the SHAPE-ID Project." *European Policy Brief.* Online at http://www.tara.tcd.ie /handle/2262/92598, accessed 9 November 2020.
Beach, C.M., R. Boadway, and R.M. McInnis, eds. 2005. *Higher Education in Canada.* Montreal; Kingston, ON: McGill-Queen's University Press.
Blyth, M. 2002. *Great Transformations: Economic Ideas and Institutional Change in the Twentieth Century.* Cambridge: Cambridge University Press.
Bothwell, R. 1988. *Nucleus: The History of Atomic Energy of Canada Ltd.* Toronto: University of Toronto Press.
Bouchard, M.J., ed. 2013. *Innovation and the Social Economy: The Quebec Experience.* Toronto: University of Toronto Press.
Bradford, N., and A. Bradwell, eds. 2014. *Governing Urban Economies: Innovation and Inclusion in Canadian City-Regions.* Toronto: University of Toronto Press.
Brassard, D. 1996. "Science and Technology: The New Federal Policy." Ottawa: Library of Parliament.
Britton, N.H., and J.M. Gilmour. 1978. *The Weakest Link: A Technological Perspective on Canadian Industrial Underdevelopment.* Background Study 43. Ottawa: Science Council of Canada.
Bubela, T.M., and T. Caulfield. 2010. "Role and Reality: Technology Transfer at Canadian Universities." *Trends in Biotechnology* 28 (9): 447–51. https:// doi.org/10.1016/j.tibtech.2010.06.002
Castle, D., and P. Phillips. 2011. "Science and Technology in Canada: Innovation Gaps and Productivity Traps." In *How Ottawa Spends, 2011–12: Life under the Knife (Again!),* ed. C. Stoney and G.B. Doern, 163–79. Montreal; Kingston, ON: McGill-Queen's University Press.
Chiappetta, M.E. 2020. "Understanding Open versus Proprietary Research and Innovation: A Case Study of Canada's Pharmaceutical Sector." PhD

diss., York University. Online at https://core.ac.uk/download
/pdf/322837945.pdf, accessed 9 November 2020.

Conteh, C. 2019. "Balancing Collaboration and Autonomy in Multilayered
Systems. Canada's Pursuit of Innovation Policy." Paper prepared for the
ICPP 2019 Conference, Montreal. Online at https://www.ippapublicpolicy
.org/file/paper/5d0aaa11259f1.pdf.

Council of Canadian Academies. 2006. *The State of Science & Technology
in Canada*. Ottawa: Committee on the State of Science & Technology in
Canada, Council of Canadian Academies.

Council of Canadian Academies. 2009. *Innovation and Business Strategy: Why
Canada Falls Short*. Ottawa: Expert Panel on Business Innovation in Canada,
Council of Canadian Academies.

Council of Canadian Academies. 2013a. *Innovation Impacts: Measurement
and Assessment*. Ottawa: Expert Panel on the Socio-economic Impacts of
Innovation Investments, Council of Canadian Academies.

Council of Canadian Academies. 2013b. *Paradox Lost: Explaining Canada's
Research Strength and Innovation Weakness*. Ottawa: Advisory Group,
Council of Canadian Academies.

Council of Canadian Academies. 2013c. *The State of Industrial R&D in Canada*.
Ottawa: Expert Panel on Industrial R&D in Canada, Council of Canadian
Academies.

Council of Canadian Academies. 2015. *Some Assembly Required: STEM Skills
and Canada's Economic Productivity*. Ottawa: Expert Panel on STEM Skills for
the Future, Council of Canadian Academies.

Council of Canadian Academies. 2017. *Science Policy: Considerations for
Subnational Governments*. Ottawa: Workshop Steering Committee, Council
of Canadian Academies. Online at https://cca-reports.ca/wp-content
/uploads/2018/08/subnatlscipol_fullreport_en.pdf.

Council of Canadian Academies. 2018. *Competing in a Global Innovation
Economy: The Current State of R&D in Canada*. Ottawa: Expert Panel on the
State of Science and Technology and Industrial Research and Development
in Canada, Council of Canadian Academies.

Council of Canadian Academies. 2019. *Building Excellence*. Ottawa: Expert
Panel on Leading Practices for Transforming Canadian Science through
Infrastructure, Council of Canadian Academies.

de la Mothe, J. 2000. "Government Science and the Public Interest." In *Risky
Business: Canada's Changing Science-Based Regulatory Regime*, ed. B. Doern
and T. Reed., 31–48. Toronto: University of Toronto Press.

de la Mothe, J. 2003. "Ottawa's Imaginary Innovation Strategy: Progress or
Drift?" In *How Ottawa Spends, 2003–2004: Regime Change and Policy Shift*,
ed. B. Doern, 172–86. Oxford: Oxford University Press.

de la Mothe, J., and G. Paquet, eds. 1998. *Local and Regional Systems of Innovation*. New York: Springer.

Doern, G.B., and R. Levesque. 2002. *The NRC in the Innovation Policy Era: Changing Hierarchies, Networks, and Markets*. Toronto: University of Toronto Press.

Doern, G.B., P. Phillips, and D. Castle. 2016. *Canadian Science, Technology and Innovation Policy: The Innovation Economy and Society Nexus*. Montreal; Kingston, ON: McGill-Queen's University Press.

Doern, G.B., and M. Prince. 2012. *Three Bio-Realms: Biotechnology and the Governance of Food, Health and Life in Canada*. Toronto: University of Toronto Press.

Doern, G.B., and T. Reed. 2001. "Science and Scientists in Regulatory Governance." *Science and Public Policy* 28 (3): 195–204. https://doi.org /10.3152/147154301781781480.

Doern, G.B., and C. Stoney, eds. 2009. *Research and Innovation Policy: Changing Federal Government-University Relations*. Toronto: University of Toronto Press.

Dufour, P., and Y. Gingras. 1988. "The Development of Canadian Science and Technology." *Science and Public Policy* 15 (1): 13–18. https://doi.org/10.1093 /spp/15.1.13.

Fischer, F. 2003. *Reframing Public Policy: Discursive Polities and Deliberative Practices*. Oxford: Oxford University Press.

Fortin, J.-M., and D. Currie. 2013. "Big Science vs. Little Science: How Scientific Impact Scales with Funding." *PLoS ONE* 8 (6) e65263. https:// doi.org/10.1371/journal.pone.0065263.

Galvin, P. 2019. "Local Government, Multilevel Governance, and Cluster- based Innovation Policy: Economic Cluster Strategies in Canada's City Regions." *Canadian Public Administration* 62 (1): 122–50. https://doi.org /10.1111/capa.12314.

Gilpin, R. 1975. "Three Models of the Future." *International Organization* 29 (1): 37–60. https://doi.org/10.1017/S0020818300017896.

Gordon, R. 2017. *The Rise and Fall of American Growth: The U.S. Standard of Living since the Civil War*. Princeton, NJ: Princeton University Press.

Grant, J., ed. 2014. *Seeking Talent for Creative Cities: The Social Dynamics of Economic Innovation*. Toronto: University of Toronto Press.

Hall, H., and K. Vodden. 2019. "Learning, Knowledge Flows, and Innovation in Canadian Regions." In *The Theory, Practice, and Potential of Regional Development: The Case of Canada*, ed. K. Vodden, D.J.A. Douglas, S. Markey, S. Minnes, and B. Reimer, 183–211. New York: Routledge.

Hall, P. 1997. "The Role of Interests, Institutions and Ideas in the Comparative Political Economy of the Industrialized Nations." In *Comparative Politics:*

Rationality, Culture and Structure, ed. M.I. Lichbach and A.S. Zuckerman,
174–207. Cambridge: Cambridge University Press.

Hawkins, R. 2012. *Looking at Innovation from a Uniquely Canadian Perspective: The Case for a New Alliance of Practice, Policy and Scholarship.* Ottawa: University of Ottawa Press.

Hayter, R., and A. Clapp. 2020. "Towards a Collaborative (Public-Private Partnership) Approach to Research and Development in Canada's Forest Sector: An Innovation System Perspective." *Forest Policy and Economics* 113: 102119. https://doi.org/10.1016/j.forpol.2020.102119.

Holbrook, J.A., and D. Wolfe, eds. 2000. *Innovation, Institutions and Territory: Regional Innovation Systems in Canada.* Montreal; Kingston, ON: McGill-Queen's University Press.

Holbrook, J.A., and D. Wolfe, eds. 2002. *Knowledge, Clusters and Regional Innovation: Economic Development in Canada.* Montreal; Kingston, ON: McGill-Queen's University Press.

Keynes, J.M. [1936] 1973. *The General Theory of Employment, Interest and Money.* Cambridge: Macmillan for The Royal Economic Society.

Kinder, J. 2010. "Government Laboratories: Institutional Variety, Change and Design Space." PhD diss., Carleton University.

Kinder, J., and P. Dufour. 2018. *A Lantern on the Bow: A History of the Science Council of Canada and Its Contribution to the Science and Innovation Policy Debate.* Ottawa: Invenire Books.

Leiss, W. 2000. "Between Expertise and Bureaucracy: Risk Management Trapped at the Science-Policy Interface. " In *Risky Business: Canada's Changing Science-Based Policy and Regulatory Regime*, ed. G.B. Doern and T. Reed, 49–74. Toronto: University of Toronto Press.

Lemay, M.A. 2020. "The Role of Expectations of Science in Shaping Research Policy: A Discursive Analysis of the Creation of Genome Canada." *Minerva* 58 (2): 235–60. https://doi.org/10.1007/s11024-020-09395-5.

MacDonald, L. 2001. *The Bombardier Story: Planes, Trains, and Snowmobiles.* New York: Wiley and Sons.

MacKinnon, P. 2014. *University Leadership and Public Policy in the Twenty-First Century: A President's Perspective.* Toronto: University of Toronto Press.

Madgett, P.J., and C. Stoney. 2009. "Universities, Commercialization, and the Entrepreneurial Process: Barriers to Industry." In *Research and Innovation Policy: Changing Federal Government-University Relations*, ed. B. Doern and C. Stoney, 148–71. Toronto: University of Toronto Press.

Majone, G. 2001. "Ideas, Interests, and Institutional Change: The European Commission Debates the Delegation Problem." *Les Cahiers européens de Sciences Po 04.* Online at https://www.sciencespo.fr/centre-etudes-europeennes/sites/sciencespo.fr.centre-etudes-europeennes/files/n4_2001_final.pdf, accessed 20 April 2020.

Migone, A., and M. Howlett. 2009. "Classifying Biotechnology-Related Policy, Regulatory and Innovation Regimes: A Framework for the Comparative Analysis of Genomics Policy-Making." *Policy and Society* 28 (4): 267–78. https://doi.org/10.1016/j.polsoc.2009.09.002.

Milley, P., B. Szijarto, and K. Bennett. 2020. "The Landscape of Social Innovation in Canadian Universities: An Empirical Analysis." *Canadian Journal of Non-Profit and Social Economy Research* 11 (1): 21–42. https://doi.org/10.22230/anserj.2020v11n1a287.

Milward, A. 1981. "Tariffs as Constitutions." In *The International Politics of Surplus Capacity: Competition for Market Shares in the World Recession*, ed. S. Strange and R. Tooze, 58–66. London: George Allen and Unwin.

Niosi, J. 2000. *Canada's National System of Innovation.* Montreal; Kingston, ON: McGill-Queen's University Press.

Niosi, J. 2005. *Canada's Regional Innovation System.* Montreal; Kingston, ON: McGill-Queen's University Press.

North, D. 1991. "Institutions." *Journal of Economic Perspectives* 5 (1): 97–112. Online at http://links.jstor.org/sici?sici=0895-3309%28199124%295%3A1%3C97%3AI%3E2.0.CO%3B2-W.

Phillips, P., and G. Khatchatourians, eds. 2001. *The Biotechnology Revolution in Global Agriculture: Invention, Innovation and Investment in the Canola Sector.* Wallingford, UK: CABI.

Phillips, P., and D. Castle. 2010. "Science and Technology Spending: Still No Viable Federal Innovation Agenda." In *How Ottawa Spends, 2010–2011: Recession, Realignment and the New Deficit Era*, ed. G.B. Doern and C. Stoney, 168–86. Montreal; Kingston, ON: McGill-Queen's University Press.

Phillips, P., and D. Castle. 2012. "Science and Technology in Canada: Government Investment at the Crossroads?" In *How Ottawa Spends, 2012–2013: The Harper Majority, Budget Cuts, and the New Opposition*, ed. C. Stoney and G.B. Doern, 81–105. Montreal; Kingston, ON: McGill-Queen's University Press.

Phillips, P., and D. Castle. 2013. "Is the Budget Action Plan and Related Harper Agenda a Coherent Plan for Economic Growth?" In *How Ottawa Spends, 2013-2014: The Harper Government, Mid-Term Blues and Long-Term Plans*, ed. C. Stoney and G.B. Doern, 19–30. Montreal; Kingston, ON: McGill-Queen's University Press.

Phillips, P., and D. Castle. 2016. "A New Government and Its 'New Innovation Agenda.'" In *How Ottawa Spends, 2016–2017: The Trudeau Liberals in Power*, ed. C. Stoney and G.B. Doern, 141–66. Montreal; Kingston, ON: McGill-Queen's University Press.

Phillips, P., G. Jobe, A.D. Gupta, S. Juma, P.T. Jacome, S.K. Karba, A. Rastogi, and M. Horvath. 2017. "Science and Innovation Policy for Canada's Next 150 Years." In *How Ottawa Spends, 2017–2018: Canada@150*, ed.

K. Graham and A. Maslove, 46–58. Montreal; Kingston, ON: McGill-Queen's University Press.

Phillips, P., G. Webb, J. Karwandy, and C. Ryan. 2012. *Innovation in Agri-food Research Systems: Theory and Case Studies*. Wallingford, UK: CABI.

Radelet, S. 2015. *The Great Surge: The Ascent of the Developing World*. New York: Simon & Schuster.

Rodrik, D. 2014. "When Ideas Trump Interests: Preferences, Worldviews, and Policy Innovations." *Journal of Economic Perspectives* 28 (1): 189–208.

Salazar, M., and A. Holbrook. 2007. "Canadian Science, Technology and Innovation Policy: The Product of Regional Networking?" *Journal of Regional Studies* 41 (8): 1129–41. https://doi.org/10.1080/00343400701530865.

Savoie, D. 1987. *Regional Economic Development: Canada's Search for Solutions*. Toronto: University of Toronto Press.

Savoie, D. 2003. "Reviewing Canada's Regional Development Efforts." In *Royal Commission on Renewing and Strengthening Our Place in Canada*. St. John's: Government of Newfoundland and Labrador. Online at https://www.exec.gov.nl.ca/royalcomm/finalreport/default.html.

Shapira, P., and Y. Youtie. 2010. "The Innovation System and Innovation Policy in the United States." In *Competing for Global Innovation Leadership: Innovation Systems and Policies in the USA, EU and Asia,* ed. R. Frietsch and M. Schüller, 5–29. Stuttgart: Fraunhofer IRB Verlag.

Sharma, P. 2013. "Social Capital in Large-Scale Projects and their Impact on Innovation: A SNA Analysis of Genome Canada (2000–2009)." MPP thesis, University of Saskatchewan. Online at https://harvest.usask.ca/handle/10388/ETD-2012-12-888, accessed 20 April 2020.

Simpson, J. 2009. "Needed urgently: More creativity from the business class." *Globe and Mail*, 25 May.

Stone, D. 1989. "Causal Stories and the Formation of Policy Agendas." *Political Science Quarterly* 104 (2): 281–300. https://doi.org/10.2307/2151585.

Tamtik, M. 2018a. "Innovation Policy Is a Team Sport: Insights from Non-governmental Intermediaries in Canadian Innovation Ecosystem." *Triple Helix* 5 (1). https://doi.org/10.1186/s40604-018-0062-8.

Tamtik, M. 2018b. "Movers and Shakers of Canadian Innovation Policy: Recognizing the Influence of University Vice-Presidents as Policy Advocates." *Journal of Tertiary Education and Management* 24 (4): 311–24. https://doi.org/10.1080/13583883.2018.1445772.

Veletanlić, E., and C. Sá. 2020. "Implementing the Innovation Agenda: A Study of Change at a Research Funding Agency." *Minerva* 58: 261–83. https://doi.org/10.1007/s11024-020-09396-4.

Wessner, C., and A. Wolff, eds. 2012. *Rising to the Challenge: US Innovation Policy for the Global Economy. NAS Committee on Comparative National Innovation Policies: Best Practice for the 21st Century*. Washington, DC:

National Academy of Sciences. Online at https://www.nap.edu/read/13386/chapter/1, accessed 9 November 2020.

Wolfe, D. ed. 2014. *Innovating in Urban Economies: Economic Transformation in Canadian City-Regions.* Toronto: University of Toronto Press.

Wolfe, D. 2018. "Experimental Governance: Conceptual Approaches and Practical Cases." Background paper for workshop series "Broadening Innovation Policy: New Insights for Regions and Cities," Paris. https://doi.org/10.13140/RG.2.2.10377.67681.

Wolfe, D., and M. Gertler, eds. 2016. *Growing Urban Economies: Innovation, Creativity, and Governance in Canadian City-Regions.* Toronto: University of Toronto Press.

Wolfe, D., and M. Lucas, eds. 2004. *Clusters in a Cold Climate: Innovation Dynamics in Canada's Diverse Economy.* Montreal; Kingston, ON: McGill-Queen's University Press.

Wolfe, D., and M. Lucas, eds. 2005. *Global Networks and Local Linkages: The Paradox of Cluster Development in an Open Economy.* Montreal; Kingston, ON: McGill-Queen's University Press.

Wright, R. 2004. *A Short History of Progress.* Toronto: Anansi Press.

Zhang, L. 2014. "Program Evaluation: A Case Study of Genome Canada Investments, 2000–2012." MPP thesis, University of Saskatchewan. Online at https://harvest.usask.ca/handle/10388/ETD-2014-01-1438, accessed 20 April 2020.

2 The Ideas

PETER W.B. PHILLIPS AND DAVID CASTLE

Science, technology, and innovation policy is the amalgam of two over-lapping and complementary conceptual framings. In the first and most general sense, the emergence of clearly structured thinking about the role and function of government and the engagement of governments with others beyond the state – what we increasingly call governance – provides the foundation for the entire system. The policy studies field, in particular, has helped frame and define the architecture of decision making, which influences what ideas surface and gain attention. Second, and more specifically to our interest, scholars have worked to frame and reframe the goals and objectives of science, technology, and innovation policy and to lay out a range of sometimes complementary but often competing paradigms for policy action. Understanding the basics of each stream of ideas will help situate what the provinces and territories think they are trying to accomplish and identify how that might influence the innovation performance of their respective economies.

Governments, Governance, and Policy

The political science literature is grounded on the search for order. Much of the focus has been on how the "state" organizes itself. This literature is itself highly organized, with streams focused on comparative politics, political economy, international relations, political theory, public administration, policy, and methodology. While many developments across the field create the context for innovation policy, we are mostly interested in the evolution of the policy stream.

Two specific developments in policy studies ground the context for the ongoing debate about the appropriate approach to effective science, technology, and innovation policy. First, both theorists and practitioners have come to accept that the focus on the state and the tools and spaces the state uniquely controls is too narrow to explain "order" in any economy. Political scientist Gilles Paquet (2001, 184) suggests that we face new forms of distributed governing arrangements "based on a more diffused pattern of power and a new valence for various meso-systems." Distributed governing "does not simply mean a process of dispersion of power toward localised decision making within each sector: it entails a dispersion of power over a wide variety of actors and groups." A seemingly infinite array of distributions of power evolves in response to pressures to adjust to rapid change. Paquet asserts that "the fabric of these new 'worlds' is defined by the new dominant logic of subsidiarity in all dimensions: it welds together assets, skills and capabilities into complex temporary communities that are as much territories of the mind as anything that can be represented by a grid map." There is extensive ongoing debate about what this means for our ability to make choice. Some assert this "hollows out" the state's traditional power (e.g. Rhodes 1994), while others see it more as a form of power sharing (Levi-Faur 2011). Horvath (2017) offers an excellent overview of the threads of this debate.

The Commission on Global Governance (1995) defines governance as: "the sum of the many ways individuals and institutions, public and private, manage their common affairs. It is a continuing process through which conflicting or diverse interests may be accommodated and co-operative action may be taken. It includes formal institutions and regimes empowered to enforce compliance, as well as informal arrangements that people and institutions either have agreed or perceive to be in their interest." The concept of governance thus does not represent a single, consistent view of how we govern. Rather, it offers an array of ways of looking at governing. In the first instance, the concept clearly suggests that there are alternatives to governing through the authority of the state or by relying on the market – the voluntary or civic sector offers an alternative approach that has different norms and objectives. Second, these alternative systems are increasingly interdependent, which has the potential to challenge traditional notions of sovereignty and accountability. Third, the diffusion of power and authority has the potential to blur the boundaries of the state, the market, and everything else. Ogilvy (cited by Paquet 2001) concludes this might be a world without a pecking order. Instead, it displays "strange loops" of authority, much like the game of paper, rock, scissors, where no one authority dominates in all circumstances, but only under limited conditions.

As our concept of governance has expanded, so has our sense of how we might go about governing (Salamon and Elliot 2002). Scholars (and to some extent practitioners) have taken this opportunity to refine our sense of how policy should be structured. The so-called policy cycle – encompassing agenda setting, policy design, decision making, implementation, and evaluation – provides a general road map of what needs to happen, even if the order is not always adhered to. Agenda setting and policy design are often the most difficult stages in the policy cycle. Stone (1989, 9) argues that "difficult conditions become problems only when people come to see them as amenable to human action. Until then, difficulties remain embedded in the realm of nature, accident, and Fate – a realm where there is no choice about what happens to us." She explores the role of causal stories in moving policy debate from the domain of fate, arguing that new models and paradigms help to motivate and focus energies. In the context of innovation, the emerging and conflicting causal stories both locally and globally lead to a mix of responses. While Downs (1972) asserts that an issues-attention cycle drives debate towards some consensus (the median), this would require a clear logic of causal action and a specific set of discrete actions with known consequences.

The challenge for innovation policy is that few of the causal stories propounded by theorists and practitioners are well defined. Overlapping but inconsistent causal stories have difficulty gaining traction, with the result that innovation policy in Canada (and in most other places) is pushed to the margins of public consciousness (see Doern, Phillips, and Castle 2016). The innovation policy agenda instead evolves more like one of Jones and Baumgartner's (2005) policies of punctuated equilibria, with long periods of inattention followed by infrequent, discrete (almost random) step changes. Much of what gets attention tends to be based on specific experiences and just-so stories, rather than validated causal stories supported by evidence. Stone is right: stories are compelling, but not all compelling stories are valid.

To model the policy process adequately, the role of the individual actor needs to be properly theorized and assessed. Arguably, policy analysis has largely neglected the individual actor and has inadequately connected aspirations and limitations at the individual level to the policy agenda. While most theories assume specific behaviours, many of those are untested or, when tested, are not realized. We are seldom if ever as rational and consistent as theory assumes (Kahneman 2011). People use context, limited cognitive processes, framing devices, and an array of heuristic practices to deal with the profound uncertainty they face in making choices. Drawing on insights from behavioural psychology, behavioural economics, and social psychology, scholars and practitioners are exploring the role of cognition in policy formulation. This literature is based on four building blocks: the role of uncertainty and indeterminacy, especially in the context of the classical ends-means choices fundamental to policy; the role of systems thinking, cognitive frames, and heuristics and their effect on decisions; the effect of aggregating individual behaviours to that of groups; and the impact of biases and heuristics on choice and the consequences for organizations. In effect, the choice architecture of the system defines the choices that are made (Thaler and Sunstein 2008).

Perhaps one of the most important insights of the combination of worldviews, policy studies, and behavioural cognition is that much of our policy effort relies on motivated thinking (Kahan 2016). We can and do ignore or differentially interpret objective data to fit with our prior beliefs. Thus, while rationality is assumed and sometimes tested for, in many cases ideas implicitly or explicitly become the handmaiden of interests, rather than the drivers of insight and direction. As the behavioural economics literature shows, our interpretation of facts and events can be prejudiced by one or more cognitive biases: affect, anchoring, availability, confirmation, and others.

Science, Technology, and Innovation Ideas

Much of the literature about technology and the economy starts with Austrian economist Joseph Schumpeter, who is credited with the first economic definition of innovation. He asserted that innovation is the introduction of a new good or new quality of an existing good, a new method of production, the opening of a new market, the introduction of a new supply of inputs to a production system, or a new organizational structure in an industry (Schumpeter 1934). Schumpeter argued that innovation involves the setting up of a new production function, while technical change is shorthand for any kind of shift in an existing production function.

There is a surfeit of other definitions and adjectives in the literature to modify this simple concept. Writers and thinkers characterize change at one extreme as major, strategic, enabling, transformative, general purpose, or macroinventions; these are juxtaposed against minor, iterative, end-use, microinventions. The general view is that macroinventions lead to a cascade of small improvements and applications (microinventions).

Two points are clear from this approach. First, as Schumpeter noted, invention is distinct from innovation: "innovation is possible without anything we should identify as invention, and invention does not necessarily induce innovation." Moreover, while some might argue that innovation delivers a "better way of doing things," one should keep in mind that many, if not most, new technologies typically emerge in a relatively primitive condition. It is increasingly becoming accepted that it is irrelevant whether an innovation offers any immediate or actual advantages over the product, technology, market, or organization it is replacing; rather, all that matters is whether individuals perceive an advantage. Regardless of these nuances, much of the literature and all of the public policy interest tends to focus on those innovations that bring something new – especially an invention – into widespread, practical, and advantageous use.

Second, Schumpeter clearly was talking about a process ("introduction") by which something new is initiated or adopted. Ruttan (2003) explicitly notes innovation is derived from science, technology, and art. Griliches (cited in Darby and Zucker 2003, 145) goes further, asserting that breakthrough change actually involves the "invention of a method of inventing," where a major new method leads to a succession of incremental inventions. A variety of researchers see creativity – defined as the production of novel and useful ideas in any domain – as the basis for innovation. The Committee for Study of Invention produced a report for the US National Science Foundation that explicitly differentiates invention – "the process of devising and producing by independent investigation, experimentation, and mental activity something that is useful and that was not previously known or existing" – from innovation, which it defines as "the complex process of introducing novel ideas into use or practice. Inventions, thus, generate value from their use (innovation) and not from their creation and existence" (CSI 2004, 9).

Currently, four discernible competing theories of innovation are driving debates and decisions in Canada and most other advanced industrial economies. These perspectives operate on different assumptions and provide different policy advice. At one end of the debate are neoclassical economic growth theorists and development economists, who abstract from the specific actors and activities in an innovation process, and assert that optimal investment will be derived in well-structured economies where marginal costs and marginal revenues balance – that is, getting the prices right. In contrast, three highly contextualized theories posit that innovation is the result of some combination of *special people* doing *special things* in *special places* (Leadbeater 2005). All theories of development, innovation, and growth make some reference to prices, place, processes, and people – what one might remember as the 4Ps of innovation policy – but each tends to focus on one driver, holding the others constant. While the neoclassical economic model underpins all the theories, most governments are attracted to do more, if for no other reason than they tell a more compelling story, with people, places, and action at the core.

Prices are implicit in each of the four theories, but only neoclassical growth theory asserts that they are often sufficient for explaining growth. This model sees innovation as an "induced" event, driven by strict economic need in generally competitive markets. British economist and Nobel Prize winner Sir John Hicks proposed as a general hypothesis that "a change in the relative prices of the factors of production is itself a spur to invention, and to invention of a particular kind – directed to economizing the use of a factor which has become relatively expensive" (Hicks 1932, 124–5). Thus, we have induced innovation driven by relative price change. Rosenberg credits Charles Babbage, the inventor of the analytic computer, with first making the point that an extensive division of labour enables a succession of applied solutions to small problems. He spent significant energy on careful cost accounting to identify areas of possible profitable innovation (Rosenberg 1997). Economists Robert Lucas (1988) and Paul Romer (1990) extended the neoclassical model by introducing embodied and disembodied knowledge; they asserted that accumulating and exploiting knowledge offers opportunities to innovate and grow beyond the resource limits of the traditional economy.

The focus in economic modelling has moved to exploring the nature and role of knowledge. The key point is that disembodied knowledge, which Romer likened to recipes, is not rivalrous, in that everyone can use it simultaneously without reducing the use-value for one another. So, as we generate more knowledge, we can accelerate our ability to produce and consume. Considerable literature has been produced to test this hypothesis. Economists tend to recommend limited interventions, most often establishing clear property rights for useful ideas through patents, copyrights, and trade secrets to incentivize private investment and for public subsidies for research, among others. Nevertheless, this approach assigns the burden of proof to the state to identify a failure and design an appropriate remedy. This was the main and sometimes only perspective taught to the economists who populate treasury departments and economic units across governments today, so that the default approach of many advisors is to advocate for minimalist interventions; economists are generally highly sceptical that any of the more deeply contextualized theories about places, processes, and people credibly justify public intervention. While this minimalist view has come to dominate in many member countries of the Organisation for Economic Co-operation and Development (OECD), more interventionist, statist approaches remain popular in many nations, including China, Mexico, Brazil, and India.

The earliest and most popular contextualized theory asserts that special places generate positive outcomes. Marshall (1890) and Porter (1990) both noticed the agglomerations of firms and industries in specific places and offered the explanation of "economies of scale." Firms co-locating in a region are likely to gain through competition and traded interdependencies, such as extensive and supportive forward and backward supply chain linkages and thick labour markets – those where both demand for and supply of skilled labour are high. Policies directed at nurturing special places tend to encourage firms, sectors, or industries to co-locate to create scale. Specific efforts include subsides, tax credits, and direct public investments in special infrastructure (such as universities, public laboratories, and industrial parks) to encourage firms to relocate and grow in a community. Firms pursuing a product-based strategy are most attracted to such centres, as they facilitate cost efficiencies that allow them to gain or sustain market share. Ironically, while the cluster model has been subsumed in the larger innovation literature, market efficiency trumps all other motives, with innovation only a by-product.

In the 1980s the special-process approach to innovation gained ascendancy. Variously described as national systems of innovation (Freeman 1995; Lundvall 1992; Nelson 1993), regional systems of innovation (Cooke 1998; Wolfe and Gertler 2004) and the triple-helix model (Etzkowitz and Leydesdorff 1995, 2000), this approach posits that "economies of scope" emerge through untraded interdependencies between people and firms that coexist in innovation systems. The frequent and complex interactions of individuals and firms as they develop and test new ideas in the market generate social capital that facilitates the transmission of information and knowledge. Unlike the special-places theory, the bulk of the important interactions happen outside of formal transactions: they emerge organically, often as an unplanned collective product of local culture and context. Policy focused on special processes tends to be supply push, involving investment in institutions, programs, or processes where research, development, and commercialization can prosper. Enterprises and entrepreneurs attracted to this type of system are likely to pursue resource-based strategies of the firm (Penrose 1959), where the focus is more on core competencies than on explicit products and market share.

At about the turn of the millennium, a group of business theorists and economic geographers broke away from the special-processes group to explore the role of special people in the innovation process (e.g. Florida 2002; Gertler et al. 2002). A set of interrelated theories assumes that creative individuals drive innovation. A mix of sociology, psychology, and economic theories assert that highly creative individuals can be nurtured and attracted to communities that invest in technology and talent, and tolerate diversity and change (for example, Florida's three Ts). The institutional and social pathways of change are not fully delimited in this literature, but those promoting this approach advocate for investments in high-quality, creative human capital through education and for investments in related research and networking programs. In contrast to the innovation system, these investments are targeted at the elite in an innovation system: the scientific and entrepreneurial "stars." Some communities promote their local quality of life to attract this talent. Firms attracted by this type of milieu tend to pursue knowledge-based strategies (Grant 2002) that put them on the leading edge of technology, product, market, and organizational innovation. The open-source, creative commons approach is often wistfully cited as the perfect environment for creative types, as it generates the space for optimal recombination of knowledge and ideas.

In practice, governments seldom limit themselves to tools supported by any single theory.

Canada's Responses

Canada's industrial landscape and science, technology, and innovation policy were profoundly influenced historically by Prime Minister John A. Macdonald's National Policy, which settled the agricultural West and created a tariff wall to encourage and protect the development of Canadian manufacturing, mostly in Ontario and Quebec (Creighton 1955). The repeal of the Corn Laws in 1846 and the loss of preferred access to Britain forced the British colonies in North America to band together to create Canada and to rationalize and generate a more robust and interconnected domestic economy. The result was that firms and sectors developed to serve domestic demand. Primary products were abundant and exported, while import tariffs were set high enough to generate domestic demand for higher-order goods and services. This had the effect of limiting the integration of most of our industrial ventures into global production systems, while the tariff wall reduced the imperative to innovate. Largely as a result of the National Policy, major new industries developed to meet domestic needs: electrical equipment and chemicals in the 1890s; pulp and paper between 1890 and 1914; cars, aluminum, and steel after 1900; radio and home appliances in the 1920s; and aircraft in the 1940s. Policy and programming was largely directed to nation building (Savoie 2003). Wars, depressions, and the uncertainly of world markets focused government attention on domestic economic stabilization and resource development. Science, technology, and innovation were only selectively used in support of these goals.

Beginning in the late 1970s, governments globally began to rethink their approaches to industrial policy. The Keynesian consensus of proactive and engaged government, initiated in the dark days of the depression in the 1930s and by all accounts successfully pursued through the mid-1960s, began to unravel in the 1970s (Harris 1985; McFetridge 1985). Economists and firms began to promote the idea that the state had expanded too far and too fast, and that many of the policies, programs, and investments did little to improve socio-economic outcomes. A few voices were highly influential. Milton Friedman and Anna Schwartz (1971) undertook a groundbreaking long-term study of US monetary policy, concluding that proactive, macroeconomic policies designed to moderate the business cycle were seldom beneficial – the leads and lags involved in detecting recessions and then stimulating demand were so long and unpredictable that society would generally be better off without proactive policies.

Rational expectations theorists (Muth 1961; Sargent 2013) added another nail in the coffin of Keynesian proactive stabilization policy, arguing that, regardless of which measures government used – spending, taxes, debt, or printing money – rational individuals and markets could and would make choices that would sterilize stimulative effects. Economists came to the view that stabilization was ineffective and often counterproductive. The tipping point came in 1979 when Margaret Thatcher and the UK Conservative government adopted the monetarist solution of high interest rates and lower public spending to choke off inflationary pressures. Ronald Reagan, Brian Mulroney, and their governments followed suit over the next few years. As global inflation dropped and discretionary, contracyclical macroeconomic stabilization wound down, theorists and governments turned to the supply side of the economy. Governments in OECD nations began to look seriously at the microeconomic foundations of successful firm growth, including the role of policies and programs related to finance, markets, technology, and skills. The public choice model became the new "economics of politics" – in effect, governments adopted an economic Hippocratic Oath, vowing to intervene only where private markets failed *and* where government action could make things better.

Canada was no exception. Since the mid-1980s, the historical statist, *dirigiste* model that dominated in Canada has been wound down. A number of causal stories have dominated since then, leading to greater support for world trade, de- or re-regulation, privatization, and tinkering with microeconomic incentives. Attention focused on innovation, specifically on the three main policy variants: clusters, innovation systems, and creative communities.

Canada has cycled over the past thirty years through the four Ps of innovation policy, directed at exploiting prices, place, processes, and people. Before 1990 the focus was primarily on getting the prices right; in an effort to get the deficit and public borrowing under control, governments cut back funds flowing for research, especially to the universities. As the fiscal situation improved in the mid-1990s, economists judged prices had come into line with expectations, but innovation remained weak, suggesting more policy action might be needed. The federal government was an early supporter of clusters: in 1990, Industry Canada hired Michael Porter and his Monitor Group to assess Canada's economy through his proprietary clusters model. Ottawa has sustained some cluster-directed support since then, with clustered programming in agriculture, the National Research Council's clusters initiative, and most recently, in the Superclusters Initiative. At other times, the government has invested in programs and activities aligned with the innovation-systems approach, including the recapitalization of scientific research through new merit-based funds in the late 1990s – for example, network grants in the Tri-Agencies, Genome Canada, the Canada Foundation for Innovation, and the Canada First Research Excellence Fund. Some government programs have also been directed to nurturing and attracting elite talent, such as the Canada Research Chairs, Canada Excellence Research Chairs, and Canada 150 Chairs, and an array of scholarship programming.

In many ways policy directed to prices, place, processes, and people is quite laissez-faire, with actual research topics largely chosen by those doing the research. Few governments anywhere in the world are content to let the resulting effort operate unguided. What is now called mission-oriented research has evolved, starting in Europe and now well embedded in most of our domestic programs. At one level Canada has always supported some of this type of work, having invested heavily over the years in science to advance nation building. Investment in mining and mineral research began with the Geological Survey of Canada in 1842, followed in the 1880s with establishment of the federal Experimental Farms; after the Second World War, the federal government invested heavily in communications research through the

Defence Research Board, which became the Communications Research Centre. But a large part of government support for research has been relatively undirected by public priorities, in that researchers or firms have made choices about what to work on without much input or incentive from governments (Doern, Phillips, and Castle 2016). Greater targeting and leveraging in grant programs and new competitively targeted programs like the Superclusters are working to introduce more federal direction and guidance for those using public funds.

There is significant debate in the Canadian policy community about the best balance between purposeful, targeted research and innovation and unguided, curiosity-led effort. The OECD (2011), among others, has recommended Canada move resources from undirected programs towards more strategic and targeted efforts; in contrast, the Naylor Report (Canada's Fundamental Science Review 2017) plumped for greater resources for investigator-defined research. The question of the value of trying to pick winners remains unresolved, and underlies the practical reality that the federal, provincial, and territorial governments have not allocated enough resources to pursue fully both opportunities, so there is a see-saw in the research and policy community about where to put the emphasis over time.

Overall, it is important to keep in mind that science, technology, and innovation policies compete with other often more pressing and compelling issues. One particular challenge is that, although governments across Canada now generally focus more on the microeconomic foundations of growth, the macroeconomy still has an enduring impact on the degree of attention, on the policy choices available, and on their impacts. The overall global macroeconomy has had its ups and downs. In the earlier part of our period under review, there were only two slowdowns that led to modest dips in North America. Then the 2007–9 banking crisis triggered a sharp, 5 per cent drop in activity across North America and a sustained rise in unemployment. That was then followed by more than a decade of growth, which pushed unemployment to record low rates across the continent. With the COVID-19 pandemic, the global and Canadian economy went into free fall, with the bottom about 5–10 per cent lower than the pre-pandemic peak. At the time of writing, the global economy had recovered much of its losses, but successive waves of the pandemic have triggered new lockdowns and attendant economic disruption. The World Bank forecasts that the global economy will not return to its pre-growth trajectory until 2022 or later.

Recessions are both threats and opportunities in the policy world. During downturns, revenues fall and force governments to review operating budgets, which often leads to squeezes on discretionary spending – especially outlays on science, technology, and innovation, which deliver results over the long term. Economic recovery, in turn, offers opportunities for new policy directions. There are active policy debates in Canada and the United States about whether to use stimulus or pandemic recovery funds to "build back better," which could include industrial incentives and research funding to reduce the carbon footprint of the two economies, to make them more resilient to future public health risks or more equitable through new social policy.

The normal gyrations of the macroeconomy, outside recessionary periods, can have an equal or larger impact on innovation policy outcomes. Canada, as a resource-rich exporter, is especially vulnerable to wild swings in commodity prices. When resource prices are rising, as in the commodity supercycle that started around 1996 and peaked in 2011, the national terms of trade rose sharply and so did export revenues, which, all other things being equal, caused the Canadian dollar to rise against other currencies. Canada is often classed in the financial markets a "petro currency," rising or falling in line with world oil prices. This triggers what is often called the "Dutch disease," whereby buoyant domestic commodity sectors bid away resources from other sectors, especially manufacturing. This is especially challenging in heavily resource-dependent provinces such as Alberta, Saskatchewan, and Newfoundland and Labrador, but has knock-on effects across the country as higher exchange rates make imports more competitive in domestic markets and exports of non-resource goods and sectors more challenging (Beine, Bos, and Coulombe 2012). Both efforts and outcomes of investments in science, technology, and innovation are challenged by these macroeconomic pressures. At the extreme, the macroeconomy so captivates our attention that all other policy priorities fall off the agenda, which leads to uneven effort over time.

Guidance for Policy Makers

Ideas unambiguously frame all action in this policy space. The challenge in the science, technology, and innovation policy space is that there is probably too much theory and related policy advice and too little empirically based evaluation.

There are strong proponents in Canada for policies based on each of the 4Ps: price, place, processes, and people. Everyone seems to have an opinion. There is a large and growing community of scholars with duelling theories, methods, interests, and advice, much of which are generalized from work focused on narrower technological, sectoral, or regional applications. Research stars are particularly visible, as governments and the media seek their opinions on issues and options, often for topics far removed from their area of expertise. University leaders have strong opinions they passionately promote. Numerous former civil servants and administrators remain active after retiring, offering both unsolicited and contracted advice. Both one-off and serial entrepreneurs who have had some success in bringing an innovation to the market frequently engage locally or nationally in trying to pass forward what they have learned. They do this on advisory groups, through lobbying efforts, through advocacy in the media, and through direct action as angels and mentors to emerging entrepreneurs. The result is a debate rife with "fuzzy concepts" and "scanty evidence" that deliver "wimpy policies" (Markusen 1999).

One of the biggest weaknesses in our policy system is the almost complete absence of structured evaluation of any policy ideas. Evaluation is at the core of professional management of the public effort. We probably have an adequate handle on the processes and activities (involving audits) and efficiency of administration, but little in the way of substantive impact evaluation. As one moves from internal assessments of processes and efficiency to consideration of impacts, attribution and incrementality become major challenges to affirming causality. One external reference for best practice is the Maryland Scientific Methods Scale, developed in the 1970s to communicate to scholars, policy makers, and practitioners in the simplest possible way to measure the methodological quality of evaluative efforts (What Works Centre for Local Economic Growth 2020). At the top of the scale (5*), we would have multiple evaluations of every policy and program using randomized trials that offer cross-sectional and before-and-after comparisons, with an untreated control group. We cannot see any major studies in Canada that meet this standard. Instead, we mostly see largely confirmatory reports (level 0) that use anecdotes, administrative data of input-output relationships, and case studies to tell just-so stories of implied causality and impact.

Given the long-term importance of this policy field, governments must strive to sort out the self-serving ideas and advice from grounded and impactful choices. More theory will not help. We need to challenge critically the myriad options with real evidence, reject those that add little or no value, and move our efforts to areas of demonstrated higher impact.

References

Beine, M., C. Bos, and S. Coulombe. 2012. "Does the Canadian Economy Suffer from Dutch Disease?" *Resource and Energy Economics* 34 (4): 468–92. https://doi.org/10.1016/j.reseneeco.2012.05.002.

Canada's Fundamental Science Review. 2017. *Investing in Canada's Future: Strengthening the Foundation of Canadian Research.* Online at http://www .sciencereview.ca/eic/site/059.nsf/vwapj/ScienceReview_April2017. pdf/$file/ScienceReview_April2017.pdf, accessed 11 November 2020.

Commission on Global Governance. 1995. *Our Global Neighbourhood: The Report of the Commission on Global Governance.* Online at https://www.gdrc .org/u-gov/global-neighbourhood/.

Committee for Study of Invention. 2004. *Invention: Enhancing Inventiveness for Quality of Life, Competitiveness, and Sustainability.* Lemelson-MIT Program and the National Science Foundation, 23 April. Online at https://lemelson-dev.mit.edu/sites/default/files/2020-04/Invention%20Assembly%20 Report%20Exec%20Summary.pdf, accessed 11 November 2020.

Cooke, P. 1998. "Introduction: Origins of the Concept." *In Regional Innovation Systems,* ed. H. Braczyk, P. Cooke, and M. Heidenreich, 2–24. London: UCL Press.

Creighton, D. 1955. *John A. Macdonald: The Old Chieftain. Toronto: Macmillan of Canada.*

Darby, M., and L. Zucker. 2003. "Grilichesian Breakthroughs: Inventions of Methods of Inventing and Firm Entry in Nanotechnology." *Annales d'économie et de Statistique* 79/80: 143–64.

Doern, G.B., P. Phillips, and D. Castle. 2016. *Canadian Science, Technology and Innovation Policy: The Innovation Economy and Society Nexus.* Montreal; Kingston, ON: McGill-Queen's University Press.

Downs, A. 1972. "Up and Down with Ecology: The Issue-Attention Cycle." *Public Interest* 28 (Summer): 38–50.

Etzkowitz, H., and L. Leydesdorff. 1995. "The Triple Helix: University-Industry-Government Relations: A Laboratory for Knowledge Based Economic Development." *European Society for the Study of Science and Technology Review* 14 (1): 14–19. Online at https://ssrn.com /abstract=2480085.

Etzkowitz, H., and L. Leydesdorff. 2000. "The Dynamics of Innovation: From National Systems and Mode 2 to a Triple Helix of University-Industry-Government Relations." *Research Policy* 29 (2): 109–23. https://doi.org /10.1016/S0048-7333(99)00055-4.

Florida, R. 2002. *The Rise of the Creative Class.* New York: Basic Books.

Freeman, C. 1995. "The National System of Innovation in Historical Perspective." *Cambridge Journal of Economics* 19 (1): 5–24. https://doi. org/10.1093/oxfordjournals.cje.a035309.

Friedman, M., and A.J. Schwartz. 1971. *A Monetary History of the United States 1867–1960.* Princeton, NJ: Princeton University Press.

Gertler, M., R. Florida, G. Gates, and T. Vinodrai. 2002. *Competing on Creativity: Placing Ontario's Cities in Continental Context.* Toronto: Institute for Competitiveness and Prosperity and the Ontario Ministry of Enterprise, Opportunity and Innovation.

Grant, R. 2002. "The Knowledge-based View of the Firm." In *The Strategic Management of Intellectual Capital and Organizational Knowledge,* ed. C. Choo and N. Bontis, 133–48. New York: Oxford University Press,

Harris, R. 1985. *Trade, Industrial Policy, and International Competition.* Toronto: University of Toronto Press.

Hicks, J. 1932. *The Theory of Wages.* London: Macmillan.

Horvath, A. 2017. "Governance – in Crisis? A Cross-disciplinary Critical Review of Three Decades of 'Governance' Scholarship." Center for Global Higher Education Working Paper 20. Online at https://www.researchcghe .org/perch/resources/publications/wp20.pdf, accessed 9 November 2020.

Jones, B.D., and F.R. Baumgartner. 2005. *The Politics of Attention: How Government Prioritizes Problems.* Chicago: University of Chicago Press.

Kahan, D.M. 2016. "The Politically Motivated Reasoning Paradigm, Part 1: What Politically Motivated Reasoning Is and How to Measure It." *In Emerging Trends in the Social and Behavioral Sciences,* ed. R.A. Scott and S.M. Kosslyn. New York: Wiley. http://doi.org/10.1002/9781118900772.etrds0417

Kahneman, D. 2011. *Thinking, Fast and Slow.* New York: Farrar, Straus and Giroux.

Leadbeater, C. 2005. "Innovation." *TED Talks.* Online at : http://www.ted.com /talks/charles_leadbeater_on_innovation.html

Levi-Faur, D. 2011. "From Big Government to Big Governance." Jerusalem Papers in Regulation & Governance Working Paper 35. Jerusalem: Hebrew University.

Lucas, R. 1988. "On the Mechanics of Economic Development." *Journal of Monetary Economics* 22 (1)L 30–42. https://doi.org/10.1016/0304 -3932(88)90168-7.

Lundvall, B-Å. 1992. *National Systems of Innovation: Towards a Theory of Innovation and Interactive Learning.* London: Pinter.

Markusen, A. 1999. "Fuzzy Concepts, Scanty Evidence, Policy Distance: The Case for Rigour and Policy Relevance in Critical Regional Studies." *Regional Studies* 33 (9): 869–84. https://doi.org/10.1080/003434003 2000108796.

Marshall, A. 1890. *Principles of Economics.* London: Macmillan.

McFetridge, D. 1985. *Canadian Industrial Policy in Action.* Toronto: University of Toronto Press.

Muth, J. 1961. "Rational Expectations and the Theory of Price Movements." *Econometrica* 29 (6): 315–35. https://doi.org/10.2307/1909635.

Nelson, R. 1993. *National Innovation Systems: A Comparative Analysis*. Oxford: Oxford University Press.

OECD (Organisation for Economic Co-operation and Development). 2011. *Business Innovation Policies: Selected Country Comparisons*. Paris: OECD Publishing. Online at https://read.oecd-ilibrary.org/science-and -technology/business-innovation-policies#page3, accessed 11 November 2020.

Paquet, G. 2001. "The New Governance, Subsidiarity and the Strategic State." In *Governance in the 21st Century*. Paris: Organisation for Economic Co-operation and Development. Online at http://www.oecd.org /dataoecd/15/0/17394484.pdf, accessed 20 August 2005.

Penrose, E. 1959. *The Theory of the Growth of the Firm*. Oxford: Oxford University Press.

Porter, M. 1990. *The Competitive Advantage of Nations*. New York: Free Press.

Rhodes R. 1994. "The Hollowing Out of the State: The Changing Nature of the Public Service in Britain." *Political Quarterly* 65 (2): 138–51. https:// doi.org/10.1111/j.1467-923X.1994.tb00441.x.

Romer, P. 1990. "Endogenous Technological Change." *Journal of Political Economy* 98 (5): S71–S102. https://doi.org/10.1086/261725.

Rosenberg, N. 1997. "Babbage: Pioneer Economist." Babbage Papers. Online at www.ex.ac.uk/BABBAGE/rosenb.html.

Ruttan, V. 2003. *Social Science Knowledge and Economic Development: An Institutional Design Perspective*. Ann Arbor: University of Michigan Press.

Salamon, L., and O. Elliot, eds. 2002. *The Tools of Government: A Guide to New Governance*. Oxford: Oxford University Press.

Sargent, T. 2013. *Rational Expectations and Inflation*, 3rd ed. Princeton, NJ: Princeton University Press.

Savoie, D. 2003. "Reviewing Canada's Regional Development Efforts." In *Royal Commission on Renewing and Strengthening Our Place in Canada*, 147–83. St. John's: Government of Newfoundland and Labrador.

Schumpeter, J. 1934. *The Theory of Economic Development: An Inquiry into Profits, Capital, Credit, Interest, and the Business Cycle*. Cambridge, MA: Harvard University Press.

Stone, D. 1989. "Causal Stories and the Formation of Policy Agendas." *Political Science Quarterly* 104 (2): 281–300. https://doi.org/10.2307/2151585.

Thaler, R., and C. Sunstein. 2008. *Nudge: Improving Decisions about Health, Wealth, and Happiness*. New Haven, CT: Yale University Press.

What Works Centre for Local Economic Growth. 2020. "The Maryland Scientific Methods Scale." Online at https://whatworksgrowth.org /resources/the-scientific-maryland-scale/, accessed 11 November 2020.

Wolfe, D., and M. Gertler. 2004. "Clusters from the Inside and Out: Local Dynamics and Global Linkages." *Urban Studies* 41 (5-6): 1055–77. https:// doi.org/10.1080%2F00420980410001675832.

3 The Institutions

PETER W.B. PHILLIPS AND DAVID CASTLE

This book is about the provinces and territories and their role in science, technology, and innovation policy, but it is impossible to talk about them without reference to the rest of the system in which they are embedded and the other actors they seek to partner with, to mobilize, or to incentivize; no single actor is truly autonomous. The business literature sometimes suggests one can understand and unpack the dynamics of innovation through the study of "unicorn" firms or "heroic" inventors or entrepreneurs. That approach offers a stylized iconography, but limited insight into the role of policies and programs. One might explain some innovation by focusing on discrete stages and actors in the innovation process, but that often leads to false precision and poor policy prescriptions. This is particularly so when the focus on process is based on the assumption that innovations follow relatively discrete, linear paths from research to development, commercialization, and sales. To suggest that innovation is generally about an exceedingly small number of individuals capitalizing on these processes is far from a complete picture. Most observers and practitioners now accept that the system is highly dynamic and densely packed with many actors that are differentially connected to specific activities. The main point is not that the system is complicated, but that at any point in time there is the potential that multiple actors are working with, competing with, or working at cross-purposes to the interests of any provincial innovation policy.

This chapter and the next unpack the structure and function of both the provincial state and those actors engaged in accelerating innovation. In this chapter, we first explore the provincial state and its relationships within the multilevel government system that operates in Canada. Then, in sequence, we review the structure of the role of the national and provincial governments, the design of the critically important higher education system, the scale and scope of the business sector, the diversity of Canada's population, and labour market conditions that affect the supply of labour, particularly skilled workers. We conclude with a brief discussion of the distribution of digital capacity to connect people, firms, and governments internally and to link with the rest of the world.

Canada's Multilevel Government System

Canada is constitutionally a federal system, with powers explicitly divided between the federal and provincial orders of government, with acknowledgment of First Nations, Métis, and Inuit, and municipal systems. Each order engages with innovation differently.

Although the system arguably was designed to assign "water-tight" authorities between the federal and provincial orders of government, the boundaries are often blurred or breached. When Canada was created as a nation state in 1867, the founders worked to balance the reality that the four colonies that were joining Confederation had varying levels of competence and capacity that warranted respect, but that, as a new nation, the national government required authority both to speak on behalf of all its residents and to work in areas that transcended the immediate reach of provincial governments.

The net effect was that "generally all Matters of a local or private Nature" were assigned exclusively to the provinces in section 92 of the British North America Act. This included direct taxation, management of public lands, health, social services, incorporation of businesses, property, family law, and civil rights. Provinces also had authority over municipal and regional governments. Education (via section 93) was uniquely also assigned to the provinces and, in an effort to finesse the dual-language challenge initially in Lower Canada (now Quebec) and New Brunswick, was structured to support denominational schools. Additionally, agriculture and immigration, both critical for nation building, were concurrently assigned to the provinces and the federal government, with the proviso that federal actions take precedence. The rest of the articulated powers were either directly assigned to the federal order of government in section 91 of the BNA Act or enumerated over time through the operation of the residual powers in that section, whereby the federal government may make "Laws for the Peace, Order, and good Government of Canada, in relation to all Matters not coming within the Classes of Subjects by this Act assigned exclusively to the Legislatures of the Provinces." The effect was to put into provincial hands most of what are the key factors in the science, technology, and innovation system: labour markets (including joint authority for immigration, which has been more formally delineated in the past few decades); property markets; local trade in goods, services, and skills; the regulation of most businesses; the entire education sector; agricultural and natural resource development; most civil litigation; and the creation and maintenance of municipal governments. Authority for marine natural resources is more complicated. The federal government via the BNA Act has responsibility for all offshore resources (such as fisheries and offshore oil and gas), albeit with a few exceptions. Beginning in the 1990s, the federal government negotiated joint-management agreements with the Atlantic provinces for some offshore oil and gas development. In 1984 the Supreme Court of Canada ruled that British Columbia has authority over the waters and submerged lands in coastal straits and submerged lands between major headlands, including the rocks, docks, attached flora and fauna, and all subsurface resources (*Reference re: Ownership of the Bed of the Strait of Georgia and Related Areas*, [1984] 1 SCR 388). The Court had ruled earlier that First Nations have rights to derive a "moderate livelihood" from coastal fisheries, which has generated significant conflict in the Maritimes in recent years as First Nations have exercised those rights.

The territories are in some ways a different order of government. Unlike the provinces, which are formally defined in the Constitution, the territories are a creation of the federal government and are very much a work in progress. For an extended period, there were two territories, the Northwest Territories (NWT), created in 1870, and Yukon Territory, created in 1898; in 1999 Nunavut was carved out the northern and eastern parts of NWT. For the most part, the territories were governed from Ottawa by commissioners appointed by the federal Minister of Indian Affairs and Northern Development. An advisory legislative assembly for the territories west of the Ontario-Manitoba border, except for the small Red River Colony, started in 1870. With the creation of the provinces of Manitoba, British Columbia, Saskatchewan, and Alberta, administration of the remaining northern areas moved to Ottawa. The first fully elected territorial council in NWT was chosen in 1975, responsible government began in 1986, and devolution was completed in 2014. Yukon Territory got responsible government in 1979, when the powers of the commissioner were devolved to the assembly and the executive council; further powers were devolved in 2003. When created in 1999, Nunavut acquired powers similar to those of the other territories. The three territories have a blend of authorities similar to that of the provinces, but not with the permanency and full scope of provincial authority.

First Nations, Métis, and Inuit maintain separate and emerging orders of government. Although constitutionally recognized through a succession of treaties, policies, statutes, and court decisions, the relationships between First Nations, Métis, and Inuit settlements and federal, provincial, and municipal governments are far from settled. Some First Nations, Métis, and Inuit have treaty lands or occupy unceded territory; others are negotiating modern treaties. A number of the chapters in this book explore the way First Nations, Métis, and Inuit communities are beginning to flex their innovative capabilities and capacities.

Until after the Second World War, provincial government policy and program capacity was underdeveloped and underresourced. In contrast, the federal government had both policy and program capability and fiscal capacity to exercise its authority, and sometimes inadvertently and sometimes wilfully took a dominant role in nation building. In a few cases, the federal system reserved rights to itself upon the accession of new territories – for example, Crown lands in Alberta and Saskatchewan were federally owned and controlled from 1905 to 1930. In other instances, the federal government arranged constitutional amendments to create new federal authority for emerging issues – for example, formal amendments affirmed federal responsibility for unemployment insurance in 1940 and old age pensions in 1964 – and throughout it used its general spending powers to invest in areas of federal interest. On the face of it, formal powers assigned to the federal government – such as regulation of trade and commerce (including interprovincial trade); all forms of taxation; most of the national infrastructure; the census and statistics; money, banking, and currency; weights and measures; patents and copyrights – give it significant capacity to set the general conditions for innovation policy, consistent with the prescriptions from price-based theory, but few of the powers related to contextualized theories of growth are exclusively in the federal domain.

Federal, Provincial, and Territorial Fiscal and Administrative Capacities

The relative fiscal and administrative capacity of the federal, provincial, and territorial governments is one way to explore the dynamics and interaction of Canada's multilevel system of governance. The fiscal power has always been uneven, partly because many important activities are federally regulated and partly because the capacity of provinces actually to levy enough taxes to meet their constitutional and policy needs has always been a challenge.

In the earliest years, the federal government had significantly more capacity than any single province to tax and borrow, so that its transfers became the base for the fiscal capacity of most provinces. In the 1930s, the federal, provincial, and some municipal governments all attempted to generate revenues through separate income tax systems, creating large variations in burdens and complex, expensive, and sometimes inefficient administration. In 1941, partly in response to recommendations for greater tax coordination in the Rowell-Sirois Royal Commission on Dominion-Provincial Relations (Smiley 1963) and partly to fund the war effort, the provinces agreed to vacate the income and estate tax fields in exchange for tax rental payments. Formal tax rental agreements ended in 1962 (Quebec created its own parallel tax system in 1954), but most provinces (except Quebec) have continued with a single administrative process that until quite recently allowed little flexibility in the calculation of the provincial tax base and the targeting of tax incentives.

The federal government continues to dominate in the generation of revenues, but its discretion is bounded. Relative to other federal systems, Canada's federal authority is quite constrained. Between 2000 and 2004 (the period of the most recent data), the federal government raised less than half of all revenues generated by federal, provincial, and territorial governments, and, after key constitutional and statutory payments – for equalization, health and social transfers, and a range of operational agreements with other orders of government – directly spent less than 37 per cent of all government revenues. In contrast, in the United States, the federal government raised about 54 per cent and directly spent about 46 per cent of government resources; in Australia, a common comparator for Canada, the Commonwealth government generated almost three-quarters of revenues and made up about 60 per cent of total government spending (Watts 2008). Recent changes in tax collection to allow for greater provincial discretion have worked to reduce further the federal government's ability to influence policy through national fiscal action.

Within these constraints, the federal government does vary its fiscal footprint. On the revenue side, in 2017 the federal government raised on average $8,400 per capita across the country, with a high of $11,700 per capita in Alberta and low of $6,150 in Prince Edward Island (PEI) (Table 3.1). Formal tax rates are the same everywhere for the same sources of income, but different industrial structure and different per capita incomes deliver widely different effective tax rates both between and within provinces. Some federal-provincial payments, including equalization and parts of the health and social transfer system, work to vary the federal footprint. The federal government payback to provinces ranges from a low of $1,870 per capita to Ontario to a high of $5,072 per capita to PEI, with the average at about $2,460 in 2017 (equal to 29 per cent of total federal revenues). The combination of differentiated effective tax rates and targeted transfers results in the federal government generating and keeping about $5,900 per capita across Canada, with a high of $9,711 per capita raised in Alberta and a low of $1,078 per capita

Table 3.1. Federal Revenues by Province, Federal Transfers to Provincial and Territorial Governments, and Share Distributed, 2017

Jurisdiction	Total Federal Revenues	Total Federal Transfers	Net Federal Revenues
		($ per capita)	
Canada	8,376	2,464	5,912
Newfoundland and Labrador	8,844	3,298	5,546
Prince Edward Island	6,150	5,072	1,078
Nova Scotia	6,862	3,866	2,996
New Brunswick	6,486	4,386	2,100
Quebec	6,397	2,714	3,683
Ontario	8,817	1,871	6,946
Manitoba	7,010	4,187	2,823
Saskatchewan	8,642	2,955	5,687
Alberta	11,738	2,027	9,711
British Columbia	8,388	1,980	6,408
Yukon	–	25,560	–
Northwest Territories	–	30,704	–
Nunavut	–	43,790	–

Note: Rows may not sum due to rounding.

Sources: Authors' calculations using Kerim-Dikeni (2018); Canada, "Federal Support to Provinces and Territories," 2 February 2017, online at https://www.fin.gc.ca/fedprov/mtp-eng.asp.

from PEI. While similar numbers are not available for the territories, it is worth noting that federal outlays there are a scalar quantity higher than the per capita transfer system working in the provinces, ranging from $37,151 per capita in Yukon to $49,330 per capita in NWT in fiscal year 2019/20.

While not the largest federal-provincial fiscal relationship, equalization is a political flash point for debate. Equalization was first introduced in 1957 and was included in the Constitution in 1992. The program is designed to bring provinces with weak fiscal capacity up to the average fiscal capacity across some representative set of provinces. The formula and reference period keep changing, such that, combined with diverging economic cycles in the provinces, different provinces get different payments in different years. Over the life of the program, every province has received an equalization payment. The most important things to note about the program over the past twenty years is that Alberta has

Table 3.2. Average Annual Equalization, by Period and Jurisdiction

Jurisdiction	2004–8	2009–13	2014–18	2019	$ per capita 2019
	($ millions)				
Canada	11,919	14,949	17,821	19,836	548
Newfoundland and Labrador	697	0	0	0	0
Prince Edward Island	292	335	382	419	2,832
Nova Scotia	1,395	1,279	1,749	2,015	2,131
New Brunswick	1,437	1,552	1,735	2,023	2,649
Quebec	5,936	7,989	10,330	13,124	1,591
Ontario	0	1,990	1,808	0	0
Manitoba	1,761	1,804	1,816	2,255	1,715
Saskatchewan	243	0	0	0	0
Alberta	0	0	0	0	0
British Columbia	577	0	0	0	0
Yukon	–	–	–	–	–
Northwest Territories	–	–	–	–	–
Nunavut	–	–	–	–	–

Note: Columns may not sum due to rounding.

Sources: Authors' calculations; Canada, Finance Canada, "Equalization Entitlements 1980–81 to 2020–21" (Ottawa, 2017), online at https://open.canada.ca/data/en/dataset /4eee1558-45b7-4484-9336-e692897d393f.

not received any payments, despite wide price swings in oil (Alberta last received payments in 1964), both Newfoundland and Labrador and Saskatchewan ceased getting payments as they exploited their increasingly valuable resources, and British Columbia and Ontario got payments when their economies were buffeted by recession. In fiscal year 2019/20, only five provinces received payments. Table 3.2 shows the recent and current range of payments by province.

While the federal footprint on the economy and society is absolutely bigger than that of any individual provincial or territorial government, the latter governments now loom larger in their own jurisdictions. But the relative balance of each order of government ranges widely across the provinces and territories. Overall, in fiscal year 2011/12, 3.6 million people were working for some order of government. The average for Canada was 98 government workers per 1,000 residents, but the ratio ranged from a high of 227 per 1,000 in NWT to a low of 81 in Alberta (Table 3.3). The federal footprint is absolutely large in Ontario and

Table 3.3. Government Employees per 1,000 Residents, Canada, Provinces, and Territories, Average, April 2011–March 2012

Jurisdiction	Total Public Sector All	General Government							Government Enterprises			
		All	Federal	Provincial Territorial	Health and Social Service Institutions	Universities, Colleges, Vocational, Trade institutions	Local	Local School Boards	All	Federal	Provincial Territorial	Local
	(government employees per 1,000 residents)											
Canada	98	89	11	10	23	10	16	18	9	3	4	2
Newfoundland and Labrador	133	124	14	23	40	21	8	18	9	5	4	–
Prince Edward Island	125	116	24	53	–	12	6	21	10	8	2	–
Nova Scotia	135	126	26	13	33	14	19	22	8	6	2	1
New Brunswick	116	108	21	38	30	8	10	–	9	2	5	1
Quebec	106	98	10	11	33	11	13	21	8	2	5	1
Ontario	93	83	13	6	17	10	19	19	10	3	3	4
Manitoba	129	109	13	13	35	9	14	24	20	10	9	1
Saskatchewan	125	111	9	13	35	12	19	23	14	2	12	–
Alberta	81	78	7	7	18	9	19	17	3	1	1	1
British Columbia	83	76	8	8	22	10	12	15	7	2	5	–
Yukon	179	154	16	114	11	–	14	–	–	–	–	–
Northwest Territories	226	202	28	105	19	–	37	–	–	–	–	–
Nunavut	157	153	12	94	–	–	46	–	–	–	–	–

Sources: Authors' calculations; Statistics Canada, table 10-10-0025-01, "Public sector employment, wages and salaries, seasonally unadjusted," online at https://www150.statcan.gc.ca/t1/tbl1/en/tv.action?pid=1010002501, accessed 26 September 2019.

Quebec, especially in the national capital region, but is relatively more important in the Atlantic provinces and northern territories. Generally, public sector employment is relatively high in smaller provinces and territories and lower in the larger provinces. In terms of government business enterprises, Manitoba is notable for its federal activity, while Saskatchewan's suite of provincial Crown utilities is significant.

Doern, Phillips, and Castle (2016) offer a full discussion of how the federal system directed to science and innovation is organized, financed, and directed. The federal effort is concentrated in Innovation, Science and Economic Development (ISED) and its portfolio of agencies, including the three academically oriented research granting councils and a foundation for infrastructure investments, but there is substantial intramural research in the line ministries, as well as significant tax support for firms to conduct research and development (R&D), especially through the Scientific Research and Experimental Development program. The single largest performer of R&D in Canada in most years has been the National Research Council, a federal research agency that spent $1 billion in fiscal year 2017/18 through its fourteen sector-targeted research centres, and employed 3,979 full-time equivalents. Overall, one way or another, the federal government invests over $10 billion annually. Some of this effort is directed and spent internally (such as on research programs at Natural Resources Canada and Fisheries and Oceans Canada), a share is managed through federal-provincial agreement (such as the five-year partnerships in agriculture), a portion is allocated to universities through the academic councils and related agencies, and some is disbursed through programs and projects (such as the Innovation Superclusters Initiative). Increasingly, merit review is supplanting peer review as a key hurdle in the allocation system – specifically, many programs now require matching funds from the provinces and territories, industry, or some other partner whose eligibility is defined by the program criteria (Doern, Phillips, and Castle 2016).

The specific policies and programs in the provinces and territories and their creations are the subjects of later chapters. They show that each province and territory has engaged in some way with the science, technology, and innovation agenda, using a mix of tax incentives, subsidies, services, infrastructure, investments, policies, and regulations to incent action. All employ an assortment of line departments, traditional Crown corporations, new partnerships, and special operating agencies. Doern, Phillips, and Castle (2016) note that, at the federal level, a movable feast of ministries, ministers, programs and priorities defines day-to-day priorities, often at the expense of long-term focus on any sustained policy effort. The stories in Part II of this book show that is also happening in the provinces and territories.

The Market and Economy

Measuring the scale, scope, and health of the economy is a perpetual challenge. We have a range of real-world data on markets (such as commodity and stock exchanges), while a host of formal statistical surveys and databases measure the firm (for example, Statistics Canada's Survey of Manufacturers), specific activities (retail sales and farm cash receipts), and sectoral activities and outputs (for example, the Labour Force Survey), all which provide us insights into the components of Canada's market economy. At the national and provincial level, we often default to gross domestic product (GDP), which provides one measure of the size of an economy over a period of time (usually one quarter or one year). Although constructed to assist with macroeconomic management, GDP increasingly is used to estimate productivity in aggregate, by sector, and for different factors of production. While we recognize that better measures are needed for innovation, that is beyond the scope of this book.

Overall, as Table 3.4 shows, about 30 per cent of value added in Canada is generated in the goods-producing sectors and 70 per cent in service industries. Agriculture, mining, and energy combined contribute about 13 per cent of the overall economy, while manufacturing accounts for about 10 per cent, mostly representing a range of high-value-added, globally linked efforts in the automobile, aircraft, and pharmaceutical sectors and a number of subsectors that produce the key inputs and process the output from our resource sectors.

The provinces and territories experience widely different prospects. Saskatchewan, with a relatively large effort in agriculture, mining, and energy, generates 52 per cent of its output in goods production, while Nova Scotia generates less than 20 per cent from goods production. Energy production is heavily concentrated in Alberta, Newfoundland and Labrador, and Saskatchewan, while manufacturing is relatively more concentrated in Quebec, Ontario, Manitoba, and New Brunswick. The national financial sector is differentially concentrated in Ontario.

Partly in response to the differentiated economic structure and opportunities in each province, there is significant diversity in the composition of the private sector (Table 3.5). While the distribution of firms across the size spectrum is virtually the same for all the provinces and territories, the number of firms per 1,000 adults ranges from a low of 35 in Quebec to a high of 49 in Alberta and PEI. Enterprises with fewer than 100 workers in 2017 employed between 67 per cent of all workers

Table 3.4. Gross Domestic Product at Basic Prices, Percentage Distribution by Industry, Canada, Provinces, and Territories, Average, 2014–18

Jurisdiction	Goods Production						Services Production	
	All	Crop and Animal Production	Mining and Quarrying	Energy	Power Generation, Transmission	Manufacturing	All	Finance and Insurance
	(% of GDP)							
Canada	30	2	2	9	0	10	70	7
Newfoundland and Labrador	49	0	7	28	2	3	51	3
Prince Edward Island	23	4	0	1	1	10	77	5
Nova Scotia	19	1	0	3	2	7	81	6
New Brunswick	25	1	1	6	4	10	75	5
Quebec	27	2	2	4	3	14	73	6
Ontario	23	1	1	2	1	12	77	9
Manitoba	30	5	1	6	3	10	70	5
Saskatchewan	52	8	10	23	2	7	48	3
Alberta	44	1	0	28	1	7	55	4
British Columbia	24	1	2	6	2	7	76	6
Yukon	21	0	6	2	2	1	79	3
Northwest Territories	43	0	29	6	1	0	57	3
Nunavut	39	0	21	2	2	0	61	2

Sources: Authors' calculations; Statistics Canada, table 36-10-0402-01, "Gross domestic product (GDP) at basic prices, by industry, provinces and territories," online at https://www150.statcan.gc.ca/t1/tbl1/en/tv.action?pid=3610040201, accessed 26 September 2019.

Table 3.5. Firm Statistics, Canada, Provinces, and Territories, Various Years

Jurisdiction	Total Firms, December 2017	Distribution of Firms by Number of Employees (%)			Firms per 1,000 Adults	Employment Share by Business Size (%)			Share of Contribution to Net Employment Growth, 2013–17 (%)		
		0–99	100–499	500+		0–99	100–499	500+	0–99	100–499	500+
	(number)	(%)			(number)	(%)			(%)		
Canada	1,177,634	98	1.9	0.2	40	70	20	10	68	18	15
Newfoundland and Labrador	16,933	98	1.8	0.3	39	76	18	6	27	21	53
Prince Edward Island	6,068	98	1.5	0.2	49	79	15	6	47	43	10
Nova Scotia	29,496	98	1.9	0.2	37	75	18	7	88	30	–17.9
New Brunswick	25,335	98	1.8	0.2	41	73	19	8	–	–	–
Quebec	241,755	98	1.8	0.2	35	67	21	13	56	29	16
Ontario	427,718	98	2.0	0.3	37	67	21	12	70	14	16
Manitoba	39,170	98	2.1	0.3	38	73	19	9	76	12	13
Saskatchewan	40,783	98	1.5	0.2	45	77	17	6	80	18	2
Alberta	163,584	98	1.8	0.2	49	74	17	9	133	–79.2	47
British Columbia	182,670	98	1.5	0.2	46	75	19	7	64	27	9
Territories	4,122	97	2.9	0.1	46	–	–	–	–	–	–

Source: Canada, Innovation, Science and Economic Development, "Key small business statistics," online at https://www.ic.gc.ca/eic/site/061.nsf/eng/h_03090.html, accessed 26 September 2019.

in Ontario and Quebec and 79 per cent in PEI, while firms employing more than 500 workers were major employers in Ontario and Quebec, generating 12–13 per cent of total employment, compared with 6–9 per cent in other provinces. Small firms everywhere generated the majority of the new jobs between 2013 and 2017; large firms absolutely shrank in Nova Scotia, while medium-sized enterprises were decimated in Alberta due to the energy price crunch.

Crown corporations and co-operatives, both collective responses to market and non-market needs, are small absolutely in Canada as a whole, but play different roles in different provinces and territories (Table 3.6). In aggregate, federal and provincial Crowns are estimated to contribute a high of around 5 per cent of GDP in New Brunswick and below 2 per cent in Alberta and Saskatchewan. Federal or provincially incorporated co-operatives, owned and operated by members who share in the returns of the enterprise, are relatively more important employers in Saskatchewan, PEI, and Quebec.

Foreign firms are important actors in many sectors in Canada: over the 2012–16 period, they controlled about 18 per cent of commercial assets, 22 per cent of shareholders' equity, 28 per cent of operating revenues, and 12 per cent of total employment (Statistics Canada 2018). While not obviously more profitable than other industries, foreign firms add more value relative to their share of assets and employees. Overall, foreign firms account for only about 10 per cent of gross expenditure on R&D – much less than their share of the economy.

There are no numbers differentiating foreign ownership by province, but the sectoral distribution of ownership mapped onto provincial industrial structure suggests those provinces with manufacturing, mining, energy, and wholesale trade have differentially larger foreign footprints (Table 3.7).

Given that Canadian manufacturing is more than 50 per cent foreign owned, it is worthwhile to delve into the details about the causes and consequences of this foreign ownership. Using the analysis by Baldwin and Rafiquzzaman (1994), Statistics Canada has divided up the sector into a range of segments. Scale-based industries, such as car manufacturing, are distinguished by higher ratios of capital to labour and advanced technologies in large-scale plants, while the science-based subsector (for example, chemicals and pharmaceuticals) has a higher R&D intensity and a greater tendency to employ knowledge workers, and natural-resource-based enterprises (such as wood and energy processing) are characterized by lower ratios of value added relative to material inputs. Labour-intensive subsectors, such as textiles, have lower wage rates and lower capital-to-labour ratios, while product-differentiated subsectors,

Table 3.6. Crown Corporations and Co-operatives, Canada, Provinces, and Territories, 2013

Jurisdiction	Crown Corporations		Co-operatives				
	As % of GDP, 2010	Assets, 2010 ($ billions)	Number, 2013	Business Volume, 2013 ($ billions)	Assets, 2013 ($ billions)	Members per 1,000 Adults, 2013	Workers per 1,000 Workers, 2013
Canada	0.7	11,316	5,276	43.2	26	285	5
Newfoundland and Labrador	2.1	8,983	19	0.1	0.2	101	2
Prince Edward Island	4.1	6,490	50	0.2	0.2	139	13
Nova Scotia	2.9	5,344	287	0.3	0.2	53	4
New Brunswick	5.2	19,576	116	1.1	0.4	130	7
Quebec	1.9	37,377	2,464	14.5	7.4	187	11
Ontario	3.3	6,979	782	3.4	3.5	16	2
Manitoba	4.0	17,352	225	2.9	1.4	527	9
Saskatchewan	1.4	12,391	582	13.1	8	624	21
Alberta	1.4	11,267	361	5.9	3.3	345	5
British Columbia	2.5	14,375	359	1.6	1.5	1151	2
Territories	–	–	31	0.2	0.2	177	14

Notes: Federal Crown corporations exclude the Bank of Canada, Canada Pension Plan Investment Board, and Public Sector Pension Investment Board. Columns may not sum due to rounding.

Sources: Authors' calculations using Crisan and McKenzie (2013); Canada, Innovation, Science and Economic Development, "Co-operatives in Canada 2013," online at https://www.ic.gc.ca/eic/site/061.nsf/eng/h_03070.html#overview, accessed 20 April 2020; Pavel (2014).

Table 3.7. Value Added of Foreign Majority-Owned Affiliates, by Major Sector, Canada, 2012–16

Sector	Average Value Added, 2012–16 ($ billions)	Foreign Share of Total Sectoral Value Added (%)	Change in Share, 2012–16 (%)
All industries	265.0	15	7
Manufacturing	104.4	56	9
Wholesale trade	33.3	35	19
Mining, quarrying, and oil and gas extraction	31.1	26	–33
Professional, scientific, and technical services	19.4	19	4
Retail trade	16.9	19	15
Finance and insurance	14.3	13	31
Information and cultural industries	7.5	13	47
Administrative and support, waste management, and remediation services	6.4	13	2
Transportation and warehousing	6.4	8	8
Construction	9.4	7	–2
All other industries	16.0	2	22

Note: Columns may not sum due to rounding.

Sources: Authors' calculations; Statistics Canada, table 36-10-0447-01, online at https://www150.statcan.gc.ca/n1/daily-quotidien/181114/t002a-eng.htm, accessed 26 September 2019.

including consumer goods, typically have higher brand capital, as measured by ratios of advertising to sales. Almost all sectors have seen declining foreign control since the mid-1970s (Table 3.8). Overall, the share of foreign control in manufacturing dropped to 45 per cent from 50 per cent between 1975 and 2011, with larger drops in product-differentiated and science-based sectors. The only sector to remain stubbornly dominated by foreign control is the scale-based sector, differentially dominated by car and steel manufacturing.

Table 3.8. Average Foreign-Controlled Market Share, Selected Manufacturing
Subsectors, Canada, 1973–75 and 2009–11

	Average Foreign-Controlled Market Share		Change, 1973–75 to 2009–11
	1973–75	2009–11	
Subsector	(%)		(percentage points)
Food, beverage, tobacco	35.8	32.8	−3.0
Natural-resources-based	57.9	48.4	−9.5
Labour-intensive	34.6	21.4	−13.2
Scale-based	57.0	58.0	+1.0
Product-differentiated	56.2	34.0	−22.2
Science-based	72.6	46.6	−26.0
All manufacturing	50.8	44.6	−6.2

Notes: The average foreign-controlled market share is the average share of a sector's output under foreign control over the three-year period specified.

Source: Baldwin and Li 2017.

Society

Canada has from its beginning in 1867 struggled to define a national identity. The prior settlement of First Nations and the French fact forced successive Canadian governments to build religious and ethnic diversity into Canadian institutions and organizations. The shared, but differentially lived, experience of Indigenous Peoples, early settlers, and modern immigrants has created a range of regional cultures (Dunn 2015). The waves of migration – the early British and French settlements, the influx of United Empire Loyalists after the Revolutionary War in the United States, the settlement of the West, and mass migration in the post–world war periods – all were linked to growth driven by export of primary products, what Harold Innis called the staples theory of development. These waves of settlement and change, punctuated by formative events (Lipset 1989), generated a range of fragmented, cultural self-images (Hartz 1964). Under the social science microscope, regional differences loom large. From a distance, however, and especially from a global view, they can appear quite modest. The most obvious divide is between the French-Canadian reality, concentrated in Quebec but distributed through northern Ontario, New Brunswick, and Manitoba, and what some assert is an anglophone majority, but which is better described as a pluralist allophone community. So-called English Canada subdivides based on ethnic and national origin. Almost half the people in Toronto, for example, are foreign born, making any single cultural identification impossible. Canada and Canadians define their society in a variety of ways, sometimes as an accommodation between First Nations and settlers and sometimes in the context of the English-French dichotomy, but overall since 1971 as an officially multicultural society where many cultures are welcome and encouraged to thrive.

With just over 38 million residents in 2020, Canada occupies the world's third-largest land mass (with the world's longest coastline), with the result that it has among the lowest population densities of any country. While we often define ourselves as a northern country, about 95 per cent of Canada's population lives within a hundred miles of the US border. As one would expect with the different geographies and migrations, density and diversity vary significantly (Table 3.9). Overall, Canada has only about 3.8 persons per square kilometre, compared with almost 20,000 in Macau and Monaco, 1,165 in Bangladesh, 418 in the Netherlands, and 36 in the United States. PEI has the highest density of any province or territory, at 24.7 per square km, while the territories have fewer than 0.1 per square km. More than 60 per cent of the population is in Ontario and Quebec, almost a third in the West, and about 6.5 per cent in the Atlantic region. The three northern territories, with 36 per cent of the national area, have fewer people than the least populous province, PEI. The population in the West and North is growing relatively quickly, while that in Quebec and the Atlantic region is relatively static. As a result of varying rates of migration, the median age is diverging, with the highest average age in Newfoundland and Labrador and New Brunswick, at 47 and 46, respectively, and the lowest in the Prairies (at 37) and in the North (26 to 39).

Process- and people-based innovation theories assert that diversity is vital to creativity and innovation. Racial and cultural backgrounds, divergent worldviews, and lived experiences all contribute to diversity. About 1.67 million people declared Aboriginal identity in the 2016 census, representing 4.9 per cent of the national population. In absolute terms, as Table 3.10 shows, the largest number of Aboriginal people live in Ontario (374,000), but they represent only 2.8 per cent of the total provincial population. The highest proportionate concentrations are in Manitoba, Saskatchewan, and the territories, where between 16.9 per cent and 85 per cent of the population is of Aboriginal descent.

Most of the rest of Canada's population can trace back to one of the successive waves of migration from elsewhere. In 2016, Canada had about 7.5 million foreign-born residents, or about 21.9 per cent of the

Table 3.9. Basic Demographics, Canada, Provinces, and Territories, 2018

Jurisdiction	Population	Share of Total (%)	Growth, 2011–18 (%)	Median Age	Population Density (persons per square km)
Canada	37,058,856	100.0	8	41	3.8
Newfoundland and Labrador	525,355	1.4	0	47	1.4
Prince Edward Island	153,244	0.4	6	44	24.7
Nova Scotia	959,942	2.6	2	45	17.4
New Brunswick	770,633	2.1	2	46	10.5
Quebec	8,390,499	22.6	5	43	5.8
Ontario	14,322,757	38.6	8	41	14.1
Manitoba	1,352,154	3.6	10	37	2.2
Saskatchewan	1,162,062	3.1	9	37	1.8
Alberta	4,307,110	11.6	14	37	5.7
British Columbia	4,991,687	13.5	11	42	4.8
Yukon	40,476	0.1	14	39	0.1
Northwest Territories	44,541	0.1	2	35	0
Nunavut	38,396	0.1	12	26	0

Source: Statistics Canada 2019a.

Table 3.10. Aboriginal Identity Population, by Province and Territory, 2016

Jurisdiction	Total Population	Aboriginal Identity Population	Aboriginal Identity Population as a % of Total Population
Canada	34,460,065	1,673,780	4.9
Newfoundland and Labrador	512,250	45,725	8.9
Prince Edward Island	139,685	2,740	2.0
Nova Scotia	908,340	51,495	5.7
New Brunswick	730,705	29,380	4.0
Quebec	7,965,450	182,890	2.3
Ontario	13,242,160	374,395	2.8
Manitoba	1,240,695	223,310	18.0

Table 3.10. (continued)

Jurisdiction	Total Population	Aboriginal Identity Population	Aboriginal Identity Population as a % of Total Population
Saskatchewan	1,070,560	175,015	16.3
Alberta	3,978,145	258,640	6.5
British Columbia	4,560,240	270,585	5.9
Yukon	35,110	8,195	23.3
Northwest Territories	41,135	20,860	50.7
Nunavut	35,580	30,550	85.9

Source: Statistics Canada, 2016 Census.

total population. As a reference, the United Nations estimates that currently about 260 million people, or about 3.5 per cent of the total world's population, live in countries other than that of their birth. In Canada, foreign-born residents reside primarily in larger centres in each province. The highest concentration is in Toronto, where more than 46 per cent of the population was born abroad. Generally speaking, at least 15 per cent of the population of all the larger metropolitan centres from Montreal westward was born abroad; east of Montreal and outside census metropolitan areas, less than 10 per cent of the population is foreign born (Table 3.11).

Labour Markets

As with demographics, the country largely divides east-west, with higher participation and employment rates and lower unemployment west of the Ontario-Quebec boundary, and vice versa. The employment-to-population ratio ranges from a low of 52 per cent in Newfoundland and Labrador to a high of 72 per cent in Yukon (Table 3.12). Labour market conditions can vary significantly depending on the state of global commodity markets: when world prices are high, resource-based provinces tend to boom at the expense of regions dependent on manufacturing and services; when prices decline, markets rebalance.

Education can be the great leveller in terms of economic opportunity, but it is not yet evenly distributed. Internationally Canada ranks highly in terms of both technical and higher education. Having said that, there are pockets of relatively low skills and low education everywhere. The population in some provinces, particularly Newfoundland and Labrador, New Brunswick, Manitoba, and Quebec, on average has

Table 3.11. Foreign-born Residents, Total and as Share of Major Census Metropolitan Area Population, Canada, 2016

Jurisdiction	Census Metropolitan Area (CMA)	Foreign Born (number)	Distribution (%)	Foreign Born as % of Population
Canada		7,540,830	100.0	21.9
Newfoundland and Labrador	St. John's	8,135	0.1	4.0
Nova Scotia	Halifax	37,210	0.5	9.4
New Brunswick	Moncton	7,955	0.1	5.6
New Brunswick	Saint John	6,645	0.1	5.4
Quebec	Quebec City	44,550	0.6	5.7
Quebec	Montreal	936,305	12.4	23.4
Ontario	Toronto	2,705,550	35.9	46.1
Ontario	Ottawa-Gatineau	255,800	3.4	19.7
Ontario	Hamilton	177,075	2.3	24.1
Ontario	Kitchener-Cambridge-Waterloo	118,615	1.6	23.0
Manitoba	Winnipeg	181,965	2.4	23.9
Saskatchewan	Saskatoon	45,155	0.6	15.6
Saskatchewan	Regina	36,910	0.5	15.9
Alberta	Calgary	404,700	5.4	29.4
Alberta	Edmonton	308,610	4.1	23.8
British Columbia	Vancouver	989,545	13.1	40.8
British Columbia	Victoria	65,610	0.9	18.3
–	Other CMAs	540,110	7.1	17.4
–	non-CMAs	670,385	8.9	6.7

Source: Statistics Canada, 2016 Census.

lower skills and education levels, while Ontario, British Columbia, and Yukon, in particular, are endowed with abundant highly educated and skilled workers (Table 3.13).

The Financial System

The financial system is a vital part of both the economy and the innovation system. Given the constitutional division of powers in Canada, the

Table 3.12. Labour Force Characteristics, by Province and Territory, 2018

Jurisdiction	Working-Age Population	Labour Force	Employment	Unemployment Rate	Participation Rate	Employment Rate
Canada	29,608,000	19,464,000	18,181,000	6.6%	66%	61%
	% of Canada			relative to Canada = 100		
Newfoundland and Labrador	1.5	1.4	1.3	202.7	91	85
Prince Edward Island	0.4	0.4	0.4	154.7	102	98
Nova Scotia	2.7	2.5	2.5	127.1	94	93
New Brunswick	2.1	2.0	1.9	137.7	95	92
Quebec	23.3	22.9	22.9	103.3	98	98
Ontario	39.0	38.6	38.7	97.9	99	99
Manitoba	3.4	3.5	3.5	86.6	103	104
Saskatchewan	2.9	3.1	3.1	83.6	106	107
Alberta	11.4	12.6	12.6	100.9	110	110
British Columbia	13.3	13.0	13.1	85.4	98	99
Yukon	0.1	0.1	0.1	68.4	114	117
Northwest Territories	0.1	0.1	0.1	114.0	111	110
Nunavut	0.1	0.1	0.1	222.8	97	88

Source: Statistics Canada, Labour Force Survey, 2019.

Table 3.13. Highest Educational Attainment of Core Working-Age Population, by Province and Territory, 2016

Jurisdiction	No Certificate, Diploma, or Degree	Secondary/High School Complete	Apprenticeship, Trade Certificate, or Diploma	College, CEGEP, Non-university Diploma	University, BA and Above
Canada	11.5	23.7	10.8	22.4	28.5
			% of all Canadians ages 25–64		
			indexed to Canada = 100		
Newfoundland and Labrador	137	96	116	121	64
Prince Edward Island	104	106	78	120	83
Nova Scotia	106	99	98	111	89
New Brunswick	121	120	87	110	71
Quebec	116	78	183	89	89
Ontario	90	103	57	106	112
Manitoba	125	118	76	95	88
Saskatchewan	106	125	109	93	79
Alberta	94	106	98	99	99
British Columbia	83	112	84	97	105
Yukon	93	88	106	105	106
Northwest Territories	178	82	103	96	86
Nunavut	357	62	89	80	50

Source: Statistics Canada, 2016 Census.

banking and financial system has become a blend of federally regulated national firms and provincially regulated market segments. Banking is a federal responsibility. Currently there are eighty-five chartered banks in Canada, but the big five control more than 89 per cent of total assets; in contrast, the United States has almost five thousand banks and the big five control only about 35 per cent of the market. Canadian banks engage in extensive financial mediation, taking deposits locally and directing loans to those areas of the highest return and lowest risk. This at times works to reallocate net funds between provinces and territories. In response, some provinces and territories and some capitalists have sought to address unmet local needs. Credit unions are a common response. In 2019, just over 5.8 million Canadians were members of at least one of the 241 credit unions and 4.6 million were members of the 239 *caisses populaires*, which collectively have about $430 billion in assets. Proportionately, credit unions/*caisses* have the most assets per capita in Manitoba ($24,500), Quebec ($21,800), Saskatchewan ($21,000), and British Columbia ($16,850). Average per capita assets in the other provinces are below $8,500 by our calculations (Canadian Credit Union Association 2019). A range of provincially and federally incorporated trust companies also does similar financial intermediation.

Equity markets are provincially regulated, but in recent years the private operators of the various regional exchanges have consolidated into a single coordinated system. In 2001 the Toronto Stock Exchange (TSX) acquired the Canadian Venture Exchange, itself a merger of the Vancouver and Alberta Stock Exchanges. Later, the Winnipeg Stock Exchange and the Bourse de Montréal (MSE) were merged into the TSX. In 2002 the TSX became a private company, and in 2019 was ranked ninth globally in terms of traded value.

There is a separate relatively small venture capital industry in Canada. The Conference Board of Canada judges that this sector moved from near the bottom of fourteen leading economies in 2009 to second-best performer, behind the United States, by 2014. The Canadian Venture Capital and Private Equity Association reports gross activity has slipped some since then. The deal flow by venture capital companies has been highly volatile, with early growth in the sector cut off by the 2007–09 recession and only recovering in recent years. The Conference Board of Canada (2020) reports that Quebec has the most sustained effort, with annual deal flow in recent years ranging between 0.1 per cent and 0.25 per cent of GDP; all provinces in almost all years were lower. Ontario is next, with a deal flow peaking at 0.19 per cent of GDP in 2016; British Columbia is usually at or below Ontario rates.

Below that, most of the provinces struggle to sustain regular flow, and few get above 0.1 per cent of GDP for any sustained time. For reference, US deal flow reached 0.36 per cent of GDP in 2016, while Australia's deal flow represented only 0.01 per cent of GDP. Community development funds and First Nations and Aboriginal Development Corporations also offer varying levels of additional support for new ventures.

To round out this brief review of the financial industry, it is important to mention the role of government-organized investments pools and public and private pension funds. The top eight funds in 2018 in aggregate had more than $1.5 trillion under management. Most of these funds operate and invest completely independently of the governments and employers that established them; the notable exception is Quebec's Caisse de dépôt et placement. With $336 billion under management, the Caisse has a nation-building role built into its management, and at times has taken significant positions in Quebec-based firms to assist them to restructure or to remain in Quebec.

In many countries, and in some contexts in Canada, the charitable and not-for-profit sector is a key funder of research and helps to set research priorities. Canada has an estimated 170,000 charitable and not-for-profit organizations, about 85,000 which are registered as charities recognized by the Canada Revenue Agency. Imagine Canada estimates that the charitable and not-for-profit sector contributes an average of 8.1 per cent of total Canadian GDP, more than the retail trade industry and close to the value of the mining, oil, and gas extraction industries. Two million Canadians are employed in the sector, and more than 13 million people volunteer some time to their causes.

As Table 3.14 shows, in 2016 the not-for-profit sector as a whole received more than $12.8 billion in charitable revenues, some from business but much from individuals. Individual donations to charities in Canada represented 0.77 per cent of GDP in 2016, behind the United States (1.44 per cent) and New Zealand (0.79 per cent), but ahead of Australia (0.68 per cent) and the United Kingdom (0.54 per cent). About 82 per cent of Canadians donate each year, with a range of 78 per cent in British Columbia to 87 per cent in Newfoundland and Labrador. The average annual donation ranges from $264 in Quebec to $863 in Alberta, with an average of about $530.

An estimated 15 per cent of donations is directed to charities engaged in some aspect of science and research. We cannot definitively identify the sectors, but the evidence suggests some of this goes to health and environmental advocacy groups, some directly to hospitals and universities, and some to privately managed research programs.

Table 3.14. Charitable Revenues, by Type of Not-for-Profit Organization, Canada, 2013

Type of Organization	Donor Rate (%)	Total Revenues ($ millions)	Share of Total Revenues (%)
Total	82	12,764	100
Religious organizations	31	5,228	41
Health	48	1,658	13
Social services	40	1,578	12
International organizations	11	1,283	10
Grant-making, fundraising & promotion	10	687	5
Hospitals	17	560	4
Environment	8	294	2
Education and research	16	286	2
Sports and recreation	13	193	2
Universities and colleges	2	161	1
Arts and culture	3	160	1
Development and housing	2	152	1
Law, advocacy and politics	3	136	1

Note: Columns may not sum due to rounding.

Source: Statistics Canada, "2013 General Social Survey on Giving, Volunteering and Participating."

Universities and the Polytechnics

By some measures, Canada is an education powerhouse, with the world's highest proportion of working-age adults having been through higher education: 55 per cent compared with an average in other major industrialized countries of 35 per cent. The higher education sector is a critical part of the R&D system. The challenge to getting a handle on the system is that universities and polytechnics are regulated at the provincial level, while much of the research funding comes from the federal government. Table 3.15 offers statistics on higher education in Canada, broken down by province and territory.

There are diverse ways of measuring and defining higher education. Universities Canada (formerly the Association of Universities and Colleges Canada) reports there are ninety-six universities, fourteen polytechnics, and an array of other post-secondary colleges, with a combined annual enrolment of more than two million students. On

Table 3.15. Higher Education General Statistics, Canada, Provinces, and Territories, 2018

Jurisdiction	Number of Universities	Number of Polytechnics	Total Students	University Students	College Students	% Total Population		
						Total Students	University	College
Canada	96	14	2,039,809	1,302,405	737,403	5.5	3.5	2.0
Newfoundland and Labrador	1	0	27,315	18,117	9,199	5.2	3.4	1.8
Prince Edward Island	1	0	6,388	4,237	2,150	4.2	2.8	1.4
Nova Scotia	9	0	55,142	43,555	11,586	5.7	4.5	1.2
New Brunswick	4	0	28,964	20,899	8,066	3.8	2.7	1.0
Quebec	19	0	529,536	310,549	218,986	6.3	3.7	2.6
Ontario	31	7	809,095	516,077	293,017	5.7	3.6	2.0
Manitoba	6	2	62,317	46,103	16,214	4.6	3.4	1.2
Saskatchewan	6	1	54,592	35,093	19,499	4.7	3.0	1.7
Alberta	8	2	187,774	129,384	58,390	4.4	3.0	1.4
British Columbia	11	2	274,953	178,388	96,563	5.5	3.6	1.9
Territories	–	–	3,733	–	3,733	3.0	–	3.0

Sources: Authors' calculations; Polytechnics Canada; Universities Canada.

average, 5.5 per cent of the national population is in the post-secondary system in a given year, ranging from 6.3 per cent in Quebec to 3.8 per cent in New Brunswick. The territories have less post-secondary training because of limited capacity. For some considerable time, northern institutions have delivered degree programs on behalf of southern universities; in May 2020, Yukon College transitioned to Yukon University with its own degree programs. Nova Scotia has the greatest intensity of students in universities (4.5 per cent) and New Brunswick the lowest (2.7 per cent), while Quebec has the highest relative enrolment in colleges at 2.7 per cent and New Brunswick the lowest at 1 per cent.

The nearly 100 universities combined are big ventures, in 2014 directly spending $35 billion and employing about 250,000 workers. Universities Canada reports that universities performed $13 billion in R&D that year, or about 40 per cent of the Canadian total; about $1 billion of that was undertaken on behalf of business. Universities also partner with entrepreneurs and firms seeking to exploit knowledge flowing from the academy. The Association of University Research Parks Canada estimates that, in 2013, there were nearly 1,500 companies and government labs located in 26 university research and technology parks, collectively employing 65,000 people (AURP n.d.).

Internet Access and Use

In many ways the internet has become a techno-social institution in its own right, and is both a product of, and crucial factor for, twenty-first-century innovation. In a world of global competitiveness, the internet is a vital link to world markets and ideas. In the digital age, there is an emerging consensus that, for many firms, market reach determines the ultimate durability and profitability of their innovations. The pressure for better service has been amplified in the COVID-19 pandemic as many workers, students, and families have had to isolate at home to control the spread of the disease. There is increased pressure for greater availability, affordability, and adoption.

At issue is both who owns or manages the internet and its platforms, and where and under what terms individuals and firms can access its services. We do not explore the ownership question explicitly in this book, but we acknowledge its saliency. Who owns the underlying search algorithms, hosts cloud-based services, and has preferred access to the data created and stored will have a privileged place in the global market. Canada, like most countries, is not endowed with many players in this space. The companies that dominate cyberspace – US-based Alphabet (Google), Amazon, Apple, Facebook, Microsoft, and Netflix, a range of mostly Chinese analogues (Biadu, Alibaba, JD.com, Xiaomi, Tencent, and iQiyi), and a growing number of regional competitors in Asia and Africa – are all based in other countries, which over time might hurt Canada's access to global markets.

A bigger immediate question is Canadians' capacity even to get on the web. While Canada ranks in the top tier for technical access globally, as Table 3.16 shows, there is significant variation in access and quality across the country. Given Canada's geography and low population density, it has always been a challenge to serve rural and remote residents and firms with radio, telephones, and television. That continues in the internet world. Looking back to 2004, 96 per cent of households in Canada had landlines, with rural and remote service spotty, poor, and costly; 59 per cent were also using mobile services. In technical terms, 99 per cent of Canadians in 2017 were covered by long-term evolution (LTE), or 4G, networks; the North was the exception, with only 63.5 per cent coverage. By that year, landline use had dropped to 63 per cent of homes, while 90 per cent of households used mobile devices (CRTC 2019), with Quebec and the Atlantic provinces differentially relying on landlines compared to Ontario and the West. Provincial use of mobile services also varied widely, with 92 per cent of Alberta households subscribing, but only 71 per cent of PEI residents using mobile devices, reaffirming that availability does not always translate to use. As of 2018, internet access was available to 91 per cent of Canadian households, ranging from 86 per cent in Newfoundland and Labrador and 94 per cent in Alberta (Statistics Canada 2019b, 2019c).

Speed varies significantly depending on where Canadians live. While 99 per cent of the total population and 97 per cent of rural communities had LTE service in 2017, the higher quality 50/10 Mbps standard was largely restricted to cities and larger rural towns. Only about 59 per cent of rural communities had access to this level of service, and rural and remote residents in the West and North were virtually excluded, which is a barrier to some forms of innovation in those regions.

Price is another barrier. A study commissioned by the Canadian Radio-television and Telecommunications Commission in 2016 reported that Canadians contracting for 150 minutes of monthly mobile service paid more than consumers in every other G7 country and Australia, and almost two and a half times as much as in Germany, the lowest-priced G7 market. Adding 10 GB of data was also costly, with Canadians paying the second most of the comparator countries. In contrast, Canadians paid the lowest price for landlines of any of the other advanced industrial economies (Nordicity Group 2016). There is little evidence that these relatively high costs have changed in the interim,

Table 3.16. Broadband Internet Service, Canada, Provinces, and Territories, 2017

Jurisdiction	50/10 Mbps Unlimited			1.5 Mbps		
	All Areas	Rural Communities	First Nations Reserve Areas	All Areas	Rural Communities	First Nations Reserve Areas
	(% of area served)					
Canada	84	37	28	99	94	91
Newfoundland and Labrador	71	47	24	92	82	96
Prince Edward Island	60	31	30	99	98	100
Nova Scotia	78	51	44	100	100	100
New Brunswick	81	63	87	96	92	99
Quebec	89	54	38	99	95	86
Ontario	87	28	15	99	94	89
Manitoba	70	10	2	99	97	98
Saskatchewan	45	1	0	96	88	93
Alberta	80	9	0	100	98	98
British Columbia	91	53	62	98	90	87
Yukon	0	0	0	91	80	43
Northwest Territories	0	0	0	98	95	74
Nunavut	0	0	0	99	98	0

Source: CRTC 2019.

and despite various policy efforts, there does not seem much prospect of this changing in the near future.

Guidance for Policy Makers and Analysts

The diversity and diffusion of interested and affected actors within and between the provinces and territories creates a variety of differentiated innovation spaces. While industrial and business systems have many similarities across Canada, most provinces and territories have clear comparative advantages and a divergent portfolio of firms with which to work. Each province and territory has a blend of federal and provincial programs and services, differentiated to fit with the structure of the local economy. A few provinces host a significant number of large firms, many foreign owned, that, as we will see in the next chapter, are significantly research intensive. Other provinces rely more on small and medium-sized firms, co-operatives, *caisses populaires*, and Crown corporations to advance measures. All but two territories have access to higher education training and research. As we will see in the chapters in Part II, provinces and territories have different priorities and pursue different strategies for how science, technology, and innovation can contribute to economic and social development. Perhaps most important, no single province is self-sufficient.

We do not believe that this inventory of institutions necessarily generates any strong case for action by itself. We have noted that those parts of our manufacturing sector that remain foreign owned tend to invest less in R&D than their share of the economy. Some might draw the conclusion that Canada should either repatriate ownership or impose benefits agreements, but there is no evidence that such moves would improve the outcome. Conversely, the fact that Canada has a proportionately larger share of its working-age population with advanced skills training and education might be an asset, but it does not suggest directly how that capacity might be better utilized. Some might assert that both weaknesses and strengths necessitate more coordination and management of innovation across the national economy. The rest of this book will illustrate, however, that where these strategies have been tried, the resulting outcomes have not been unambiguously better.

References

AURP (Association of University Research Parks). n.d. "What Is a Technology Park? Economic Impact." Online at http://aurpcanada.com/canadas-rt-parks/what-is-a-technology-park/, accessed 20 April 2020.

Baldwin, J.R., and Jiang Li. 2017. "The Changing Importance of Foreign Control in Canadian Manufacturing." Ottawa: Statistics Canada, Economic Analysis Division. Online at https://www150.statcan.gc.ca/n1/pub/11f0019m/11f0019m2016387-eng.htm.

Baldwin, J.R., and M. Rafiquzzaman. 1994. "Structural Change in the Canadian Manufacturing Sector: 1970–1990." Analytical Studies Branch Research Paper Series 61. Cat. no. 11F0019M. Ottawa: Statistics Canada.

Canadian Credit Union Association. 2019. "National Sectoral Results, 3rd Quarter Results." Online at https://ccua.com/about-credit-unions/facts-and-figures/national-system-results/.

Conference Board of Canada. 2020. "How Canada Performs: Venture Capital." Ottawa. Online at https://www.conferenceboard.ca/hcp/provincial/innovation/venture-capital.aspx#ftn2, accessed 2 December 2020.

Crisan, D., and K. McKenzie. 2013. "Government-Owned Enterprises in Canada." *School of Public Policy Research Papers* 6 (8): 11–12. Online at https://www.policyschool.ca/wp-content/uploads/2016/03/government-owned-enterprises-final.pdf, accessed 4 May 2020.

CRTC (Canadian Radio-television and Telecommunications Commission). 2019. *Communications Monitoring Report 2019*. Ottawa. Online at https://crtc.gc.ca/eng/publications/reports/policymonitoring/2019/cmr1.htm#f1.2, accessed 4 May 2020.

Doern, G.B., P. Phillips, and D. Castle. 2016. *Canadian Science, Technology and Innovation Policy: The Innovation Economy and Society Nexus*. Montreal; Kingston, ON: McGill-Queen's University Press.

Dunn, C. 2015. *Provinces: Canadian Provincial Politics*, 3rd ed. Toronto: University of Toronto Press.

Hartz, L. 1964. *The Founding of New Societies; Studies in the History of the United States, Latin America, South Africa, Canada, and Australia*. New York: Harcourt, Brace and World.

Kerim-Dikeni, S. 2018. "Distribution of Federal Revenues and Expenditures by Province." Ottawa: Library of Parliament. Online at https://lop.parl.ca/sites/PublicWebsite/default/en_CA/ResearchPublications/201701E.

Lipset, S.M. 1989. *Continental Divide: The Values and Institutions of the United States and Canada*. New York: Routledge.

Nordicity Group. 2016. *2016 Price Comparison Study of Telecommunications Services in Canada and Select Foreign Jurisdictions*. Ottawa: Canadian Radio-television and Telecommunications Commission. Online at: https://crtc.gc.ca/eng/publications/reports/compar/compar2016.pdf, accessed 4 May 2020.

Pavel, J. 2014. "Crown Corporations and Government Divestment." Policy Series 159. Winnipeg: Frontier Centre for Public Policy. Online at https://fcpp.org/sites/default/files/crowndivestment.pdf, accessed 20 April 2020.

Smiley, D.V., ed. 1963. *The Rowell-Sirois Report: An Abridgment of Book I of the Royal Commission Report on Dominion-Provincial Relations*. Montreal; Kingston, ON: McGill-Queen's University Press.

Statistics Canada. 2018. "Activities of foreign majority-owned affiliates, as a share of the Canadian economy." Table 36-10-0356-01. Online at https://www150.statcan.gc.ca/n1/daily-quotidien/181114/cg-a001-eng.htm. https://doi.org/10.25318/3610035601-eng, accessed 26 September 2019.

Statistics Canada. 2019a. "Annual Demographic Estimates: Canada, Provinces and Territories, 2018." Cat. no. 91–215X. Ottawa.

Statistics Canada. 2019b. "Internet use by province." Table 22-10-0083-01. Online a: https://www150.statcan.gc.ca/t1/tbl1/en/tv.action?pid=2210008301, accessed 20 April 2020.

Statistics Canada. 2019c. "Internet use, by location of access by geography." Table 22-10-0058-01. Online at https://www150.statcan.gc.ca/t1/tbl1/en/tv.action?pid=2210005801, accessed 20 April 2020.

Watts, R.L. 2008. *Comparing Federal Systems*, 3rd ed. Montreal; Kingston, ON: McGill-Queen's University Press for the Institute of Intergovernmental Relations.

4 The Interests

PETER W.B. PHILLIPS AND DAVID CASTLE

Science, technology, and innovation policy engages a bundle of actors and agents with a range of motivations and interests. Few actors in the system are disinterested; everyone has something they wish to achieve directly or indirectly, and honest brokers are relatively rare. Some researchers and inventors simply seek to satisfy their own curiosity, but few reject the spoils of discovery, be they fame or fortune. For-profit firms are almost always blatantly self-interested, making investments to achieve some very specific goal. Motivations at play include the desire to minimize costs (especially of scarce and increasingly costly inputs), to manage risks, to increase profit, or simply to serve some economic, social, or cultural need. Some new outcome is always sought. There is also a range of actors and agents, variously investing, researching, financing, marketing, managing, governing, or consuming, all seeking to contribute to or gain from the search for new ways of doing things.

While ideas and institutions set the stage, interests motivate the action. Effective policy engages to advance the interests of broad segments of the economy and society. Given Canada's heterogeneity, different jurisdictions have markedly different contextual factors underpinning science, technology, and innovation, and different interactions among actors, organizations, and institutions. Quebec, for instance, has built a relatively independent architecture of institutions and systems that mirrors the nation state and that it uses to pursue a sometimes competing but often complementary agenda to the federal effort. Ontario, which is vested with significant resources for science, technology, and innovation, has its efforts significantly intertwined with the federal system, partly because the province represents about 39 per cent of the national economy and population and partly because the national capital and the bulk of the intramural research effort and the special operating entities are sited in the province. Beyond central

Canada, different actors lead in different regions, with federal and a few provincial agencies dominating the agenda in some provinces or territories while industry or the higher education sector leads in others.

Given the expansive and diffuse nature of the Canadian science, technology, and innovation system, it is valuable to map aspects of the system. One place to start is with the funding of research and development (R&D). In 2016, Canada funded approximately $33.5 billion of R&D, equal to about 1.66 per cent of gross domestic product (GDP), down from a peak of about 2.2 per cent earlier in the decade. In 2016, business enterprises contributed about 45 per cent of the total funding, higher education about 19 per cent, the federal government just over 17 per cent, and private not-for-profits 4 per cent. About 8 per cent of the funds came from foreign sources, including firms, other governments, granting agencies, and not-for-profits (Table 4.1).

Gross expenditure on R&D (GERD) as a percentage of GDP varied widely across provinces, with Quebec at the top with 2.17 per cent and the territories at the bottom with 0.81 per cent. Business R&D as a percentage of GDP averaged 0.75 per cent across the country, from a high of 1.07 per cent in Quebec to 0.20 per cent in New Brunswick. Federal GERD as a percentage of GDP, averaged 0.29 per cent but ranged from 0.14 per cent in Alberta to 0.42 per cent in Prince Edward Island (PEI). Provincial governments in Quebec and Alberta were the most significant relative investors. Post-secondary institutions are relatively more important in the Atlantic provinces, while foreign funding is more significant in the territories, British Columbia, Ontario, and Quebec.

Funding tells us half of the story; the other half involves who actually performs the research and development (Table 4.2). Ontario, Quebec, Alberta, and British Columbia combined undertake 91 per cent of the R&D in Canada. Business performs more than half the R&D in Ontario, Quebec, Alberta, British Columbia, and the territories, while the higher education sector dominates in Atlantic Canada and Manitoba. The federal government is a relatively large player in PEI (20 per cent of activity), the territories (17 per cent), Manitoba (14 per cent), Saskatchewan (12 per cent), New Brunswick (11 per cent), and Ontario (10 per cent), but directly undertakes only about 3 per cent of activity in Quebec, Alberta, and British Columbia.

Understanding the dynamics in the national system requires moving beyond these high-level observations. The policy evaluation literature offers a useful rubric for unpacking who does what, why, when, and where. Scholars and practitioners suggest that one can parse the impact of any effort by identifying the actors and their inputs to the system, the array of activities undertaken with those resources, the direct outputs

Table 4.1. Gross Expenditure on Research and Development as a percentage of GDP, by Province, 2016

| Jurisdiction | Total, All Funders | Government | | Provincial Research Organizations | Business Enterprise | Higher Education | Private Non-profit | Foreign |
		Federal	Provincial					
Canada	1.66	0.29	0.09	0.00	0.75	0.32	0.07	0.13
Newfoundland and Labrador	1.14	0.20	0.06	–	0.39	0.44	0.01	0.03
Prince Edward Island	1.20	0.42	0.04	–	0.29	0.40	0.03	0.04
Nova Scotia	1.39	0.40	0.04	–	0.28	0.56	0.06	0.06
New Brunswick	0.90	0.23	0.03	–	0.20	0.37	0.03	0.04
Quebec	2.17	0.31	0.15	–	1.07	0.39	0.08	0.16
Ontario	1.88	0.38	0.07	–	0.84	0.33	0.08	0.19
Manitoba	1.12	0.28	0.05	–	0.36	0.31	0.07	0.05
Saskatchewan	0.91	0.21	0.05	0.01	0.36	0.24	0.03	0.02
Alberta	1.19	0.14	0.13	–	0.65	0.20	0.04	0.03
British Columbia	1.31	0.23	0.05	–	0.55	0.27	0.07	0.15
Territories	0.81	0.15	0.07	–	0.49	–	0.04	0.29

Sources: Authors calculations; Statistics Canada, table 27-10-0273-01, "Gross domestic expenditures on research and development, by science type and by funder and performer sector (x 1,000,000)."

Table 4.2. Gross Expenditure on Research and Development by Performing Sector, Canada, Provinces, and Territories, 2012–16

Jurisdiction	Total	Government		Provincial Research Organizations	Business Enterprise	Higher Education	Private, Non-profit
		Federal	Provincial				
Gross expenditure	29,932	2,082	268	30	15,677	11,736	139
	(% Canada)			($ millions)			
Canada	100	7	1	0	52	39	–
				(average percentage distribution by sector)			
Newfoundland and Labrador	1	5	–	–	27	67	–
Prince Edward Island	<1	20	3	–	28	52	–
Nova Scotia	2	9	–	–	20	71	–
New Brunswick	1	11	–	1	28	59	–
Quebec	26	3	1	0	58	39	–
Ontario	44	10	0	–	53	36	–
Manitoba	2	14	1	–	35	50	–
Saskatchewan	2	12	1	2	40	45	–
Alberta	11	3	4	–	55	38	–
British Columbia	10	3	1	–	54	42	–
Territories	<1	17	–	17	67	–	–

Note: Columns and rows may not sum due to rounding.

Sources: Authors' calculations; Statistics Canada, table 27-10-0273-01, "Gross domestic expenditures on research and development, by science type and by funder and performer sector (x 1,000,000)."

of those activities, and the direct, indirect, and induced outcomes arising from the effort. We combine this with some of the guidance from the Organisation for Economic Co-operation and Development (OECD) Oslo Manual, which posits that a general set of "framework" conditions and institutions (for example, education, financial, legal, public, scientific, and cultural endowments) establishes the range of opportunities for innovation. Innovation is thus a nested activity with a complex set of factors within the firm that rely directly on an array of human, social, and cultural processes and systems external to the enterprise. There is significant blurring of the line between activities and actors in innovation: some see it as fundamentally an intrafirm event, while others see innovation as an industrial event, a community event, a national event, or a collective event involving arrays of institutions – for example, the triple helix of industry, government, and university articulated by sociologists Etzkowitz and Leydesdorff (1995, 1997). Innovation is seldom limited to local ecosystems, but encompasses a wide range of actors who are geographically dispersed within communities and across the world.

In what follows we discuss the motivations of each of the institutions explored in Chapter 3, and position their interests on the spectrum from inputs to outputs. Through this approach, we hope to deliver a somewhat nuanced set of narratives about the respective interests of the various institutions, their contributions to the overall innovation agenda, and the resulting individual and cumulative outcomes in the socio-economic system.

Politics

While innovation policy has seldom captured the imagination of voters or dominated the public agenda in Canada, partisan politics can and does have an effect on why and where innovation policy advances. The nature of our constitutional system, which unifies power in the hands of an executive responsible to the legislature and the people by regular elections, often works to delay consideration of policy matters that are longer term, are more difficult to define, and involve a diffuse set of actors that are hard to mobilize.

All governments in Canada elect representatives through first-past-the-post (FPTP), single-member constituencies. As Elections Canada (Canada 2018) explains, this system tends to drive out third parties and fringe issues, as candidates must appeal to a broad spectrum of voters to get elected; once elected, representatives generally have little power unless they are part of the government or in an opposition caucus. Special interests often get diluted or marginalized in this system. There have been a few efforts to reform the system, but so far none has advanced. British Columbia dabbled with a variety of alternate systems (such as multimember constituencies), but converged on the single-member FPTP system by 1990. Both British Columbia and Ontario have aggressively explored electoral reform, including referenda – in British Columbia in 2005, 2009, and 2018, and in Ontario in 2007 – to solicit voters' opinions on if or how to implement single, transferrable voting, mixed-member proportional representation (PR), and a range of other PR systems. None of the referenda passed the threshold for implementation.

The political system accommodates a wide variety of interests, but actually empowers a narrow range of parties. Historically Canada has had two large, broadly based centrist parties, the Liberals and Conservatives – sometimes called "big tent," "catch-all," or "broad church" – that contest for and have held power at the national level, mostly with majority governments, although party schisms and third parties have emerged and endured for extended periods. Provincial politics has been a bit more dynamic, with local interests leading to unique provincial parties and governments (Table 4.3). Alberta had a Social Credit government for an extended period. Social democracy emerged in Saskatchewan in the 1930s, where the Co-operative Commonwealth Confederation (CCF), later the New Democratic Party (NDP), have governed for extended periods; the NDP has held power at times in five other provinces. Quebec has had extended periods with nationalist governments: first, the Union nationale off and on from 1936 to 1970, and then the sovereigntist Parti Québécois. Recently a nativist movement has been taken up by centre-right parties that have gained power in Quebec, Alberta, and Saskatchewan, while the Green Party held the balance of power in British Columbia between 2017 and 2020, and became the official opposition in PEI in 2019. Elections in the provinces and territories are contested by as many as nineteen official parties, with up to five represented in the various assemblies. Majority governments have tended to be the norm, although in 2020 the federal government and four provinces had minority governments.

Despite concerns that the FPTP system tends to mute electoral change, Canada's electoral system delivers dynamic outcomes. Parties started as integrated federal-provincial units, but few now are. Most provinces have set up separate party organizations even if they share the same name, and some (Quebec, Saskatchewan, Alberta) have created provincial-specific parties. Every province and the federal government had at least two changes of governing party between 1990 and 2020, with

Table 4.3. Politics in Canada, May 2021

Jurisdiction	Government Party *Minority	Loyal Opposition	Other Parties with Seats	Parties without Seats	Date Prime Minister/Premier Appointed	Number of Premiers, 1990–2021	Number of Changes in Party, 1990–2021
Canada	Liberal*	Conservative Party of Canada	Bloc Québécois, NDP, Green	11	2015	6	3
Newfoundland and Labrador	Liberal	Progressive Conservative	NDP, Independent	1	2020	10	2
Prince Edward Island	Progressive Conservative*	Green	Liberal	1	2019	7	3
Nova Scotia	Liberal*	Progressive Conservative	NDP, Independent	2	2021	9	4
New Brunswick	Progressive Conservative	Liberal	Green, People's Alliance	2	2018	8	4
Quebec	Coalition Avenir Québec	Liberal	Québec Solidaire, Parti Québécois	18	2018	9	5
Ontario	Progressive Conservative	NDP	Liberal, Green, New Blue	19	2018	7	4
Manitoba	Progressive Conservative	NDP	Liberal	3	2016	4	2
Saskatchewan	Saskatchewan Party	NDP	–	5	2018	5	2
Alberta	United Conservative	NDP	–	9	2019	8	2
British Columbia	NDP	Liberal	Green	13	2017	9	3
Yukon	Liberal*	Yukon Party	NDP	2	2016	7	5
NWT	–	–	–	–	2019	10	–
Nunavut	–	–	–	–	2018	5	–

Sources: Various public sources; authors' calculations.

Quebec and Yukon having five changes in the period. Alberta is a bit of an outlier, as it has been governed for extended periods by parties with overwhelming mandates: Liberals (1905–21), United Farmers of Alberta (1921–35), Social Credit (1935–71), and Conservatives (1971–2015). But even Alberta has had two changes of government in the past five years. Parties are even more dynamic: parties in power renew their leaders three times more frequently than elections change governments. Provinces and territories have had between four and ten premiers over the past thirty years. The average tenure of sitting government leaders in May 2021 is about three years, with Manitoba premier Brian Pallister, in his fifth year of governing, the longest serving as of May 2021. Only Prime Minster Justin Trudeau has led a government longer in current federal-provincial politics.

Some enduring elements of government emerge from this system. Governing political parties in the Atlantic provinces contest for the median voter, which leads to small changes in policy when governments change. In contrast, Quebec politics delivers sharply divergent governments, swinging between nationalist and federalist parties that differentially pursue social democratic or liberal policies. Ontario and Nova Scotia are the only provinces with sustained three-party politics, both having had Liberal, Progressive Conservative, and NDP governments in the past thirty years. Saskatchewan and British Columbia traditionally have had left-right, rural-urban conflicts that drive policy, and both have spawned new national movements (CCF/NDP and Social Credit, respectively). Manitoba recently has settled into this left-right pattern in its governments. The territories have some parties, and Yukon has a government formed of parties, but party politics is less important than elsewhere in Canada. Interestingly, Canadian cities are governed largely by non-partisan elected councils consisting of independents. Only municipalities in Quebec (Montreal, Quebec City, and Longueuil) and British Columbia (Vancouver, Victoria, Surrey, and Richmond) have locally based political parties or election slates, few of which affiliate with any provincial or federal party.

Politics everywhere is becoming more structured. In the not-so-distant past, parties were less formally organized and their leaders elected in a wider array of ways, often only by party insiders. In particular, parties recently have formalized how leaders are chosen and removed, which often limits the opportunity for elected caucuses to change leaders – a common practice in the United Kingdom and Australia. The electoral system itself is now more rules bound. Until the last decade, the only limit to the timing of elections was that they had to be held within five years of the previous election, with the actual timing up to the government. Fixed election laws started in Alberta and are now almost universal – only Nova Scotia and Yukon do not have one. These laws set either a fixed date every four years or specify that the next election be four years after the previous one. At the municipal level, all the provinces have moved to scheduled elections every four years.

As the following chapters on the provinces and territories will show, partisan politics has a variety of effects on innovation policy. In some provinces, parties actively promote new approaches to innovation; in others, innovation policy is largely isolated from partisan influence.

Provincial Government Interests

Governments undoubtedly have the broadest mandates and legal powers, and the widest range of policy interests of all institutions. They generally want to do right by the public, and to do their work properly, equitably, efficiently, and sustainably. The literature on agenda setting, however, and, to a lesser extent, evaluation, illustrates that it is challenging to define what problem is being solved or what goal is being pursued, as there is no limit to the permutations and combinations of demands and opportunities facing governments.

Provinces and territories are probably the most exposed of all the orders of government. National governments have the protection of large numbers of interested institutions competitively engaging, plus the luxury of distance from most of those they govern. This allows federal administrations to go beyond the narrow interests of specific firms and sectors and engage in ways that address larger concerns. Cities can be, and usually are, parochial. Given the uneven distribution and concentration of many sectors in Canada, cities often have only a few entrepreneurs, firms, or emerging sectors they can usefully champion. Provinces, in contrast, are too local to avoid the chumminess of local interests, but too large to ignore the necessity of structured policy and programming. Territories in some ways are probably more like cities, in that personalities and individual circumstances might be impossible to ignore due to their thin economic and social systems; on the upside, such small, personal governments can be more responsive to citizens' needs.

As noted in Table 3.4 in Chapter 3, the provincial economies differ widely, with goods production contributing between 19 per cent of GDP in Nova Scotia and 52 per cent in Saskatchewan, and individual sectors are concentrated in different provinces. A complementary way to examine the economic base is to look at the distribution of specific sectors across provinces, rather than within each province (Table 4.4).

Table 4.4. Distribution of Canada's Sectoral GDP, by Province and Territory, 2014–18

Jurisdiction	All Goods production	Goods production	Crop & Animal Production	Forestry & Logging	Mining & Quarrying	Energy	Power Generation	Manufacturing	Services	Finance & Insurance
	(average percentage share of Canadian value added in sector)									
Newfoundland and Labrador	2	3	0	1	7	5	2	0	1	1
Prince Edward Island	0	0	1	0	0	0	0	0	0	0
Nova Scotia	2	1	1	2	0	1	2	1	2	2
New Brunswick	2	1	1	8	1	1	3	2	2	1
Quebec	19	17	18	23	21	8	33	25	19	17
Ontario	37	29	22	9	20	10	31	45	41	53
Manitoba	3	3	10	1	3	2	5	3	3	3
Saskatchewan	4	8	21	1	24	11	4	3	3	2
Alberta	18	26	16	11	3	55	8	13	14	10
British Columbia	13	10	10	46	15	8	11	9	14	11
Yukon	0	0	0	0	0	0	0	0	0	0
NWT	0	0	0	0	4	0	0	0	0	0
Nunavut	0	0	0	0	2	0	0	0	0	0

Sources: Author's calculations; Statistics Canada, table 36-10-0402-01, "Gross domestic product (GDP) at basic prices, by industry, provinces and territories," online at https://www150.statcan.gc.ca/t1/tbl1/en/tv.action?pid=3610040201, accessed 10 September 2019.

A few provinces have the lion's share of some sectors and often are the national champion for policy in those areas. Quebec has particular vested interests in forestry, mining, power generation, and manufacturing. Ontario is vested in manufacturing and services, especially finance. Manitoba, arguably one of the more diversified economies – or, as our chapter authors say, the most "average" – still has particular interests in agriculture and power generation. Saskatchewan has a plurality of activity in agriculture and mining. Alberta's laser focus on primary energy arises from its 55 per cent market share of all such activity in Canada. Finally, although British Columbia has moved heavily to a services economy, it still contributes almost half the value added in the national forestry sector. All the other provinces and territories have above-average effort in certain sectors, but none contributes more than 10 per cent of the national activity in any sector.

Almost all provinces and territories accept that they need more productivity and growth to sustain and realize their economic and social aspirations. Innovation, especially innovation driven by science and technology, is a go-to strategy to achieve that goal. In some instances, the innovation is directed to resolving barriers to development – for example, Alberta's R&D investments in heavy oil extraction and Saskatchewan's efforts to overcome barriers to potash mining. Other efforts are designed to assist and support new economic activity, such as information technology, biotechnology, advanced materials, and artificial intelligence, where provinces have sought to exploit new technologies to accelerate innovation and growth. Some effort is targeted to sustain or improve factor productivity – that is, the efficient use of land, labour, and capital – in existing firms and sectors such as agriculture, forestry, and mining, all of which face declining marginal productivity due to the depletion of resources. But provinces have more than economic motivations. Innovation is also desired for what it can offer in terms of new fiscal capacity and new technical opportunities for improving the social and cultural fabric of society and, increasingly, for how it helps to improve or enhance environmental sustainability.

The challenge for most provinces, especially the smaller ones, is that the structure of their economy limits their influence and reduces the incentives to invest alone in most developments. Flows of inputs and outputs within and between provinces work to distribute the benefits of any specific provincial venture well beyond the host province. As Table 4.5 shows, the average multiplier for economic activity in each province is less than 1, with the result that $1 million spent by a government will yield something less in terms of net overall economic activity in that province. Much of the impact is distributed elsewhere in

Table 4.5. Input-Output Multipliers, Total Output Multiplier (Level 4), Canada, Provinces, and Territories, 2016

Jurisdiction	Total Industries	Lowest Sectoral Multiplier	Highest Sectoral Multiplier
Canada	1.94	1.62	2.25
Newfoundland and Labrador	0.79	0.48	1.15
Prince Edward Island	0.88	0.64	1.07
Nova Scotia	0.92	0.54	1.20
New Brunswick	0.77	0.33	1.14
Quebec	0.95	0.66	1.14
Ontario	0.94	0.58	1.16
Manitoba	0.90	0.64	1.22
Saskatchewan	0.86	0.61	1.13
Alberta	0.95	0.76	1.11
British Columbia	0.98	0.77	1.25
Yukon	0.87	0.55	1.02
NWT	0.71	0.33	0.97
Nunavut	0.71	0.25	0.91

Source: Statistics Canada, table 36-10-0013-01, "Input-output multipliers, summary level," online at https://www150.statcan.gc.ca/t1/tbl1/en/tv.action?pid=3610001301.

Canada: the overall national multiplier is almost 2, meaning that more than a half of the impact of any development in a province will flow elsewhere in Canada. The subnational multipliers range from 0.71 in NWT and Nunavut to 0.98 in British Columbia. The sector targeted for development also matters. Sectors with limited forward and backward linkages in the province generally deliver much lower multipliers (often less than half the average provincial multiplier). But each province has at least one sector, and some have more, that should yield some positive multiple of impact for any investment. A recent study of the Protein Industries Canada supercluster initiative located in the Prairies illustrates this effect. The input-output analysis revealed that about 35 per cent of the total GDP impact would arise outside the Prairies, more than 60 per cent of the new employment would be located in the rest of Canada, and almost half of the government revenues would accrue to governments elsewhere. The inexorable logic of this is that few provinces would have a strong economic argument for investing in new developments, except in a few narrow and highly competitive sectors.

The flip side of low provincial multipliers is the high cost of raising public funds through various taxation rates. Dahlby and Ferede (2011) estimate that the marginal cost of public funds is relatively high everywhere, with wide variations both over time and across provinces. For 2006 they estimate that the marginal cost of public funds from personal income taxes ranged from 1.45 in Alberta to 3.85 in Quebec, with rates generally higher in the Atlantic provinces but lower in the West.

Science, technology, and innovation policy is complicated, as it is often woven into the fabric of the political rhetoric and cultural self-image of a province. Quebec's extensive and aggressive approach to science and innovation is at least partly a manifestation of the clarion call of the Quiet Revolution in the 1960s to be *maîtres chez nous* ("masters of our own house"). Other provinces in different ways have framed their self-image around various specific technologies, such as biotechnology, advanced manufacturing, and digital technologies. Regardless of the clarity of purpose, however, government motives often get clouded by local politics, as different opportunities become personified with individual entrepreneurs, firms, locations, and political parties.

Turning provincial and local inspirations into action is challenging. Governments attempt to influence the system by a mix of leadership, selected capital investments, new infrastructure, and education. As the individual provincial and territorial chapters illustrate, most jurisdictions have a balance of policies in support of science, technology, and innovation, sometimes wrapped up in a coherent and consistent policy statement and sometimes simply discernable from the actions of the government.

The most visible and watched measure of engagement is provincial and territorial government investments in R&D (Table 4.6). On average in the 2012–16 period, the provinces and territories allocated more than $1.8 billion annually, albeit on a downward trend over the period. Almost two-thirds of these funds went to the higher education sector, about 17 per cent was spent directly by provincial departments, agencies, and provincial research organizations, and 15 per cent was disbursed to businesses to support in-house R&D. The distribution across the provinces is mostly proportionate to population, with two notable exceptions. Compared with their share of the national economy, Quebec and Alberta unambiguously fund a higher portion of R&D than other provinces or territories – Quebec flows those funds to industry and higher education and Alberta to intramural research and universities.

Provinces also invest significantly in training and recruitment of educated and skilled labour. The main partners for provinces are universities and polytechs that educate and train the majority of new labour market entrants. As noted in Chapter 3, there is significant diversity in

Table 4.6. Provincial government funding for R&D by performing sector, by province and territory, average distribution, 2012–2016

Jurisdiction	Total	Government		Provincial Research Organizations	Business Enterprises	Higher Education	Private Non-profit
		Federal	Provincial				
Canada ($ millions)	1,830	3	298	12	282	1,174	61
(% distribution)	100.0	0.1	16.3	0.7	15.4	64.2	3.3
	(percentage distribution of total by performing sector)						
Newfoundland and Labrador	1.0	–	–	–	0.6	1.5	–
Prince Edward Island	0.1	–	0.7	–	0.5	0.1	–
Nova Scotia	0.8	–	–	–	0.9	1.0	–
New Brunswick	0.5	–	–	–	0.9	0.6	–
Quebec	33.3	40.0	24.8	–	53.2	32.2	–
Ontario	28.3	80.0	18.2	–	32.0	31.7	–
Manitoba	1.7	–	2.5	–	0.8	1.8	–
Saskatchewan	2.2	–	1.3	–	1.8	2.4	–
Alberta	21.5	–	45.1	–	4.7	20.8	–
British Columbia	7.1	–	7.8	–	4.5	7.9	–
Territories	0.1	–	–	16.4	–	–	–

Note: Columns and rows may not sum due to rounding.

Sources: Authors' calculations; Statistics Canada, table: 27-10-0273-01, "Gross domestic expenditures on research and development, by science type and by funder and performer sector (x 1,000,000)."

the distribution of educated and skilled workers among the provinces. Training more is one way to address the gap; another is through the migration of skilled workers. While interprovincial migration is generally unimpeded, cities and provinces are making significant effort to retain or attract educated and highly skilled workers to support economic development. These efforts involve a range of direct incentives (such as tax deductibility of post-secondary tuition for graduates who stay in a province) and indirect supports (such as superclusters and industrial research parks). Nevertheless, no province would say it has closed its skills gaps. In response, the federal government and, since the late 2000s, the provinces have worked aggressively to attract skilled immigrants. The federal immigration program has moved to increase the total number of immigrants to over 400,000 by 2021, with over 70 per cent of those economic migrants. Until the 1970s, all immigrants were selected by federal officers to meet national goals. Since then, first Quebec and then the rest of the provinces have negotiated agreements to have a greater say in the selection of economic migrants. Provinces have used this capacity differently (Table 4.7). Manitoba was the first and most aggressive province to use the nominee system, with Saskatchewan not far behind. Interestingly, Ontario, Alberta, and British Columbia have each used the program, but more selectively perhaps than other provinces, as they targeted only a modest portion of total economic migrants landing over the 2011–17 period.

Most politicians are to a great extent judged on whether their policies generate and sustain highly paid jobs. Whether or not this is a reasonable expectation deserves some thought. The challenge is that most of the labour market is disconnected from R&D and innovation in two possible ways: first, labour markets, especially in the resource sectors, can be geographically distanced if R&D is not *in situ*, but in cities that host research universities and technology parks; and, second, labour markets can experience the impact of R&D and innovation some time after technologies mature or pass through regulatory approval. Somewhat perversely, many innovations appear creatively to destroy employment and wealth as they emerge and challenge existing production systems; net job growth often lags significantly. This dampens public and government enthusiasm about innovation, irrespective of whether or not it is generally viewed as important.

Overall, the provinces aspire to drive and benefit from R&D, and have a broad and expansive set of expectations of how success in this field could contribute to their socio-economic development. But the structure and function of the national economy and relatively limited capacity of the provinces themselves mean their reach often exceeds their grasp.

Table 4.7. Total Provincial Nominee Program Immigrants as Share of All Economic Immigrants, Canada, Provinces, and Territories, Cumulative Totals, 2011–17

Jurisdiction	Provincial Nominee Program	Total Economic Migrants	Provincial Nominee Program Migrants as % of Total
Canada	307,292	1,115,865	28
Newfoundland and Labrador	2,521	4,075	62
Prince Edward Island	9,604	10,029	96
Nova Scotia	11,056	15,852	70
New Brunswick	13,043	14,706	89
Quebec	179*	235,769*	0
Ontario	23,351	354,573	7
Manitoba	72,562	77,937	93
Saskatchewan	62,042	68,758	90
Alberta	65,271	181,774	36
British Columbia	45,555	150,093	30
Yukon	219	319	69
NWT	1,210	1,450	83
Nunavut	243	516	47

* Quebec has a separate system for selecting migrations other than the Provincial Nominee Program.

Note: Columns may not sum due to rounding.

Source: Trujillo 2019.

Federal Interests

The federal government overwhelms provincial and local efforts in many jurisdictions, partly due to its sheer size and level of engagement and partly because of its aspirations. As discussed in some detail in Doern, Phillips, and Castle (2016), the federal government has come to the innovation agenda in a series of fits and starts, frequently reformulating and adding to the objectives of the policy file. As noted in that book, the federal government has an abiding interest in science, technology, and innovation, is both absolutely and relatively a major actor in the national system, has acknowledged the imperative for Canadian industry to be responsive, and has worked to create policy and market conditions to support national innovation.

Where the federal government obviously differs is in the scope of its ambition. Unlike at the provincial level, where limited fiscal capacity constrains effort and large import leakage dissipates the returns, the federal government can and usually does look at the full effects of its ventures. In that sense, it can expect its investments to be more afford-able, less risky, and likely to generate higher net returns to the national economy and federal treasury. Moreover, in contrast to the provinces and local governments, federal policies, programs, politicians, and administrators can usually abstract or distance from the specific inter-ests, needs, or pressures of individual entrepreneurs, firms, or sectors. Federal decision makers are usually more physically distant from those exerting pressure and are bound by increasingly stringent conflict-of-interest and lobbying rules that control overt lobbying.

One might expect that this would allow a more coherent and sus-tained policy effort at the federal level. In some ways it has, but the effort remains diffuse. Overall, the federal system directly invested annually almost $6 billion in the 2012–16 period, about half of that to the higher education sector, about $500 million a year directly to firms and the rest to intramural research inside the federal system (Table 4.8).

To get a better sense of the interests at play in the federal system, it is worthwhile unpacking the outlays and efforts. At the core is the Department of Innovation, Science and Economic Development (ISED), which has a large portfolio of agencies, including the three federal granting councils, the Canada Foundation for Innovation, the National Research Council, and about twenty third-party orga-nizations such as Genome Canada, the Communications Research Centre, and Canarie. The ministry and its portfolio directly spends or disburses more than half the federal effort. But its efforts do not always align – each of the separate operating agencies has its own arm's-length governance system, which often makes them compet-ing voices both inside government and in the larger economy. The granting agencies, in particular, have a special relationship with the post-secondary education sector that broadens the conversation, while the special operating agencies bond with their clients. Beyond ISED, many line departments have intramural research, either to advance some aspect of science and technology – for example, the Research Branch of Agriculture and Agri-Food Canada (AAFC), which does breeding and agronomy – or to support policy and regulation. AAFC, Environment and Climate Change, Fisheries and Oceans, Global Affairs, Health Canada, Natural Resources Canada, and National Defence all are major investors in research and science (see Table 4.9).

Table 4.8. Federal Funding for R&D Allocated to Performing Sectors, Canada, Provinces, and Territories, 2012–16

Jurisdiction	Total	Federal Government	Provincial Research Organizations	Business Enterprises	Higher Education	Private Non-profit
Canada ($ millions)	5,935	2,289	1	502	3,108	34
(% distribution)	100	39	0	8	52	1
			(average percentage distribution of federal resources to preforming sector)			
Newfoundland and Labrador	1.0	0.8	–	1.7	1.1	–
Prince Edward Island	0.5	0.7	–	0.5	0.3	–
Nova Scotia	2.8	2.3	–	2.0	3.3	–
New Brunswick	1.3	1.5	–	2.1	1.0	–
Quebec	21.0	11.0	–	37.3	25.9	–
Ontario	49.9	66.3	–	30.6	41.5	–
Manitoba	3.2	4.6	–	1.4	2.5	–
Saskatchewan	2.7	3.5	–	2.0	2.3	–
Alberta	7.0	5.0	–	5.0	8.8	–
British Columbia	10.1	4.2	–	18.7	13.2	–
Territories	0.1	0.1	100.0	0.0	–	–

Note: Columns may not sum due to rounding.

Sources: Authors' calculations; Statistics Canada, table 27-10-0273-01, "Gross domestic expenditures on research and development, by science type and by funder and performer sector (x 1,000,000)."

Table 4.9. Federal Program and Tax Expenditures on Science and Technology, by Major Department and Agency, fiscal years 2015/16 to 2017/18

	Fiscal Years			Change, 2015/16 to 2017/18
	2015/16	2016/17	2017/18	
	($ millions)			(%)
All Federal Program Spending	10,363	11,439	11,297	9.0
Innovation, Science and Economic Development portfolio				
Department	366	558	855	133.6
Canada Foundation for Innovation	341	336	367	7.6
Canadian Institutes of Health Research	1,026	1,084	1,087	5.9
Canadian Space Agency	389	383	333	−14.4
National Research Council	981	1,094	1,002	2.1
Natural Sciences and Engineering Research Council	1,115	1,196	1,207	8.3
Social Sciences and Humanities Research Council	720	778	775	7.6
Statistics Canada	640	864	583	−8.9
Portfolio sub-total	5,578	6,293	6,209	11.3
Other science-based departments and agencies				
Agriculture and Agri-Food	496	492	447	−9.9
Environment & Climate Change	621	658	652	5.0
Fisheries and Oceans	235	300	299	27.2
Global Affairs	456	486	453	−0.7
Health Canada	373	381	386	3.5
Natural Resources Canada	494	528	505	2.2
Atomic Energy of Canada	389	406	418	7.5
National Defence	261	277	294	12.6
Other departments and agencies	1,460	1,618	1,634	11.9
Subtotal	4,785	5,146	5,088	6.3
Scientific Research and Experimental Development Investment Tax Credit				
Non-refundable portion for corporate income tax	1,385	1,445	1,500	8.3
Refundable portion	1,305	1,350	1,405	7.7
Total tax credits	2,690	2,795	2,905	8.0

Source: Statistics Canada, table 27-10-0026-01, "Federal expenditures on science and technology, by major departments and agencies - Intentions," online at http://www5.statcan.gc.ca/cansim/a26?lang=eng&id=3580163.

These GERD numbers capture only cash payments, not the large tax expenditures through the Scientific Research and Experimental Development Tax Incentive Program (SR&ED). While tax expenditures often go unnoticed for long periods because they are not formally budgeted and often are perpetual, the sheer size of the SR&ED, which peaked at over $3.4 billion in 2009, has evoked extensive comment and criticism. There is extensive debate about whether the funds are focused enough, whether they are helping the firms most in need, and whether they might be better managed (see Doern, Phillips, and Castle 2016).

The federal government plays another important role: through investments in scholarly research in general and through a number of policy-engaged institutions in particular, the federal government supports research and dialogue to frame the national debate. As early as the 1960s, Canada created an Economic Council and then a separate Science Council to advise on policy options and strategies. Both councils were wound down in the early 1990s and replaced with advisory boards tasked with offering advice on biotechnology, science, technology, and innovation, the environment and the economy, and a range of technical questions about appropriate incentives for commercialization and growth. In 2005, the Council of Canadian Academies was formed to respond to the government's need for assessments of evidence related to arising policy questions. The combined effort of these ventures and their impact on the national conversation is significant, but their impact on policy itself is largely an open question. In many ways, these forums provide an outlet for venting the array of demands from both inside and outside the federal system that cannot be accommodated in the policy system.

In 2015 the then new Liberal government added inclusivity to the federal innovation agenda, which is variously defined in demographic, geographic, sectoral, and social terms. The new goal works to moderate the common tendency in science, technology, and innovation policies to focus on the first and best among inventors and innovators using cutting-edge technologies, often to the exclusion of later adaptors and adopters or more socially engaged researchers. While the goal has been set, there is little concrete evidence of how priorities and activities are shifting at the federal level. Nevertheless, one can see their effect on the structuring of ventures funded by the federal government, in that project teams and boards are beginning to become gender, racial, and geographically diverse.

Local Governments

Local governments are beyond the scope of this book, but they cannot be ignored. Most science and research is undertaken in cities, almost all the firms and sectors heavily engaged in innovation are located in urban settings (or at least their head offices are), most universities and research institutes are anchored in cities, and most knowledge-economy jobs are created in metropolitan areas. Moreover, most of the clusters that can be identified statistically are anchored on cities, which host the systems and creative communities that drive innovation. Spencer (2014) estimates that, in 2010, Canada had 230 measurable economic clusters, virtually all of them in urban settings. Generally, the number of clusters in a province is proportionate to their economic size, with employment in British Columbia and New Brunswick notably more heavily clustered than the rest (Table 4.10).

Regardless of the size of the urban area, ranging from metro Toronto with 5.9 million people to towns of as few as 5,000, local politicians are boosters for economic development – and sometimes innovation. Limited fiscal capacity, inherent leakiness of municipal economies (which all have multipliers smaller than their province), and the pressure of other inescapable priorities means there is little energy and few resources to devote to innovation. Municipal governments' main roles are planning and zoning, both of which can be an asset or a hindrance to some ventures. Sustained municipal level policy and programming effort most often comes from sectoral or community-based associations that mobilize local industry and connect it with the system of supporting services. Communitech in the Waterloo region, the Ottawa Centre for Research and Innovation in the National Capital Region, and AgWest Bio in Saskatoon all have long-term, demonstrated capacity to assist local development.

Universities

As shown in the GERD data, the higher education sector is a large part of our national, provincial, and territorial research systems. Etzkowitz and Leydesdorff (1995) characterize contemporary universities as bound into a triple helix of state, market, and university engagement that advances innovation. Canadian universities and polytechs have been variously pushed and pulled along this path, sometime enthusiastically and aggressively moving towards the entrepreneurial university model, at other times digging in their heels and resisting the pull of the market. This has led different universities at different times to exhibit and act on a mix of motives and interests.

We think it is fair to say that, at its core, the university system is grounded in the disinterested search for knowledge and finding ways to disseminate knowledge through teaching, partnerships, and

Table 4.10. Industrial Clusters in Canada, by Province, 2010

Jurisdiction	Total	Agriculture	Maritime	Forestry & Wood	Mining	Oil & Gas	Construction & Logistics	Manufacturing	Services
Canada	230	19	8	18	16	13	32	86	38
Newfoundland and Labrador	4	–	1	–	–	–	–	1	2
Prince Edward Island	1	–	–	–	–	–	–	–	1
Nova Scotia	3	–	2	–	1	–	–	–	–
New Brunswick	10	–	–	2	1	–	1	1	5
Quebec	42	5	–	4	3	–	1	25	4
Ontario	86	9	1	1	4	1	7	49	14
Manitoba	5	1	–	–	1	–	–	3	–
Saskatchewan	6	1	–	–	2	1	1	–	1
Alberta	30	1	–	–	2	10	10	4	3
British Columbia	43	2	4	11	2	1	12	3	8

Note: Columns and rows may not sum due to rounding.

Source: Spencer 2014, revised by authors.

community engagement. Were it the case that universities aspired to operate on Robert Merton's (1973) norms of communalism, universalism, disinterestedness, and organized scepticism (giving rise to the acronym CUDOS), one approach would be to resource the scholarly research system suitably and let curiosity rule. Researchers are self-starting and curious, and with time and other resources, they will happily set about deepening our understanding of the world around us and create opportunities to do new things. But we cannot ignore the fact that universities are large, expensive enterprises with a multitude of operating units and many audiences. These institutions have developed identities and purposes that far exceed the aggregation of individual interests. Boards of directors and alumni associations want to see their institutions grow in stature, reputation, and impact, both academically and socially. Senior administrations are now branding their university aspirations, such as "the university the world needs" and producing "research that makes a vital impact."

Universities have become large commercial enterprises, comparable in some respects to small towns. Generally, human resources account for upwards of 80 per cent of a university's operating budget, but on an activity basis, teaching makes up less than 25 per cent of the total effort and budget. Beyond the classroom, faculty and staff undertake curiosity-led and contract research; the university projects into the community and market with various outreach, extension, and commercial ventures; many universities are significant landlords, operating housing developments or industrial parks; and universities run substantial businesses on-campus to feed, house, and support students and staff. Each of these business units is motivated to ask for funding, and universities operate extensive endowments, undertake charitable campaigns, and are in continual negotiations with governments, industry, and alumni to secure funding for students, research, infrastructure, and maintenance. Because of their commercial footprint, universities are often drawn into the policy debate about the role of universities and innovation in their community, in Canada, and across the globe.

Higher education performs about 40 per cent of all R&D in Canada, second only to industry, and is the only performer of R&D that has posted annual growth relative to GDP in the past while. Canada has the fourth-highest higher education R&D as a percentage of GDP among OECD countries. The sector as a whole amasses almost $35 billion annually to support operations. Overall, grants from the provinces are the single-largest source of revenue, followed by tuition and federal transfers (in the form of grants, contracts, and other support). An estimated $13 billion, or about 38 per cent of the total sector effort, is booked as research. Of that, about $6 billion is counted as "undefined" research, in that it is the typically imputed value of 39–45 per cent of the average salary of a tenured faculty member. Because research time is neither paid by, nor formally budgeted in, research grants, it is only notionally allocated. The big question for policy is how much of this notional allocation is actually directed to research activities – those with external grants or publications clearly are engaged in research, but the majority of faculty at any point do not hold consecutive grants, and many publish infrequently.

Taking the full $30 billion of Tri-Council grants between 1999 and 2018, we can see that, generally speaking, there are some minor economies of scale in the allocation of grants, with larger provinces getting marginally more than their share of the Canadian population or the economy while smaller provinces got less (Table 4.11). One explanation is that smaller provinces often have fewer and smaller institutions, with the result that research is squeezed by teaching demands. Interestingly, the scale effect does not translate directly to outputs. Overall, Canadian universities produced 1.1 million publications from 1999 to 2018. Ontario, British Columbia, and Alberta leveraged their funds into a larger share of publications, but Quebec produced significantly fewer publications for the money it got. Smaller provinces that got less grant money than the size of their economy in most cases produced a relatively larger share of publications.

There are no easily accessible and universally accepted measures of the impact of this work. The Scopus academic literature database shows that Canada as a whole produces a higher proportion of scholarly work than its size in the global economy or share of world population. Across almost all major groupings by subject, Canada produces at least 2 per cent of the world's research publication output – compared with its shares of less than 0.4 per cent of the global population and 1.4 per cent of the global economy. In many fields, including health sciences, economics, decision sciences, and biological sciences, Canada produces more than 4 per cent of world output. Another measure commonly used is the citation-to-publication ratio, which in Canada is particularly high for space sciences, clinical medicine, environmental sciences, and various plant, animal, and microbial applications (Council of Canadian Academies 2018).

University patent data show significant concentrations of both invention and ownership of results in the larger provinces, anchored on the larger universities (Table 4.12). This might increase in coming years with large-scale investments in funded research chairs and networked grants, many of which will be hosted by large universities.

Table 4.11. Academic Grants and Publications, Canada, Provinces, and Territories, 1999–2018

	Tri-Agency Grants		Publications, 1999–2017	
	($ millions, 1999–2018)	(% distribution, 1998–2018)	Total	Share of Total (%)
Canada	30,645	100.0	1,113,294	100.0
Newfoundland and Labrador	298	1.0	13,842	1.2
Prince Edward Island	51	0.2	3,399	0.3
Nova Scotia	913	3.0	39,271	3.5
New Brunswick	271	0.9	14,587	1.3
Quebec	8,280	27.0	226,174	20.3
Ontario	12,212	39.8	459,836	41.3
Manitoba	794	2.6	35,939	3.2
Saskatchewan	806	2.6	36,382	3.3
Alberta	2,997	9.8	131,648	11.8
British Columbia	4,024	13.1	150,696	13.5
Yukon	0	0.0	474	<0.1
NWT	0	0.0	683	0.1
Nunavut	0	0.0	359	<0.1
Other	0	0.0	4	<0.1

Note: Columns may not sum due to rounding.

Sources: Observatoire des sciences et des technologies, December 2018; Observatoire des sciences et des technologies, Tri-Council Database, February 2019.

Universities are vitally interested in whether their inventions are used. The Association of University Technology Managers estimates that Canadian universities and research institutions generate modest income on their research portfolios. All universities combined reported income of less than $100 million a year between 2008 and 2017, which barely covered the out-of-pocket expenses of running the technology transfer programs at those institutions (Smyth, Williams, and Vasilescu 2016). Universities use a range of strategies, including licensing only to Canadian firms, investing in start-ups, and licensing exclusively to global market leaders. The choice is

Table 4.12. Patent Activity, Canada, Provinces, and Territories, 1990–2017

Jurisdiction	Patent Owners (number)	(%)	Patent Inventors (number)	(%)
Canada	89,834	100.0	128,998	100.0
Newfoundland and Labrador	189	0.2	344	0.3
Prince Edward Island	70	0.1	125	0.1
Nova Scotia	736	0.8	1,155	0.9
New Brunswick	629	0.7	1,076	0.8
Quebec	20,541	22.9	23,055	17.9
Ontario	45,486	50.6	70,105	54.3
Manitoba	1,796	2.0	2,402	1.9
Saskatchewan	1,721	1.9	2,288	1.8
Alberta	8,260	9.2	11,872	9.2
British Columbia	10,097	11.2	16,041	12.4
Yukon	22	<0.1	19	<0.1
NWT	10	<0.1	12	<0.1
Nunavut	0	0	0	0
Unknown	277	0.3	504	0.4

Source: Observatoire des sciences et des technologies, USPTO database, December 2018, online at https://www.ost.uqam.ca/en/service/bases-de-donnees/.

driven by the nature of both the technology and the market and the likelihood of the technology's reaching the market and delivering returns.

Industry

The business sector is both the workhorse for innovation and often the scapegoat for low business expenditure on R&D and the lack of innovation in Canada (Council of Canadian Academies 2018). The private sector invests almost as much as all other sectors combined, but relative to other jurisdictions, business underinvests in and underperforms doing research. Business in Canada invests only about 0.8 per cent of GDP in R&D, just about half of what business does across the OECD countries and just about one-fifth of what business expends in Israel, the highest performer.

Domestic firms in Canada invest on average $15 billion annually in R&D, of which 93 per cent is directed to in-house work or to commercial partners. Although only about 7 per cent of total outlays is directed to higher education, this represents about $1 billion of commercial funds flowing to the academy. More than 94 per cent of commercial research in Canada is directed to efforts in Ontario, Quebec, Alberta, and British Columbia. Business expenditure on R&D is vanishingly small both in absolute and proportionate terms in the other provinces and territories (Table 4.13). Bombardier has been Canada's single largest R&D undertaker, with a gross outlay of $1.6 billion in 2017. As a reference, Samsung was the top global firm, spending almost $30 billion in 2018, and twenty global firms each invested more than $8.5 billion that year.

While one solution would be for every firm and every sector to spend more on R&D, the evidence does not support this as either necessary or sufficient. Business expenditure on R&D as a share of value added in each sector varies widely. Some Canadian firms and sectors are world leaders in investing in R&D, others are laggards. One way to assess Canada's performance is by comparing its business expenditure on R&D to that of the global leaders in each sector and then estimating the gap by multiplying the difference in research intensity in the sector by the value added generated in Canada in that sector. The challenge for this analysis was finding the right comparators with data. We found five OECD countries with significantly higher business expenditure on R&D to use as comparators – the United States, France, Germany, the United Kingdom, and Italy – albeit with some gaps in sectoral coverage. Our analysis shows that Canada is a world leading investor in R&D in mining, manufacturing of paper products and computer electronics, wholesale and retail trade, and transportation and storage. In many other sectors, Canada is close to the best in either percentage or gross terms. Where we fall down is in many of the world's most research-intensive sectors, such as pharmaceutical products and medical devices, vehicles and related sectors (fabricated metal, machinery and equipment, and motor vehicles), telecommunications, manufacturing of chemicals, aerospace, and general scientific R&D. The biggest single deficit, equal to more than 40 per cent of the measured gap, is in the automotive sector and related industries.

We estimate the gap between Canada and the world's best in terms of business expenditure on R&D at just over $7 billion, or equal to about 50 per cent of current R&D performed by business in Canada. It likely would be higher if we could get evidence on the missing sectors (for an overview by sector, see Table 4.14). Even if all the firms and sectors in Canada that now expend less on R&D than the world's best were to

Table 4.13. Domestic Business Enterprise Funding for R&D and Performing Sector, Canada, Provinces, and Territories, 2012–16.

Jurisdiction		Total	Federal Government	Provincial Research Organizations	Business Enterprise	Higher Education	Private Non-profit
Canada	($ millions)	15,090	31	14	14,034	1,000	11
	(% distribution)	100	0	0	93	7	0
		(average percentage distribution across Canada, 2012–16)					
Newfoundland and Labrador		0.8	–	–	0.5	4.6	–
Prince Edward Island		0.1	–	–	0.1	0.2	–
Nova Scotia		0.8	–	–	0.6	3.3	–
New Brunswick		0.5	–	–	0.4	0.6	–
Quebec		28.2	7.0	–	28.5	25.4	–
Ontario		43.6	85.4	–	43.6	44.0	–
Manitoba		1.6	–	–	1.6	1.5	–
Saskatchewan		1.8	–	–	1.8	1.7	–
Alberta		13.0	3.2	–	13.1	12.0	–
British Columbia		9.5	3.2	–	9.7	6.8	–
Territories		0.1	–	–	–	–	–

Note: Columns may not sum due to rounding.

Sources: Authors' calculations; Statistics Canada, table: 27-10-0273-01, "Gross domestic expenditures on research and development, by science type and by funder and performer sector (x 1,000,000)."

Table 4.14. Gap in Business Expenditure on R&D by Sector, Canada, average 2012–16

Sector	R&D Intensity		Difference from World Leader	
	Canada	World Leader		
	(average %, 2012–16)		(%)	($)
Mining and quarrying	1.15	1.15	0.00	0
Manufacturer (Mfr) of textiles	2.33	2.33	0.00	0
Mfr of wearing apparel	0.75	0.75	0.00	0
Mfr of paper and paper products	1.88	1.88	0.00	0
Mfr of computer, electronic, and optical products	26.10	26.10	0.00	0
Electricity, gas, steam, etc.	0.50	0.50	0.00	0
Wholesale and retail trade	0.80	0.80	0.00	0
Transportation and storage	0.11	0.11	0.00	0
Publishing, video, and television, etc.	5.13	5.13	0.00	0
IT and other information services	6.43	6.43	0.00	0
Construction	0.08	0.08	0.00	−1
Education	0.02	0.02	0.00	−2
Printing and reproduction of recorded media	1.07	1.13	−0.06	−2
Real estate activities	0.00	0.01	0.00	−6
Mfr of wood and of products	0.97	1.16	−0.19	−12
Accommodation and food service activities	0.01	0.07	−0.06	−18
Mfr of furniture	0.61	1.48	−0.87	−31
Mfr of basic metals	1.87	2.39	−0.52	−48
Financial and insurance activities	0.32	0.38	−0.06	−61
Human health and social work activities	0.08	0.15	−0.07	−63
Administrative and support service activities	0.24	0.41	−0.16	−71
Arts, entertainment, and recreation	0.04	0.80	−0.76	−78
Mfr of electrical equipment	4.19	7.24	−3.05	−92
Agriculture, forestry, and fishing	0.34	0.86	−0.52	−105
Mfr of other non-metallic mineral products	0.85	3.10	−2.25	−130
Mfr of coke and refined petroleum products	0.06	3.77	−3.71	−183

(*Continued*)

Table 4.14. (Continued)

| Sector | R&D Intensity | | Difference from World Leader | |
	Canada	World Leader	(%)	($)
	(average %, 2012–16)			
Mfr of rubber and plastic products	1.45	4.71	–3.27	–243
Mfr of pharmaceutical products	9.78	16.71	–6.93	–260
Mfr of fabricated metal products, except machinery and equipment	1.71	3.85	–2.14	–278
Telecommunications	1.28	2.86	–1.59	–397
Mfr of medical and dental instruments and supplies	1.48	11.87	–10.39	–403
Mfr of chemicals and chemical products	2.29	8.20	–5.91	–557
Mfr of air and spacecraft and related machinery	14.32	22.01	–7.69	–617
Mfr of machinery and equipment not elsewhere classified	3.90	9.43	–5.53	–654
Scientific research and development	38.58	57.71	–19.13	–789
Mfr of motor vehicles, trailers, and semi–trailers	0.95	16.31	–15.36	–1,913
Estimated total gap				–7,013

Note: Data are missing data for food products and beverages; tobacco products; leather and related products; ships and boats; railway locomotives and rolling stock; military fighting vehicles; transport equipment n.e.c.; architectural and engineering activities, technical testing and analysis; other professional, scientific, and technical activities; public administration and defence; and compulsory social security.

Source: Organisation for Economic Co-operation and Development, "Business enterprise R&D expenditure by industry (ISIC Rev. 4)." Paris. Online at https://stats.oecd .org/

meet the standards of the world's best, Canada would still reach only about 1.2 per cent of business expenditure on R&D as a percentage of GDP, about 75 per cent of the OECD average and still only about 30 per cent of that of the top spenders.

Getting even that far would be challenging, for three reasons. First, most sectors where business expenditure on R&D lags are largely foreign owned. There is a long-standing practice for multinational enterprises (MNEs) to locate R&D and other higher-order management functions at head offices, which in these sectors are abroad. Changing that practice would be challenging but not necessarily insurmountable, as MNEs increasingly are implementing world product mandates. On most scores, Canada is an attractive place to do much of that work. Second, at least half of the lower overall rate of business expenditure on R&D is due to the structure of the Canadian economy. Canada has more value added in sectors that globally are relatively low investors in R&D and vice versa. Changing that would take time and effort. Third, in some sectors, Canada is both a global leader in production and business expenditure on R&D is leading edge, but investment is absolutely low. Agriculture, mining, oil and gas, and forestry are key sectors in this context. Government subsidies for research and infrastructure to reduce the cost of research and policy reforms that speed commercialization or increase market size are often mooted, and occasionally tried, to increase the return on R&D investment.

Firms and sectors engaged in R&D are estimated to earn good returns on R&D, albeit with peak returns lagging decades in some sectors, such as agriculture (Alston et al. 2011). Hall, Mairesse, and Mohnen (2009), after a survey of the literature on returns, conclude that, while a simple return to R&D cannot be calculated, the overall returns to R&D is positive in many countries — and usually higher than returns to ordinary capital. They also find that social returns are almost always substantially greater than commercial returns, albeit asymmetrically distributed among industries. The issue for many enterprises is not whether they earn returns, but whether firms that actively engage in research earn more than firms that wait to adapt and adopt inventions generated by others; there is less conclusive evidence on this.

Somewhat counterintuitively, despite lagging research, recent surveys in Canada suggest most firms are innovative: somewhere between 78 per cent and 86 per cent of all firms adopted at least one innovation over the 2015–17 period. Larger firms in better capitalized sectors were more aggressive. Goods-producing industries are relatively more engaged with process innovation, while services-producing industries are more focused on organization and marketing innovations (Table 4.15).

Foreign Business

As discussed in Chapter 3, Canada has significant foreign investment in its business sector, with about 20 per cent of the economy under control of foreign owners. Like our domestic industry, these firms are motivated by profit, with the proviso that their comparative opportunities often are much greater, as these enterprises operate in multiple

Table 4.15. Innovations by Type, Industry, and Enterprise Size, Canada, 2015–17

Firm Size	Type of Innovation	All firms	Agriculture etc.	Mining, oil & gas	Utilities	Construction	Manufacturing	Wholesale trade	Retail trade	Transportation	Information and Communications Technology	Finance	Professional services
		(percent of firms reporting innovation, by type)											
Small (20–99 employees)	All	78	66	68	80	75	85	84	79	68	87	85	87
	Product (good or service)	52	29	34	44	45	57	60	53	42	74	63	66
	Process	51	51	39	52	45	65	59	44	46	61	62	59
	Organizational	58	48	56	64	55	59	64	56	52	69	71	69
	Marketing	54	36	43	42	40	50	65	66	40	67	62	63
Medium (100–249 employees)	All	84	81	80	73	79	88	90	82	82	88	88	86
	Product (good or service)	53	41	48	40	36	59	64	43	46	73	74	69
	Process	58	62	50	60	48	72	61	45	63	60	71	63
	Organizational	64	58	66	67	65	67	70	50	68	72	74	71
	Marketing	56	46	39	60	42	51	61	65	50	72	69	65

Large (250+ employees)												
All	86	83	85	93	78	87	88	84	80	90	95	88
Product (good or service)	59	53	37	59	43	63	64	50	49	76	76	69
Process	64	64	71	72	54	70	62	55	57	69	76	66
Organizational	70	64	70	79	66	71	68	64	69	73	81	73
Marketing	61	56	39	52	42	57	73	68	52	66	74	64

Source: Statistics Canada, table 27-10-0155-01, "Introduction of different types of innovation by industry and enterprise size," online at https://www150.statcan.gc.ca/t1/tbl1/en/tv.action?pid=2710015501, accessed 2 October 2019.

markets. This leads to firms investing only in areas where Canada has particular technological or economic strength.

Foreign enterprises contribute approximately $2.7 billion annually to R&D, 95 per cent of which is for intramural research in business. As Table 4.16 shows, in contrast to expenditure by domestic business, foreign firms direct about 93 per cent of their attention to just three provinces: Ontario, Quebec, and British Columbia. Alberta, which nets about 13 per cent of domestic business R&D, attracts only about 3 per cent of foreign business outlays. Of particular concern is that those foreign firms gain a larger share of the rents from R&D. Statistics Canada (n.d.) reports that, over the 2014–18 period, foreign firms accounted for about 24 per cent of total business activity in Canada, but for more than half of all merchandise and commercial exports and imports; in the 2012–16 period, foreign enterprises generated about 63 per cent of

Table 4.16. Foreign Business Expenditure on R&D by Performing Sector, Canada, Provinces, and Territories, 2012–16

Jurisdiction		Total	Provincial Research Organizations	Business Enterprise	Higher Education	Private Non-profit
Canada	($ millions)	2,694	1	2,565	120	8
	(% distribution)	100	0	95	5	0
		(average percentage distribution across Canada, 2012–16)				
Newfoundland and Labrador		0.4	–	0.4	4.5	–
Prince Edward Island		0.1	–	0.1	1.7	–
Nova Scotia		0.7	–	0.7	0.0	–
New Brunswick		0.5	–	0.5	1.3	–
Quebec		24.1	–	24.1	0.0	–
Ontario		54.4	–	55.1	26.7	–
Manitoba		1.2	–	1.0	43.2	–
Saskatchewan		0.6	–	0.6	8.6	–
Alberta		3.1	80.0	3.0	0.8	–
British Columbia		14.6	–	14.5	5.2	–
Territories		0.3	–	0.3	17.7	–

Sources: Authors' calculations; Statistics Canada, table 27-10-0273-01, "Gross domestic expenditures on research and development, by science type and by funder and performer sector (x 1,000,000)."

international technological receipts and made more than 72 per cent of technological payments.

Outcomes

Ultimately, research and investment are one way or another targeted to raising the productive capacity of the economy, generating jobs, and increasing the quality of life of Canadians. The challenge is that the outcome measures – particularly productivity, growth, employment, and quality of life – are a product of more than just research.

Capacity, measured as multifactor productivity, has grown variably in the past twenty years (Table 4.17). Resource depletion in mining, oil, gas, and utilities caused a sharp drop in multifactor productivity in this significant Canadian sector. In contrast, agriculture and manufacturing posted strong gains, albeit with high volatility in the weather-dependent agricultural sector. While overall business sector multifactor productivity rose everywhere except Alberta, Saskatchewan, and New Brunswick, gains were modest. In aggregate, the national economy added only 4 per cent to its productive capacity over twenty years, or only about 0.2 per cent per year, which is very low in international terms.

Despite generally modest productivity gains, compound real growth continued above 2 per cent from 1998 to 2019. Nunavut led the way with 4.6 per cent annual growth, while the Northwest Territories posted only 0.4 per cent average growth (Statistics Canada n.d.). The range among the provinces was narrower, with British Columbia the highest at 2.6 per cent and New Brunswick the lowest at 1.3 per cent. Employment also rose: overall, over a third more workers were employed in 2018 than twenty years previously. All provinces had some growth, but the strongest growth was in Alberta (54 per cent), British Columbia (34 per cent), Ontario (33 per cent), and Quebec (31 per cent). Looked at by sector, one can see that those industries with the most R&D and where Canada is relatively strong – specifically the goods-producing sectors – largely lost employees, suggesting innovation in this period might have creatively destroyed more employment than it created.

Growth in material prosperity over the period was significant and relatively widely distributed. Average GDP per capita is now over $51,000 per annum, with particularly strong results in Alberta, Saskatchewan, the North, and, most recently, Newfoundland and Labrador (Table 4.18). Resource rents are undoubtedly a major part of this story. Provinces most heavily invested in science, technology, and innovation, especially Quebec, Ontario, and British Columbia, have lagged.

Table 4.17. Multifactor Productivity Growth by Industry, Canada and Provinces, 1997–2017

	Business Sector Industries	Agriculture, Forestry, Fishing & Hunting	Mining and Oil & Gas Extraction	Utilities	Construction	Manufacturing	Wholesale trade	Retail Trade	Transportation & Warehousing	Information & Cultural Industries	Finance, Insurance & Other Services	Professional, Scientific & Technical Services	Administrative, Waste Management, etc.	Arts, Entertainment & Recreation	Accommodation & Food services	Other Private Services
						Index 1997 = 100										
Canada	104	158	54	83	108	123	137	133	92	115	114	96	88	76	115	98
Newfoundland and Labrador	112	151	265	81	108	144	198	140	76	202	106	72	161	51	119	95
Prince Edward Island	107	101	3	113	109	122	159	135	136	158	90	71	105	95	122	95
Nova Scotia	106	137	110	83	83	142	155	141	72	147	94	78	86	57	97	87
New Brunswick	99	171	16	115	117	96	147	122	99	126	92	97	123	41	92	87
Quebec	108	140	72	129	112	111	124	127	96	111	109	94	87	65	116	95
Ontario	112	132	49	77	109	137	177	134	85	118	116	93	84	86	121	91
Manitoba	117	154	72	92	121	109	155	153	141	130	109	116	80	61	110	111
Saskatchewan	81	85	37	85	84	138	178	140	112	136	118	93	98	23	97	102
Alberta	81	121	49	75	88	115	111	156	75	133	112	111	84	58	100	115
British Columbia	114	142	48	92	121	167	161	153	119	136	104	110	98	59	100	94

Sources: Authors' calculations; Statistics Canada, table 36-10-0211-01, "Multifactor productivity and related variables in the aggregate business sector and major sub-sectors, by industry," online at https://www150.statcan.gc.ca/t1/tbl1/en/tv.action?pid=3610021101, accessed 9 October 2019.

Table 4.18. Relative per capita Nominal GDP, Canada, Provinces, and Territories, 2014–18

	Average per capita Nominal GDP($)	Per capita Incomes indexed to Canada = 100
Canada	51,353	100
Newfoundland and Labrador	58,967	115
Prince Edward Island	36,644	71
Nova Scotia	37,630	73
New Brunswick	38,904	76
Quebec	42,413	83
Ontario	49,898	97
Manitoba	45,955	89
Saskatchewan	70,867	138
Alberta	78,245	152
British Columbia	47,877	93
Yukon	64,510	126
NWT	106,415	207
Nunavut	69,087	135

Sources: Authors' calculations; Statistics Canada, table 36-10-0402-01, Gross domestic product (GDP) at basic prices, by industry, provinces and territories," online at https://www150.statcan.gc.ca/t1/tbl1/en/tv.action?pid=3610040201.

Guidance for Policy Makers and Analysts

The basic challenge for science, technology, and innovation policy everywhere is the lack of conclusive proof that any particular mix of inputs or activities uniquely influences desired outputs and outcomes. One can use theory and data to construct causal stories to justify almost any configuration of policy and programming. Nevertheless, the evidence reviewed in this chapter offers some insights for policy makers.

The first observation is that few provinces have a full slate of actively engaged and adequately resourced actors. Many provinces are missing critical elements that are needed to generate better performance. Collaboration with federal actors or with others might be necessary to advance effective policy. Second, the higher education sector is a core part of each provincial innovation system, but universities in particular are struggling to identify if or how their research is being translated and used. Given that these institutions are creations of the provinces, this is a part of the system within the purview of provincial governments. As the following chapters show, some provinces and territories have begun to engage more aggressively with their higher education sector. Third, the business sector is performing variably: it does the lion's share of R&D and most of the commercialization, but some sectors and firms are short of the technology frontier. Given the small size of Canadian domestic industry, increased emphasis on internal R&D probably will not be enough. Attention needs to be paid to how we can better access and import technology, either by domestic firms and sectors or through multinational enterprises operating in Canada.

Analysts could note that there is a lot to do to advance sound policy for innovation. While there are some interesting and compelling studies of firm and sectoral impacts of research, lacking is a body of evidence that policy makers can use to make choices. There is a surplus of theory but a deficit of evidence that any theoretically derived causal links actually work. Testing and validating that theory is the first step. Equally important is to calibrate the sensitivity of firms and economic performance to different volumes and types of investment.

References

Alston, J., M. Andersen, J. James, and P. Pardey. 2011. "The Economic Returns to US Public Agricultural Research." *American Journal of Agricultural Economics* 93 (5): 1257–77. https://doi.org/10.1093/ajae/aar044.

Canada. 2018. Elections Canada. "Plurality-Majority Electoral Systems: A Review." Online at https://www.elections.ca/content.aspx?section=res&dir=rec/fra/sys/courtney&document=courtney&lang=e, accessed 2 December 2020.

Council of Canadian Academies. 2018. *Competing in a Global Innovation Economy: The Current State of R&D in Canada.* Ottawa: Expert Panel on the State of Science and Technology and Industrial Research and Development in Canada, Council of Canadian Academies. Online at https://cca-reports.ca/wp-content/uploads/2018/09/Competing_in_a_Global_Innovation_Economy_ExecSumm_EN.pdf, accessed 20 April 2020.

Dahlby, B., and E. Ferede. 2011. "What Does It Cost Society to Raise a Dollar of Tax Revenue? The Marginal Cost of Public Funds." *C.D. Howe Institute Commentary* 324. Toronto: C.D. Howe Institute. March.

Doern, G.B., P. Phillips, and D. Castle. 2016. *Canadian Science, Technology and Innovation Policy: The Innovation Economy and Society Nexus.* Montreal; Kingston, ON: McGill-Queen's University Press.

Etzkowitz, H., and L. Leydesdorff. 1995. "The Triple Helix: University-Industry-Government Relations: A Laboratory for Knowledge Based Economic Development." *European Society for the Study of Science and Technology Review* 14 (1): 14–19.

Etzkowitz, H., and L. Leydesdorff. 1997. *Universities and the Global Knowledge Economy: A Triple Helix of University-Industry-Government Relations.* London: Pinter.

Hall, B., J. Mairesse, and P. Mohnen. 2009. "Measuring the Returns to R&D." NBER Working Paper w15622. Cambridge, MA: National Bureau of Economic Research. Online at SSRN: https://ssrn.com/abstract=1530078.

Merton, R. 1973. *The Sociology of Science: Theoretical and Empirical Investigations.* Chicago: University of Chicago Press.

Smyth, S., A. Williams, and J. Vasilescu. 2016. "An Assessment of Canadian University Technology Transfer Offices." *International Journal of Intellectual Property Management* 9 (1): 32–50. http://doi.org/10.1504/IJIPM.2016.079584.

Spencer, G. 2014. *Clusters Atlas of Canada.* Online at https://localideas.files.wordpress.com/2014/05/cluster-atlas.pdf, accessed 2 October 2019.

Statistics Canada. n.d. "Activities of multinational enterprises in Canada, Canadian and foreign multinationals, as a share of the Canadian economy." Table 36-10-0356-01. Online at https://www150.statcan.gc.ca/t1/tbl1/en/tv.action?pid=3610035601. https://doi.org/10.25318/3610035601-eng.

Trujillo, P.J.C. 2019. "Immigration Federalism: A Comparative Analysis of Policy in Canada (Saskatchewan) and in Australia (Western Australia)." PhD diss., University of Saskatchewan. Online at https://harvest.usask.ca/handle/10388/12916, accessed 2 December 2020.

PART II

The Provinces and Territories

5 Newfoundland and Labrador: Missed Opportunities, but Glimmers of Hope

KEN CARTER, HEATHER M. HALL,
AND ROB GREENWOOD

Over the past two decades, there have been many missed opportunities and some glimmers of hope with regards to science, technology, and innovation (STI) policy in Newfoundland and Labrador (NL). Four themes stand out. First, there are STI opportunities in the province's resource sectors, especially the large resource-based benefits agreements that support research and development (R&D) and innovation in those sectors. These offer a number of success stories, particularly in local supply chain development (Stantec Consulting 2019). Benefit agreements, however, have underachieved on creating new R&D, expanding value-added processing capacity and developing export potential that creates sustainable employment and business spin-offs (Hall and Vodden 2019). Second, current STI policy has focused on supporting highly motivated start-ups through a collaborative regional approach that aligns with innovation and entrepreneurship ecosystems, and this policy is bearing fruit. Third, the province is recognized for its vibrant culture and strong sense of place, providing rich, untraded interdependencies (Greenwood, Pike, and Kearley 2011; Vodden, Carter, and White 2013). These strengths, however, have not led to substantial innovation outcomes or to commercialization in the provincial context (Walsh and Winsor 2019). Finally, and perhaps most important, provincial politics has created discontinuity and inconsistency in the development of STI policy relative to other jurisdictions. The provincial political landscape has been dominated by strong personalities who have inhibited broader engagement within the innovation ecosystem – particularly industry partners as well as broader coalitions of community, Indigenous, and other partners. This chapter provides a brief socio-economic overview of Newfoundland and Labrador, outlines the key actors in the innovation ecosystem, offers an overview of provincial STI policy since the 1980s, discusses the implications, and offers some key conclusions.

Context

Newfoundland and Labrador has a complex socio-economic situation. There are some signs of growth and prosperity, coupled with troubling fiscal and investment trends. The province last received equalization payments from the federal government in fiscal year 2007/8 (Bernard 2012). Historically the federal government has had lower levels of spending in NL than in the other Atlantic provinces (Harris Centre 2006) while NL has contributed more to federal revenue per capita than any other Atlantic province. NL is confronted by high provincial taxation, spending, and deficits compared with other provinces, leading Schroeder and Hallett (2019) to argue that, without federal intervention, the province could be facing bankruptcy.

In 2017, the goods-producing sector accounted for 43 per cent of the province's gross domestic product (GDP) (Newfoundland and Labrador 2019a). Oil and gas extraction (14 per cent of GDP) and mining (6 per cent) are the major drivers, with oil and gas extraction dominating the economy and provincial government revenues for close to two decades. After a lengthy period of decline, the fisheries have stabilized, with reductions in the wild fishery mitigated by a growing aquaculture sector. Forestry has also declined significantly over the past twenty years, with two paper mill closures. The loss of jobs in the fishery and forestry has been only partially compensated by gains in oil and gas, mining, and their related supply sectors, which together represent only 3.5 per cent of total provincial employment (Newfoundland and Labrador 2019a). As a result, unemployment has remained high, in part attributed to a lack of value-added development in these extractive industries.

Non-extractive industries contribute significantly to the provincial economy. One particularly bright spot is growth in the St. John's–based tech sector. The Newfoundland Association of Technical Industries (NATI) estimates that the sector has revenues of $1.6 billion, making it larger than the fisheries, forestry, or tourism. Employment in the sector is estimated at 4,000 (NATI 2020), which makes the sector an important employment generator in the province. This urban-based sector helps St. John's rank seventeenth overall in the country on technology talent, tenth in technology concentration, and thirteenth in educational attainment (CBRE 2019).

One huge success story is Verafin, the world's largest financial crime management company, which secured $515 million in equity and debt recapitalization, representing "one of the largest ever growth financings of a Canadian software business," and which was acquired in 2020 by NASDAQ for $2.75 billion (CBC 2020). The founders, Jamie

King, Raymond Pretty, and Brendan Brothers, were doing graduate work in the Faculty of Engineering at Memorial University of Newfoundland, where they had developed robotic software for the mining industry. They decided to apply their technology to fight financial crime. Verafin spent its first few years at Genesis, an incubator at Memorial University, and the NASDAQ buyout will see $1 million invested in start-ups at Genesis (CBC 2020). Local firm Killick Capital was one of the company's earliest investors. With 600 employees and significant growth, one challenge for Verafin is attracting talent, and it is currently working with the College of the North Atlantic (CNA) and Memorial University to train the programmers needed to support this growth.

Other non-extractive industries include tourism, which generated $567 million in non-resident spending in 2018. It also provides a much-needed economic diversification opportunity and generates significant employment, particularly in rural areas of the province.

NL has a higher proportion of smaller firms to larger firms (over 500 employees) relative to other provinces, but those larger firms contributed disproportionately to employment between 2013 and 2017 (see Chapter 4). This is partly a result of construction at the Voisey's Bay nickel mine and Long Harbour processing facility, the Muskrat Falls hydro development, and oil platform construction during that period. The predominance of smaller firms perhaps is a factor in the weak capacity of business to organize and support STI policy input.

In 2016, NL had a population of 519,880, but population modelling suggests it could decline to roughly 495,000 people by 2036 (Simms and Ward 2017). The Harris Centre has shown that the province is home to Canada's most rapidly aging population, with high out-migration of young people, significant rural migration to urban centres, and declining birth rates (Simms and Ward 2016). These trends converge to create a population challenge that will dramatically affect the economy, governance, and quality of life for residents as most regions, with the exception of Northeast Avalon in the St. John's region and some parts of Labrador, will see significant population decline (Simms and Ward 2017).

The largest city in the province, St. John's, had a census metropolitan area population of 205,955 according to the 2016 census. As the provincial capital, it has stronger policy and fiscal capacity than cities of similar size in other provinces, but it is geographically remote and peripheral in the Canadian context (Lepawsky, Phan, and Greenwood 2010). The St. John's city-region has had significant growth as a headquarters and supply base for offshore oil and gas development, a growing tech sector, tourism, and a mix of non-resource–based industries. As a result, the city has a relatively healthy labour market, pulling rural residents to the area. The city has greater capacity for government, university, industry, and community collaboration, as well as co-construction of innovation and regional development goals, although there is no guarantee this will happen. One challenge is the "come from away" – a local expression for someone who moves to the province – or insider/outsider dynamic, which can act as a barrier to the integration of newcomers to the province (Lepawsky, Phan, and Greenwood 2010).

NL also has a high percentage of rural residents per capita. In 2011, 42 per cent of residents lived in rural regions – areas with fewer than 1,000 inhabitants and a population density below 400 people per square kilometre (Statistics Canada 2020). These smaller communities generally have weak municipal capacity and lack regional governance structures that could provide a base for regional innovation partnerships. Long distances within regions and to service centres, low and declining population density, and the challenge of responding to climate change are challenges for rural regions (Reimer and Bollman 2010). Carter and Vodden (2017) find that on the Great Northern Peninsula, one of the most remote regions of the province, there is limited capacity in the private sector or municipal governments, creating a void in the partnerships needed to spur innovation.

The periodic pull of high-wage employment in other provinces, most notably Alberta, has led to a higher rate of long-distance commuting in sectors such as mining, quarrying, oil and gas extraction, utilities, and construction (Hewitt, Haan, and Neis 2018). From an innovation perspective, this mobile workforce, or "been aways" (Greenwood and Hall 2016), has the potential to bring back valuable entrepreneurial experience and skills to the province. It has also created a new kind of single-industry town in rural NL, one that is dependent on a geographically distant employer (see Storey and Hall 2018), where residents build houses and have families locally but work elsewhere (most often in Alberta).

Finally, NL is known across Canada and internationally for its rich culture. The cultural renaissance began in the 1960s with arts collectives such as the Mummers Troupe and Codco, which tackled mainland misconceptions and celebrated a positive sense of identity among Newfoundlanders and Labradorians (Higgins 2012). Alongside this cultural revival was a stirring of resource nationalism connected to the Churchill Falls deal with Hydro-Québec in the late 1960s (Collins and Reid 2015). This "place making" generated a nascent pride and emergent nationalism in the province (Hiller 2007), and led to calls for the province to attain a more favourable relationship with Ottawa and other provinces, partly to right perceived wrongs, particularly the Churchill Falls contract and ownership of offshore resources. It also created a strong sense of place and connection to "home" (Greenwood and Hall 2016) that could be used to support and facilitate innovation.

The Innovation Architecture

An innovation ecosystem describes the complex relationships among actors across the quadruple helix of government, post-secondary education, industry, and community. Adner and Kapoor (2010) use the innovation ecosystem terminology to make interdependencies more explicit. Relationships among players in the ecosystem are critical to enhancing the development of technology and innovation (Hall et al. 2014). The innovation ecosystem in NL is dominated by the provincial and federal governments, Memorial University, and CNA. These larger organizations have significant institutional capacity to fund and do science, to promote the use of technology, and to innovate. The provincial government relies heavily on federal fiscal support for innovation policy and practice, and while both industry and civil society actors generally have fewer resources and more limited capacity to contribute to the ecosystem, they are increasingly active.

The current provincial government lead on innovation policy is the Department of Tourism, Culture, Industry and Innovation (TCII). Innovate NL – formerly the Research and Development Corporation (RDC) – was relaunched within TCII in 2016, and has maintained funding levels similar to the RDC in support of entrepreneurship and regional economic development. The RDC was originally a creation of the Danny Williams Progressive Conservative (PC) government during a period of significant oil and gas revenues. It was intended to direct provincial government R&D investments into strategic sectors, but became a lightning rod for top-down provincial dominance of the ecosystem. After the demise of the RDC as a stand-alone government entity, the innovation agenda became more widely dispersed across other departments within the provincial government, with Fisheries and Land Resources, Natural Resources, and others active in the innovation ecosystems underpinning the fisheries and aquaculture, agriculture and agri-food, and oil and gas sectors. The provincial government has become increasingly important to the innovation ecosystem with its greater capacity to fund initiatives and infrastructure, although that capacity has waxed and waned with oil revenues and is currently in a weakened state. Policy prior to 2000 tended to focus on employment

Table 5.1. Gross Expenditure on Research and Development by Performing Sector, average $ millions, Newfoundland and Labrador, 2013–17

		Performers					
		Government		Provincial			Private
				Research	Business	Higher	Non-
Funders	Total	Federal	Provincial	Organizations	Enterprise	Education	profit
Total sectors	314	17	–	–	87	209	–
Federal government	55	17	–	–	8	30	–
Provincial government	13	–	–	–	2	11	–
Business enterprise	112	–	–	–	70	42	–
Higher education	123	–	–	–	–	123	–
Private non-profit	4	–	–	–	1	4	–
Foreign	8	–	–	–	8	–	–

Note: Columns and rows may not sum due to rounding.

Source: Statistics Canada, table 27-10-0273-01, "Gross domestic expenditures on research and development, by science type and by funder and performer sector (x 1,000,000)."

generation as the province struggled with high unemployment. Since then, the focus has been more clearly on innovation and firm development. The key innovation policy initiative of the current Liberal provincial government is *The Way Forward* process (more on this below).

The federal government is a critical player in NL, especially through its lead agency, the Atlantic Canada Opportunities Agency (ACOA). Since its inception in 1987, ACOA has made major investments in business support, the innovation ecosystem, and infrastructure. ACOA was designed to be more flexible than previous federal regional development entities – an arm's-length agency with a focus on innovation, education, entrepreneurship, training, and local development (Dewolf, McNiven, and McPhail 1988). Other federal organizations in the innovation ecosystem include the Tri-Agencies, which fund university-based research, including some important industry-partnered projects, and the Canada Foundation for Innovation, which has provided funding for infrastructure related to ocean research, often partnered with off-shore industries that offer access to their research infrastructure. The National Research Council's Ocean, Coastal, and River Engineering Centre in St. John's studies ice and wave effects on marine transportation and coastlines, while the Department of Fisheries and Oceans and Natural Resources Canada both contribute to research in the province.

The 2015 Atlantic Growth Strategy, launched by four provincial premiers and the prime minister, has worked to broaden collaboration and linkages across the region. Some key initiatives in the strategy include supporting the Ocean Supercluster, accelerated growth service, a network of incubators and accelerators, sectoral funding for industry research and innovation, the Atlantic Fisheries Fund to support innovation, infrastructure, and science partnerships, and skills development in the fish-harvesting and -processing sectors.

Memorial University, the province's only university, is an active collaborator in the innovation ecosystem, particularly around ocean science, fisheries, forestry, mining, and oil and gas research. With 80 per cent of its operational funding coming from the provincial government, the university acknowledges a special obligation to the people of the province. Memorial is a uniquely locally embedded university, with a multicampus structure that promotes public engagement within the province and beyond. Over the past ten years, Memorial has focused on increasing research intensity and has doubled graduate enrolment to over 4,000 students, including 900 PhDs, 75 per cent coming from outside the province (Memorial University 2019). Engineering enrolment has doubled, and major science infrastructure has been built on the St. John's campus. The increased capacity at Memorial is a major addition to the innovation ecosystem.

Memorial's Marine Institute is a key contributor to fisheries and oceans research, with world-class infrastructure and research capacity focused on collaborating with industry. When the fishery in the province faced an existential crisis in the early 1990s, Marine Institute played a significant role in undertaking research and training to refocus the offshore fishery from groundfish to primarily crab and shrimp and in spurring aquaculture development, and supported the innovative shifts in fishing gear, technology, and training required to accommodate these changes. Landed values increased dramatically, and employment stabilized at more than 21,000, albeit at the cost of more than 16,000 jobs in the offshore fisheries (Williams 2019). In this case, crisis was a huge motivator to innovation.

C-Core, a separately incorporated R&D organization on Memorial's St. John's campus, offers key expertise in ice engineering, geotechnical engineering, and remote sensing. Collectively, the province has significant infrastructure and research capacity related to oceans research, and is recognized federally through ACOA as a key leader in Atlantic Canada in oceans technology. According to Warrian and Wolfe (2016, 2017), the approaches of Marine Institute and C-CORE in supporting firms that are reaching and implementing technology readiness levels (Mankin 1995) are unique in Canada, effectively linking post-secondary research and development capability with industry commercialization.

R&D and training related to fisheries and ocean technology have seen collaboration among regional universities and industries in Atlantic Canada, leading to larger, ocean-based funding arrangements. The Ocean Frontier Institute, a partnership between Memorial, Dalhousie University, and the University of Prince Edward Island, supported by the Canada First Research Excellence Fund, has generated world-leading scale in ocean innovation capability. The momentum of the Ocean Frontier Institute and the demonstration that the Atlantic provinces can collaborate on innovation have helped advance other ventures. The successful private-sector–led application to the federal supercluster program, the Ocean Supercluster, brings together oil and gas, fishery, aquaculture, marine transportation, and other ocean technology firms in partnership with universities, Indigenous organizations, and governments.

Memorial is a key supporter of entrepreneurship and start-ups, through Genesis, a high-growth technology incubation, acceleration, and co-working group, owned by Memorial but with a standalone governance structure; the Memorial Centre of Entrepreneurship, a pan-university student entrepreneurship facilitator led jointly by the business and engineering faculties; Navigate, a partnership between Corner Brook's Grenfell Campus of Memorial and CNA; and additional start-up programs in the health sector and for graduate students. The university also operates a Technology Transfer and Commercialization Office and collaborates with Springboard, an Atlantic Canada network to build stronger relationships between university research and industry commercialization. A recent example of entrepreneurship and innovation is the Lab2Market program, designed to support science-based graduate student start-ups. Memorial has also launched a new intellectual property framework for the university, established a multilevel innovation strategy, and launched the Emera Innovation Exchange in downtown St. John's.

The College of the North Atlantic, the public college system, provides training and encourages applied research and technology adoption. Formed in 1997 out of an amalgamation of five community colleges,

CNA has more direct policy linkages to the provincial government and its development is more connected to political aspirations than is Memorial. The college supports industry and community engagement, external partnerships, and applied research, particularly with local firms and sectors. Applied research and innovation at CNA is administered under the college's Office of Applied Research and Innovation, housed within the broader Office of Partnerships, Innovation and Entrepreneurship. This office runs the College Innovation Network, which works to provide equipment, infrastructure, students, graduates, and staff to support applied R&D and business development. It also supports the planning, execution, and management of applied industry projects that address challenges limiting firm-level competitiveness and growth. The College Innovation Network both mentors firms and performs the role of innovation intermediary, helping to bridge the gap between small and medium-sized enterprises (SMEs) and to support resources both internal and external to the college. The network offers SMEs a continuum of support services, including assistance with sourcing funding, networking and collaboration, technology transfer, and innovation management. CNA operates a number of key applied research and innovation facilities, including the Wave Environment Research Centre, Manufacturing Technology Centre, Centre for Energy and Thermal Systems, Innovative Product Development Lab, Applied Mineralogy Lab, Mineral Processing Lab, and Hyperspectral Imaging for Geological Applications Lab. These and other knowledge infrastructure promote a skilled workforce and support applied research partnerships with industry. While CNA is not as active in research as Memorial, it is more industry driven and is an active partner in the innovation ecosystem.

Industry associations in the oil and gas, mining, technology, manufacturing, fisheries, forestry, environmental, aerospace, and tourism sectors also play key roles in the innovation ecosystem. They are usually supported financially by their membership and by the provincial and federal governments to bring industry views to the policy table, facilitate industry collaboration, and disseminate best practices. One key industry player is Petroleum Research NL, which manages joint industry investments in R&D through resource benefits agreements. In addition to multinational firms, the ecosystem has a number of larger local firms, including DF Barnes, the Cahill Group, and PAL (which grew from Provincial Airlines), all the result of oil and gas industry R&D that generated supply chain opportunities within and beyond the resources sector and local market (Stantec Consulting 2019). Numerous technology start-ups, mostly led by Memorial alumni – usually engineering and often Genesis incubator graduates – have been supported by available local business mentors and investors as well as by university, industry associations, and governments. Many of these start-ups and corporate leaders are no longer beholden to government, which represents a positive shift in the business and innovation culture.

Indigenous governments across the province – including the Qalipu First Nation and Miawpukek First Nation on the island and the Nunatsiavut government, the Innu Nation, and the NunatuKavut Community Council in Labrador (Memorial University 2020) – are playing more strategic roles as key innovation actors. As resource beneficiaries and critical governance actors in the province, Indigenous governments have distinct strengths and challenges in addressing innovation and economic development. For example, the Nunacor Development Corporation, the business development corporation for the NunatuKavut Community Council, owns and operates a number of Indigenous companies throughout Labrador. Other Indigenous governments have similar development arms.

Finally, municipalities are important community players, and those with resources are active participants in their regions. The local boards of trade and chambers of commerce are particularly active in St. John's and larger centres, but they have broad and diffuse agendas not focused solely on innovation. In St. John's, these organizations have had a long-term commitment to ocean sector development, oil and gas, and R&D, but this has been focused – consistent with the municipality's resources and authority – on promotion and marketing. St. John's also played a role in fostering the development of OceansAdvance, a quadruple-helix cluster organization of industry, governments, post-secondary institutions, and community organizations that has helped to make the St. John's region a leading ocean cluster (Shearmur 2010; Lepawsky, Phan, and Greenwood 2010). Various industry associations, however, vie for leadership: the emergence of the Ocean Supercluster, with its own staff and alliances, combined with the usual ebb and flow of government policy, has affected the ability of OceansAdvance to maintain its cluster role.

There are other examples of small municipalities proactively supporting innovation in their regions: Holyrood, thirty minutes from St. John's, at the head of Conception Bay, is collaborating with Marine Institute to brand itself as an ocean industry community; Corner Brook Pulp and Paper, the province's last pulp and paper facility, is working closely with Grenfell Campus and CNA on an innovation, training, and entrepreneurship facility for the bioeconomy; Grand Falls-Windsor, in the centre of the island, has focused on health care and partnerships with the Memorial faculties of medicine and nursing, to foster rural health care innovation and harness the province's unique founder population for genetics research; and Labrador North Chamber of Commerce partners with its counterpart in Nunavut to host the bi-annual Northern Lights conference in Ottawa to promote Arctic and Indigenous development. For the most part, local activity is rare; most small communities in the province lack capacity to engage in the innovation ecosystem (Greenwood 2017; Greenwood and Hall 2016).

There are encouraging indications of impact from the collective efforts across the quadruple helix on innovation. Recent initiatives such as the provincial Innovation Week, held annually since 2014, have engaged industry and entrepreneurs in a more active role in championing innovation. In addition, the provincial government's sector strategy initiatives in *The Way Forward* explicitly include members of civil society as co-chairs of the collaborative industry-government working groups. Workplans have been developed across sectors, including agriculture, business innovation, technology, oil and gas, and mining (Newfoundland and Labrador 2020). There is increasing recognition of the importance of including industry and community partners in these processes.

Although it is still too early to assess, there are signs of a growing entrepreneurial spirit in the province, born during the boom years of oil and gas development but sustained by Genesis, the Memorial Centre for Entrepreneurship, and Navigate, as well as a myriad other entrepreneurial supports (such as Community Business Development Corporations, the Newfoundland and Labrador Organization of Women Entrepreneurs, and Futurpreneur). There has also been growing leadership by entrepreneurs themselves, a critical element to building start-up communities (Feld 2012). One area of identified opportunity is encouraging more peer-to-peer connections among entrepreneurs in the St. John's and Corner Brook regions (Winsor and Carter 2018).

Investments in Memorial University are showing early success, with a new wave of younger entrepreneurs who are succeeding across technology- and oceans-related sectors. Studies on the impact of the offshore petroleum industry on firm development in NL show many successes: Provincial Aerospace has connected to the offshore sector and achieved significant company growth; Kraken Sonar Systems is developing seabed imaging technology; and SubC Imaging is producing optical imaging systems for offshore markets (Stantec Consulting 2019). More and deeper interaction that leads to lasting change in the innovation ecosystem, particularly among firms, is required, however, to turn early successes into permanent innovation effects.

The Policy Efforts

STI policy efforts in Newfoundland and Labrador have gone through several phases since the 1980s, shaped by different premiers. This period includes resource nationalism, the rise of an innovation technocracy, an effort to exploit resource benefits and investment, and now a focus on smart specialization (Foray et al. 2012). We turn now to a discussion of each of these phases, with particular emphasis on the interests shaping STI policy.

From a political standpoint, the 1980s set the stage for resource development that has had a significant impact on the province's fiscal and innovation capacity. The 1980s were dominated politically by PC premier Brian Peckford's battles with the centralist model of federalism. As long as the federal Liberal party was in power, Peckford made little headway on oil development, fisheries jurisdiction, or addressing the Churchill Falls hydro agreement with Quebec. A breakthrough came only with the Progressive Conservative win in the 1984 federal election and the signing of the Atlantic Accord on 11 February 1985. The deal gave the province greater decision-making powers and created the Canada-Newfoundland Offshore Petroleum Board. Motivated by the growing perception that the province should be the prime beneficiary of its abundant natural resources, the Atlantic Accord gave the provincial government the right to tax offshore resources in the same way as those onshore and ensured local preference in hiring, which set the stage for the oil boom in the province almost two decades later. Peckford's efforts were championed by federal cabinet minister John Crosbie, a fellow Newfoundlander. As Collins and Reid (2015) note, Peckford hoped that "have not will be no more" in Newfoundland and Labrador.

In 1986, Peckford established the Royal Commission on Employment and Unemployment, chaired by Memorial University sociologist Doug House. The House Commission conducted an extensive review of the NL economy and called for a balanced approach of leveraging emerging information technologies for SME development, diversification, and rural development, while continuing to advance large-scale developments in oil and gas, mining, and modernization of the fishery. The provincial public service was sceptical of the approaches offered by House, and the Peckford government largely ignored the report (House 1999). Despite his efforts on oil and gas, Peckford resigned in 1989 amid controversy around a failed greenhouse that lost $22 million in taxpayer funding – a top-down initiative led by a premier frustrated by little progress to achieve his vision of resource nationalism.

The 1990s, under Liberal leaders Clyde Wells and Brian Tobin, saw the first benefits from the Atlantic Accord and offshore oil development through the Hibernia platform construction. Wells's early tenure included a prominent role in the demise of the Meech Lake Accord, persistently high unemployment, and budget cuts (Dunn 2005; House 1999) that delivered the province's first balanced budget. Wells was impressed by the House Commission and had campaigned with its recommendations as his economic policy platform in the 1989 election. Once elected, he created the Economic Recovery Commission (ERC) as a small, action-oriented think tank outside the mainstream bureaucracy, with Doug House as commissioner, reporting directly to the premier. The ERC led the creation of Enterprise NL (ENL) as a Crown corporation combining sections of line departments and a pre-existing business finance Crown. The ENL board, led by the ERC with an independent chair, significantly decentralized decision making for SME business and regional development support through five regional offices and 17 satellite offices.

Meanwhile, the ERC advanced a number of ventures, including: a New Opportunity for Growth Sector Strategy in concert with industry, post-secondary, and community organizations; establishing or strengthening private sector–led industry associations to champion sectoral diversification; leading a major pilot project on a guaranteed annual income (which was not implemented); working to establish a network of telecentres to foster the new information economy; and facilitating the establishment of Regional Economic Development Boards in twenty economic zones throughout the province. House played a key role in developing a Strategic Economic Plan for the province, which was then mirrored by a Strategic Social Plan (Close 2007).

These efforts were just getting traction when the federal government implemented a groundfish moratorium in 1992 due to the collapse of cod stocks on the Grand Banks that saw the layoff of over 30,000 people in the fisheries in NL. This triggered a flood of out-migration from rural areas that continued for thirty years (Williams 2019). Wells's approach to policy making allowed policy innovations to be advanced despite frequent objections from the more steadfast bureaucracy. The massive economic, demographic, and community restructuring induced by the moratorium reinforced the need for innovation, but the election of Brian Tobin as Liberal premier in 1996 saw the return of a top-down charismatic politician in NL. The ERC was shut down and ENL was absorbed into a line department under strict political control and traditional bureaucratic oversight (House 1999).

The greatest benefits of the Atlantic Accord came in the PC era, which lasted from 2003 to 2015. Offshore oil revenues grew from $127 million in fiscal year 2003/4 to almost $2.8 billion in 2011/12 (Masoudi 2017). This period saw the re-emergence of the resource nationalism of the Peckford years, under the theme of "no more giveaways" (Collins and Reid 2015). The Atlantic Accord and royalties triggered an era of investment in innovation infrastructure. Spending on knowledge infrastructure and operating increases in the budgets of Memorial and CNA were a hallmark of this period. While the focus was on energy development, with large, resource-based projects dominating the economy – Muskrat Falls hydroelectric development in Labrador was the biggest and most controversial – targeted investments in infrastructure and the innovation ecosystem led to many high-profile successes in knowledge-based sectors.

In 2006, the Williams administration released *Innovation NL: A Blueprint for Prosperity*, which highlighted a range of innovation-related challenges, including: a relatively low level of investment in R&D by the private sector; limited access to risk capital and financing for commercialization; limited linkages and collaboration among post-secondary institutions, industry, and communities; a lack of innovation experience among entrepreneurs, managers, and professionals; and continuing out-migration of the knowledge industry and other skilled workers (Newfoundland and Labrador 2006). The blueprint offered four strategic directions: 1) fostering a culture of innovation to encourage new ideas and collaboration among industry, labour, government, educational institutions, and other stakeholders; 2) positioning NL as a competitive economy with recognized international strengths and advantages; 3) broadening education and skills development and aligning skills to future economic and labour market needs; and 4) supporting enhanced R&D capacity through improved financing and investment. The Innovation Strategy prompted a series of innovation programs directed at industry and academic partners. With oil revenues rising after 2007, new funding flowed to Memorial and CNA, the RDC was founded and provincial dollars were used to leverage federal research funding on innovation in oceans, mining, and oil and gas. One issue from the RDC era was that the policy instruments were never formally evaluated, leading to a lack of clarity as to whether these investments had the impact intended.

Despite best efforts, the economy remained largely resource based and continued to ship mostly unprocessed oil, ore, fish, and lumber during this period. Towards the end of the PC era, oil revenues began to fall and a new round of fiscal restraint and budget deficits emerged. Williams copied the top-down, charismatic leadership of Joey Smallwood, Peckford, and Tobin. In addition to his resource focus, he made no effort to decentralize decision making. Then, when the Harper government cut federal funding to regional economic development organizations in 2012, the provincial government under Premier Kathy Dunderdale immediately cut support to the REDBs. As Hall, Vodden, and Greenwood (2017) argue, the demise of the REDBs – created under the Liberals – shifted the governance of regional development from dysfunctional to destitute.

After 2015, Premier Dwight Ball's Liberal administration focused largely on dealing with the fiscal legacy of the PC era. The provincial government faced a fiscal squeeze through dwindling oil revenues, which dipped to $515 million in fiscal year 2015/16, mounting debt, and pressures related to financing the Muskrat Falls project. Ball's innovation policies during the first five years shifted towards strengthening the microeconomic underpinnings of firm-level growth. The policies and realigned programs of the Department of Tourism, Culture, Industry and Innovation focused on firm-level innovation and entrepreneurship, including a pilot of European-style regional innovation systems (Newfoundland and Labrador 2020).

The current provincial Liberal government's innovation policy, *The Way Forward*, identifies four priorities: a more efficient public sector; a stronger economic foundation; better services; and better outcomes to promote a healthy and prosperous province. In 2017, following an extensive stakeholder engagement process, the province delivered the Business Innovation Agenda, which put forward new initiatives to support the accelerated growth of key businesses, five regional innovation pilots, and a regional trade network. The goal is to enhance product development and commercialization, increase productivity through technology and lean manufacturing, accelerate business development and internationalization, and develop workforce skills and talent (Newfoundland and Labrador 2017).

The Regional Innovation Systems pilot projects, building on the European Union's Smart Specialization Strategy, is a first for North America. The adoption of this approach was a direct result of the work of the Advancing Innovation in NL project led by researchers at Memorial University (including the authors of this chapter; see Hall et al. 2014). The application of these pilots is a policy experiment for the province. It remains to be seen if it will be a boutique policy innovation forgotten by the next administration or if it will influence regional innovation policy going forward.

The provincial government also commissioned McKinsey & Company to make recommendations on increasing economic growth. The report, *Economic Growth Strategy for Newfoundland and Labrador*, was released in February 2019 with recommendations across nine priority sectors, as well as three enabling areas of investment attraction; education, skills, and workforce development; and digitization (Newfoundland and Labrador 2019b). The strategy is very much a top-down exercise, building on existing provincial strategies and initiatives, and it is unclear what policy influence it will have.

Andrew Furey became premier in August 2020 with an economy ravaged by the COVID-19 pandemic and a projected deficit of $1.8 billion. Furey, an orthopaedic trauma surgeon from a prominent St. John's political family, initiated the Premier's Economic Recovery Team (PERT) led by Dame Moya Greene, former chief executive officer of Canada Post and the Royal Mail in the United Kingdom. In May 2021, PERT released its final report, *The Big Reset*, which makes for grim reading, pointing to NL's having the highest per capita revenues and debt of any province, the highest per capita health care costs, the oldest population, and the worst health care outcomes (Green 2001). The report argues for extensive resets to governance, the economy, social programs, and government finances. From the perspective of innovation policy, we highlight two elements of the report: economic transition and governance change. The report calls for a transition to a green economy and provincial climate change plans. These issues are well known, with significant discussion and debate (Harris Centre 2021a, 2021b). The report envisions a smaller provincial government footprint with the recognition that the government does not and cannot do everything by itself (Greene 2021). Instead, greater industry, university, government, and community collaboration is proposed. The Big Reset also acknowledges continued provincial dependence on oil revenues and the need to reduce the carbon footprint of exploration and development of new fields. New oil projects, such as Bay de Nord, envision high-tech production that generates a smaller carbon and ocean footprint with fewer employees (Greene 2021).

The shifts between PC to Liberal regimes has generated significant changes in innovation policy. As noted, the Wells Liberal government's ERC and ENL were collapsed by the Tobin Liberal government into line departments. The Dunderdale PC government then shut down the Wells government's REDBs. Similarly, the PC government's RDC, founded in 2007, was recast in 2016 by the Liberals as Innovate NL. These swings in policy have put the staying power of newer innovative policy initiatives, such as the regional innovation pilots, in doubt. Many of these swings were influenced not by any consistent policy or ideological direction, but by the "that was them, this is us" syndrome that demands change – or the appearance of change – as each government tries to make its policy mark (Greenwood 2017).

Politics has also played a major role in provincial STI policy. The federal government is a key investor, albeit with a relatively smaller footprint than in other provinces. The provincial government is the strongest and best-resourced participant in the governance structure of NL, but with weak municipal-level governance outside a handful of urban centres and no regional-level governance structures. Partly because of the overwhelming centrality of the provincial government in the ecosystem, political shifts at this level have led to wholesale changes in policy. While the innovation literature highlights the importance of collaboration among innovation stakeholders, including governments, post-secondary institutions, industry, and community partners, the NL system is dominated by government (Hall et al. 2014). A better system of multilevel collaborative governance might support continuity (Vodden et al. 2019).

The recent calls from PERT for greater collaboration, characterized as a quadruple helix of dialogue and action, highlight the current imbalanced stakeholder dynamic, with industry input particularly weak. The predominance of small firms with limited resources to contribute to industry associations and the paucity of larger local firms make organizing input more difficult. Industry associations, community groups, and other interest groups, often starved for funding, are forced to broaden their agenda, which dilutes their focus on innovation. These actors need adequate and regular funding to mobilize support for strong, multilevel innovation policy – in the absence of strong civic associations, government is often a critical funder.

The returns on investments in knowledge infrastructure are difficult to measure and track. Most are indirect and with significant lags, so tracing impact is challenging. The oceans cluster is one example where increased knowledge infrastructure and research capacity have led to new opportunities, new funding, and increased commercialization. The early investments in federal labs, at Memorial University and elsewhere, created the base for the recent Ocean Supercluster. The big challenge is to link this to downstream commercial activity. The recent Ocean Startup Project's Engage Cafés events to link the supercluster to entrepreneurs is one attempt to broaden the impact. Memorial and the province's college system, despite significant investments, are suffering from a lack of infrastructure renewal and aging assets. The weaker fiscal situation in the province due to lower oil revenues could create a significant policy challenge for sustaining and renewing capacity.

As noted earlier, NL has a strong culture, attachment to place, and high scores on happiness and resilience. While these indicators are positive, out-migration remains high. In addition, while the indicators suggest people are committed to local success, this has not led to a stronger economy through innovation and commercialization. Walsh and Winsor (2019) argue that NL has good ideas and great people, but poor commercialization skills. Commitment to place can provide a cultural underpinning for innovation, but it has yet to be harnessed fully (Vodden et al. 2019). Building a culture of innovation and entrepreneurship alongside, and inspired by, culture and commitment to place is needed.

Over time, the oil-fuelled boom in private sector activity, university, and college R&D and the more recent focus on ocean technology changed the innovation culture of NL, particularly in the Northeast Avalon region around St. John's. Post-secondary graduates during the boom enjoyed work-term placements in Houston, Calgary, Aberdeen, and beyond, where they graduated into six-figure salaried positions and benefited from mentors who are worlds away from the historic model of business success based on government contracts and patronage. Larger-than-life charismatic politicians and system-serving controlling bureaucrats have little place in the consciousness of these new entrepreneurs, tech specialists, and corporate managers who understand global supply chains and global finance. This could signal a shift in the politics of STI policy in NL.

In this chapter, we have outlined several key ideas driving provincial policy over the past thirty years. The first of these is resource nationalism: the fight for control over offshore resources, including the fishery and oil. This collectivist effort to become the primary beneficiary of provincial resources, mobilized by the Atlantic Accord, generated massive financial benefits that helped develop significant research capacity at CNA and Memorial and strengthen the entrepreneurial class in industry supply chains. Connected to this has been a cultural reawakening in the province and a growing confidence in its ability to succeed. However, decisions such as the Sprung greenhouse and Muskrat Falls remind everyone that large investment decisions aimed at greater self-sufficiency can fail spectacularly if not carefully thought through. As in other provinces, there has been a championing of entrepreneurship, but it has been perhaps too specifically connected to technology start-ups and has had less impact on resource industries. Championing a culture of entrepreneurship is critical to embracing innovation fully.

In examining the interests of key actors, we argued that the provincial government has been a dominant player at the expense of other members of the innovation ecosystem. This has been tied to charismatic leaders and top-down agendas. Recent studies on innovation stress the social nature of innovation and note that a flourishing ecosystem requires input across governments, universities/colleges, industry, and community – that is, the quadruple helix. NL has weaker industry and community capacity and needs to strengthen these critical components of civil society. This is why we have stressed the importance of the Regional Innovation Systems pilots currently under way, as they prioritize broader community consensus while promoting entrepreneurial discovery linked to academic institutions. The goal is more diffused power across a wider variety of actors and groups at the regional level.

Finally, the province is still in "institutional building mode" and perhaps behind other provinces with respect to institutional strength beyond the provincial and federal governments. The university and college systems have benefited from significant investments, are regionally embedded in the economy, and are well positioned to support innovation across key sectors. The contributions of oil and gas, oceans, and tech start-ups have been particularly significant. Having said this, both Memorial and CNA need to become more flexible and nimble to support industry applied research and training needs. Industry associations are growing and have been asserting more influence on the innovation agenda, championing lean manufacturing, tech start-ups, human resource constraints, and innovation initiatives, but they continue to need strong government support due to weak membership of mostly smaller firms. Perhaps the biggest gap is the lack of regional voices at the community level. Regionalization has been discussed for a long time and championed by Municipalities NL, but little has been achieved since the demise of the Regional Economic Development Boards.

Conclusions and Lessons

Newfoundland and Labrador has a distinct Atlantic Canadian advantage in major offshore oil and mining, with beneficiary agreements providing large budgets earmarked for innovation. There have been some key successes in this area, including the examples of SubC, Kracken Sonar Systems, and Provincial Airlines (Stantec Consulting 2019). Nevertheless, these benefits agreements could be better used to drive new intellectual property and new secondary processing capacity in the resource sectors, which would pull the province out of the staples trap.

The benefits agreements could be aligned to leverage other financial resources for R&D, including the federal government's capacity through the Tri-Agencies, ACOA, line departments, and special initiatives. They could also align better with the provincial TCII and Innovate NL.

The provincial focus on building entrepreneurship, coupled with investment in knowledge infrastructure, through Genesis and MCE in St. John's and Navigate on the west coast, has assisted highly motivated entrepreneurs, particularly from Memorial University. The doubling of engineering students, research intensification, and graduate program expansion, coupled with an entrepreneurial focus, is generating some success in the knowledge economy. A small but vibrant group of entrepreneurs is succeeding within emerging entrepreneurial ecosystems (CBC 2019). Where policies are aligned effectively, there is immense potential to support entrepreneurial place-based innovations, as we see in cases such as Anaconda, the Fogo Island Inn, or Verafin. Despite some successes and encouraging signs, however, Walsh and Winsor (2019, 278) conclude that the province is "impeded from embracing the benefits of innovation-driven entrepreneurship as a means of fostering economic development." They argue that innovation-driven entrepreneurial activity in NL is lower than in the rest of Canada due to enduring sociocultural factors.

The challenge for Newfoundland and Labrador is to build and implement sound policy and practice with respect to science, technology, and innovation, based on collaboration among key institutions and partners. Studies such as the Harris Centre's *Advancing Innovation in NL* offer guidance to policy makers, recommending that quadruple-helix partners spur new joint initiatives with distinct roles for a wide range of interests (Hall et al. 2014). These studies influence new efforts by key partners, including the provincial government's Regional Innovation Pilots, but more is needed. Innovation policy has also sometimes suffered under charismatic politicians. The lack of continuity on innovation policy arguably can be connected to political shifts, where strong leadership styles snuff out the social underpinnings of innovation. Pendulum swings due to partisan interests, however, would be harder to sustain if the innovation ecosystem were to become truly a four-part partnership.

Overall, the evidence that innovation is taking root in the province is mixed, with plenty of missed opportunities, but also glimmers of hope. Newfoundland and Labrador has great potential to use a combination of financial resources (often from resource-based industries) and a growing group of younger entrepreneurs ready to engage. Yet, the province has not fully embraced an entrepreneurial culture, and there is only weak networking among key ecosystem participants. It is imperative, therefore, to enhance a culture of entrepreneurship and build more strategic networking among key stakeholders in the innovation ecosystem, particularly given the current decline in the offshore oil and gas industry and the resulting effects on the provincial economy, coupled with a decline in mobile work associated with the oil and gas downturn in Alberta.

Given these realities, which have been intensified by the global pandemic, innovation actors in NL need to focus on new opportunities for science, technology, and innovation. In particular, there is real opportunity for investments in the sector that build on local knowledge related to cold oceans and Arctic science and the industry know-how developed in the province. For example, value-added innovation in the fisheries could provide a competitive advantage for the province – with similar circumstances, Iceland has supported turning fish waste into leather, pharmaceuticals, and skin care products (CBC 2017). The St. John's region, in particular, is seeing vibrant activity in the tech sector, as new grads, experienced knowledge workers, and entrepreneurs look for opportunities in the face of the post–oil boom. The challenge is to link these actors to traditional sectors beyond St. John's and to apply their knowledge and skills in new, expanding areas such as green technology and alternative energy.

References

Adner, R., and R. Kapoor. 2010. "Value Creation in Innovation Ecosystems: How the Structure of Technological Interdependence Affects Firm Performance in New Technology Generations." *Strategic Management Journal* 31 (3): 306–33. https://doi.org/10.1002/smj.821.

Bernard, J.T. 2012. "The Canadian Equalization Program: Main Elements, Achievements and Challenges." The Federal Idea: A Quebec Think Tank on Federalism. Online at https://ideefederale.ca/documents /Equalization.pdf.

Carter, K.L., and K. Vodden. 2017. "Applicability of Territorial Innovation models to Declining Resource-based Regions: Lessons from the Northern Peninsula of Newfoundland." *Journal of Rural and Community Development* 12 (2/3): 74–92.

CBC. 2017. "Fish skin for fashionistas: How this clever leather is hooking customers." *CBC News*, 17 November. Online at https://www.cbc.ca/news /canada/newfoundland-labrador/eye-on-iceland-fish-skin-leather-1.4399985.

CBC. 2019. "N.L. tech startups had a wildly successful 2019. Can they keep it up?" *CBC News*, 25 December. Online at https://www.cbc.ca/news /canada/newfoundland-labrador/tech-startups-2019-nl-1.5401391

CBC. 2020. "Nasdaq buying N.L. online security company Verafin in $2.75B US deal" *CBC News*, 19 November. Online at https://www.cbc.ca/news /canada/newfoundland-labrador/verafin-nasdaq-deal-1.5807866.

CBRE (Coldwell Banker Richard Ellis). 2019. "Scoring Canadian Tech Talent." Online at https://researchgateway.cbre.com/Layouts/GKCSearch /DownLoadPublicUrl.ashx.

Close, D. 2007. "The Newfoundland and Labrador Strategic Social Plan: The Life Cycle of an Innovative Policy." Prepared for presentation to the Midwest Political Science Association 2007 Conference, Chicago, 13 April. Online at http://www.envision.ca/pdf/cura/CloseMPSA2007_final.pdf.

Collins, J.F., and S. Reid. 2015. "No More Giveaways! Resource Nationalism in Newfoundland: A Case Study of Offshore Oil in the Peckford and Williams Administrations." *Newfoundland and Labrador Studies* 30 (1). Online at https://journals.lib.unb.ca/index.php/NFLDS/article /view/24519.

Context Energy Examined. 2019. "Social and economic benefits of NL oil and natural gas." 25 February. Online at https://context.capp.ca /energy-matters/2019/itn_nl-socio-economic-study/.

Dewolf, G., J. McNiven, and D. McPhail. 1988. "ACOA in an International and Historical Context." *Canadian Journal of Regional Science* 11 (2): 313–25.

Dunn, C. 2005. "Why Williams Walked, Why Martin Baulked: The Atlantic Accord Dispute in Perspective." *Policy Options* 26 (2): 9–14.

Feld, B. 2012. *Startup Communities: Building and Entrepreneurial Ecosystem in Your City.* Hoboken, NJ: Wiley.

Foray, D., J. Goddard, G.B. Xabier, M. Landabaso, P. McCann, K. Morgan, C. Nauwelaers, and R. Ortega-Argilés. 2012. *Guide to Research and Innovation Strategies for Smart Specialisation (RIS 3).* Luxembourg: European Union.

Greene, M. 2021. *The Big Reset: Report of the Premier's Economic Recovery Team.* May. Online at https://thebigresetnl.ca/wp-content/uploads/2021/05 /PERT-FullReport.pdf.

Greenwood, R. 2017. "Managing the Impacts of Openness on Island Economies." *Islands Economic Cooperation Forum Annual Report on Global Islands 2017.* Charlottetown: Island Studies Press and University of Prince Edward Island.

Greenwood, R., and H. Hall. 2016. "The Social Dynamics of Economic Performance in St. John's: A Metropolis on the Margins." In *Growing Urban Economies: Innovation, Creativity, and Governance in Canadian City-Regions*, ed. D.A. Wolfe and M.S. Gertler, 363–88. Toronto: University of Toronto Press.

Greenwood, R., C. Pike, and W. Kearley. 2011. *A Commitment to Place: The Social Foundations of Innovation in Newfoundland and Labrador.* St. John's: Harris Centre.

Hall, H.M., and K. Vodden. 2019. "Learning, Knowledge Flows, and Innovation in Canadian Regions." In *The Theory, Practice, and Potential of Regional Development: The Case of Canada*, ed. K. Vodden, D.J. Douglas, S. Markey, S. Minnes, and B. Reimer, 183–211. New York: Routledge.

Hall, H.M., K. Vodden, and R. Greenwood. 2017. "From Dysfunctional to Destitute: The Governance of Regional Economic Development in Newfoundland and Labrador." *International Planning Studies* 22 (2): 49–67. https://doi.org/10.1080/13563475.2016.1167585.

Hall, H.M, J. Walsh, K. Vodden, and R. Greenwood. 2014. *Challenges, Opportunities and Strategies for Advancing Innovation in Newfoundland and Labrador. Final Report of the Advancing Innovation in Newfoundland and Labrador Project*. St. John's: Memorial University of Newfoundland, Leslie Harris Centre of Regional Policy and Development.

Harris Centre. 2006. *Federal Government Presence in Newfoundland and Labrador: Final Report*. St. John's: Memorial University of Newfoundland, Leslie Harris Centre of Regional Policy and Development. Online at https://www.mun.ca/harriscentre/reports/research/2006/federalpresence/HC_FP_FINAL.pdf.

Harris Centre. 2021a. *Session 2 Climate Change Impacts and Actions in NL*. Forecast NL, 10 March. St. John's: Memorial University of Newfoundland, Leslie Harris Centre of Regional Policy and Development. Online at https://www.harriscentreforum.ca/forecast-nl/forum_topics/session-2-climate-change-impacts.

Harris Centre. 2021b. *Scenario Sessions*. St. John's: Memorial University of Newfoundland, Leslie Harris Centre of Regional Policy and Development. Online at https://www.mun.ca/harriscentre/whatwedo/publicpolicy/scenariosessions.php.

Hewitt, C.M., M. Haan, and B. Neis. 2018. "Interprovincial Employees from Newfoundland and Labrador." On the Move Partnership. Online at http://www.onthemovepartnership.ca/wp-content/uploads/2019/01/NL-IPE-Final-web.pdf.

Higgins, J. 2012. "Cultural Renaissance." St. John's: Heritage Newfoundland and Labrador. Online at https://www.heritage.nf.ca/articles/politics/cultural-renaissance.php

Hiller, J.K. 2007. "Robert Bond and the Pink, White, and Green: Newfoundland Nationalism in Perspective." *Acadiensis* 36 (2): 113–33.

House, J.D. 1999. *Against the Tide: Battling for Economic Renewal in Newfoundland and Labrador*. Toronto: University of Toronto Press.

Lepawsky, J., Phan, C., and Greenwood, R. 2010. "Metropolis on the Margin: Talent Attraction and Retention to the St. John's City-Region." *Canadian Geographer* 54 (3): 324–46. https://doi.org/10.1111/j.1541-0064.2010.00315.x.

Mankin, J. 1995. "Technology Readiness Levels." Online at https://aiaa.kavi.com/apps/group_public/download.php/2212/TRLs_MankinsPaper_1995.pdf, accessed 8 December 2020.

Masoudi, N. 2017. "Oil and Gas Development in Newfoundland." Paper presented at the Norwegian School of Economics (NHH) and Memorial University of Newfoundland Joint Workshop on Offshore Oil and Gas Development, St. John's, 3–5 May. Online at https://www.mun.ca/econ/more/events/Nahid_Masoudi_Nor_M2017.pdf.

Memorial University of Newfoundland. 2019. "Historic growth: Graduate student applications, enrolment grow at record pace." *Gazette*, 4 October. Online at https://gazette.mun.ca/campus-and-community/historic-growth/.

Memorial University of Newfoundland. 2020. "Primer on Indigenous Peoples and Protocols in Newfoundland and Labrador." Online at https://www.mun.ca/research/Indigenous/primer.php.

NATI (Newfoundland and Labrador Association of Technical Industries). 2020. "Facts and Figures." Online at https://www.nati.net/facts-and-figures/.

Newfoundland and Labrador. 2006. *Innovation Newfoundland and Labrador: A Blueprint for Prosperity*. St. John's. Online at https://www.tcii.gov.nl.ca/innovation/pdf/full_report.pdf.

Newfoundland and Labrador. 2017. *The Way Forward: Business Innovation Agenda*. St. John's. Online at http://www.nlinnovationagenda.ca/pdf/business_innovation_agenda.pdf.

Newfoundland and Labrador. 2019a. *Budget 2019: The Economy*. St. John's. Online at https://www.gov.nl.ca/fin/files/e2019-theeconomy2019.pdf.

Newfoundland and Labrador. 2019b. *Economic Growth Strategy for Newfoundland and Labrador: Recommendations to the Government of Newfoundland and Labrador*. St. John's. Online at https://www.fin.gov.nl.ca/fin/publications/pdf/MCK_Final_Report.pdf.

Newfoundland and Labrador. 2020. "Implement Regional Innovation System Pilots." St. John's. Online at https://www.gov.nl.ca/thewayforward/action/identify-five-regional-innovation-systems-pilot-project-areas/.

Nunacor. 2020. "About Nunacor." Online at https://www.nunacor.com/about-nunacor/

Reimer, B., and R. Bollman. 2010. "Understanding Rural Canada: Implications for Rural Development Policy and Rural Planning Policy." In *Rural Planning and Development in Canada*, ed. D. Douglas, 10–52. Toronto: Nelson Education.

Schroeder, W., and B. Hallett. 2019. "Newfoundland and Labrador needs Ottawa's help, soon." *Globe and Mail*, 22 November. Online at https://www.theglobeandmail.com/business/commentary/article-newfoundland-and-labrador-needs-help-soon/.

Shearmur, R. 2010. "Maritime Clusters: A Comparative Perspective." Memorial University of Newfoundland, Leslie Harris Centre of Regional Policy and Development, Synergy Session, with Oceans Advance, 9 June.

Simms, A., and J. Ward. 2016. *Regional Projections for Labrador & the Northern Peninsula.* St. John's: Memorial University of Newfoundland, Leslie Harris Centre of Regional Policy and Development, Regional Analytics Laboratory. Online at https://www.mun.ca/harriscentre/Population Project/Final_Labrador_Report.pdf.

Simms, A., and J. Ward. 2017. *Regional Population Projections for Newfoundland and Labrador 2016–2036.* St. John's: Memorial University of Newfoundland, Leslie Harris Centre of Regional Policy and Development, Regional Analytics Laboratory. Online at https://www.mun.ca/harriscentre /PopulationProject/Population_Projections_for_NL.pdf

Statistics Canada. 2020. *Canada Goes Urban.* Ottawa. Online at https:// www150.statcan.gc.ca/n1/pub/11-630-x/11-630-x2015004-eng.htm.

Storey, K. and H.M. Hall. 2018. "Dependence at a Distance: The New Single-Industry Community and the Implications for Policy." *Canadian Geographer* 62 (2): 225–37. https://doi.org/10.1111/cag.12390

Vodden, K., K. Carter, and K. White. 2013. "A Primer on Innovation, Learning, and Knowledge Flows." *Canadian Regional Development: A Critical Review of Theory Practice and Potentials,* August. Online at http://cdnregdev.ruralresilience.ca /wp-content/uploads/2014/12/Innovation_Primer-WP-CRD6.pdf.

Vodden, K., D. Douglas, S. Markey, S. Minnes, and B. Reimer. 2019. *The Theory, Practice and Potential of Regional Development: The Case of Canada.* New York: Routledge.

Walsh, J., and B. Winsor. 2019. "Socio-Cultural Barriers to Developing a Regional Entrepreneurial Ecosystem." *Journal of Enterprising Communities: People and Places in the Global Economy* 13 (3): 263–82. https://doi.org /10.1108/JEC-11-2018-0088.

Warrian, P., and D. Wolfe. 2016. "C-CORE as a Networked Industrial Policy." St. John's: Memorial University of Newfoundland, COASTS Initiative. July.

Warrian, P., and D. Wolfe. 2017. "Research and Technology Transfer at the Marine Institute, Memorial University of Newfoundland. St. John's: Memorial University of Newfoundland, COASTS Initiative. April.

Williams, R. 2019. *A Future for the Fishery: Crisis and Renewal in Canada's Neglected Fishing Industry.* Halifax: Nimbus.

Winsor, B., and K. Carter. 2018. *Mapping Knowledge Seeking in the St. John's and Corner Brook Entrepreneurial Ecosystems.* St. John's: Memorial University of Newfoundland, Leslie Harris Centre of Regional Policy and Development, Regional Analytics Laboratory. Online at https://www.mun.ca /harriscentre/reports/WINSOR_CARTER_ARF_15-16.pdf.

6 Prince Edward Island: From Gentle to Mighty Island

MARK LEGGOTT AND H. WADE MACLAUCHLAN

For much of its history Prince Edward Island (PEI) has been described, both formally and informally, as the *Gentle Island*. This stemmed from the small, pastoral nature of this "Island in the Gulf," which has a strong rural economy built from the natural resources of the island and surrounding waters as well as a tourist industry with roots in the Anne of Green Gables stories of Lucy Maud Montgomery. In economic terms, PEI's "gentle" nature has been underscored by the fact that it has the lowest per capita gross domestic product (GDP) in the country.

More recently, PEI has been rebranded the *Mighty Island*, a reference to the considerable increase in GDP over the past half-century and the emergence of innovative economic sectors and small business entrepreneurship that have helped drive this growth. PEI's small size has been both a benefit and a detriment to driving innovation and economic growth, and, to a large degree, has helped to frame the science, technology, and innovation (STI) strategies advanced in the province over the past three decades.

Key to the innovation agenda have been the development of provincial post-secondary institutions and an enhanced emphasis on exports. Many of the leading STI efforts have emerged from collaborations among private sector companies, research institutions, and provincial and federal government agencies. These efforts have benefited from a robust immigration program: between 2011 and 2017, PEI recruited 96 per cent of its immigrants through the Provincial Nominee Program, the highest rate among the provinces (see Chapter 4).

Context

Some might consider it extravagant for Canada's smallest province in terms of size and population to call itself the *Mighty Island*, but there is some justification for this claim. At the core of PEI's "might" is the advantage of scale and an increasingly diversified and integrated economy. While GDP per capita averaged only $36,644 over the 2014–18 period, the lowest of all the provinces and territories (see Chapter 4), PEI has demonstrated impressive catch-up over the years. In the 1960s, the province earned less than 50 per cent of the national average; today, it earns about 71 per cent of the average province. For the years 2015–18, PEI's economic growth was second only to that of British Columbia, and in 2019 PEI led all provinces with 2.8 per cent real economic growth, leading RBC Economics (2019) to acknowledge the brand: "Mighty growth continues for the island." Scotiabank Economics (2020, 3) described the economy as "firing on all cylinders."

The transition from gentle to mighty island is about much more than numbers. The change is not simply about getting bigger: in today's global economy, it is not feasible to expect PEI will gain enough scale to compete against the largest economic regions. Its claim to be the *Mighty Island* is founded instead on a diverse economy, integration among institutions and other key actors, and a focus on strategic sectors. STI-based development has been closely tied to a shared narrative of environmental awareness and effective stewardship, reinforced by a sense of appropriately scaled effort. In one area of concerted development, PEI's bioscience cluster tripled from 20 to 60 firms between 2005 and 2019, with employment rising to 1,800 well-paying jobs (Atlantic Business 2020). A second area of focus is aerospace and marine technologies, with comparable growth over a period extending from the early 1990s. Over the most recent five-year period, PEI's economic growth strategy combined with population growth and a focus on immigration to achieve cumulative GDP growth of 11.2 per cent, second only to that of British Columbia among the provinces (Statistics Canada n.d.c).

Being small presents challenges that can limit the province's ability to respond to growth opportunities or to develop a competitive edge in technology and innovation. Chief among these challenges are the comparatively small population and workforce, and constraints of small scale on some types of trade or transportation. The economies of scale and scope that are evident in larger centres are clearly missing. Some are absolute impediments, but, to some degree, these have been balanced by a narrative of resiliency and local resourcefulness that has shaped PEI's history. In some instances, smallness helps to increase engagement and interaction, the foundation for many dynamics that underpin innovation processes. When combined with a history of research and development (R&D) partnerships between the university and island companies, this closeness and increased interaction might be a unique stimulus for the absorptive capacity of island firms, or even of the island as a whole.

Population and workforce are core to the future of the province. PEI's median age increased from twenty-five in 1970 to forty-four in 2016 – clearly not an ideal trend for the long term, but not unambiguously bad, as maturing workers tend to drive the economy towards peak productivity. There has been significant effort to overcome this challenge, including strategies linking immigration to economic opportunity and attempts to generate greater opportunities for youth through, for example, the Aerospace Academy Program. There is evidence that the trends are shifting. In 2015–16 PEI led the other provinces with a population growth rate of 13.6 per 1,000, and in 2019 the median age of Islanders dipped to forty-three, defying the aging demographic trend for Canada and most other provinces. From 2015 to 2019, PEI saw the creation of 8,500 new full-time jobs, equal to 14.2 per cent of the local labour market (Statistics Canada n.d.a).

In the past three decades, the island economy has become more diverse, with greater reliance on manufacturing, services, and the knowledge economy. Goods production contributes only about 23 per cent of GDP, compared with 30 per cent for the national economy. Within the goods sector, the province is differentially dependent on primary agriculture and its processing. Services have taken up the slack, leading employment and GDP growth.

PEI's goal is to close the gap with the rest of Canada by above-average growth. Over the past sixty-five years, the PEI economy has grown at an average of 3.1 per cent per annum, compared with only 2.2 per cent for the national economy and second only to Newfoundland and Labrador (see Chapter 4). At that rate of convergence, however, it would still take almost forty years for the province to reach the national level of GDP per capita. Mobilizing existing and new labour and capital to exploit the island's natural resources will not be sufficient to meet that goal. Innovation and productivity growth need to be part of the solution.

Innovation Architecture

Prince Edward Island's economy historically has been built on doing the best you can with whatever is "at hand" on the land and sea: shipbuilding during the days of sail; the breeding of silver foxes for export to fashion capitals of the world; seed potato expertise; themed tourism; mussel and oyster aquaculture; dairy innovation; and, most recently, nutrisciences and the harnessing of wind energy. PEI today remains the most rural of Canada's provinces, with 53 per cent of its population living outside urban areas. Agriculture remains a significant contributor to the provincial economy – only in Saskatchewan is the farm and food sector more important to the overall economy (Statistics Canada 2015).

In general, while policy and investment have had an impact on the province's STI, the greater impact has come from a hardscrabble combination of subsistence and entrepreneurship. The combination of smaller players and the island's physical scale and close community means collaborations are more obvious or natural. For decades, PEI has had both the lowest level of wealth and the lowest income inequality of any province (Statistics Canada 2017). Larger firms also represent a smaller share of the number of firms in the province and employ a smaller number of workers than in most other provinces. In their place, co-operatives and government Crown corporations contribute relatively more than in other provinces. Not insignificantly, the lack of dominant families or firms has meant that the spirit of innovation and enterprise is widespread.

The formally structured innovation effort is relatively small in PEI, representing less than 1 per cent of the national effort and only about 1.20 per cent of provincial GDP (Table 6.1). The federal government is the largest single funder, much of it directed to federal facilities in the province. More than 50 per cent of the R&D is done in post-secondary educational institutions. No single enterprise cracks the list of 100 top research-intensive firms in Canada.

Many of PEI's key economic developments have come through a natural scrappiness – a willingness to put up a fight to get ahead. At its tamest, this might be thought of as island pride – that is part of the image of the *Gentle Island*. Its essence is that we know that we have to get better, that we can succeed, and that material progress will come only through hard work and competitive excellence. We also know that none of that will be given to us without struggle; this is not a fight where we prevail by force but because we draw on our scrappy essence. We do not expect others to give us our fair share, but we believe that, given a chance, we can and will get ahead.

PEI has been actively directing resources to STI targets in its economic development policy since the early 1990s. The province has variously targeted industries with financial support, mainly with tax rebate programs to return corporate income and property taxes to firms that have twenty or more employees and an annual payroll of at least $700,000. The aerospace and defence rebate program was launched in 1993, followed by the bioscience rebate in 2006 and the advanced marine technologies program in 2018. It was initially envisaged that the

Table 6.1. Gross Expenditure on Research and Development by Performing Sector, average $ millions, Prince Edward Island, 2013–17

		Performers					
		Government		Provincial			Private
				Research	Business	Higher	Non-
Funders	Total	Federal	Provincial	Organizations	Enterprise	Education	profit
Total sectors	68	14	–	–	19	35	–
Federal government	24	14	–	–	2	8	–
Provincial government	2	–	–	–	1	1	–
Business enterprise	16	–	–	–	15	2	–
Higher education	22	–	–	–	–	22	–
Private non-profit	2	–	–	–	1	1	–
Foreign	2	–	–	–	2	–	–

Note: Columns and rows may not sum due to rounding.

Source: Statistics Canada, table 27-10-0273-01, "Gross domestic expenditures on research and development, by science type and by funder and performer sector (x 1,000,000)."

tax rebate programs would each have a ten-year sunset, but they have been extended several times. The annual cost of the rebate programs to the province is now in excess of $20 million, but this has to be put into context: the aerospace and bioscience firms now achieve annual sales in excess of $300 million. The aerospace rebate program is currently set to expire in 2022.

The province has also directly invested in island businesses through two Crown corporations: Finance PEI and Island Investment Development Inc. (Grant Thornton 2018). In the past three decades, support for industry has focused on five key sectors: aerospace; food technology/ advanced manufacturing; information technology; bioscience/tech; and marine technology. We tell the story below of PEI's STI strategy using four specific examples: Standard Aero, PEI Mussel King, discoverygarden Inc., and Diagnostic Chemicals.

One visible impact of these efforts is the 28.9 per cent growth in industrial production in PEI from 2013 to 2017, twice the rate of any other province. In its review of provincial economies for 2019, Scotiabank Economics found that PEI also outperformed other provinces in growth in domestic exports and manufacturing shipments, suggesting "that resilience in part reflects the breadth of the island's industrial base and its geographic export diversification" (Scotiabank Economics 2020, 3).

Policy Efforts

In the early 1960s, PEI's per capita GDP was 50 per cent of Canada's. The province operated with institutions, social systems, and an economy that had been subsisting since the late 1800s. There were select areas of competitive advantage, such as silver foxes, wooden ships, or seed potatoes, but, in the main, off-island transportation was a barrier. As the 1960s began, new technologies were making an appearance, the Baby Boom was doing its thing, and the economy was growing, although not as dynamically as in most of Canada.

A key turning point in PEI's development was signing of the *Prince Edward Island Comprehensive Development Plan* (CDP) in 1969 by Jean Marchand, the federal minister of forestry and rural development, and Alexander B. Campbell, PEI's longest-serving premier. The significance of the Plan (as it became known), is best summed by University of Prince Edward Island (UPEI) history professor Dr Ed MacDonald (2000, 313): "It may be an overstatement, but no lie, to say that the postwar history of Prince Edward Island can be divided into two epochs: before "the Plan" and after it. On one side of the Development Plan era lies the Island that was; on the other, still too close to see clearly, looms the Island of today. In popular memory, the Comprehensive Development Plan is thus both coffin and cradle."

The CDP identified four priorities: resource adjustment and development, social development, resource support and commercial services, and implementation (Nemetz 1982, 159). The CDP's main contribution to STI development, not in the forefront of thinking at the time, came through institution building – specifically UPEI as a single provincial university and Holland College as a college of applied arts and technology. These institutional investments have been essential contributors to PEI's development ever since. This strategy was further advanced in the 1970s and 1980s with the creation of the Atlantic Veterinary College (AVC), a joint venture of the four Atlantic provinces. AVC and UPEI developed a series of technology transfer entities, starting with AVC

Inc., followed by UPEI Inc., Three Oaks Innovations, and, most recently, Synapse Applied Research and Industry Services. All four entities have contributed to the incubation and spin-off of efforts of island researchers and entrepreneurs.

People still look back on the creation of UPEI as an act of political leadership and bravery. Going back into the early decades of the nineteenth century, PEI had two post-secondary colleges: Saint Dunstan's University and Prince of Wales College. During the mid-1960s, with the Baby Boom coming to its crest and the impetus of new federal spending in post-secondary education, the two colleges embarked on ambitious plans of growth and spending. This was a matter of concern to the provincial government, which ultimately had to write the cheques. With a one-seat majority in the PEI legislature, Premier Campbell came to the view that the only solution was to form a single provincial university. In parallel, and with vision, he introduced Holland College as the provincial college of applied arts and technology. This transformative move was presented to the legislature in the form of a White Paper on post-secondary education at a time of particular tension and rivalry in terms of institutional expansion, and very few expected the Campbell government to move forward. The initial reaction to the White Paper was revealing. Most of the public, including many of the key players associated with the two colleges, voiced support. With an indication that there would be leadership support and new institutional capacity created – including significant new resources spent – the reaction was mainly, "Great, let's get on with it" (MacLauchlan 2014).

The formation of the Atlantic Veterinary College, starting in the mid-1970s and culminating with its opening in 1986, is a further example of scrappiness and determination. The new institution was to serve the four Atlantic provinces, but Nova Scotia felt strongly that the college belonged in Truro, linked to the Nova Scotia Agricultural College. An independent committee recommended AVC be established on the UPEI campus; that view ultimately prevailed, with PEI picking up a larger fraction of the operating and capital costs. AVC brought professional and graduate studies in the field, as well as close ties to the productive sectors in animal and fish health. While serving as UPEI president from 1999 to 2011, co-author Wade MacLauchlan was known to comment on more than one occasion, "It's like having a medical school without the egos."

By the late 1990s, UPEI, AVC, and Holland College, with support from provincial and federal economic development agencies, were well positioned to compete for expanding national R&D and innovation funding. When the Canada Research Chairs program was unveiled

in the spring 2000 federal budget, there was a notional allocation of two
Tier II chairs for UPEI. By 2008, UPEI/AVC had been awarded six Canada Research Chairs and in 2009 secured one of ten inaugural Canada
Excellence Research Chairs, in the relatively new discipline of aquatic
epidemiology.

In the summer of 2000, the federal government announced the Atlantic Investment Partnership, a $700 million, five-year initiative designed
to help Atlantic Canadians innovate and compete in an increasingly
global, knowledge-based economy. Two primary initiatives were the
$300 million Atlantic Innovation Fund and new resources to support
the National Research Council (NRC) to expand its activities and
facilities in the region. While PEI was not on the initial list of intended
NRC investments, an active partnership of institutional, industry, federal, and provincial players worked with the NRC through a technology road-mapping exercise to identify the need for federal-provincial
resources to establish the Institute for Nutrisciences and Health on the
UPEI campus. It opened in 2003.

PEI proposals have been recognized for their above-average success
in securing Atlantic Innovation Fund support, often through a creative
combination of federal, provincial, institutional, and private sector
resources. The success came mainly because the proposals and partnerships proactively have focused on the funds' objectives – namely, to
increase R&D being carried out in Atlantic research facilities, leading
to the launch of new ideas, products, processes, and services; improve
the region's capacity to commercialize R&D; strengthen the region's
innovation system by supporting R&D and commercialization partnerships and alliances among private enterprises, universities, research
institutions, and other organizations; and enhance the region's ability
to access national R&D programs (ACOA n.d.).

UPEI was recognized as the top Canadian undergraduate university in research funding growth from 2002 to 2007, with a 154 per cent
increase from $5.2 million to $13.2 million in annual funding (Research
Infosource 2008). From 1996 to 2005, spurred by strong federal investment and success in university research competitions, annual R&D
expenditures in PEI almost quadrupled from $17 million to $63 million
(Mayne 2008, 38). These R&D investments were focused particularly on
the biosciences, food innovation, and advanced manufacturing, translating into sectoral economic growth that outpaced overall growth of
the PEI economy.

In 2008, following public and sector engagement, PEI released a new
economic development plan, the *Island Prosperity Strategy* (IPS), which
defined the challenge: "In the past, our wealth has been drawn from

the resources of our land and surrounding waters. To ensure continued wealth, we must strengthen the new factors of competitiveness in today's economy – people and technology – and apply them across the full range of our economy. Our traditional industries and our new industries are not two separate worlds. They must act together, just as one hand strengthens the other" (Mayne 2008, 5).

After underscoring that the traditional and new industries would work hand in hand and strengthen each other, the IPS identified four sectors for investment and growth: biosciences, aerospace, information technology, and renewable energy. The IPS laid out a five-year investment strategy in people ($40 million), innovation ($100 million), and economic infrastructure ($60 million), and created Innovation PEI as a new Crown corporation. The strategy outlined a series of workforce initiatives, including labour market development programs, graduate and post-doctoral awards, and industry-leveraged research chairs. The two big infrastructure investments were the BioCommons Industry Park in Charlottetown and an e-Health Centre of Research Excellence in Summerside. The innovation pillar involved: (a) the Pilot Fund to provide funds to test high-risk projects with commercial potential; (b) the Discovery and Development Fund to support research projects upstream of traditional development and commercialization funding; (c) the Prototype Fund to support proof of concept or prototype studies to move promising ideas towards commercialization more quickly; (d) the Regulatory, Management, and Marketing Program to provide firms with expertise and mentoring to get their products to market; (e) selected tax incentives to spur further business development in priority sectors; and (f) a review of corporate taxation approaches to maximize competitiveness in advancing key sectors (Mayne 2008, 52–4).

During the first five years, the IPS did not achieve its stated goals in terms of employment and earnings – far from surprising given the world economic crisis of 2008–9. While PEI was the only province whose economy did not slip into recession in that downturn, the global market was not conducive to much progress. In the subsequent five years, 2014–19, PEI generated more than 8,000 full-time jobs, equal to 14 per cent growth, which in proportionate terms was greater than any other province. This helped boost per capita population growth. In both 2017–18 and 2018–19, PEI experienced population growth in excess of 2 per cent annually, leading all provinces, while Canada saw relatively high population growth of 1.4 per cent annually (Statistics Canada n.d.c). During this three-year period, the median age of the PEI population declined from 43.9 to 43.2, a remarkable achievement in demographic terms, as Canada's overall median age rose from 40.7 to 40.8 over the same period (Statistics Canada, n.d.b).

This recent expansion contrasts favourably with the 1960s and 1970s, when investments in industrial parks and firm expansion generated limited success and sometimes spectacular failure, a pattern that repeated itself elsewhere in the Atlantic provinces (Bickerton 1990; Savoie 2006). There was the Bricklin car-making fiasco in New Brunswick, the failure of Clairtone Sound's stereo-manufacturing operations in Nova Scotia, and numerous enterprises of developers financed by Newfoundland and Labrador premier Joseph Smallwood. The most notorious PEI failure was the investment by the Walter Shaw government in shipbuilding and food processing in Georgetown in the early1960s (MacLauchlan 2014, 67–9). Some of those earlier investments generated a return only when they were repurposed. A success of particular note in this context was the fight in the early 1990s to salvage the Slemon Park aerospace initiative out of the closure of CFB Summerside. Today the Park houses a number of aerospace companies, as well as operations in advanced manufacturing and security training.

Transportation and connectedness to the bigger world has always been a challenge for PEI, one now largely overcome by the Confederation Bridge and the internet. The bridge emerged from a protracted and, at times, emotional process. Construction started in the late 1980s, and the bridge opened in 1997. Today, five hundred trucks per day move across in each direction. Meanwhile the expansion of the internet has begun to open the province to the world; access is virtually universal, but narrow bandwidth continues to limit the province's capacity to exploit its strengths. One positive outcome of this greater connectivity is that, since 1992, PEI's exports have grown at a rate more than double those of Canada as a whole.

The Policy Efforts

The combined efforts of federal and provincial programming and growing post-secondary sector capacity have helped to advance a number of industrial developments in PEI. Four stand out: aerospace, mussels, information technology, and biotechnology. Environmental technologies represent a fifth, emerging, area of focus.

Manufacturing is a significant player in PEI's changing economy, with 6,800 workers and over $2 billion of shipments in 2018, overall contributing about 10 per cent of GDP. This reflects double-digit growth in the manufacture of aerospace products and parts, chemicals, and machinery. PEI's aerospace and defence sector had its genesis in the response to the announced closure of CFB Summerside in 1989. The community and province rallied, with support from the federal government, to create the Slemon Park Corp. utilizing the hangar and runway facilities as a site for business growth. Today there are approximately twenty companies operating throughout PEI offering aerospace, defence, marine, and security products and services, predominantly for national and international clients. Standard Aero is the largest employer in the sector, with almost five hundred workers. The firm, operating then as Atlantic Turbines, was one of the first tenants at Slemon Park when it started in 1991 with a handful of employees. The company specializes in the maintenance, repair, and overhaul of gas turbine engines. The PEI government has supported the sector with two test cell facilities and the aerospace corporate tax rebate. Other firms have grown around the nucleus. MDS Coating Technologies has operated at Slemon Park since 2003, providing erosion/corrosion resistant coating to compressor components of gas turbine engines. The technology was developed for the Soviet military in Afghanistan in the 1980s to protect aircraft propellers and engines from sand corrosion. With government support, MDS has invested in equipment and technology enhancements to maintain a competitive advantage in serving military and commercial clients worldwide.

The blue mussel is both one of PEI's best-known ambassadors and a major growth opportunity. The province produces 80 per cent of cultivated mussels in Canada and supplies markets throughout North America, Europe, and parts of Asia. A significant part of the innovative energy behind the launch of the PEI mussel industry in the 1970s and 1980s was adapted from agriculture. Using a longline system, naturally collected mussel seed is placed in mesh sleeves suspended in water columns. The mussels grow over a 12- to 24-month period in nutrient-rich, sometimes ice-covered, waters without feed or additives. Because a mussel is a living creature meant for discerning consumers, handling and shipping call for innovation and science. PEI Mussel King, owned and continuously operated by the Dockendorf family since 1978, has innovated and invested, with government support, in the development of frozen mussel products. In the late 1980s, the industry faced a crisis of food poisoning related to domoic acid in blue mussels. Government and academic researchers collaborated with industry to discover the cause and develop new standards of food safety and quality assurance. UPEI and the Atlantic Veterinary College have also worked with industry and international partners to develop expertise in aquatic animal health, while the provincial and federal governments have supported the industry through development of a leasehold regime, subsidies for plant and equipment, food safety, quality-assurance programming, and export development assistance. In 2015, PEI Mussel King was recognized as "Exporter of the Year" by Trade Team PEI.

As elsewhere, information technology is a target. By 2008 over one hundred information technology (IT)–focused companies were operating in the province, employing over twelve hundred workers. IT firms ranged from those that sprang from the well-educated island community to large national firms such as CGI Consulting. One unusual island start-up was discoverygarden Inc., which emerged from a team at the Robertson Library at UPEI. A series of projects designed to make cultural heritage materials (such as books, newspapers, and music) available to a wide audience resulted in the development of an open-source platform called Islandora. Some of the original development was supported by the library's budget and private donations and led to an ever-more sophisticated system. Support for the university from the Atlantic Canada Opportunities Agency's Atlantic Innovation Fund helped to develop a product based on freely available software. In 2010 the university spun out the start-up firm discoverygarden, with the goal of developing a fee-for-service/cloud platform to take Islandora to the international market. discoverygarden continues today, employing mostly island-born and -trained software developers and engineers. In addition, there are over a dozen international companies and consortia that provide Islandora services to their clients and community members, as well as hundreds of institutions that run the software with their own resources. The decision to ensure that the intellectual property that emerged from the university sector remained open, with the help of federal and provincial programs, offers a good example of how the traditional model of IT commercialization need not be the only mode.

Prince Edward Island's bioscience sector is a significant feature of the province's modern economy, comprising more than 50 firms, upwards of 1,600 highly qualified personnel, $250 million in annual revenues, and over $70 million in R&D expenditures. The genesis of the sector can be traced to the founding in 1970 of Diagnostic Chemicals Ltd. (DCL) by Dr Regis Duffy, who, as dean of science at UPEI, set out to create employment opportunities for his students. Dr Duffy also played a leadership role as founding chair of the PEI BioAlliance, a public-private partnership coordinating bioscience cluster development, and through the Regis Duffy BioScience Fund, which invests in bioscience-related businesses nearing commercialization and provides guidance to emerging businesses. Today, DCL has grown and evolved into two firms, BioVectra Ltd. and Sekisui Diagnostics PEI, with a total of almost seven hundred employees. DCL's core expertise was the manufacture and sale of synthetically challenging chemicals, biochemicals, chemical reagents, and point-of-care tests for the pharmaceutical industry and health care providers. With the growth of competitors in India and China, DCL reinvented itself to produce smaller quantities of high-value chemicals, supported by a biopharmaceutical manufacturing facility that is compliant with current Good Manufacturing Practices. DCL's growth was assisted by provincial loans and federal support from the Atlantic Innovation Fund. The labour rebate program, in particular, provides refundable support equal to 25 per cent of eligible wages and salaries paid to develop or commercialize any product, process, or service new to PEI. The PEI bioscience sector also benefits from a provincial corporate income tax exemption introduced in 2006.

While each of the four priorities of the *Island Prosperity Strategy* continues, the future is increasingly being framed around the environment. As in most jurisdictions, the impacts of climate change have become compelling, and are especially noticeable on a small island in the warm waters of the Gulf of St. Lawrence. In the past one hundred years, PEI's average air temperature has warmed by 0.5 C degrees and sea levels have risen by 30 cm (Prince Edward Island n.d.). Its "islandness" means that PEI is especially alert to the challenges of climate change. Two recent developments at UPEI demonstrate this connection to the land and a new direction for the province. In 2014, the Faculty of Sustainable Design Engineering was established. It has taken an innovative approach to an engineering baccalaureate, including the opportunity for students to focus on sustainable energy or bioresources. The Canadian Centre for Climate Change and Adaptation at UPEI, launched in 2019, will "provide skills to help mitigate and adapt to climate change, as well as drive innovation in green technology." The impact of these forward-looking developments remains to be seen. The commitment to a sustainable approach can also be seen in the various programs and partnerships with the Abegweit and Lennox Island First Nations. For example, the Abegweit Biodiversity Enhancement Hatchery raises indigenous fish species to restock island rivers, and the Bideford Shellfish Hatchery, owned and operated by the Lennox Island Development Corporation, is a key source of brood stock for the oyster industry. These and other projects highlight the importance of a collaborative and sustainable approach to development.

Conclusions and Lessons

Seamlessly balancing a pattern of positive STI momentum and economic growth with what it means to be an Islander will be the most important challenge for the next thirty years. More than any other characteristic, PEI's size has been both a challenge and a strength. A low cost of living and a high quality of life have supported a successful population growth strategy, attracting skilled immigrants and investors and stemming long-standing trends of domestic out-migration. This would not have been possible without a strategic focus on STI.

As a province of limited land and natural resources, PEI identified the need to develop a knowledge-based economy to support a modern lifestyle and population. Because of its small scale and relative geographic isolation, the province was able to identify areas of strategic focus and concerted investment without spending an undue amount of time persuading key actors that "we can't do everything." In larger jurisdictions, arguments over both the principles and the principal beneficiaries of STI specialization can consume a great deal of time and goodwill. In PEI, the anchoring sense of place and size has shaped the ideas and institutions that helped drive the province's approach to STI.

The industry cameos highlighted above demonstrate a history of innovation reflecting a range of interests, approaches, and supports, from federal and provincial investment, transformative efforts stemming from the university context, to the determination of entrepreneurs. These are just a few of the examples that continue to help drive economic development in PEI. The growth over the recent past would not have been possible without an active population strategy and proactive immigration policies.

The province's small scale served to bring to the fore a further, common barrier to STI-based growth: the need for housing. By 2018, PEI had the lowest rental vacancy rate in Canada, at 0.2 per cent (CBC 2020). In 2019, a record number of new residential units was constructed and the provincial rental vacancy rate rose to 1.2 per cent. For STI growth, housing is especially challenging because housing supply tends to lag or be out of sync with demand. As recently as 2013, PEI's rental vacancy rate was 7.1 per cent (CMHC 2018). An important parallel is the availability, speed, reliability, and affordability of internet broadband service, as important for social and community reasons as for business. Again, PEI's small size is an advantage, with the province scheduled by 2023 to be the first to have universal broadband service (Neatby 2020).

Recent investments and developments will help PEI continue to leverage its "Island nature," including environmental awareness, sense of scale, and effective stewardship. The main strategic areas of STI-based growth, notably biosciences, renewable energy, the digital community, and food innovation, relate well to Islanders' sense of place and PEI's history and scale. Even in advanced manufacturing, where PEI's growth has been impressive, the main areas of growth have been related to food production and processing. PEI's experience with STI investments and growth offers a case in point of the theories of innovation discussed in Chapter 2 – notably, that STI does well when it is place sensitive and place specific, and when it builds around core competencies.

The PEI experience with STI can be considered evidence of a larger point made in the opening chapters: ideas matter. In concert with specific STI policies, investments, and initiatives, it helps to have an identity or an aspiration that answers the question, "Who do you think you are?" Prince Edward Islanders have no difficulty with the concept that PEI is "Canada's Food Island." This self-image stands up well in terms of both heritage and contemporary strengths. It naturally embraces biosciences, human and animal health and nutrition, hospitality and culture, as well as the human capital, investments, and policies required to succeed. It mobilizes the population to see itself more as a Mighty Island than as the Gentle Island.

PEI has demonstrated an impressive economic performance over the past decade. Its diversity and resilience have served the province well in challenging times. During the great recession of 2008–9, PEI was squeezed economically, but it was the only province that did not experience a year of negative growth. Since 2014, PEI has been a leader among the provinces for year-over-year growth, a foundation that bodes well for future development.

In pandemic times, it is also an advantage to have a smaller, more rural population and to be geographically isolated. Eight months after the COVID-19 pandemic hit Canada in mid-March 2020, PEI was the only province to have no community spread and zero cases requiring hospitalization. Needless to say, the pandemic disrupted early 2020 economic forecasts for Canada and all provinces and territories. This unparalleled health crisis and economic setback will test the rootedness of STI culture, the resiliency of institutions, and the allegiance of workforces and communities. It will be telling to see how long it takes to emerge from the crisis and what is required for the Mighty Island to get its "mojo" back.

References

ACOA (Atlantic Canada Opportunities Agency). n.d. "Atlantic Innovation Fund: FAQ." Online at https://www.canada.ca/en/atlantic-canada-opportunities/services/aiffaq.html#objectives, accessed 11 May 2020.

Atlantic Business. 2020. "PEI BioAlliance clears global path for regional firms." 8 January. Online at https://www.atlanticbusinessmagazine.net /article/pei-bioalliance-clears-global-path-for-regional-firms/.

Bickerton, J. 1990. *Nova Scotia, Ottawa, and the Politics of Regional Development.* Toronto: University of Toronto Press.

CBC (Canadian Broadcasting Corporation). 2020. "P.E.I. vacancy rate improved, but still lowest in country." 15 January. Online at https:// www.cbc.ca/news/canada/prince-edward-island/pei-vacancy -rate-improves-january-2020-1.5427715.

CMHC (Canada Mortgage and Housing Corporation). 2018. "Rental Vacancy Rates: Canada, Provinces and Metropolitan Areas." Ottawa. Online at https://www.cmhc-schl.gc.ca/en/data-and-research/data-tables/rental- vacancy-rates-canada-provinces-metropolitan-areas, accessed 11 May 2020.

Grant Thornton LLP. 2018. "The Fiscal 2016 Economic Impact of Finance PEI and Island Investment Development Inc. Supported Firms." Online at https://www.princeedwardisland.ca/en/publication/fiscal-economic- impact-finance-pei-and-island-investment-development-inc-supported-1.

MacDonald, E. 2000. *If You're Stronghearted: Prince Edward Island in the Twentieth Century.* Charlottetown: Prince Edward Island Museum and Heritage Foundation.

MacLauchlan, H.W. 2014. *Alex B. Campbell: The Prince Edward Island Premier Who Rocked the Cradle.* Charlottetown: Prince Edward Island Museum and Heritage Foundation.

Mayne, M. 2008. *Island Prosperity Challenge: A Focus for Change.* Charlottetown, PEI: Government of Prince Edward Island. Online at http://www.gov .pe.ca/photos/original/IPS.pdf, accessed 11 May 2020.

Neatby, S. 2020. "Updated: P.E.I. releases details of plan to fix rural internet." *Guardian,* (Charlottetown), 13 March. Online at https://www.theguardian .pe.ca/news/local/updated-pei-releases-details-of-plan-to-fix-rural-internet -423682/.

Nemetz, D. 1982. "Managing Development." In *The Garden Transformed: Prince Edward Island, 1945–1980,* ed. V. Smitheram, D. Milne, and S. Dasgupta, 155–75. Charlottetown: Ragwood.

Prince Edward Island. n.d. "Our Changing Climate." Charlottetown. Online at https://www.princeedwardisland.ca/en/information/communities -land-and-environment/our-changing-climate.

RBC Economics. 2019. "Provincial Outlook." Online at https://royal-bank-of -canada-2124.docs.contently.com/v/provincial-outlook-december-2019.

Research Infosource. 2008. "Canada's Innovation Leaders 2008." 7 November. Online at https://researchinfosource.com/pdf/CIL08_CIL_2008.pdf.

Savoie, D. 2006. *Visiting Grandchildren: Economic Development in the Maritimes.* Toronto: University of Toronto Press.

Scotiabank. 2020. "Provincial Outlook, January 14, 2020." Online at https://
   www.scotiabank.com/content/dam/scotiabank/sub-brands/scotia
   bank-economics/english/documents/provincial-pulse/provincial
   _outlook_2020-01-14.pdf, accessed 11 May 2020.
Statistics Canada. 2015. "Agriculture and Agri-Food Economic Account,
   2015." Ottawa. Online at https://www150.statcan.gc.ca/n1/daily
   -quotidien/190730/dq190730a-eng.htm.
Statistics Canada. 2017. "Annual Wages, Salaries and Commissions of T1 Tax
   Filers." Ottawa. Online at https://www150.statcan.gc.ca/n1/daily
   -quotidien/190129/dq190129e-eng.htm.
Statistics Canada. n.d.a. "Labour Force Characteristics by Province,
   Seasonally Adjusted." Ottawa. Online at https://www150.statcan.gc.ca/n1
   /daily-quotidien/200110/t003a-eng.htm
Statistics Canada. n.d.b. "Population Estimates on July 1st, by Age and Sex."
   Table 17-10-0005-01. Ottawa. Online at https://www150.statcan.gc.ca/t1
   /tbl1/en/tv.action?pid=1710000501.
Statistics Canada. n.d.c. "Population Growth Rate, Canada and Provinces."
   Table 17-10-0009-01. Ottawa. Online at https://www150.statcan.gc.ca/t1
   /tbl1/en/tv.action?pid=1710000901.

7 Nova Scotia: Capitalizing on the Atlantic University Advantage

RICHARD ISNOR

The policy environment for science, technology, and innovation (STI) in Nova Scotia has been influenced over the past decade by two extensive multistakeholder engagement exercises and several influential studies and reports. Provincial innovation system strengths include the research capacity of the post-secondary education (PSE) sector and strengthened venture capital support for start-up companies (Duruflé 2014). Weaknesses exist in business-performed research efforts and a lack of overall STI policy focus and capacity within the provincial government. Successful sectoral efforts include energy, life sciences, and oceans. The creation in 2019 of Research Nova Scotia holds potential to strengthen the provincial innovation system and create new synergies between innovation system partners in the province.

Nova Scotia generally has followed an *implicit* (rather than *explicit*) STI policy approach, typical of most Canadian provinces (Council of Canadian Academies 2017). Provincial policy attention is diffused across several sectoral ministries (business, health, labour and advanced education, agriculture, fisheries, natural resources, and energy), none which has a clear policy lead for science or innovation within the government. Reports by the Commission on Building Our New Economy (Nova Scotia 2014), the ONE Nova Scotia Coalition (2016), and the Research, Development and Commercialization (RDC) Working Group (Nicholson and Larsen 2016) provided renewed attention to STI as an area more deserving of provincial policy attention, and highlighted the need for more integrated efforts to address economic and social issues. The provincial government, however, possesses limited internal STI policy capacity, and central government agencies have not focused significant attention on this area. Health, education, and economic development (particularly job-creation or protection efforts) have tended to capture political, policy, and budget attention in successive Nova Scotia governments. As a result, per capita provincial government research spending lags significantly behind that in most other Canadian provinces. Successive provincial governments have implemented various innovation-oriented programs via numerous agencies and departments in the absence of an overall policy framework or strategy (Traves 2014). Government policy towards what is arguably the province's strongest STI asset, its post-secondary education institutions, frequently has been indifferent or focused on rationalization efforts.

Market forces have influenced Nova Scotia innovation efforts, especially in the energy and ocean sectors. Federal investments, business attraction, efforts to preserve employment in particular companies or regions, and experiments with cluster-based approaches – in life sciences, information communication technologies, and the oceans technology sector – have also been part of the province's focus and motivation. Given a lack of STI focus within the government, as well as its limited fiscal capacity in this area, provincial policies and programs have often been shaped by external actors, including the federal government, post-secondary education institutions, voluntary advisory councils, government-appointed commissions, influential business leaders, and consultants (Table 7.1).

Provincial governments since the early 1990s have taken a largely incremental approach towards STI, adding new elements over time to the provincial innovation system and tinkering with organizational structures and program responsibilities. No provincial government has been able to develop and sustain focus on a formal or overarching (explicit) STI policy agenda. STI policy efforts in general have tended to be crowded out by more dominant policy issues (health, education, unemployment), crises (such as the impending closure of a major employer), struggles to control provincial debt, and frequent provincial elections and changes of government. Provincial STI efforts only recently have begun to address historical areas of weakness, including Canada's worst level of business-performed R&D, lacklustre levels of cooperation between PSE institutions and the private sector, weak financing support for start-up technology-based companies, a lack of attention to retaining skilled immigrants and university-educated students, and poor efforts by companies to invest in technology. Progress is starting to be made in these areas as a result of efforts in the aftermath of the ONE Nova Scotia Coalition process.

Provincial STI programs and investments tend to be spread across a range of ministries such as Energy and Mines, Health and Wellness, Fisheries and Aquaculture, and Agriculture, as well as agencies such as Nova Scotia Business Inc. (NSBI) and Innovacorp, resulting in a system

Table 7.1. Gross Expenditure on Research and Development by Performing Sector, average $ millions, Nova Scotia, 2013–17

		Performers					
		Government		Provincial			Private
				Research	Business	Higher	Non-
Funders	Total	Federal	Provincial	Organizations	Enterprise	Education	profit
Total sectors	522	48	–	–	112	363	–
Federal government	150	48	–	–	10	93	–
Provincial government	13	–	–	–	2	11	
Business enterprise	105	–	–	–	77	28	–
Higher education	211	–	–	–	–	211	–
Private non-profit	23	–	–	–	5	20	–
Foreign	19	–	–	–	19	2	–

Note: Columns and rows may not sum due to rounding.

Source: Statistics Canada, table 27-10-0273-01, "Gross domestic expenditures on research and development, by science type and by funder and performer sector (x 1,000,000)."

that is generally the sum of its parts without much overall coordination or central policy attention. The provincial government occasionally has set ambitious policy goals related to STI, but has failed to sustain the long-term investments necessary to achieve them. Modest provincial STI investments have also had to compete against established (and better-financed) traditional forms of economic development support, such as financial bailouts, business loans, and payroll rebates directed towards established, rather than emerging, sectors of the economy, although NSBI and Innovacorp are making concerted efforts to focus greater attention on emerging sectors. While the higher education sector in Nova Scotia performs more R&D as a share of gross domestic product (GDP) than in any other Canadian jurisdiction, provincial governments and the public frequently view the PSE sector as a drain on the provincial purse, rather than as a strategic contributor to social and economic development.

As a result, provincial innovative performance remains mixed, with some distinct strengths and several weaknesses. The McNeil Liberal government made some important structural changes, including the creation of Research Nova Scotia – announced in the 2016 Speech from the Throne and operational since 2019 – that could affect overall STI efforts significantly, but it is too early to assess the impact of this organization.

Context

Outside Halifax, the province's one major urban centre, Nova Scotia has a small, relatively decentralized population, and generates low levels of economic activity compared with provinces in central and western Canada. Traditionally dependent on natural resource industries, Nova Scotia governments frequently have resorted to reactive, rather than anticipatory, policy making in an effort to protect jobs and firms (Haddow 2000). The conventional view is that the provincial government has very limited fiscal capacity (or at least discretionary capacity) due to high debt and related interest payments, as well as the high percentage of the provincial budget committed to spending in areas such as health and education (Steele 2014). Traves (2014, 7) however, noted in a review of economic development programs that "[w]e do not lack resources. The Province spends more than $170 million annually… to promote growth and manages an investment and loan portfolio of almost $800 million. If government spending on economic development, workforce development and resource fields from all provincial ministries is included, the total exceeds $1.7 billion in 2012–13." Hence, mobilizing and focusing provincial fiscal efforts in support of an innovative economy and society remain key challenges, but also distinct possibilities if backed by sound policy analysis and political will.

Demographically, the province is experiencing a number of challenges. Population peaked at close to 950,000 persons in 2011, then started to decline – a trend that only recently has shown signs of reversal due to international immigration. Nova Scotia also has a rapidly aging population and workforce. From 2002 to 2012 the share of seniors age sixty-five and older grew by over 26 per cent, and in 2016 made up over 17 per cent of the population (ONE Nova Scotia Coalition 2016). Nova Scotia remains one of the most rural provinces in Canada, with approximately 40 per cent of the population living in rural areas, compared with the national average of approximately 19 per cent. Although Halifax has experienced population growth, it is one of Canada's slowest-growing urban centres.

Close to 85 per cent of the Nova Scotia economy is in services industries. Key sectors are financial, insurance and real estate services; ocean industries, including fisheries, seafood, and naval operations; health care and life sciences; agriculture and agri-food production; forestry, information communications technology; public administration and education; and tourism, including food services (Nova Scotia 2018a). Provincial research and innovation-related investments tend to prioritize many of these sectors, but have also focused on manufacturing, offshore oil and gas development, and tidal energy development. Oil and gas extraction and mining, while historically important, have experienced significant declines recently.

Business attraction has been a key element of economic policy for successive provincial governments, with mixed results. Michelin Canada, attracted during the 1980s, now has three manufacturing plants and 3,200 employees, and plays a key role in the provincial economy (Withers 2019). The government's business-attraction efforts have also experienced key failures, including stereo manufacturer Clairtone (1966–71) and a heavy-water plant in Glace Bay, Cape Breton, which started in the 1960s but was abandoned within a decade (Haddow 2000; Johnstone and Haddow 2003). Over the 2010–15 period, the province invested more than $60 million (through tax incentives, grants, loans and loan guarantees, import incentives and help with land leases) in Daewoo Shipbuilding & Marine Engineering Trenton Ltd., a joint venture to build wind turbine components and towers in the former Trenton rail car facility (Laroche 2018). Despite these efforts and investments, the company went bankrupt by 2016, leaving the provincial government to find buyers for the converted industrial facility and its equipment; in 2020, the two oldest of the five buildings on site were demolished, as they were beyond repair.

Provincial post-secondary institutions have been major anchors and quartermasters of innovation (MacNeil 2018). Universities have attracted significant funding through federal programs or federal-provincial joint initiatives, including the Ocean Tracking Network, the Marine Environmental Observation Prediction and Response Network of Centres of Excellence, based at Dalhousie University, and the National Collaborating Centre for the Determinants of Health, based at St. Francis Xavier University. The federal government has also allocated over $94 million through the Canada First Research Excellence Fund program to the $225 million Ocean Frontier Institute led by Dalhousie University in partnership with Memorial University of Newfoundland and the University of Prince Edward Island. Dalhousie, together with Memorial, was also instrumental in developing the Ocean

Supercluster, which was awarded $153 million in 2018 (to be matched by private sector investments) under the federal Supercluster Initiative.

Reports and multistakeholder consultation exercises focused on the province's economic and social challenges have led to a renewed recognition of the value of its geographically diverse PSE sector as an asset within the provincial innovation ecosystem. These efforts represent a fundamental shift away from the previous preoccupation with studies of PSE amalgamation and rationalization (O'Neill 2010; Turner 2011). The Ivany Report (Nova Scotia 2014) stated that the province "should view its high concentration of universities and colleges as a fundamental asset in growing our economy." The subsequent report by the ONE Nova Scotia Coalition (2016, 32) added:

> universities and colleges play a key constructive role in regional economic and social development, particularly in less-prosperous parts of the province ... making contributions to regional economic development that go well beyond the traditional emphasis on teaching and research. They are often anchors of local economies in their roles as major employers, purchasers of local goods and services, and contributors to cultural life and the built environment. They contribute to building human capital through specialized curricula, customized training, and lifelong learning. Faculty often engage in contract research and consulting that provide technical assistance and problem solving to local firms, acting as business advisors and network builders, supporting business incubation, as well as taking leadership roles in regional development.

The report for the RDC Working Group (Nicholson and Larsen 2016) took these arguments further and concluded that advanced education is a Nova Scotia "strength." The province's eleven PSE institutions have more than 55,000 students, almost 20 per cent from abroad and a third from other provinces, making this an important export business with growth potential. In fiscal year 2014/15, the PSE sector performed $411 million in R&D, including $175 million funded from external sources. The provincial government invested only $11.4 million (about 6.5 per cent) in university research, while the federal government spent $109 million, which Nicholson and Larsen (2016) concluded were de facto "export services." Leading provincial university researchers, such as Dalhousie physicist Dr Jeffrey Dahn, have had a significant effect on the provincial innovation ecosystem. Dr Dahn's research on advanced battery materials and testing has led to several successful spin-off companies created by his students in the province, as well as important collaborative research with industry.

Despite this relatively recent change in the provincial government's perspective of PSE institutions, more work is needed to strengthen the financial stability of Nova Scotia's universities, enhance collaboration across institutions in areas of provincial research strength, and connect these efforts with businesses and entrepreneurs. A strong convening and facilitation role by government has been largely absent, although there are indications that Research Nova Scotia is focusing on this need, complementing the efforts of such organizations as Springboard Atlantic.

The province is also focusing attention on boosting entrepreneurial efforts – Nova Scotia ranked last among the provinces in a Conference Board of Canada (2018) Provincial Innovation Report – with investments in incubators, sandbox initiatives, and a social enterprise strategy. The provincial government has also begun to reassess and substantially upgrade R&D funding infrastructure and investments. In 2016, it established the Research Nova Scotia Trust, a first step towards the creation of Research Nova Scotia, with initial investments totalling $45 million directed to sectoral and health research. While these are positive short-term signs, the longer-term financial commitment to STI is uncertain at this point. Annual provincial government spending on R&D would have to roughly triple from current levels to reach the average spending of other provinces.

Innovation Architecture

The Nova Scotia innovation ecosystem is characterized by a relatively diverse set of organizations considering the small size of the province. With only 2.6 per cent of the national population and 2 per cent of national GDP, Nova Scotia is home to close to 10 per cent of Canada's universities, over 55,000 post-secondary students (2.7 per cent of the national total), and over 43,500 university students (3.4 per cent of the national total). In 2017, Dalhousie University, with its main campus in Halifax and agricultural campus in Truro, ranked fifteenth among Canada's research-intensive universities with $150 million in sponsored research (Research Infosource 2018). Saint Mary's University, Mount Saint Vincent University, the University of King's College, and the Nova Scotia College of Art and Design are also located in Halifax, while Acadia University, Cape Breton University, St. Francis Xavier University, and the Université Sainte-Anne are located in rural and smaller urban communities across the province. Nova Scotia Community College (NSCC), with fourteen campuses across the province, has expanded its applied research efforts over the past decade in line with trends across

Canada due to the greater availability of dedicated funding available for college R&D from the federal government. In 2019, NSCC ranked twenty-second in Research Infosource's list of Top 50 Research Colleges in Canada.

The federal government exerts a strong STI influence in Nova Scotia. The Atlantic Canada Opportunities Agency (ACOA) plays a key role in supporting business development and innovation, exemplified by its 2006 investment of $10 million towards a $92 million R&D project at Michelin Tire's Waterville plant for the development of new transport truck tires (*CBC News* 2006). The National Research Council (NRC) facility in Halifax has played an important role in marine-related research and the creation of research-intensive companies such as Acadian Seaplants Ltd., while the Bedford Institute of Oceanography and Defence R&D Canada are key federal contributors to the province's ocean science sector. The NRC network of Industrial Technology Advisors based across Nova Scotia is also an important component of the innovation system. Agriculture and Agri-food Canada's Atlantic Food and Horticultural Research Centre in Kentville has helped develop and commercialize new fruit varieties, and is now involved in the growing wine industry.

Given a general lack of central agency oversight for STI, provincial policy leadership has usually come from the ministry (and minister) responsible for economic development. Haddow (2000) notes that this ministry has had a "tumultuous" history, with frequent reorganizations and name changes, as well as changes in responsibility for diverse agencies and funding programs targeted at a wide range of economic sectors and objectives. Provincial governments led by the New Democratic Party (2009–13) and Liberals (2013–21), each commissioned independent studies of provincial economic development programs to better understand the organization, impacts, and shortcomings of these efforts (Savoie 2010; Traves 2014). As a line department, the economic development ministry has had to contend with the sectoral and competing interests of other line departments such as Energy and Mines, Natural Resources, Agriculture, Health, and Fisheries and Aquaculture. Finally, the Department of Labour and Advanced Education (preceded by the Department of Education), with responsibility for Nova Scotia universities and community colleges, historically has neglected the research and innovation potential of PSE institutions in order to focus on institutional financial management issues, student issues (loans, tuition), and questions of university rationalization and/or amalgamation.

Although the provincial government operates few research facilities and conducts little intramural research, it has created several provincial

STI organizations, programs, and services. Innovacorp, a provincial Crown corporation, operates several incubation facilities for technology-oriented companies, and provides financial support for start-up companies through Early Stage Venture Capital and Clean Technology Funds, the Early Stage Commercialization Fund, and the I-3 Technology Start-up Competition. Provincial Crown corporation NSBI focuses on business attraction using loans, loan guarantees, equity financing, and payroll rebates. NSBI has also assumed responsibility for administering the Productivity and Innovation Voucher program, which allows private sector firms to "purchase" research and technical services from Nova Scotia universities and NSCC.

Several provincial research-funding organizations have been established over the past couple of decades. The Nova Scotia Health Research Foundation, an arm's length provincial agency, was created in 2000 to support and mentor provincial health research efforts while the Nova Scotia Research and Innovation Trust was created at about the same time to provide matching funds to Canada Foundation for Innovation projects in PSE institutions. The Offshore Energy Research Association of Nova Scotia (OERA) was created in 2012 from the merger of the Offshore Energy Environmental Research and the Offshore Energy Technical Research Associations – both of which had been created in 2006 as independent, not-for-profit corporations focused on environmental, renewable, and geoscience energy research. The provincial government was also instrumental in developing the Fundy Ocean Research Centre for Energy (FORCE), a test facility to support tidal power technology demonstration in the province. FORCE provides test infrastructure, as well as a series of "berths" that require industry investment. In a reversal of normal practice, FORCE and OERA have helped attract federal and industry research investments to the province.

Nova Scotia also contributes to important components of the Atlantic regional innovation architecture, including ACENET, the regional advanced research-computing arm of Compute Canada, and Springboard Atlantic, an Atlantic-wide network of Industry Liaison Offices at nineteen Atlantic Canadian post-secondary institutions (financially supported by ACOA). Springboard Atlantic facilitates research and innovation partnerships between Atlantic post-secondary researchers and the private sector, as well as overseeing commercialization of PSE-developed intellectual property.

A number of innovation-oriented organizations and incubation centres have recently emerged in Nova Scotia, complementing the efforts of organizations such as Innovacorp and the NRC to support entrepreneurs and the growth of start-up companies in emerging sectors. These include Volta, which has evolved into a full-service innovation hub in the centre of Halifax, providing learning resources, mentors, infrastructure, and entrepreneur-oriented events. The Creative Destruction Lab (CDL-Atlantic), based in the Rowe School of Management at Dalhousie University, is part of a network of similar centres in Canada, the United States, and the United Kingdom that provide access to successful technology and business mentors who help start-up companies with a range of challenges, including raising venture capital. Ignite is another new organization, with centres in Yarmouth and Stellarton, that helps new businesses in rural communities innovate by providing access to technology, resources, and mentorship support.

Nova Scotia has also been home to innovative ideas around community organization and development, which are frequently overlooked in conventional analyses of STI policy. These initiatives include the Antigonish Movement and development of the Coady International Institute at St. Francis Xavier University, as well as organizations such as Engage Nova Scotia, Common Good Solutions, and other community-based endeavours for social enterprise and revitalization, such as New Dawn Enterprises in Sydney. In April 2017, the Nova Scotia government released a formal strategy for advancing social innovation and enterprise in the province, and has invested in linking post-secondary efforts in this area through the Change Lab for Action Research Initiative.

Federal-provincial collaboration and cost sharing have contributed to the province's innovation architecture, particularly in PSE institutions, but also in the creation of the Centre for Ocean Ventures & Entrepreneurship (COVE). Located in a former Canadian Coast Guard facility on the Halifax Harbour, COVE features two large deepwater piers, office space, an incubator, and space for shops and labs. Companies have access to shared equipment and infrastructure and the resources of a management team to support ocean technology projects.

Provincial government partnerships with the private sector have been important to the Nova Scotia innovation system. For example, significant provincial support was provided in the 2011–13 period to Irving Shipbuilding to support its successful bid to anchor a Centre of Excellence under the National Shipbuilding Procurement Strategy. The company was then selected to build the Royal Canadian Navy's new combat fleet of twenty-one vessels worth $25 billion over the thirty-year program, an initiative that is generating local research spin-off opportunities through the federal shipbuilding value proposition initiative. In 2012, the province signed an agreement with IBM Canada that resulted in IBM's contributing multi-million-dollar cloud-computing capability and software access to several PSE institutions in Nova Scotia, effectively creating a shared computing platform to support new curricula and research in data analytics. In 2018, the province and the federal government again partnered with IBM Canada to create Deepsense at Dalhousie University, an initiative focused on data analytics related to ocean industries.

Several advisory bodies, not-for profit organizations, and industry associations have also contributed to the innovation effort in Nova Scotia. The Voluntary Planning Board, established in 1963 to assist and advise the minister of finance on economic growth, frequently focused attention on STI issues (Voluntary Planning 2004). In December 2010, however, the VPB office was closed and staff moved to the Provincial Office of Policy and Priorities. Meanwhile, NovaKnowledge, a not-for-profit organization founded in the late 1990s and involving representatives of government, industry, and the education sector, carried out a series of annual benchmarking assessments, or report cards, on the state of the province's knowledge economy. The aim was to help facilitate innovation-related policy discussions related to access to capital, skills development, and sector opportunities. The organization closed in 2008 after its executive director was elected to Halifax City Council. The loss of NovaKnowledge created a key gap in generation of STI-relevant policy analysis, and the provincial government was unable or unwilling to take on the role of convening innovation stakeholders or conducting ongoing analysis and insight with respect to provincial STI efforts. An ongoing contribution, in contrast, is that of the Discovery Centre, a not-for-profit entity that operates a youth-oriented science centre, promotes STI culture and education, and hosts an annual awards gala recognizing the achievements of Nova Scotia researchers, scientists, and innovators.

Several of Nova Scotia's larger companies, as well as technology-oriented industry associations, play key roles in the province's innovation architecture. These include: Irving Shipbuilding Inc.; DSM Nutritional Products Canada Inc. (formerly Ocean Nutrition Inc.); Acadian Seaplants Ltd.; Clearwater Seafoods Ltd.; Michelin Canada Inc.; Nautel Ltd.; Ultra-Electronics Marine Systems Inc.; LED Roadway Ltd.; IMP Group; Lockheed Martin Canada; and Stelia North America (formerly Composites Atlantic). A growing number of technology-based companies such as CarbonCure, ABK Biomedical, Metamaterial Technologies, Protocase, and Simplycast are influential innovation actors by virtue of their success. Industry associations such as BioNova, the Ocean Technology Council of Nova Scotia, the Aerospace and Defence Industry

Association of Nova Scotia (ADIANS), and Digital Nova Scotia are key business-oriented groups focused on STI and the knowledge economy.

The Policy Efforts

The Liberal government of 1993–97 led by Premier John Savage pursued a number of initiatives related to STI, although it did not develop a formal policy or strategy in this area. Innovacorp replaced the Nova Scotia Research Foundation, and was tasked with providing early-stage funding for start-up companies, as well as business advice and mentoring services. The Savage Liberals also created the Agri-Tech Park in Truro, oversaw the merger of the Technical University of Nova Scotia with Dalhousie University (completed in 1997), expanded the NSCC system, and established a Science and Technology Secretariat that focused on the use of information and communications technology (ICT) and data systems within government. Meanwhile, the province collaborated with the federal Community Access Program to launch new access points for internet access in an effort to ensure rural communities were not left behind on the information superhighway. ACORN-NS, one of twelve regional advanced networks providing access to the CANARIE Information Technology Network, was also created in this era.

Key themes of the Savage government were to reinvent the operations of the provincial government, reduce patronage, reform public service delivery, transform the provincial budgeting process, and institute expenditure management. A new Priorities and Planning Secretariat was created to assist with overall policy and planning. Economic development was a prominent policy issue in the 1993 election campaign, and the Savage Liberals had promised a comprehensive economic development strategy (Haddow 2000). Once in power, however, their focus turned to devolution of economic development efforts and reorganization of the Department of Economic Development, which involved the transfer of key economic responsibilities to other departments and agencies. The new central policy and planning apparatus within the bureaucracy placed little emphasis on science and innovation. The Savage Liberals also inherited the Nova Scotia Higher Education Council, established under the previous Progressive Conservative government, which focused considerable effort on studying potential mergers, rationalizations, and other cost-saving measures in post-secondary institutions (Turner 2011). In concluding this process, the Savage Liberal government worked to strengthen the research focus of Dalhousie University – including creating a new Faculty of Engineering by merging the former Technical University of Nova Scotia with Dalhousie – while retaining provincial distribution of other PSE institutions and programs.

Federal-provincial economic development agreements also underwent significant changes during the early 1990s. In 1994, the Canada/ Nova Scotia Cooperation Agreement on Economic Diversification was created, and amended two years later to focus on the development of technology, stimulating strategic economic sectors, and improving the business climate. The two levels of government released a joint strategy, *Economic Development in Nova Scotia,* which specified five areas of focus, including education and research, centred on expanding provincial university R&D capacity and research links between university and business. According to Haddow (2000), these changes provided a more strategic focus, but also coincided with major cuts in federal economic development programming. The Russell MacLellan Liberal government of 1997–99, much of it a minority, shifted focus to social issues. One distinct area of attention was the continuing expansion of access to ICT and the internet throughout the province in partnership with the federal Community Access Program.

John Hamm became premier with the election of a PC majority government in 1999 that shifted the provincial policy focus again towards economic growth and innovation. The new government promised to establish an Energy Council to pursue the development of the oil and gas industry and to ensure that all regions of Nova Scotia benefited from offshore resources. In 2000, the Hamm government released *Opportunities for Prosperity* (Nova Scotia 2000a, 2000b), the province's first economic growth strategy in over a decade, which included a deliberate "clustering" strategy. The strategy identified priority sectors for the province, including the digital economy, oil and gas, advanced manufacturing, education and knowledge services, and the life sciences. In 2000, the Hamm government created the Nova Scotia Health Research Foundation and Nova Scotia Research and Innovation Trust, both of which resulted in new provincial research investments in PSE institutions. The 2001 Speech from the Throne announced that the government would develop a new skills agenda by undertaking a comprehensive assessment of new and developing job demands in co-operation with business, labour, industry, and education stakeholders. The government also reorganized provincial agriculture extension services into Perennia Food and Agriculture Inc., a specialized technical development agency with a mission to help farmers, fishers, and food processors be more profitable. Also in 2001, the Hamm PC government created and invested $8.5 million in NSBI, a new arm's-length Crown corporation, to attract investment, help existing businesses expand, and spread economic activity across the province.

In June 2003, just before Premier Hamm called an election, the province launched *Green Plan: Towards a Sustainable Environment*, a cross-government policy strategy linking environmental, health, and economic objectives with energy efficiency and production of renewable energy; and released the policy document *Innovative Nova Scotia: An Innovation Policy for the Nova Scotia Economy* (Nova Scotia 2003). This provincial innovation policy, the only *explicit* STI strategy produced in the past thirty years, reflected up-to-date analysis on the process of innovation, which recognized that innovation occurs not through a linear process starting with research, but rather through systems of interactions and knowledge flows involving numerous organizations (Gibbons et al. 1994; Holbrooke and Wolfe 2002). The province's innovation policy of 2003 set a bold goal of "growing and expanding innovation in Nova Scotia so that it matches or exceeds the innovation performance of the leading regions in the nation" (Nova Scotia 2003). It identified five areas of focus: R&D; innovation infrastructure; human resource development; commercialization; and direct government action. The government simultaneously launched the Premier's Advisory Council on Innovation, chaired by Dr Kelvin Ogilvie, former president of Acadia University (later appointed to the Senate). In October 2005, in its only report, the Advisory Council recommended focusing on environmental technologies, increasing the provincial scientific R&D tax credit to 40 per cent (from 15 per cent), expanded broadband service, K–12 educational programming to support entrepreneurism, innovation, and literacy, and implementation of a more strategic and coordinated approach to advancing R&D activity (Premier's Advisory Council on Innovation 2005).

In August 2003, the Hamm PCs were re-elected as a minority government. Shortly thereafter, a group of key university, business, and government organizations formed the Life Sciences Research Association (LSRA) to promote the emerging life sciences sector. The LSRA responded to policy signals from governments, particularly the new provincial innovation policy and the NRC's focus on technology clusters, the latter of which led to expanded NRC laboratory and business incubation facilities at its facility in Halifax and the establishment of a new medical imaging centre at the Queen Elizabeth II Health Sciences Centre. The LSRA promoted the idea of a Life Sciences Research Institute (LSRI), a new research and commercialization centre that would be the focal point for the life sciences and biomedical district. Plans for the LSRI in turn inspired a group of prominent physician-researchers in Halifax to launch the Brain Repair Centre (BRC), a partnership of Dalhousie University, Capital Health, the IWK Health Centre, and the NRC, with support from the Nova Scotia government. The BRC became an anchor tenant within the LSRI, which helped boost the Institute's fundraising. In 2007, the federal government made a key contribution to LSRI, which finally opened on the Dalhousie campus in 2011. The LSRI remains an important piece of Nova Scotia's innovation system; although not exclusively focused on life sciences, it houses the BRC, incubation facilities for technology-based start-up companies, as well as offices for Innovacorp, the Dalhousie University Industry Liaison and Innovation Office, Springboard Atlantic, Genome Atlantic, and BioNova, the Nova Scotia Life Sciences Industry Association.

While the *Innovative Nova Scotia* strategy provided a more *explicit* provincial innovation policy framework that helped inspire the development of initiatives such as the LSRI, the momentum of this policy was short lived. In February 2006, John Hamm resigned as premier and Rodney MacDonald was appointed in his place. In May, the minority MacDonald PC government indicated that it would take new steps to make the environment a greater priority, with a focus on renewable electricity from wind and tidal sources. By that time, *Opportunities for Prosperity* and the 2003 *Green Plan* framework had been integrated into a new policy framework, *Opportunities for Sustainable Prosperity*. In 2007, the provincial legislature passed the Environmental Goals and Sustainable Prosperity Act, marking a move away from a focus on STI in support of economic growth towards embedding STI within a sustainable development policy. The Premier's Council on Innovation was dissolved and the policy agenda narrowed. In April 2009, just before the end of the MacDonald premiership, the province launched the Play Fairway Analysis, a $15 million research contract managed by OERA to stimulate renewed offshore petroleum exploration activity. The final report, completed in 2011, helped generate new private sector oil and gas exploration activity offshore. A final innovation-relevant initiative of the MacDonald PC government was the creation of the Productivity and Innovation Voucher pilot program, launched in the 2008 budget. This modest program – designed by the Department of Economic and Rural Development and Tourism to strengthen research linkages between PSE institutions and the private sector by simplifying businesses access to provincial PSE technical services – has proven resilient, although it has been shuffled from its original department to Innovacorp, and then again to NSBI.

In June 2009, the province elected its first New Democratic Party (NDP) majority government, led by Darrell Dexter. The new government set a policy goal of generating 25 per cent of Nova Scotia's electricity from renewable sources by 2015 (later raised to 40 per cent), and promised a comprehensive renewable energy strategy by 2010 to sharpen the focus on tidal, biomass, wind, solar, and geothermal opportunities. This included legislation to promote the development, transmission, and use of clean energy sources. The new government also promised to establish a graduate tax incentive, providing up to $15,000 to incentivize university and community college graduates to stay in Nova Scotia. In response to a 2010 report on the provincial PSE sector undertaken by Scotiabank economist Tim O'Neill, the province merged the Nova Scotia Agricultural College with Dalhousie University to create Dalhousie's Agricultural Campus in Truro. The 2010 provincial budget also contributed: $31.5 million over two years for PSE infrastructure supported by the federal Knowledge Infrastructure Program; $25 million to a new Manufacturing and Processing Investment Credit to boost innovation and productivity in the province's manufacturing and processing sectors; $60 million to entice Daewoo to Pictou County; and over $300 million in financial support for Irving Shipbuilding's successful bid under the federal shipbuilding procurement initiative. In addition, the province concluded efforts begun under the Hamm PC government to develop a skills strategy, called *jobsHere*, an "innovation-oriented" approach to help Nova Scotia compete in the global marketplace.

The 2011 provincial government budget unveiled significant additional expenditures to support innovation, including a new $25 million Productivity Investment Program; a $2 million Innovation and Competitiveness Fund for business; a $15 million financial commitment for Build Ventures (via Innovacorp), a new Atlantic regional venture capital fund; and $5 million for the Nova Scotia Research and Innovation Trust. Budget 2012 built on these investments, adding: a $15 million Capital Investment Incentive to fund technologically advanced machinery, clean technology, equipment, software, and hardware for companies; a $9 million Workplace Innovation and Productivity Skills Incentive to encourage companies to invest in skills development and certification; and a $1.8 million Strategic Co-operative Education Incentive to increase the number of work placement opportunities for PSE students. In 2013, the provincial government organized an Innovation Summit, and launched the Commission on Building Our New Economy, led by five eminent leaders outside government and chaired by Ray Ivany, the president of Acadia University. The government followed up with legislation for a Community Feed-In Tariff Program to provide economic incentives for communities and the private sector to invest in renewable energy.

Despite all these efforts, many targeted towards acknowledged weaknesses in the provincial innovation system and informed by the earlier PC government's short-lived innovation policy, the Dexter NDP government was undermined by a number of unpopular decisions (such as tuition increases for university and college students, and budget cuts to health care), scandals (MLAs' expenses), and opposition to the growing influence of unions in provincial governance. The 2013 provincial election thus saw another substantial change, with the election of a majority Liberal government led by Stephen McNeil.

In February 2014, the Commission on Building Our New Economy released its report, *Now or Never – An Urgent Call to Action for Nova Scotians* (Nova Scotia 2014), which provided a stark assessment of Nova Scotia's economic prospects. Dubbed the "Ivany Report," after the commission's chair, it outlined the cumulative impacts of poor business innovation and productivity, an aging population and youth outmigration, cultural barriers (such as an unwelcoming attitude towards immigrants), and heavy reliance on government. The report proposed nineteen specific goals to direct economic and social transformation to address these challenges. In response, the McNeil government formed the ONE Nova Scotia Coalition, involving fifteen leaders from business, labour, municipalities, First Nations, the voluntary sector, social enterprises, the health sector, and universities and colleges. The resulting action plan was entitled *We Choose Now – A Playbook for Nova Scotians* (ONE Nova Scotia Coalition 2016). The province also commissioned a substantive review of economic development assistance, led by former Dalhousie University president Dr Tom Traves, which resulted in the creation of Invest Nova Scotia, a new arm's-length initiative governed by an independent board of directors. The McNeil government also replaced the Department of Economic and Rural Development and Tourism with a new Department of Business.

In response to *We Choose Now*, the McNeil Liberals undertook a range of measures, including: expanded investments in innovation infrastructure, entrepreneurship, and venture capital; creation of a new Nova Scotia Graduate Scholarships program; adding more apprenticeships, internships, and co-op programs for PSE students; establishing a Graduate to Opportunity program to help new graduates land their first job with a Nova Scotia employer; and developing a Sandbox Initiative that funded several university- and college-based spaces where students and members of the public could assess the commercial potential of their ideas.

Also in response to the Ivany and ONE Nova Scotia Coalition reports, the province launched an "Innovation Table" of senior deputy ministers and PSE presidents who then organized several thematic working groups. The RDC Working Group commissioned Peter Nicholson and Jeff Larsen to undertake an up-to-date innovation policy study. The resulting report, published in 2016, provided a set of recommendations aimed directly at the provincial innovation ecosystem, including: amalgamating provincial research organizations; substantially increasing provincial research funding; increasing coordination among provincial research and innovation organizations; strengthening provincial procurement from start-up companies; placing a strong sectoral policy focus on oceans; and vesting central-agency-level government responsibility for innovation within the Department of Business (Nicholson and Larsen 2016). The 2016 Speech from the Throne announced that the government would create Research Nova Scotia, an organization to help Nova Scotia researchers unlock federal and commercial funding. Research Nova Scotia absorbed the functions of the Nova Scotia Research and Innovation Trust and the Nova Scotia Health Research Foundation, and promised a new Research Opportunities Fund to support research-based projects in areas of particular importance to the province. Research Nova Scotia Trust was established with a $25 million initial investment – a further $20 million was invested in 2017 – to help PSE institutions attract federal research funding requiring a matching provincial contribution. The Nova Scotia government also launched a $12 million strategy to help grow the province's wine industry, provided $19.7 million in funding for COVE, and established a new procurement process to encourage provincial departments to purchase innovative goods and services from small and medium-sized enterprises.

In a concerted effort to address other specific weaknesses identified in the Ivany Report and ONE Nova Scotia Coalition action plan, the provincial Liberal government upped its innovation investments. In December 2017, the premier announced: $2.25 million to expand the ICT incubator Volta Labs; funds for Ignite labs, a rural incubation facility based in Yarmouth, to branch out to other mid-sized communities across Nova Scotia; a Building Tomorrow Fund to help farmers and fishers create new products; and a Wine Development Program to encourage producers to double grape production by 2020. The 2017 budget saw an increase of $1.7 million for the Graduate to Opportunity program, incentivizing employers to hire recent Masters and PhD graduates from Nova Scotia universities. In Budget 2018, the province committed additional funding for student research internships through the Mitacs Accelerate program, added $2.5 million to the private sector Innovation Rebate program, and provided $3 million for the new

Building Tomorrow Fund. The McNeil government further strengthened venture capital in the province, initially with a $40 million contribution to Innovacorp's Nova Scotia First Fund in 2016, then with an additional $15 million in 2017 for late-stage start-ups and $15 million in 2018 for early-stage start-ups.

It remains too early to assess the cumulative impact of these innovation policy efforts and investments, although they do appear to address many of the historic challenges identified in recent analyses. They simultaneously emphasize gaining advantage from the considerable strengths in the PSE system – particularly with respect to retaining highly qualified graduates – encouraging entrepreneurship, and strengthening PSE-business research and innovation linkages.

Despite the absence of a distinct policy framework or *explicit* STI-oriented strategy, therefore, provincial governments of all stripes in recent years have undertaken greater efforts to increase immigration, retain youth – particularly those attending Nova Scotia–based universities – and make targeted investments to address some of the key recommendations in the Ivany, ONE Nova Scotia Coalition, and Nicholson and Larsen reports. A number of structural changes have also been made to complement key innovation organizations, while support for new such organizations has further strengthened the province's innovation and entrepreneurship ecosystem. Provincial support continues for oil and gas, renewable energy, life sciences, ICT, advanced manufacturing, and oceans technologies. In particular, there has been more attention on the oceans sector, reflecting, in part, Dalhousie University's success in attracting oceans-related research funding from the federal government.

The province has also taken tenuous steps to address provincial R&D spending levels, and has embraced a more positive outlook towards the social and economic contributions of its relatively strong and geographically diverse PSE system. Taking ONE Nova Scotia Coalition's advice to treat PSE institutions as community innovation hubs, the province has directed increased support for entrepreneurial sandboxes and incubators, strengthened work-integrated learning for PSE students, provided greater support for Nova Scotia graduate scholarships and internships, and expanded provincial vouchers for business-university research collaborations.

The McNeil government did not, however, create a strengthened policy or coordination capacity within the Department of Business or move to improve mechanisms for increased knowledge flows and connections between key innovation stakeholders in the province. The concluding chapter of the report of the RDC Working Group shines a light directly on the importance of this type of government leadership:

The innovation strategy proposed in this report can ultimately only be implemented by the businesses, the educational and research institutions, the risk investors, and the working people of Nova Scotia. But without the animating force of political leadership there is no reason to believe that the course we have been on will, by itself, change for the better. If it could have, it would have. So the indispensable role of government is to be an enabler of the innovation needed for Nova Scotia to change course. Through well-designed policies and programs, government can alter the incentives that arise from the market and from other social and institutional processes – away from incentives that are frustrating innovation and toward those that promote innovation. (Nicholson and Larsen 2016, 117)

Part of the story is performance. With a wide variety of factors contributing to innovative performance, it takes time to observe or measure policy efforts aimed at strengthening an innovation system's architecture and performance. R&D performance represents a provincial strength, with Nova Scotia ranking third among all provinces in terms of R&D spending as a share of provincial GDP. The aggregate data, however, mask some important nuances. Nova Scotia has the highest percentage of R&D performed by the higher-education sector in Canada (67 per cent), as well as the lowest percentage of R&D performed by the business sector (23 per cent), while the portion of R&D performed by the government sector has declined significantly – from 24 per cent in 2000 to only 7 per cent in 2016, primarily due to reductions and redistributions of federal intramural research capacity.

Nova Scotia leads all provinces in per capita production of scientific articles, contributing 4 per cent of the national total – illustrating relatively strong research capacity that potentially is available to the private sector. The province has, however, a relatively weak record of production or ownership of intellectual property, as measured by patents. As the Conference Board of Canada (2018) reports, from 2008 to 2013, Nova Scotia's patenting rate declined by 6 per cent, while in Canada as a whole the number of patents (per million population) grew by 15 per cent. Historically, the province has also been relatively weak in terms of levels of entrepreneurial ambition, as measured by the share of the population (ages eighteen to sixty-four) that reports being involved in early-stage entrepreneurial activity. Nova Scotia also underperforms most other provinces in the number and staying power of new firms entering the marketplace: between 2004 and 2014, new firm starts were lower than company exits in Nova Scotia, while most provinces outside the Maritimes had an average entry rate that exceeded the exit rate. These latter areas have been the target of provincial policy efforts, so it

will be of interest to see if trends in entrepreneurship and company sur-
vivability improve over time. On a more positive note, venture capital
investment in Nova Scotia has increased substantially in recent years,
with Nova Scotia moving up to fourth place among all provinces (Conference Board of Canada 2018).

Conclusions and Lessons

The STI contributions of successive provincial governments in Nova
Scotia since the early 1990s have been largely incremental: adding
discrete new elements to the innovation system, while tinkering with
policy and program responsibilities, particularly in the Department
of Economic Development (now Business). Ideas have had only limited saliency. Efforts to develop formal *explicit* STI policy frameworks
have been short lived; instead, STI policy has mostly remained implicitly embedded within broader provincial policy frameworks (such as
Sustainable Prosperity), with program responsibilities spread across
numerous line ministries and Crown agencies.

Although operating without a formal overarching STI policy framework, the McNeil government benefited from efforts of previous governments, as well as the recommendations and advice of five major
reports and two major multistakeholder public engagement exercises
conducted over a decade. In response, it made some important structural changes and investments designed to improve STI performance.
It is still too early to assess the impacts of these efforts, particularly with
respect to the private sector, but also in the degree to which universities and the college system are supporting a more innovative provincial
economy.

One positive outcome of recent reliance on market-based approaches
is that Nova Scotia has been able to leverage its natural strengths (some
might call them "clusters") related to ocean science and technology to
support the establishment and growth of firms in this sector. The province has also successfully attracted investment in the nascent area of
tidal energy – although with mixed results to date. Another strength is
the province's universities, which anchor the innovation system. Dalhousie University, especially, has demonstrated leadership and success
in leveraging federal support for the development of clusters related
to life sciences and oceans. More work remains to be done, however, to
maximize available research and innovation capabilities of PSE institutions, foster research collaboration with industry, and create entrepreneurial and work-integrated learning opportunities for provincial PSE
students.

The actors are now in a state of flux. The McNeil government aggressively reorganized itself, particularly in economic development responsibilities, engaged with non-governmental and private sector organizations, and tinkered with design and resourcing for innovation system components. The creation of Research Nova Scotia represented a significant opportunity to stabilize and focus the provincial effort to link PSE capabilities with firms and mobilize efforts to address provincial challenges. As a lead provincial research agency, Research Nova Scotia has the potential – together with Innovacorp, NSBI, OERA, the PSE sector, and businesses – to deliver a critical convening function to increase the synergies and collaborations needed for long-term success, as outlined in its 2020 Mission-Oriented Research Strategy (Research Nova Scotia 2020). An early success was a rapid-response research initiative to address the COVID-19 pandemic, involving the Nova Scotia Health Authority, Dalhousie University, QEII Health Sciences Centre Foundation, Dalhousie Medical Research Foundation, IWK Foundation, IWK Health Centre, and Dartmouth General Hospital Foundation. The partners collectively committed $1.5 million to support the Nova Scotia research community, funding forty projects to inform COVID-19 practices and support related health care decision making and planning in Nova Scotia.

While the PSE system in Nova Scotia remains a strength in terms of STI potential, effective policy making to maximize the innovation impact of the PSE sector cannot be left to universities themselves (Usher 2016) or to an ever-evolving set of external advisors. As Nicholson and Larsen (2016) noted, ongoing policy and political leadership within the provincial government is necessary for long-term STI policy success – the history of government changes, incremental efforts, and diffused STI responsibilities has not helped. In a positive direction, Research Nova Scotia is building a network of policy linkages across government agencies and departments, linked to PSE institutions and other key organizations such as the Nova Scotia Health Authority, OERA, Springboard Atlantic, and Genome Atlantic. This undoubtedly will help provide missing coordination and facilitation within the provincial STI system. Without a clear lead or stronger focus on STI in the provincial bureaucracy, however, it is unclear whether the day-to-day work needed to sustain provincial policy in support of social and economic progress will endure. Stephen McNeil announced his intention to step down as premier of Nova Scotia launching a leadership race within the Liberal party and a provincial election soon followed on 17 August 2021. Tim Houston's Progressive Conservatives won a majority but with the smallest popular vote share in Nova Scotia history. Difficult fiscal circumstances await the province in a post–COVID-19 Canada, so cautious optimism is in order with respect to future STI prospects in Nova Scotia.

References

CBC News. 2006. "ACOA give 10M loan to Michelin." 6 September. Online at https://www.cbc.ca/news/canada/nova-scotia/acoa-gives-10m-loan-to-michelin-1.627009.

Conference Board of Canada. 2018. *Innovation Report – Provincial and Territorial Ranking.* Ottawa. Online at https://www.conferenceboard.ca/hcp/provincial/innovation/sci-articles.aspx.

Council of Canadian Academies. 2017. *Science Policy: Considerations for Subnational Governments.* Ottawa, ON: A Workshop Steering Committee Report, Council of Canadian Academies.

Duruflé, G. 2014. *Fueling Entrepreneurship and Innovation: A Review of the Nova Scotia Government Role in Venture Capital Provision.* Department of Economic and Rural Development: Halifax.

Gibbons, M., C. Limoges, H. Nowotny, S. Schwartzman, P. Scott, and M. Trow, M. 1994. *The New Production of Knowledge: The Dynamics of Science and Research in Contemporary Societies.* London: SAGE.

Haddow, R. 2000. "Economic Development Policy: In Search of a Strategy." In *The Savage Years: The Perils of Reinventing Government in Nova Scotia,* ed. P. Clancy, J. Bickerton, R. Haddow, and I. Stewart, 80–115. Halifax: Formac.

Holbrooke, A., and D. Wolfe, eds. 2002. *Knowledge, Clusters and Regional Innovation Economic Development in Canada.* Montreal; Kingston, ON: McGill-Queen's University Press.

Johnstone, H., and R. Haddow. 2003. "Industrial Decline and High Technology Renewal in Cape Breton: Exploring the Limits of the Possible." In *Clusters Old and New: The Transition ot a Knowledge Economy in Canada's Regions,* ed. D. Wolfe. Montreal: McGill-Queen's Press: 187–213.

Laroche, J. 2018. "Crown corporation may inherit failed Pictou County wind turbine plant." *CBC News,* 4 April. Online at https://www.cbc.ca/news/canada/nova-scotia daewoo-dsme-trenton-nova-scotia-lands-wind-turbine-dstn-1.4604846.

MacNeil, R. 2018. "Public Organizations as Anchors and Quartermasters of Innovation: The Case of Ocean Science Instrumentalities in Nova Scotia, Canada." PhD diss., Saint Mary's University, Halifax.

Nicholson, P., and J. Larsen. 2016. *New and Better Ways – Field Guide for Nova Scotia's Innovation Ecosystem: An Innovative Growth Strategy for Nova Scotia.* Halifax: Policy Wonks. Online at https://policywonks.ca/reports-publications/.

Nova Scotia. 2000a. *Opportunities for Prosperity – A New Economic Growth Strategy for Nova Scotia*. Halifax: Communications Nova Scotia.

Nova Scotia. 2000b. *Towards Prosperity – Developing an Economic Growth Strategy for Nova Scotia*. Halifax: Communications Nova Scotia.

Nova Scotia. 2003. *Innovative Nova Scotia: An Innovation Policy for the Nova Scotia Economy*. Halifax: Department of Economic Development.

Nova Scotia. 2014. Commission on Building Our New Economy. *Now or Never: An Urgent Call to Action for Nova Scotia*. Halifax: Communications Nova Scotia.

Nova Scotia. 2018a. Finance and Treasury Board. "Daily Statistics: Provincial GDP by Industry." Online at https://novascotia.ca/finance/statistics /archive_news.asp?id=13805&dg=&df=&dto=0&dti=24, accessed 2 May 2018.

ONE Nova Scotia Coalition. 2016. *We Choose Now – A Playbook for Nova Scotians*. Halifax: Communications Nova Scotia.

O'Neill, T. 2010. *Report on the University System in Nova Scotia*. Halifax: Premier's Office.

Premier's Advisory Council on Innovation. 2005. *Interim Report of Council*. Halifax: Communications Nova Scotia.

Research Infosource Inc. 2018. *Canada's Top 50 Research Universities*. Toronto: Research Infosource Inc.

Research Nova Scotia. 2020. *A Mission-Oriented Approach to Research*. Halifax: Research Nova Scotia.

Savoie, D. 2010. *Invest More, Innovate More, Trade More, Learn More: The Way Ahead for Nova Scotia*. Halifax: Premier's Officer.

Steele, G. 2014. *What I Learned about Politics: Inside the Rise – and Collapse – of Nova Scotia's NDP Government*. Halifax: Nimbus.

Traves, T. 2014. *Review of Economic Development Assistance Tools: Assessment of Current Practices and Future Potential for Nova Scotia*. Halifax: Department of Economic and Rural Development and Tourism.

Turner, K.W. 2011. "Silos and Stovepipes: The Rationalization of Higher Education in the 1990s." Master's thesis, Saint Mary's University, Halifax.

Usher, A. 2016. "Innovation Policy: Are Universities Part of the Problem?" *Higher Education Strategy Associates, Daily Blog*, 15 September. Online at: www.higheredstrategy.com/blog.

Voluntary Planning. 2004. *Closing Our Prosperity Gap: Working Paper of the Voluntary Planning Sector Committee on Economic Growth and Competitiveness*. Halifax: Voluntary Planning.

Withers, P. 2019. "Why John Buchanan was an era-ending politician in Nova Scotia." *CBC News*, 4 October. Online at https://www.cbc.ca/news/canada /nova-scotia/paul-withers-john-buchanan-obituary-legacy-1.5293657.

8 New Brunswick: Beyond the Family Compact

DAVID FOORD, GREGORY S. KEALEY,
AND JOHN MCLAUGHLIN

The federal and provincial governments supported science, technology, and innovation (STI) policies in New Brunswick well before 1980, but it was not until the 1985 Speech from the Throne that the public policy vocabulary and funding models changed to emphasize growth and new products and processes embodying science and technology. Since then, New Brunswick Throne Speeches routinely have announced new research and development (R&D), technology, and innovation initiatives in support of economic development. Underlying the change in the mid-1980s was the execution of a Memorandum of Understanding on Science and Technology between the governments of Canada and New Brunswick, and the announcement of $300 million new federal funding for fiscal years 1984/85 to 1989/90. While the federal and provincial governments articulated visions of a new innovation society for New Brunswick, they have been typically vague on the details, leaving it open for local actors to define the methods to produce and apply new ideas to practice.

In examining the negotiation of differing ideas of innovation in New Brunswick public policy, we have sought to answer a number of questions. First, what STI policies were formed during the period of our study – from 1960 to the present? Second, how did the actors work together or at cross-purposes in creating policy? Third, how has science-and-technology-based innovation policy changed over the study period?

The authors gratefully acknowledge the contributions of Drs Herb Emery and R. Steve Turner, who reviewed and offered helpful criticism and suggestions for improvement of this chapter.

Context

The federal and provincial governments act under the influence of the vague idea that scientific activity can contribute directly to growth of industrial productivity (Friedman and Friedman 1990). The idea that innovation "is both explicitly mentioned but ambiguously defined" has been a continuing theme in studies of Canadian STI policy (Metcalfe and Fenwick 2009, 222). It is also the case in New Brunswick.

As in many places in Canada, the innovation systems approach is popular in New Brunswick. Holbrook and Salazar (2004), who adapted Cooke's (1998) regional innovation systems framework to examine Canada's effort, distinguished between governance structures, characterized as either locally organized networks of provincial and national actors, and the product of central government policies. The authors found that New Brunswick's innovation governance is largely centrally determined and oriented to basic or fundamental research. The other dimension in their analysis is business innovation, delivered by (i) small and medium-sized enterprises (SMEs) highly connected with local policy makers; (ii) a balance between large and small firms, and public and private research institutes; and (iii) global firms with mainly private R&D. The authors found that, in New Brunswick, business innovation comes from SMEs with little in-house capacity for innovation or R&D. Not surprisingly, Holbrook and Salazar found no evidence of a regional innovation system in New Brunswick or even in the Maritime provinces as a whole (Holbrook and Salazar 2004).

This is an incomplete story, however, as it overlooks the role of local actors in innovation policy and practice, including federal interventions that anchor a "collaborative governance of innovation policy involving various levels of jurisdiction and the multiple ideas and resources of nongovernmental stakeholders" (Conteh 2013, 144). Conteh finds, from the late 1960s to the formation of the Atlantic Canada Opportunities Agency (ACOA) in 1988, a "transition from a bureaucratic delivery of firm subsidies to collaborative and decentralized networks of innovation governance in New Brunswick." The provincial government engaged more in the late 1980s and early 1990s as ACOA's programs were used to support every conceivable provincial scheme, and later the Atlantic Innovation Fund was used to fund university R&D projects. Shanahan and Jones (2007) found a major shift started with the 1995 federal budget – specifically, the change from indirect support through transfer payments to research grants and contributions to advance the innovation agenda. We argue that the changes in

New Brunswick started earlier, during the 1980s, and extended to the late 1990s.

In examining the emergence of STI policy in New Brunswick from 1960 to the present, it is clear that "innovation" and related polices are artefacts of differing interpretations over time (Pinch and Bijker 1989). Within the higher education sector, innovation has been interpreted as a first attempt to carry into practice a new idea (Fagerberg 2005), with practice-oriented methods of research leading the way. The linear model of innovation (Balconi, Brusoni, and Orsenigo 2010), despite scholarly criticism, has continued to influence understandings of innovation, although newer, practice-oriented models have become popular, including translational research (Woolf 2008), triple-helix partnerships and the entrepreneurial university (Etzkowitz and Leydesdorff 2000), embedded research (McGinity and Salokangas 2014), and alternate modes of knowledge production (Nowotny, Scott, and Gibbons 2003). For advocates of business-led innovation – in particular, the information and communications technology (ICT) industries – innovation is seen to conform to Schumpeter's ([1934] 2008) classical definition of new goods, methods of production, markets, sources of supply, and organization of industry, with the focus on remedying the causes of slow growth of the economy (Pond 2016). For government and business leaders, innovation has often meant the use of new equipment or processes from third-party suppliers to generate value-added products (McGuire and Lepage 2007), with the goal of assisting small firms incapable of in-house R&D to access state-of-the-art equipment and technologies. The Atlantic Innovation Fund, in particular, identifies the value in nurturing and building clusters to accelerate innovation. Finally, some social advocates define the issue in terms of social innovation and inclusiveness (New Brunswick Business Council 2018; New Brunswick RPC 2013), focusing on projects excluded from science and engineering R&D funding programs.

The Innovation Architecture

The historical roots of the New Brunswick economy are in privately held family businesses in forestry, agriculture, fisheries, mining, resource processing, and small-scale manufacturing. These roots reflect the province's geography and political economy. Eighty per cent of the landmass is forested, and forestry has been the province's largest industry. Pulp and paper is the largest segment, generating more than $1.5 billion of export revenues in 2018, and the major rural employer. The industry is dominated by J.D. Irving Limited (JDI) in Saint John, a multi-billion-dollar, family-run business. Despite, and partly in response to, wide swings in the market, with the last big drop in the mid-2000s (Bogdanski 2014), forestry has become increasingly capital intensive. Technological innovation has largely substituted equipment and capital for labour (Parenteau 2013). Meanwhile, both private and public investors have sought to diversify the sector from its low-value, commodity-based orientation: JDI has moved up the value chain to manufacture tissue and converted tissue, and expanded from newsprint to calendar stock paper. The Atholville and Nackawic mills, owned by the Aditya Birla Group of Mumbai, also produce pulp to make rayon. But for the sector as a whole, government assistance has contributed to complacency and an industry "with an extraordinary sense of entitlement to the public forest and financial resources of the province" (Parenteau 2013, 107).

The other approximately 20 per cent of the provincial landmass is suitable for agriculture, of which about one-third is cultivated. Total revenues for the sector in 2018 were about $450 million (New Brunswick 2018a). Potato and potato products are the main goods, dominated by McCain Foods, which started in the province but is now headquartered in Toronto.

New Brunswick's largest industry in terms of export gross domestic product (GDP) is oil refining. About $18.5 billion of the province's manufacturing revenues and about half of all provincial export revenues come from refined oil products, sold mostly to the United States (New Brunswick 2018b). New Brunswick's export dependence on oil products is compounded by its reliance on a single-family business, Irving Oil, which runs Canada's largest refinery in Saint John and operates a system of gasoline stations in eastern Canada and the northeastern United States.

Seafood products and mining are the other large, resource-based industrial sectors in New Brunswick. In 2018, seafood exports earned $1.7 billion, accounting for about 14 per cent of the province's total exports, with the largest revenues from lobster, salmon, and crab. Mining of lead, peat, gypsum, iron, and some minor ores generated about $350 million in exports in 2018 (New Brunswick 2018b).

The outlier among the large, export-oriented industries is the ICT sector: it is neither old nor staples based. By 2019, provincial revenues had grown to $2.1 billion, with employment of over 30,000 in 700 companies, two to three times larger than eight years earlier (Export NB 2019). The sector consists of mostly small and medium-sized organizations, with the few large firms, such as IBM and SalesForce, resulting from acquisition of local start-up companies. The exceptional quality of the ITC industry in New Brunswick is reflected in Conference Board of Canada rankings of innovation (Conference Board of Canada 2018a). While New Brunswick, along with Prince Edward Island, rated a D– on the overall scale – lowest of all the provinces and lower than sixteen international peers, mostly European states, Australia, and Japan – it was among the top-three provinces, scoring C along with Ontario and Alberta, for ITC investment, putting it in the middle of the twenty-six comparators (Conference Board of Canada 2018b). Moreover, Fredericton and Moncton have two of Canada's eleven statistically significant ICT service clusters (Spencer 2014). While small in national terms, they posted the fastest employment growth of all of Canada's regional ICT clusters.

The Policy Efforts

The federal government has been a major investor in research in New Brunswick for more than a century. Through its marine, potato, and forestry research stations, it has played an active role in science, technology, and innovation. The Atlantic Biological Station at St. Andrews, now the St. Andrews Biological Station (SABS), has conducted research in support of commercial fisheries since 1908. A key milestone came in 1981, when its research demonstrated that overwintering penned salmon was possible and economically viable, which proved pivotal for the emergence of the farmed-salmon industry in the province (Hubbard 2016). In its dual role as industry watchdog, it has applied "the tools of scientific monitoring to collect information on the effects of pollution, over-exploitation, and inadequate or tardy regulation" (Turner 2016), including investigation of the effects of DDT and heavy metal pollution on fish populations. Even its mistakes have had profound influence in the regional economy: its research on the "maximum sustainable yield" of the ocean stocks contributed to overfishing and collapse of the fishery (Hubbard 2014 , 2016). Likewise, potato research at the Dominion Experimental Station, established in 1912 in Fredericton, led to new cultivars for local producers, such as the Shepody, registered in 1980, which has enjoyed vast commercial success (Turner and Molyneaux 2004). Overall, the fortunes of federal research operations in New Brunswick have been on the wane since the 1970s. St. Andrews staff were transferred into federal line departments, resulting in "a loss of autonomy for science and scientists to set research agendas, a new and dangerous reliance on commercial and private funding to support public science, and an imbalance of applied over fundamental research" (Turner 2016). Similarly, the Fredericton Forest Experimental Station, established in 1912 to research forest insect populations, began in the late 1970s to transition entomological research to the universities.

The National Research Council's (NRC's) Institute for Information Technology (IIT) started in 2002 after a battle between the federal and provincial government over whether it would operate at a single location or multiple sites. Ultimately, the province convinced NRC "to ensure that all New Brunswickers benefit," as the 2000 Throne Speech put it, by locating a major operation on the University of New Brunswick (UNB) Fredericton campus, with satellite centres at the UNB campus in Saint John, the Université de Moncton, and the New Brunswick Community College campus in Miramichi. Research at the Institute was aligned with provincial economic development initiatives in digital commerce, e-learning, health, and infrastructure. The budget was about $50 million for its first five-year term, with $37 million from the NRC and $12 million from the New Brunswick government and ACOA. A decade later, the budget and staffing were slashed as a result of restructuring within the NRC and IIT, with all NRC institutes recast into a technology platform and managed in a matrix model. The much-diminished capacity of the IIT was rearranged to work on cybersecurity with UNB's Canadian Institute for Cybersecurity, aligning it with the current provincial economic priorities.

ACOA has had the largest budget for STI policy in the province over the past forty years. Established in 1987 as a result of the restructuring of regional agencies in western Canada and northern Ontario, its mission is to help Atlantic business become more competitive, innovative, and productive, and to diversify local economies (ACOA 2019). It also has a policy development mission, which has been shaped by scholarship that has argued for decentralization of programs and engagement of local actors in regional development (Savoie 1992). Long-standing ACOA programs support everything from oyster festivals to tourism and cluster development workshops (Canada 2019).

The emphasis on R&D and innovation funding emerged in 2001 in the Atlantic Innovation Fund. From 2005 to 2013, $414 million was spent, with annual appropriations of $31–55 million for the Atlantic region (ACOA 2015). The AIF mandate arose from negotiations among local stakeholders, including federal and provincial governments and academic representatives. The resulting broadly framed policy mission was to increase connections between R&D, technology-based economic development, and commercialization (ACOA 2019). The overall goal was to grow strategic sectors or clusters and accelerate the transition from traditional industries to a knowledge-based economy. Sectors were broadly conceived, including everything from ICT to ocean technologies, aquaculture, biotechnology, health and medical technologies, and environmental technologies. Program objectives embraced everything from developing new products, whether radical or incremental innovation, within firms to leveraging funds from national research programs. One key challenge was that this differed markedly from the provincial approach, which made a sharp distinction between research and innovation in its flagship funding initiative.

Judged by provincial Throne Speeches since 1960, there was little concern with STI policy until 1985. Before then, the preoccupation of Richard Hatfield's Progressive Conservative (PC) government was with industrial development, productivity, and modernization, including development of fish-processing plants and pulp and paper mills. As in other Atlantic provinces, the 1985 Memorandum of Understanding on Science and Technology, individualized to New Brunswick, introduced a focus on STI policy. In 1987, Incutech, a technology-based incubator hosted by UNB and affiliated with the New Brunswick Research and Productivity Council (RPC) was announced. Thereafter, there was an announcement every year or two of some new provincial STI initiative. In 1987, the new Liberal government under Frank McKenna seized on ICT as a growth industry for the province. The mostly bilingual workforce, low wages, and the Atlantic time zone were touted as attractions for call centres and related industries to locate or develop in the province. ICT has remained a target ever since and, as discussed below, is a notable success for provincial policy. In 1987, the province formed the Minister's Advisory Board on Science and Technology to provide direction on the application of science and technology to economic and social development, including how to provide firms with the latest technological and business models. In 1991, a formal science and technology policy was introduced, with a twin focus on technology transfer and industrial technology adoption. Over the next twenty years, the government launched: a biotechnology innovation centre (1996, now called BioNB); a workforce training initiative for information technology firms (1997); a Premier's Roundtable on eNB and Innovation, made up of representatives of business, academia, and government (2001); an *Innovation Agenda* focused on clustered knowledge industries such as life sciences, advanced manufacturing, and value-added natural resources (2002); the New Brunswick Innovation Foundation (NBIF), to invest in university research and commercialization (2003); a tax credit for investing in R&D (2003); a life sciences and bio-economy strategy (2004); the New Brunswick Health Research Foundation (2008); and a centre of excellence in advanced learning technologies (2009).

To implement its strategies, the province created two innovation funding bodies. The NBIF, established by the Bernard Lord PC government (1999–2006) in 2002 with $20 million in provincial seed money (New

Brunswick 2003), was given the mission to create a culture of innovation by funding start-ups and researchers. Unlike the federal Atlantic Innovation Fund, it separated research and innovation funding into two discrete pots. By 2019, the Foundation had invested more than $100 million in more than 110 companies and awarded about $52 million for applied research (NBIF 2017, 2018, 2019). It recently expanded its definition of innovation to encompass social innovation, in 2019 launching a pilot program in partnership with the New Brunswick Social Policy Research Network to fund projects "to positively impact the province" by "creating lasting changes to systematic challenges that have left vulnerable people behind; better quality of life for all New Brunswickers; or solving a complex social problem in the province" (NBIF 2019). The other provincial research granting agency is the New Brunswick Health Research Foundation. Created by the Shawn Graham Liberal government in 2008, its mission is to "promote, coordinate and support all aspects of health research and innovation" (NBHRF 2019). It funds health-related research, with the goal of leveraging federal funding dollars. Its aim is both to support research that will produce health services to meet New Brunswick's most pressing needs and to grow the knowledge economy. Over its first ten years, it granted about $15 million for research and incurred nearly $7 million in operational expenses (Boyne 2019).

As with federal policy, innovation has been broadly defined in provincial policies. In the 2012 *Strategies for Innovation*, innovation was defined as the economic element that is "continually pushing back the boundaries of what is possible" (New Brunswick 2012, 3). While acknowledging Schumpeter's classical definition, the strategy asserted that innovation "at its core is about people: people who are willing to make changes, people who are willing to take chances, and people who are willing to build and support an ecosystem for individual and community prosperity." The industry focus included aerospace and defence, adding to the earlier list of ICT, biosciences, advanced manufacturing, and value-added natural resources. The strategy acknowledged that work was needed to raise R&D expenditures, venture capital investment, scores on standardized tests of high school students, citizen awareness, and, ultimately, low per capita GDP. A provincial program was introduced to provide direct funding to companies for innovation projects, as well as an innovation voucher fund covering costs for New Brunswick businesses to contract with local universities and research organizations to conduct research (New Brunswick 2012). The following year, the David Alward PC government (2010–14) formed the Research and Innovation Council to provide a wide array of advice, but it lasted only a year, as the new Brian Gallant Liberal government in 2014 shifted its focus to a different set of knowledge sectors, including financial services, insurance, health sciences, professional services, and contact centres.

The most recent update to provincial policy was the 2018 *Innovation Agenda*, introduced in the last months of the Gallant government. As with the 2012 strategy, the goal was to boost R&D and foster innovation: "invention converts money into ideas and innovation converts ideas into money" (New Brunswick 2018c, 2). The agenda took a broad view of innovation, including delivering local innovation experiences (for instance, at the science centres), supporting enhanced educational technology integration into First Nations communities, upgrading the information technology infrastructure in elementary schools, developing cybersecurity coding programs for delivery in provincial classrooms, running a province-wide annual celebration of innovation, promoting the province's history of innovation, and expanding support for social innovation. The Blaine Higgs PC government, installed as a minority in late 2018 and re-elected with a majority in 2020, has not materially changed the policy.

New Brunswick is one of the few provinces to operate its own provincial research organization continually. The New Brunswick Research and Productivity Council was established by a statute in 1962 with a mandate for "scientific and industrial research" (New Brunswick RPC 1963, 2). It has since emerged as the primary industrial contract research body in the province, with a particular focus on service to local SMEs (Schramm and Cook 2020). In its first year of operation, it ran two programs, one for research and another for productivity. The former provided grants to university faculty members, primarily for supporting student research, and the latter involved collaboration with the NRC to run work-study programs, an industrial research assistance service to industry (a forerunner of the contemporary NRC-Industrial Research Assistance Program), and short courses on management. From 1962 to 1980s, the RPC expanded to offer contract research for industrial and commercial firms in the province, with programs to support natural science research (such as mineral resource exploitation, forestry productivity, water pollution, and hydroelectric dam development) and industrial research (such as analytical chemistry, food technology, chemical engineering, and highway technologies). During the 1970s, contract R&D effort expanded, growing from 8 per cent to 38 per cent of the RPC's revenue by the end of the decade. The majority of contract funding came from industry, with the balance from federal and provincial governments. Innovation came to the RPC beginning in 1983 – before then, the term had never been used, but afterward it was in every statement over the decade. Innovation was originally framed by the RPC chairman as a catch-all term for the organization's technical services, contract R&D, and technology transfer in support of product design and manufacturing processes, but by the early 1990s "technological innovation" had been added to the mission, leading to new initiatives such as the incubator run with UNB. The RPC's annual contract revenue stayed steady at just under $7 million during the 1980s and 1990s, with declining revenue from large firms and increases from SMEs and the federal government. By 2010, the RPC's revenues had grown to about $9.5 million, with SMEs contributing 70 per cent, while its provincial operating grant nearly disappeared. Revenue continued to grow over the decade, reaching $13.3 million in 2018, driven most importantly by contract research for cannabis. Influenced by its long-standing mission of industrial research, in the face of dwindling government support in a period of innovation-oriented science and technology policy, the RPC emerged in the 2010s as a champion of market-pull or customer-driven innovation as the key to economic development in the province, seeking redress for what it saw as an overemphasis on university research.

Firms and non-governmental organizations have contributed to regional STI policy in innumerable ways. Local firms have shaped policy through advocacy and innovation projects proposed to government. They have worked to create incubators in Fredericton (Planet Hatch) and Moncton (Venn Garage), and supported the Fredericton Knowledge Park, Atlantic Canada's largest research and technology park. Venture capital firms East Valley Ventures in Saint John and Technology Venture Corporation in Moncton have invested in high-growth technology firms in the province. The Fredericton Joint Economic Development Initiative, created in 1995, has also worked to support Indigenous participation in the emerging economy. Advocacy for innovation policy varies by organization. Supporters such as the Fredericton Chamber of Commerce have called for innovation strategies to support the local cybersecurity industry (Fredericton Chamber of Commerce 2019), while the common growth platform of the New Brunswick Business Council and regional chambers of commerce (Atlantic, New Brunswick, and Fredericton, Moncton, and Saint John regions) have emphasized the role of private sector job creation and growth, with no mention of research, development, or innovation.

The provincial telephone company, NBTel, was a key player in the province. As with the timing of initial federal and provincial innovation investments, 1985 was a pivotal year for the utility, with Bruncor formed as its parent company. Recognizing that NBTel needed to prepare for the end of its monopoly, driven by the emergence of wireless service, Bruncor began to diversify from provincial telephone operations into export-oriented software development (Bruncor 1985). An early initiative involved a test-bed relationship with Nortel Networks to digitize the telecommunications network, which laid the foundation for the call centre industry in the province. Bruncor's software development began with internal businesses, such as computer-based white and yellow pages, and expanded into subsidiary ventures, such as e-learning company Genesys Labs and ImagicTV, the first to offer television over the internet in the 1990s. The most profound legacy of NBTel, however, was the training of a generation of managers who went on to finance or lead many of the new ICT-based software companies, innovation funding bodies, and incubators. With deregulation of the telephone industry in the late 1990s and acquisition of NBTel by Aliant in 1999 and then Bell Canada in 2014, a cohort of mid-to-late career technology managers was released into New Brunswick's fledgling ICT industry. Saint John–based Mariner Partners was one destination for many of these skilled managers. Mariner Partners is the most influential private actor in the innovation space in New Brunswick, with five business units, including Propel, an Atlantic regional accelerator supported by ACOA, and East Valley Ventures, a venture capital enterprise. In effect, deregulation of the telephone industry was a key driver for the growth of the ICT industry, freeing up entrepreneurial and management talent that might otherwise have been constrained in discovering new resources and opportunities.

The higher education sector consists of four publicly supported universities (Mount Allison University, St. Thomas University, Université de Moncton, and UNB), two community college systems (the English-instruction New Brunswick Community College and the French-language Collège communautaire du Nouveau-Brunswick), the New Brunswick College of Craft and Design, and the Maritime College of Forest Technology. In addition, there are three private-charter, religiously affiliated universities and two private universities, each with little or no science and technology research capacity.

UNB is the most research intensive of these institutions, although, by the standards of larger research institutions in other provinces, its expenditures are modest: currently about $40 million annually, down from a peak of about $60 million earlier in the 2010s. One of the unique features of UNB is its high percentage of contract revenue relative to other Canadian universities: in fiscal year 2013/14, contracts surpassed grant funding (UNB 2018). This phenomenon reflects declining Tri-Council grants, the prominence of ACOA and other federal funding, and the reliance of local industry on provincial research institutions to conduct their R&D. Start-up companies from UNB include a mix of faculty research–based ventures (for example, CARIS, Envenio, and Green Imaging Technologies), staff or student projects (such as Beauceron Security, Mathis Instruments, Potential Motors, Q1 Labs, and Stash Energy), and those that combined both (such as Inversa Systems and Smart Skin). The earlier ventures involved faculty or students exploiting their own intellectual property through their campus homes, where they had access to resources such as data, laboratories, and mentors. More recently, universities have created incubators and accelerators for both on- and off-campus ventures, including Université de Moncton's Centre Assomption de recherche et de développement en entrepreneuriat, UNB's Faculty of Management's International Business & Entrepreneurship Centre and Venture Analyst Program, and UNB's Technology Management and Entrepreneurship (TME) Program's Summer Institute and Energia Ventures. UNB's Pond-Deshpande Centre also created a social venture accelerator with the NB Social and Public Innovation Lab. UNB's Atlantic Institute for Policy Research and its JDI Roundtable on Manufacturing Competitiveness emphasize technological transformation and the role of modernization on the economy (Balcom and Wang 2019). As projects reach the commercialization stage, all of these ventures can draw on ACOA-funded Springboard Atlantic, the regional technology transfer network that serves UNB and other Atlantic Canadian universities and colleges.

This policy agenda has delivered mixed performance for New Brunswick. The ratio of gross expenditures on R&D (GERD) to GDP for all sectors is below the national average and most other benchmark provinces, but the ratio nearly doubled from 0.6 per cent in 1981 to 1.0 per cent in 2014, with peaks of 1.2 per cent in 1989 and 2009 (Statistics Canada 2020). The biggest increase occurred between 1985 and 1989. Changing federal funding has been an issue, as federal support for R&D relative to GDP fell in New Brunswick from 0.4 per cent in 1981 to 0.3 per cent in 2014 (Statistics Canada 2020). Meanwhile, business expenditure on R&D (BERD) performed erratically over the period. There was a spike in business R&D in 1989, when BERD in New Brunswick surpassed the national average (0.6 per cent versus 0.5 per cent) but apart from a secondary high of 0.5 per cent in 2009, New Brunswick business has invested well below the national average and below the average for most benchmark provinces throughout the past few decades (Table 8.1).

The data suggest that much of the increase in R&D expenditures in New Brunswick from 1980 to 2018 was due to internal funding for

Table 8.1. Gross Expenditure on Research and Development by Performing Sector, average $ millions, New Brunswick, 2013–17

Funders	Total	Government Federal	Provincial	Provincial Research Organizations	Business Enterprise	Higher Education	Private Non-profit
Total sectors	280	32	–	3	82	163	–
Federal government	70	32	–	–	10	28	–
Provincial government	9	–	–	–	3	6	–
Business enterprise	63	–	–	2	54	6	–
Higher education	113	–	–	–	–	113	–
Private non-profit	11	–	–	–	3	10	–
Foreign	15	–	–	–	14	–	–

Note: Columns and rows may not sum due to rounding.

Source: Statistics Canada, table 27-10-0273-01, "Gross domestic expenditures on research and development, by science type and by funder and performer sector (x 1,000,000)."

research in higher education institutions (HERD). Such funding in New Brunswick in 1981 was below $1 million – virtually 0 per cent of GDP – but has risen since to 0.35 per cent of GDP, just slightly below the average for the smaller provinces (Statistics Canada 2020). Behind this change were increases in the number of university faculty members hired with doctoral degrees and expectations that all faculty would develop research programs. Faculty members benefited from growing Tri-Council research programs over the thirty-year period as well as from greater investment of internal university resources for research. Tri-Council funding in New Brunswick rose from about $6 million in fiscal year 1999/2000 to a peak of about $20 million in 2011/12, before falling back to about $13.5 million in 2017/18. The gap has been filled with more contract research from industry and the province. Interestingly, this has not had much effect on scholarly publications: whereas New Brunswick researchers received 0.9 per cent of Tri-Council funding in

1999/2000, rising to 1.1 per cent by 2011/12, before declining to 0.6 per cent in 2017/2018, publications hovered between 1.4 per cent and 1.6 per cent of Canadian scholarly output over the same period. This was consistent with performance in other smaller provinces, many of which receive less grant money than the size of their economy as measured by GDP, but still produce publications proportionate to their share of Canada's population.

Data on New Brunswick patenting show a significant increase from 11 assignees and 15 inventors in 1990 to 52 assignees and 105 inventors in 2017. Publicly available reports on venture capital financing from the Canadian Venture Capital and Private Equity Association, limited to the 2014–18 period, show an increase from $9 million to $78 million over that time. As was the case for Canada as a whole, most venture capital investing in New Brunswick was in the ICT industry.

The best-known venture capital exits in recent history have all been ICT start-ups acquired by US buyers. Q1 Labs, founded in 2001 and based in Fredericton and Saint John, was bought by IBM in 2011 for a reported $650 million (Dobby 2012). Radian6, incorporated in 2006 in Fredericton, was purchased by Salesforce in 2011 for an estimated US$326 million (Taylor 2016). Spielo Gaming, established in 1990 in Moncton, was bought by GTECH in 2004 for US$150 million (Jones 2013). Beyond these, there have been many smaller technology exits, including a number of engineering consulting firms (for example, ADI, Jacques Whitford, and Neill and Gunter) and software developers (such as Blue Spurs, Brovada, CARIS, EhEye, Envenio, iMagicTV, Measureand, and Whitehill). Common to many of these firms is senior management, directors, or investors with NBTel backgrounds (Brovada, iMagicTV, Q1 Labs, Radian6, and Whitehill), NBIF investments (EhEye, Envenio, and Radian6) or affiliation with public universities in the province (ADI, CARIS, Q1 Labs, Spielo Gaming, and Envenio).

Conclusions and Lessons

Bradford and Wolfe (2013, 345) assert that, if "history has taught anything it is that the course of Canadian regional policy evolves over time through an unpredictable mix of economic pressures, new ideas and political calculations." In New Brunswick, the major political calculation by both the federal and provincial governments has been that universities, research institutions, and firms would know what to do with any funds provided. And they have, acting on economic opportunities and new research ideas based on their diverse disciplinary and corporate cultures. Changes in provincial policy have seldom been driven by new ideas of innovation (such as user innovation, open innovation, or ambidexterity); rather, they have been more tactical responses to federal funding opportunities. Ideological differences between the dominant Progressive Conservative and Liberal parties in New Brunswick rarely have made their way into innovation policy and practice. For instance, both the Lord PC and Graham Liberal governments in the 2000s looked to new R&D and innovation funding bodies to leverage federal dollars, while both the Alward PC and Gallant Liberal governments in the 2010s emphasized business-driven innovation and close alignment of university research funding with provincial economic growth.

The year 2012 marked a turning point in New Brunswick, when the public policy problem of science, technology, and innovation was reframed from a lack of R&D to a lack of firm-based innovation. In contrast to the 1985 policy trajectory triggered by the Canada-New Brunswick Memorandum of Understanding on Science and Technology, this one was formulated within the province, albeit drawing on ideas from the Organisation for Economic Co-operation and elsewhere. The new provincial policy no longer included "science and technology" or "R&D" in the title. Instead, it focused on supporting innovative firms and government practices through measures to make New Brunswick a better place to start and grow a business, by changing the mindset of New Brunswickers to be innovative thinkers and by building an innovation ecosystem. Post-secondary institutions were challenged to gear all research activities towards priority sectors to maximize commercialization opportunities, complemented with basic research in social and human sciences. Even the Research and Productivity Council was pleased with the changes at both the provincial and federal levels, noting the shift from strategies "mostly focused on funding and support for discovery, or curiosity-driven research ... to a more balanced approach ... that support[s] business expenditure on research and development" (New Brunswick RPC 2014, 2). The 2018 *Innovation Agenda* continued this policy. The emphasis remains on business-driven innovation, framed as the conversion of ideas into money, while encouraging R&D, referred to the conversion of money into ideas, echoing statements from the RPC (New Brunswick 2018c, 1–8). Its associated R&D strategy is to leverage investments in higher education from the federal government and industry for projects that fit with provincial growth areas – specifically, cybersecurity, cannabis, and smart grids.

New Brunswick both diverges from and converges towards models of successful regional innovation systems. In terms of its institutions, it diverges in its low GERD/GDP ratio and low percentage of corporate R&D expenditures. To be positive and consistent with successful models, capitalization practices and equity holdings of start-ups have changed from the old dominant model of family-owned businesses, and there is more widespread experience of competition in international markets. New Brunswick's commercial, government, non-profit, and academic actors are less siloed. This marks a change from the 1980s, when the province's most innovative utility, NBTel, had little or no involvement with UNB in science, technology, and innovation projects. Some institutional elements of the system have been intentional, such as the federal and provincial innovation funds and foundations, university commercialization and innovation programs, incubators, and accelerators. Others, such as the flow of skilled managers from NBTel to ICT start-ups, were unforeseen.

In terms of policy ideas, there is a longer period of continuity with federal policy in New Brunswick, back to the old experimental stations of the early twentieth century. The transition to the new model of outsourcing and collaborative R&D with higher education institutions, ascendant in the province from the 1980s until funding began to decline in the early 2010s, now seems like a policy *cul de sac*. The use of broad-based R&D funding programs from 1980s to 2010s, supporting research in a wide variety of fields, has narrowed to a few provincially designated growth areas, echoing the sectoral focus of the experimental stations. While university vice presidents still use "innovation" to refer to linear and research-based models, the federal and provincial governments increasingly adopt the more common sense of "innovation" derived from Schumpeter.

This transition in policy ideas reflects the interests of the innovation system actors. Local actors have sought to use STI policies for everything from scientific monitoring of pollution and overexploitation of resources to accelerating industrial modernization, pursuing basic university research, generating new products, and getting a "fair share" of federal funding programs. This most recent innovation rhetoric, built around heroic mentalities and individual entrepreneurship, with the ICT industry as the prime example in the province, has served well as a poor-province innovation policy. If all it takes is grit, market insight, a good idea, and a little private venture capital to innovate, then there is no real need for all those expensive government laboratories, costly R&D investments, complicated government-industry collaborations, and highly qualified personnel (MacNeil 2018; Pitts 2020) – a few computer science graduates will do. It is no accident that New Brunswick's R&D funding rates have declined over the years just as this new innovation policy has come along.

One challenge is that New Brunswick's capacity to participate in new federal R&D-intensive health and climate change programs is constrained to a few priority areas. The current policy approach also stands in contrast to new public policy ideas to address the climate emergency. For instance, in the sociotechnical transition frameworks emanating from Europe (Geels 2002; Sovacool et al. 2020) and mobilization models discussed in Canada and the United States (Bartels 2001; Delina 2016), the state and its institutions have central roles in decarbonization. In the sociotechnical transition literature, government contributes to the formation of new niches by choosing new technologies for experimentation, scaling up proven systems and products, and breaking down or forming policy and regulation to support the transition (Kemp, Schot, and Hoogma 1998). In mobilization models, government provides financing to engineer, procure, and construct new infrastructure (National Research Council 2011), as well as shape public behaviour (Cohen 2011). Either approach, if pursued in New Brunswick, would mark a major departure for science, technology, and innovation policy, similar to the "1985" moment when policy makers were challenged to adapt to the advice flowing from the new endogenous growth theory.

To end on a positive note, we conclude that New Brunswick is better prepared for new policy ideas than it was in 1985. Local universities and colleges participate with NB Power and provincial hospitals in collaborative innovation projects (albeit with relatively low rates of R&D investment), a marked change from the two solitudes of NBTel and UNB in the 1980s. Federal innovation policy makers are now embedded in New Brunswick, specifically within ACOA, one of the legacies of Donald Savoie's advocacy for more policy capacity in the Maritimes (Savoie 2006). There is also more communication and commonality of interests between provincial and federal government innovation policy makers and an increasing awareness in the province that innovation of regulatory and legal frameworks is an often-overlooked variable in successful STI policy. If "transition" or "mobilization" frameworks emerge as a federal policy focus like "innovation" did a generation ago, we can at least expect greater coordination of interests among institutions in the implementation of these new ideas in New Brunswick.

References

ACOA (Atlantic Canada Opportunities Agency). 2015. *Evaluation of ACOA's Innovation and Commercialization Sub-program Final Report*. Ottawa: ACOA, Evaluation Unit, Evaluation and Risk Directorate.

ACOA (Atlantic Canada Opportunities Agency). 2019. "Details of Transfer
    Payment Programs." Online at http://www.acoa-apeca.gc.ca/eng
    /publications/ParliamentaryReports/Pages/DPR_2011-12_TPP.aspx,
    accessed 25 November 2019.
Balcom, A., and L. Wang. 2019. "Adding Horsepower: Capital Stocks and
    Productivity Measure in New Brunswick's Manufacturing Sector, 2019."
    Online at https://www.unb.ca/roundtable/_assets/documents/unb-jdi-round
    -table-wp-investment-final.pdf, accessed November 25 2019.
Balconi, M., S. Brusoni, and L. Orsenigo. 2010. "In Defence of the Linear
    Model: An Essay." Research Policy 39 (1): 1–13. https://doi.org/10.1016/j
    .respol.2009.09.013.
Bartels, D. 2001. "Wartime Mobilization to Counter Severe Global Climate
    Change." Human Ecology 10: 229–32.
Bogdanski, B. 2014. "The Rise and Fall of the Canadian Pulp and Paper
    Sector." Forestry Chronicle 90 (6): 785–93. https://doi.org/10.5558/tfc2014-151
Boyne, J. 2019. "New Brunswick Health Research Foundation 10-Year Impact
    Assessment Report – Phase 1 – Short Term Impact." Online at https://
    www.nbhrf.com/files/page-files/2019-links//nbhrfimpactreport2019.pdf,
    accessed 5 November 2019.
Bradford, N., and D. Wolfe. 2013. "Governing Regional Economic
    Development: Innovation Challenges and Policy Learning in Canada."
    Cambridge Journal of Regions, Economy and Society 6 (2): 331–47. https://doi
    .org/10.1093/cjres/rst006
Bruncor. 1985. Annual Report 1985. Saint John, NB: Bruncor.
Canada. 2019. "Grants and Contributions." Ottawa. Online at https://search
    .open.canada.ca/en/gc/?search_api_fulltext=.https://www.ic.gc.ca/eic
    /site/062.nsf/eng/00088.html, accessed 25 November 2019.
Cohen, M.J. 2011. "Is the UK Preparing for "War"? Military Metaphors,
    Personal Carbon Allowances, and Consumption Rationing in Historical
    Perspective." Climatic Change 104 (2): 199–222. https://doi.org/10.1007
    /s10584-009-9785-x
Conference Board of Canada. 2018a. "ICT Investment." Ottawa. Online at
    https://www.conferenceboard.ca/hcp/provincial/innovation/ict.aspx,
    accessed 23 January 2020.
Conference Board of Canada. 2018b. "Provincial and Territorial Ranking:
    Innovation." Ottawa. Online at https://www.conferenceboard.ca/hcp
    /provincial/innovation.aspx, accessed 23 January 2020.
Conteh, C. 2013. "Navigating Canada's Federal Maze: Regional Development
    Policy Governance in New Brunswick." Regional & Federal Studies 23 (2):
    129–49. https://doi.org/10.1080/13597566.2012.742070.
Cooke, P. 1998. "Introduction: Origins of the Concept." In Regional Innovation
    Systems: The Role of Governances in a Globalized World, ed. P. Cooke, M.
    Heidenreich, and H.-J. Braczyk, 214–33. New York: Routledge.

Delina, L.L. 2016. *Strategies for Rapid Climate Mitigation: Wartime Mobilization as a Model for Action?* New York: Routledge.

Dobby, C. 2012. "CVCA investment award goes to New Brunswick-born company for second year in a row." *Financial Post*, 20 September.

Etzkowitz, H., and L. Leydesdorff. 2000. "The Dynamics of Innovation: From National Systems and "Mode 2" to a Triple Helix of University–Industry–Government Relations." *Research Policy* 29 (2): 109–23. https://doi.org/10.1016/S0048-7333(99)00055-4.

Export NB. 2019. "Why Key Export Sectors?" Online at https://exportnb.com/key-sectors/information-communications-technology/, accessed 9 November 2019.

Fagerberg, J. 2005. "Innovation." In *The Oxford Handbook of Innovation*, ed. J. Fagerberg, D.C. Mowery, and R.R. Nelson, 1–27. New York: Oxford University Press.

Fredericton Chamber of Commerce. 2019. "Commentary – 2019–2020 NB Throne Speech." Fredericton, NB. Online at https://www.frederictonchamber.ca/chamber-blog/2019/11/22/commentary-2019-2020-nb-throne-speech/, accessed 22 November 2019.

Friedman, R.S., and R.C. Friedman. 1990. "The Canadian Universities and the Promotion of Economic Development." *Minerva* 28 (3): 272–93. https://doi.org/10.1007/BF01096292.

Geels, F.W. 2002. "Technological Transitions as Evolutionary Reconfiguration Processes: A Multi-Level Perspective and a Case-Study." *Research Policy* 31(8–9): 1257–74. https://doi.org/10.1016/S0048-7333(02)00062-8.

Holbrook, A., and M. Salazar. 2004. "Regional Innovation Systems within a Federation: Do National Policies Affect All Regions Equally?" *Innovation* 6 (1): 50–64. https://doi.org/10.5172/impp.2004.6.1.50.

Hubbard, J. 2014. "In the Wake of Politics: The Political and Economic Construction of Fisheries Biology, 1860–1970." *Isis* 105 (2): 364–78. https://doi.org/10.1086/676572.

Hubbard, J. 2016. "The Gospel of Efficiency and the Origins of MSY: Scientific and Social Influences on Johan Hjort and AG Huntsman's Contributions to Fisheries Science." In *A Century of Maritime Science: The St. Andrews Biological Station*, ed. J. Hubbard, A.J. Wildish, and R.L. Stephenson, 78–117. Toronto: University of Toronto Press.

Jones, L. 2013. "GTech acquires Spielo – 2004." *World Casino News*, 22 January 2013.

Kemp, R., J. Schot, and R. Hoogma. 1998. "Regime Shifts to Sustainability through Processes of Niche Formation: The Approach of Strategic Niche Management." *Technology Analysis & Strategic Management* 10 (2): 175–98. https://doi.org/10.1080/09537329808524310.

MacNeil, R.T. 2018. "Public Organizations as Anchors and Quartermasters of Innovation: The Case of Ocean Science Instrumentalities in Nova Scotia, Canada." Diss., Saint Mary's University, Halifax.

McGinity, R., and M. Salokangas. 2014. "Introduction: 'Embedded Research as an Approach into Academia for Emerging Researchers." *Management in Education* 28 (1): 3–5. https://doi.org/10.1177%2F0892020613508863.

McGuire, F., and G. LePage. 2007. *The New Brunswick Reality Report Part 1: At the Crossroads*. Fredericton: Government of New Brunswick.

Metcalfe, A., and T. Fenwick. 2009. "Knowledge for Whose Society? Knowledge Production, Higher Education, and Federal Policy in Canada." *Higher Education* 57 (2): 209–25. https://doi.org/10.1007/s10734-008-9142-4.

National Research Council. 2011. *Informing an Effective Response to Climate Change*. Washington, DC: National Academies Press.

NBHRF (New Brunswick Health Research Fund). 2019. "About the New Brunswick Health Research Fund." Online at https://www.nbhrf.com/en/about-new-brunswick-health-research-foundation.

NBIF (New Brunswick Innovation Fund). 2017. *Annual Report 2016–2017*. Fredericton. Online at https://nbif.ca/about#annual-reports.

NBIF (New Brunswick Innovation Fund). 2018. *Annual Report 2018*. Fredericton. Online at https://nbif.ca/about#annual-reports.

NBIF (New Brunswick Innovation Fund). 2019. *Annual Report 2019*. Fredericton. Online at https://nbif.ca/about#annual-reports.

New Brunswick. 2003. "Innovation Foundation unveils new funding for province's innovators." News release. Fredericton. Online at https://www.gnb.ca/cnb/news/pre/2003e0258pr.htm, accessed 8 December 2019.

New Brunswick. 2012. *Strategies for Innovation: A Framework for Accelerating the Province of New Brunswick*. Fredericton. Online at https://www.gnb.ca/legis/business/pastsessions/57/57-2/LegDocs/2/en/StrategiesInnovation.pdf, accessed 10 November 2019.

New Brunswick. 2018a. "New Brunswick Agrifood and Seafood Export Highlights 2018." Fredericton. Online at https://www2.gnb.ca/content/dam/gnb/Departments/10/pdf/Publications/Aqu/ExportHighlightsforNewBrunswickAgrifoodandSeafood2018.pdf, accessed 9 November 2019.

New Brunswick. 2018b. "The New Brunswick Economy: 2018 in Review." Fredericton: Department of Finance and Treasury Board. Online at https://www2.gnb.ca/content/dam/gnb/Departments/fin/pdf/esi/NBEconomy2018InReview.pdf, accessed 9 November 2019.

New Brunswick. 2018c. "New Brunswick's Innovation Agenda." Fredericton. Online at https://www2.gnb.ca/content/dam/gnb/Departments/eco-bce/pdf/en/NBInnovationAgenda.pdf, accessed 10 November 2019.

New Brunswick Business Council. 2018. *We Choose Growth*. Fredericton. Online at https://nbbc-cenb.ca/en/blog/44-we-choose-growth, accessed 7 November 2019.

New Brunswick RPC (Research and Productivity Council). 1963. *Annual Report.*
    Fredericton.
New Brunswick RPC (Research and Productivity Council). 2013. *Annual Report.*
    Fredericton.
New Brunswick RPC (Research and Productivity Council). 2014. *Annual Report.*
    Fredericton.
Nowotny, H., P. Scott, and M. Gibbons. 2003. "Introduction: 'Mode 2'
    Revisited: The New Production of Knowledge." *Minerva* 41 (3): 179–94.
    https://doi.org/10.1023/A:1025505528250.
Parenteau, B. 2013. "Looking Backward, Looking Ahead: History and Future
    of the New Brunswick Forest Industries." *Acadiensis* 42 (2): 92–113.
    https://www.jstor.org/stable/24329554.
Pinch, T., and W. Bijker. 1989. "The Social Construction of Facts and
    Artefacts: Or How the Sociology of Science and the Sociology of
    Technology Might Benefit Each Other." In *The Social Construction of
    Technological Systems: New Directions in the Sociology and History of
    Technology*, ed. W.E. Bijker, T.P. Hughes, and T.J. Pinch., 17–50. Cambridge,
    MA: MIT Press.
Pitts, G. 2020. *Unicorn in the Woods: How East Coast Geeks and Dreamers Are
    Changing the Game.* Fredericton: Goose Lane Editions.
Pond, G. 2016. "Pond's Two-Pronged Growth Strategy." *Entrevestor*,
    21 December. Online at https://entrevestor.com/home/entry
    /pondstwo-pronged-growth-strategy.
Savoie, D.J. 1992. *Regional Economic Development: Canada's Search for Solutions.*
    Toronto: University of Toronto Press.
Savoie, D.J. 2006. *Visiting Grandchildren: Economic Development in the Maritimes.*
    Toronto: University of Toronto Press.
Schramm, L.L., and E. Cook. 2020. *Research and Development in New Brunswick:
    A History of the Research and Productivity Council.* Fredericton: New
    Brunswick Research and Productivity Council.
Schumpeter, J. [1934] 2008. *The Theory of Economic Development: An Inquiry
    into Profits, Capital, Credit, Interest and the Business Cycle, trans. R. Opie*, New
    Brunswick, NJ: Transaction Publishers.
Shanahan, T., and G. Jones. 2007. "Shifting Roles and Approaches:
    Government Coordination of Post-Secondary Education in Canada, 1995–
    2006." *Higher Education Research & Development* 26 (1): 31–43. https://doi
    .org/10.1080/07294360601166794.
Sovacool, B.K., D.J. Hess, S. Amir, F.W. Geels, R. Hirsh, L.R. Medina, C. Miller,
    et al. 2020. "Sociotechnical Agendas: Reviewing Future Directions for
    Energy and Climate Research." *Energy Research & Social Science* 70: 101617.
    https://doi.org/10.1016/j.erss.2020.101617.

Spencer, G. 2014. *Cluster Atlas of Canada*. Toronto: University of Toronto, Munk School of Global Affairs.

Taylor, M. 2016. "Remembering the Radian6 Exit." *Entrevestor*, 6 April 2016. Online at http://entrevestor.com/ac/blog/remembering-the-radian6-exit.

Turner, R.S. 2016. "Review of A Century of Maritime Science: The St. Andrews Biological Station, by Jennifer Hubbard, Avid J. Wildish and Robert L. Stephenson." *Journal of New Brunswick Studies* 7.

Turner, R.S., and H. Molyneaux. 2004. "Agricultural Science, Potato Breeding and the Fredericton Experimental Station, 1912–66." *Acadiensis* 33 (2): 44–67.

UNB (University of New Brunswick). 2018. "Research Matters: 2017–18 Year-in-Review." Online at https://www.unb.ca/research/_assets/documents/vpr/newsletters/researchmatters-f17-18.pdf, accessed 8 December 2019.

Woolf, S. 2008. "The Meaning of Translational Research and Why It Matters." *JAMA* 299 (2): 211–13. http://doi.org/10.1001/jama.2007.26.

9 Quebec: The National Research and Innovation System

YVES GINGRAS

The basic structure of the contemporary Quebec research system has been developed over the past fifty years in response to the generally accepted (though often implicit) conviction that the Quebec society is distinct in the Canadian federation and must possess all the institutions needed for the autonomous development of a francophone society. In response, contrary to the other provinces, where English is the common language – except for New Brunswick, which is officially bilingual, even though francophones are a minority – Quebec has created many organizational structures, some of which seem to duplicate federal ones in the domain of scientific research and innovation. In order to justify their existence, Quebec granting agencies are usually presented as "complementary" to their federal homologues. This strategic choice aims at creating a leveraging effect. One can see a result of that in the fact that about 23 per cent of Canadian faculty are in Quebec, yet Quebec receives about 27 per cent of grants from the three federal granting councils.

Context

For historical and cultural reasons, successive Quebec governments have, since the beginning of the 1960s, taken for granted that the province must develop its own "national" policy in matters of research and development (R&D) and innovation, as well as in university research.* Nevertheless, federal budgets and policies still represent about 70 per

The author thanks Benoit Sévigny, Directeur du service des communications et de la mobilisation, Fonds de recherche du Québec, for providing data for Figure 9.1 and Table 9.2 and detailed information about the recent R&D policies of the Quebec government.

* The reference to the "national" and not merely "regional" character of Quebec's science, technology, and innovation policies reflect the idea that Quebec forms a distinct nation with its unique character and is more than a "region" in Canada.

Table 9.1. Gross Expenditure on Research and Development by Performing Sector, average $ millions, Quebec, 2013–17

		Performers					
		Government		Provincial			Private
				Research	Business	Higher	Non-
Funders	Total	Federal	Provincial	Organizations	Enterprise	Education	profit
Total sectors	7,804	226	64	10	4,508	2,997	–
Federal government	1,117	224	–	–	178	716	–
Provincial government	536	1	64	5	130	336	–
Business enterprise	3,809	2	–	4	3,576	228	–
Higher education	1,419	–	–	–	–	1,419	–
Private non-profit	302	–	–	–	42	271	–
Foreign	621	–	–	–	593	29	–

Note: Columns and rows may not sum due to rounding.

Source: Statistics Canada, table 27-10-0273-01, "Gross domestic expenditures on research and development, by science type and by funder and performer sector (x 1,000,000)."

cent of total R&D investment in Quebec in higher education – excluding industry contributions and the imputed value of the time university professors are supposed to be dedicating to research (Statistics Canada 2020). Contrary to education, which, according to the Constitution, is explicitly a provincial jurisdiction, scientific research as such was not included in the original 1867 text, and is thus considered a domain of joint jurisdiction, where both the federal government and the provinces can play a role. Given its traditional defence of autonomy, there are sometimes conflicts with federal programs when Quebec considers they impinge on its own prerogatives – as was the case, for example, with the programs of the Canada Foundation for Innovation, which demands that 40 per cent of the budget comes from the province – but both jurisdictions usually find a way to collaborate or complement each other in matters of R&D as well as university research (Table 9.1).

This concept was recognized by the Canadian Parliament under the government of Stephen Harper, which adopted a motion in 2006 affirming that "the Québécois form a nation within a united Canada."

In the following sections, I briefly recall the origins of the major organizations that make up the contemporary Quebec research and innovation system (Albert and Laberge 2007), and then present the basic data
on the economic structure of the province and the most recent policy
efforts aimed at sustaining a strong culture of innovation in the sectors
identified by the government as priorities.

Innovation Architecture

The basic structure of the contemporary Quebec research and innovation system emerged first in the health sciences with the creation
in 1964 of the Conseil de recherches médicales. That was followed
in 1969 with technological assistance for small and medium-sized
enterprises (SMEs) through the Centre de recherche industrielle du
Québec. At the beginning of the 1970s, government grants for university research in the natural and social sciences and humanities
began through the FCAC (Formation des chercheurs et action con-
certée) program. To complement the federal granting councils that
focused on individual grants to researchers, this program focused
on team research, although it also provided fellowships to graduate
students.

Over the years, there have been a number of administrative changes.
The FCAC program became the Fonds pour l'aide et le soutien à la
recherche in 1981 and the Fonds pour la formation de chercheurs et
l'aide à la recherche (FCAR) in 1984. The Conseil de recherches médicales became the Conseil de la recherche en santé du Québec in 1974 and
the Fonds de recherche en santé du Québec (FRSQ) in 1981. In 1979, the
Conseil québécois de la recherche sociale (CQRS) was created to cover
research in applied social sciences. These three organizations (FRSQ,
FCAR, and CQRS) evolved in the following decades, with a major
reorganization in 2001 into three distinct research councils, mirroring
the federal ones: the Fonds de recherche du Québec – Santé (FRQS),
dedicated to medical research; the Fonds de recherche du Québec sur la
nature et les technologies (FRQNT), directed to the natural sciences and
engineering; and the Fonds de recherche du Québec sur la société et la
culture (FRQSC), supporting the social sciences and humanities. Each
supports the research of young (recently appointed) scholars to help
them start their careers and become part of a team, as well as teams of
researchers and graduate students (Master's, PhD, and post-doctoral
fellow).

Table 9.2 shows the evolution of investments in the three Quebec
research funds. We observe a major boost of 17 per cent in the budgets since 2016. Health research now accounts for 42 per cent of the

Table 9.2. Budgets of the Three Fonds de recherche du Québec, fiscal years 2011/12–2019/20.

	Fiscal Year								
	2011/ 12	2012/ 13	2013/ 14	2014/ 15	2015/ 16	2016/ 17	2017/ 18	2018/ 19	2019/ 20
Funder	($ millions)								
FRQNT	50.2	52.2	42.2	49.3	49.3	49.4	56.0	62.7	62.7
FRQS	78.3	75.6	75.4	76.8	77.6	77.6	84.6	91.0	91.0
FRQSC	49.1	47.9	43.9	47.6	47.4	47.5	53.9	60.8	60.8
Total	177.6	175.7	161.6	173.6	174.4	174.5	194.5	214.5	214.5

Source: Author's calculations.

total outlays of $215 million, while the other two sectors share the remaining budget relatively evenly. About 80 per cent of these funds support mostly non-targeted programs and basic research in all fields, with about 20 per cent for targeted projects. They also facilitate partnerships at all levels in Quebec, in Canada (with the federal councils), and internationally with equivalent organizations. The three funds at times create new programs to explore emerging avenues for research – such as Audace, which focuses on more risky projects, and Engagement and Dialogue, which promotes interactions between researchers and citizens.

An important step towards a better integration of strategic thinking in matters of science, technology, and innovation was the creation in 2011 of the position of Scientifique en chef du Québec, who acts as president of the three funds regrouped as Fonds de recherche du Québec (FRQ). Each of the three entities continues to have its own scientific director and board. In addition to directing the three funds, the chief scientist also advises the minister of the economy and innovation on the development of research and innovation and how to stimulate intersectoral research linked to major societal challenges – such as demographic changes and aging of the population, sustainable development and climate change, and artificial intelligence and the digital economy. More generally, the chief scientist promotes international research partnerships, and careers in research, entrepreneurship, and creativity.

Apart from these governmental structures, Quebec scientists have created their own representative organizations. The oldest is Acfas, created in 1923 as the Association canadienne-française pour l'avancement des sciences, on the model of the American and British Associations for the Advancement of Science. Since 2019, its name is simply Acfas, with the motto *"Faire avancer les savoirs."* Acfas includes all disciplines, and each year since 1933 has organized an annual meeting in different cities. Its elected board and president offer a strong voice for science in Quebec, and promote research and training of graduate students as well as public understanding of science through its magazine *Découvrir*. It also stimulates the scientific community by offering annual prizes to recognize researchers as well as students in different disciplines at the annual Gala de l'Acfas. All eighteen Quebec universities – including HEC Montréal, École nationale d'administration publique, and École de technologie supérieure – play an active role in Acfas through organizing its activities on different campuses across the province.

With the development of university and industrial research, a community of managers also emerged that created their own organizations. In 1978, the Association des directeurs de recherche industrielle du Québec was formed to promote industrial research and make better known to governments the needs of industry in matters of R&D. In 2011, it added innovation to its name to make it more visible, becoming the Association pour le développement de la recherche et de l'innovation du Québec. For their part, university administrators of research also regrouped and in 1983 formed the Association des administratrices et administrateurs de recherche universitaire du Québec to promote university research as well as science policies. These organizations make their views known to the government and universities through informal relations and through more official documents during periods of consultations on budgets and policy revisions. Figure 9.1 provides a global view of the diversity of organizations active in funding, production, and transfer of knowledge and innovation in the province.

The turn towards innovation policies in the 1980s was triggered by Quebec's economic structure and the relatively low level of industrial research. The Quebec government actively promoted college-industry and university-industry relations to facilitate technology transfer. With eighteen universities and forty-nine colleges in Quebec, each institution tends to collaborate with local industries. Two kinds of organizations have been created to that effect. The program of the Centres collégiaux de transfert technologiques (CCTTs), created at the beginning of the 1980s, applies to CEGEPs. There are now fifty-nine government-supported CCTTs across the province, focused on a diversity of industrial sectors, including agri-food, advanced manufacturing, advanced materials, resources of the future, health and biotechnologies, clean technologies, and social innovation (Quebec 2018). For universities, the Sociétés de valorisation de la recherche universitaire, founded in 2001, aim at facilitating technology transfer and the creation of new

Figure 9.1. Diversity of Organizations in the Quebec Research and Innovation System.

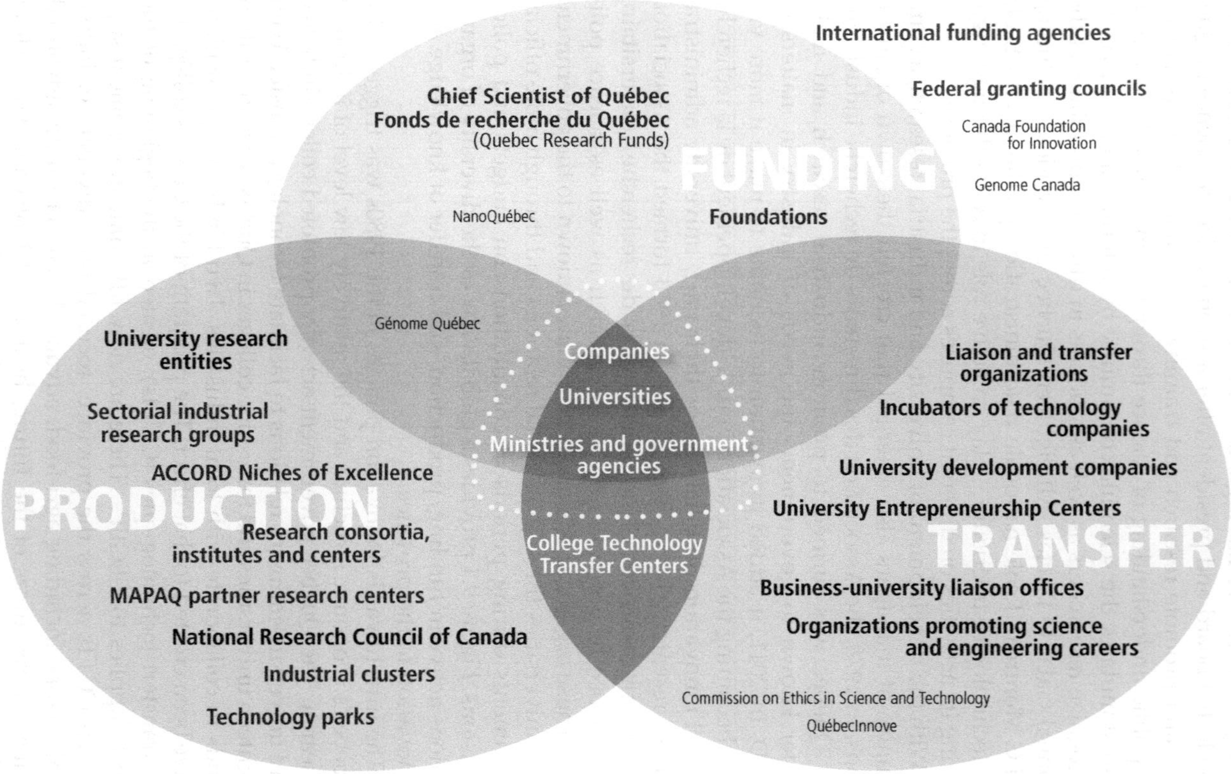

International funding agencies

Federal granting councils
Canada Foundation for Innovation
Genome Canada

FUNDING

Foundations

Chief Scientist of Québec
Fonds de recherche du Québec
(Quebec Research Funds)

NanoQuébec

Companies
Universities
Ministries and government agencies
College Technology Transfer Centers

Génome Québec

TRANSFER

Liaison and transfer organizations
Incubators of technology companies
University development companies
University Entrepreneurship Centers
Business-university liaison offices
Organizations promoting science and engineering careers
Commission on Ethics in Science and Technology
QuébecInnove

PRODUCTION

University research entities
Sectorial industrial research groups
ACCORD Niches of Excellence
Research consortia, institutes and centers
MAPAQ partner research centers
National Research Council of Canada
Industrial clusters
Technology parks

Source: Fonds de recherche du Québec.

enterprises. Five such valorization societies were created at first, but they are now consolidated under three organizations – Aligo Innovation, SOVAR, and Univalor – that manage for their partner universities the innovations they think are marketable and contribute to strengthen their relations with industries.

The Policy Efforts

All the organizations in Figure 9.1 have played an active role in defining both a national structure and sectoral strategies for advancing science and innovation in Quebec.

National Policies

The definition of the current Quebec science and innovation policy system emerged from the first interministerial committee on science policy in 1971, which defined the *Principes pour une politique scientifique du Québec*. This document was followed in 1979 by the green paper, *Pour une politique québécoise de la recherche scientifique,* which led the following year to the creation of a Ministry of State for Scientific Development. The 1980s saw a turn towards research in the service of the economy with the publication of the policy document *Bâtir le Québec: le virage technologique* (1982). This policy led to the creation of a series of new organizations, such as the Centre de recherche informatique de Montréal, the Centre facilitant la recherche et l'innovation dans les organisations, which specialized in the use and adoption of digital technology, and the Centre québécois de valorisation des biotechnologies for the development of plant biotechnology. Under a new government but in continuity with previous actions, the 1988 policy document, *La maîtrise de notre avenir technologique,* led to the creation of generous R&D tax credits as well as a program contributing up to 50 per cent of salaries to facilitate hiring of researchers by industry. A year later, a new investment fund for technological development was created with a five-year budget of $350 million to finance industrial and technological research partnerships.

More recently, the 2013 Quebec national policy on research and innovation was based on a large consultation of all the stakeholders of the Quebec research and innovation system, under the aegis of Acfas and the Association pour le développement de la recherche et de l'innovation du Québec. As these organizations are representative of most stakeholders of the research and innovation system whose propositions the government usually considers, the resulting policies tend to be perceived as reflecting a large consensus in the community of researchers and managers. For this reason, there tends to be continuity over time despite changes in government and changes of terminology (for example, "strategy" instead of "policy"). It was updated in 2017 as the *Stratégie québécoise de la recherche et de l'innovation*, with actions for specific industrial sectors. The government has published action plans for the 2018–2022 period for the health sciences, aerospace, and artificial intelligence, all based on its priorities for the economic development of the province.

All of these policies aim at sustaining economic development in emerging technologies as well as consolidating fields considered strong in the province. The policy and priorities also take into account the basic reality that the Quebec economy is structured around SMEs, which, in 2015, were responsible for 92 per cent of employment in the province. According to Entreprises Québec, the main sectors of activities are aerospace, agri-food, mines and metallurgy, information and communications technologies, life sciences, and surface transport (Enterprises Québec n.d.).

With the Quebec economy in good shape over the past few years and the provincial budget in surplus, new investments began in 2017 and are expected to continue over the next few years. For the current five-year planning period (2018–22), the Quebec government has announced that it will increase its total cumulative investment in the three FRQs by $180 million, or about 16 per cent. Generally speaking, Quebec investment in higher education has remained strong compared to the averages of both Canada and the member countries of the Organisation for Economic Co-operation and Development (OECD), averaging at about 0.9 per cent of gross domestic product (GDP) in the past decade or more. In contrast, Canada as a whole has bounced around 0.6 per cent, while the OECD average is about 0.4 per cent. It is probable that provincial programs have helped Quebec scientists over the past twenty years to receive, on average, about 27 per cent of the competitive grants from the three federal councils. In terms of publications, however, Quebecers produce only about 23 per cent of the Canadian total publications, or about equal to Quebec's share of both the Canadian population (Statistics Canada 2018) and its proportion of academic researchers. It is to be expected that these plans probably will have to be revised in light of the major and unexpected economic impact of the COVID-19 pandemic.

The weakest link in both Quebec and Canada is the R&D expenditures of firms. After real growth in the 1990s to a peak of about 1.8

per cent of GDP in 2005, we observe a continuous decline in Quebec to about 1.2 per cent of GDP in 2017. Over the same period, Canada peaked only at 1.2 per cent, and is now below 0.8 per cent, while the OECD has risen steadily over the past twenty years, peaking in 2017 at 1.6 per cent.

Quebec is home to twenty-six of the top one hundred commercial investors of R&D in Canada. The single largest funder of R&D in the province is Bombardier, which in 2017 spent more than $1.6 billion. Other major investors are Bell Canada and a number of major transportation and pharmaceutical companies. Looking at patents, we observe that Quebec has declared fewer inventions than its weight in the Canadian population, having only about 19 per cent of total Canadian patents over the past thirty years. As far as owners of these patents are concerned, the situation is better: about 23 per cent of Canadian patents are owned by Quebec companies or inventors. The most important sector using patents is electronics, accounting for about 45 per cent of total Quebec patents, followed by machinery, mechanics, and transport (18 per cent), instrumentation (17 per cent), and pharmaceutical and biomed (11 per cent). The averages mask a sharp run-up in Quebec patent ownership in the early 2000s, peaking at 32 per cent of all Canadian patents in 2004 and then falling sharply to about 14 per cent in 2013. The rise and then decline reflects the lifecycle of Nortel, which until 2006 used to contribute about 40 per cent of Quebec patents – and at its peak represented more than a third of the total valuation of companies on the Toronto Stock Exchange – but then filed for bankruptcy in 2009, was wound down, and its patents sold in 2010 and 2011. The share of patents owned in the province then stabilized, and recovered to over 17 per cent by 2019. While Bombardier, the single-largest R&D investor, was quite stable until 2018, we can expect another decline in the coming years with the demise of its aircraft division and the transfer of its C-series aircraft to Airbus.

Another important element of any complete national system of research and innovation is government laboratories. This aspect of R&D has been neglected over the past fifteen years in both Quebec and Canada. Government funding for R&D as a percentage of GDP has been declining for the past fifteen years to below 0.1 per cent in Quebec and only about 0.1 per cent in Canada, compared with the OECD average of more than 0.25 per cent. Recent announcements suggest a new period of growth might be on the horizon. As noted, however, this will probably be revised in light of the sharp downturn caused by the COVID-19 pandemic.

Sectoral Initiatives

At the beginning of the 1990s, Gérald Tremblay, the then Liberal minister of industry, commerce and technology, launched the idea of *grappes technologiques* (technological clusters) based on "consultation tables" for each industrial sector, regrouping government, industry, and unions to define priorities (Bourque 2000). This consultation approach has, over the decades and beyond party differences, been at the core of government planning strategies. In 2014, for example, as part of its industrial policy, the Parti Québécois government defined three new clusters in fashion, industrial design, and electricity (*La Presse* 2014). The Quebec policy defines specific strategies for different industrial clusters (aerospace, life sciences, information technology, artificial intelligence) that are then combined with models of public-private partnerships (health, optics and photonics, advanced materials, electrical energy).

In 2016, the government renewed its strategy for the aerospace industry for the next decade, accompanied by an investment of $500 million. With 39,000 workers, this industry is important, accounting in 2016 for 50 per cent of the Canadian presence in this sector. With the recent debacle of Bombardier, that industry in Quebec will probably be scaled down, although the French operator is supposed to keep the construction expertise of the C-series, renamed Airbus-220, in the province.

Other sectors have been targeted and stimulated through government industrial policy. In 1998, for example, Minister of Industry Bernard Landry launched the Cité du multimédia in Montreal, defining a part of the city where companies could get government subsidies for salaries and lower rent for occupying buildings in the defined sector (*TVA Nouvelles* 2000). Though criticized for its largesse, the program scored a success with the emergence of video game development in the city, first with companies such as Softimage, sold to Microsoft in 1994 and now defunct, and later Ubisoft, the creator of the popular *Assassin's Creed* and Tom Clancy games, which now ranks among the forty biggest enterprises in Quebec in terms of employees (*Les Affaires* n.d.). In 2016, the Quebec video game industry had about 230 companies, while in 2017, more than 11,000 people were employed in the sector in Quebec. The province hosts 33 per cent of studios in Canada and employs 46 per cent of the workforce in that sector (Investissement Québec International 2021).

Quebec has also established renowned research centres in digital arts, including the Society for Arts and Technology and the International Network for Research-Creation in Media Arts, Design, Technology and Digital Culture. More recently, École Polytechnique and Ubisoft created the Science and Video Games Chair. In the same logic of sectorial development, a Cité du commerce électronique was launched in 2000, but so far with less success than observed for multimedia (*La Presse* 2012). Quebec governments also make strategic use of the billions provided by the Caisse de dépôt et placement du Québec, which is formally independent but in practice is used to support strategic industrial development in Quebec in addition to its first aim of maximizing its investments for sustaining Quebecers' pension plans.

In 2017, the provincial government announced a more general five-year Quebec Strategy for Research and Innovation supported by more than $2.8 billion in investments, including $585 million for the implementation of specific measures (Quebec 2017). The three main objectives of the strategy remain quite general: to develop talent, skills, and the next generation of researchers ($133 million); to increase Quebec's research capacity and support innovation in all its forms ($267 million); and to accelerate and enhance the transfer and commercialization of innovations ($185 million). Also in 2017, the strategy for life sciences over the ten-year period 2017–27 was published with the aim of attracting $4 billion in investments before the end of 2022, to make Quebec among the top five North American poles of excellence in this sector by 2027 (Quebec 2020b). Drawing on $205 million in funding over the first five years, the strategy focuses on two niches recently promoted around the world: precision medicine and the use of big data in health care. In 2016, the health research sector comprised 630 companies and accounted for some 30,800 jobs and nearly as many at public research centres and related service companies. In 2014, its impact on Quebec's GDP was estimated at $5.6 billion. The major actors here are Pfizer, Pharmascience, and GlaxoSmithKline, which, in 2019, figure among the top 150 biggest companies in Quebec in terms of employees (*Les Affaires* n.d.).

Another field in which major funds have recently been invested is artificial intelligence (AI). Between 2016 and 2019, the Quebec government invested more than $200 million, including $83 million in SCALE AI, Quebec's supercluster, $32.5 million in the Montreal Institute for Learning Algorithms (MILA), $35 million in IVADO, and $25 million in the company Element AI. The federal government has also invested heavily in this emerging sector, with total investment in the province of $365 million, including $230 million for SCALE AI, $94 million for IVADO, and $41 million for MILA. A large portion of the grants were made on the basis of competitions opened to all sectors of research, but it is clear that active media buzz and the lobbying of researchers and AI companies have played a role in concentrating resources. According to the Ministry of Innovation, the private sector has also invested more than $1 billion in Montreal, though it is difficult to pinpoint exactly the amount of private money devoted to R&D in that sector, which is otherwise dominated by Google and Facebook, which are also investing in Montreal and collaborating with local universities (Quebec n.d.).

Other policies and strategies have also been defined and directed to managing innovation in other sectors and priorities, including international policy (2017–22); digital strategy (2019–23); leadership in entrepreneurship (2018–22); maritime (2015–20); aluminum development (2015–25); aerospace (2016–26); and agriculture (2018–25).

Policy Limits of Resource Concentration

Having described the most recent Quebec policies in support of research and innovation, I now take a step back to reflect more generally about the limits of policies that tend to concentrate resources on a particular sector that happens to be promoted by interested actors. We have observed since the end of the 1980s a new rhetoric of "excellence" that is accompanied by the idea of concentrating resources on a small number of priorities in order to get more "bang for the buck," to use the rhetoric of policy circles. This conception of policy probably explains in good part how Quebec's (and often Canada's) priorities in R&D have been influenced by successive fads based on exaggerated predictions of social and economic impact. After the biotechnology revolution of the 1980s and nanotechnology revolution in the 1990s, we saw a bandwagon effect on artificial intelligence in the 2010s. We also can expect a surge of interest in autonomous electric vehicles in the coming years.

All this is predicated on the idea that Quebec (or even Canada) can "compete" with major US or global firms that invest billions in those projects. As noted in Chapter 4, twenty global firms each invested more than $8.5 billion in 2018, any one of which is more than the entire investment of all actors in the innovation system in Quebec. In the AI space alone, the US government agency DARPA recently announced it would invest US$2 billion in a new program, AI Next (DARPA 2018). Moreover, despite the recent and trendy investments in AI, we still observe a general decline (or at best stagnation) in private R&D investment from Quebec and Canadian firms as well as in government laboratories.

The concentration of spending in a very limited number of fields supported with over-enthusiastic public announcements of forthcoming "major breakthroughs" might not be the best use of public funds for a province that produces only about 1 per cent of world publications (Canada produces 4 per cent). Rather than go it alone, Quebec (and Canada) should make sure it has the capacity to use and profit from the 99 per cent of knowledge produced by the rest of the world. Moreover, many studies show that, given the law of diminishing returns, it is economically and scientifically inefficient to concentrate resources on a too limited number of researchers (Fortin and Currie 2013; Gordon and Poulin 2009; Larivière 2013).

The recent major provincial investments in AI should recall to our minds the history of the previous concentration of public resources in the biotechnology sector. Let us recall briefly here the history of IAF Biochem, created in 1986 and renamed BioChem Pharma in 1992. It profited handsomely over the years from Quebec government (and to a lesser extent federal government) R&D subsidies, stock share tax breaks, support from the Caisse de dépôt et placement and investment from the Fonds de solidarité des travailleurs created and managed by the Fédération des travailleurs et travailleuses du Québec (the federation of Quebec workers). All of these partners were elements of the so-called Quebec model. By supporting local investors to keep control inside the province, the Quebec government policies allowed BioChem Pharma to grow to the point of being noticed, then bought, by foreign investors. Quebec's flagship biomedical research company was purchased in 2001 by the British pharmaceutical giant Shire, and then, on 31 July 2003, the company announced it would close its Quebec operations, which sent a shock wave through Quebec's scientific community.

From the market perspective, there is, strictly speaking, nothing wrong with such a decision, as long as public funds are not involved. However, those who believe that the state (be it Québécois or Canadian) must play a role in stimulating the growth of local firms are faced with a structural contradiction: entrepreneurs often use public funds to expand local firms, which, once they are sufficiently profitable, fall prey to huge multinationals that often only want to buy up their assets and move their research capacities abroad (Gingras 2003).

The following period of "nano hype" did not fare much better. After having been created with great fanfare in 2001, Nano Québec changed its name in 2015 to the less visible and less glamorous Prima Québec. We can expect further retrenchment as the US National Cancer Institute has decided to close its Centers of Cancer Nanotechnology Excellence that it created in 2005, a measure of the failure of the grandiose predictions of the nanotechnology revolution (Berube 2005; Service 2019). In this case, the technology simply did not deliver on its promise.

The same approach is now being repeated with AI. Without any critical distance between lobbyists and policy makers, investments are flowing in search of the AI revolution. To measure the intensity of the concentration of resources on a field essentially based on promising future applications, let us recall that, for 2019 alone, the three recently created provincial organizations in the field of AI (Ivado, MILA, and Scale.AI) had a combined budget of $82.5 million. On top of that, the Caisse de dépôt et placement and the provincial government have invested more than $130 million in Element AI, a company that has not yet a single product on the market (Silcoff 2019). The budget for the rest of the provincial research effort pales in comparison. The total budget of the FRQNT for the same year was only $62.7 million for research in all the disciplines in the natural sciences and engineering, while health research had for its part only $90 million to cover research in all fields of biomedical research.

The Fear of "Lagging Behind"

These government strategies are a response to the rhetoric of "lagging behind the competitors." Throughout its history, Quebec has been particularly sensitive to the idea of *retard*, particularly in the economic domain (Durocher and Linteau 1971). Since the end of the nineteenth century, discourse based on this idea can be found in many countries. Bouchard (2008), for example, has shown how this rhetoric played a central role in France's science and innovation policy after the Second World War.

Successive Quebec government priorities thus seem to be strongly influenced by lobbies that promise major economic growth, thanks to innovations generated by new technologies. Government actions are too often based on the fear of having to play "catch-up" with other countries. In such a context, politicians invest to show that they are doing things, knowing that even if the promises do not materialize in the near future, citizens will have forgotten about them anyway. By contrast, any government pushback to moving in the directions suggested by lobbies and well-known public scientific figures is often denounced as a lack of will and courage and "risking the future of the country." We have come to expect that every few years the organizations that already get millions of dollars of public money will simply say that they need even more money to keep or regain "leadership" in the "global competition." Hence, less than two years after the Quebec government announced a first wave of investment in AI, a report by a committee promoting AI stated in May 2019 that those investments "would not be sufficient to position Quebec as a leader" and that an additional $300 million would be necessary to "stabilize MILA." This in many ways was a self-interested effort, as the committee was closely associated with the Université de Montréal, one of the two key partners in MILA, and its rector was actually a member of the orientation committee that made the recommendation. MILA's chief executive officer asserted that the money it had secured was only a "starting investment" and that, to assure its full development, "much more money" would be required in the coming years (Rettino-Parazelli 2019).

The rhetoric of "global competition" plays a key role in convincing many who think that even a small province like Quebec can really "compete" at the global level. They always seem to ignore that, as noted above, most important global competitors invest hundreds of times the amount that Quebec R&D can afford in these fields. Despite the recent flood of Quebec and Canadian investments in AI, Canada is not even among the top five countries in terms of publications and number of researchers in the field (O'Meara 2019). One could, of course, respond that recent investments will change that, but it should be recalled that the presence in a given city of only a few major researchers in a given field is not enough in itself to make that city dominant in a field on a global scale.

Gartner Consultancy's "hype model" (Gartner n.d.) provides a useful – though simplified – representation of the life cycle of the rhetoric accompanying new technologies promoted as revolutions. Each goes through three phases: hype, hope, and disillusion. Biotech and nanotech have gone through all these phases and are now forgotten. In the case of AI, hype is already being replaced by more rational hopes and even the beginnings of disillusion. The technology of "deep learning," which obviously has varied useful applications, faces many limitations that now threaten to swamp the exaggerated predictions of its capacities (see Borup et al. 2006 for a critique of the model).

Conclusion and Lessons

Government has played a central role in the construction of the Quebec research and innovation system for political, social, and cultural reasons. The global ambitions of Quebec are qualitatively different than those of other parts of Canada, which have helped to ground and sustain focus in its science, technology, and innovation policy, unlike in other provinces. In terms of institutions, Quebec has developed a wide range of actors, including three granting councils. The central idea has been to create and support *grappes industrielles*, responding to the interests of emerging or new technologies over the decades: biotech, nanotech, video games, and now AI. The motives of actors in such a system, however, create fashions that have not endured. In light of the above analysis, the province's science and innovation policies should take a better measure of the objective possibilities, especially given the limited resources and the global economic context in which they are embedded. This undoubtedly requires a more broadly based approach to investments in R&D directed to identify, adapt, and support local adoption of future innovations that will continue to come mostly from abroad.

References

Les Affaires. n.d. "Les 500 au Québec." Online at https://www.lesaffaires.com/classements/les-500-plus-grandes-societes-au-quebec-2019/liste.

Albert, M., and S. Laberge. 2007. "The Legitimation and Dissemination Processes of the Innovation System Approach: The Case of the Canadian and Quebec Science and Technology Policy." *Science Technology & Human Values* 32 (2): 221–49. DOI 10.1177/0162243906296854.

Berube, D.M. 2005. *Nano-Hype: The Truth Behind the Nanotechnology Buzz*. Amherst, NY: Prometheus Books.

Borup, M., N. Brown, K. Konrad, and H. Van Lente. 2006. "The Sociology of Expectations in Science and Technology." *Technological Forecasting and Social Change* 18 (3–4): 285–98. https://doi.org/10.1080/09537320600777002.

Bouchard, J. 2008. *Comment le retard vient aux français: analyse d'un discours sur la recherche, l'innovation et la compétitivité, 1940–70*. Villeneuve-d'Ascq, France: Presses universitaires du Septentrion.

Bourque, G.L. 2000. *Le modèle québécois de développement industriel: de l'émergence au renouvellement*. Sainte-Foy: Presses de l'Université du Québec.

DARPA (Defence Advanced Research Projects Agency). 2018. "DARPA announces $2 billion campaign to develop next wave of AI technologies." 9 July. Online at https://www.ai.gov/darpa-announces-2-billion-campaign-to-develop-next-wave-of-ai-technologies/.

Durocher, R., and P.-A. Linteau. 1971. *Le retard du Québec et l'infériorité économique des canadiens-français*. Montreal: Boréal.

Fortin, J.M., and D.J. Currie. 2013. "Big Science vs. Little Science: How Scientific Impact Scales with Funding." *PLOS ONE* 8 (6): e65263. https://doi.org/10.1371/journal.pone.0065263.

Gartner. n.d. "Gartner Hype Cycle." Online at https://www.gartner.com/en/research/methodologies/gartner-hype-cycle, accessed 15 April 2020.

Gingras, Y. 2003. "The 'Quebec Model' and the End of BioChem." *Re$earch Money* 17 (4). Online at http://www.chss.uqam.ca/Portals/0/docs/articles/QuebecModel.pdf, accessed 15 April 2020.

Gordon, R., and B.J. Poulin. 2009. "Cost of the NSERC Science Grant Peer Review System Exceeds the Cost of Giving Every Qualified Researcher a Baseline Grant." *Accountability in Research: Policies and Quality Assurance* 16 (1): 13–40. https://doi.org/10.1080/08989620802689821.

Larivière, V. 2013. "La concentration des fonds de recherche et ses effets." *Découvrir* 2 (September). Online at https://www.acfas.ca/publications /decouvrir/2013/09/concentration-fonds-recherche-effets, accessed 15 April 2020.

O'Meara, S. 2019. "Will China lead the world in AI by 2030?" *Nature* 572: 427–8. https://doi.org/10.1038/d41586-019-02360-7.

La Presse. 2012. "Cité du commerce électronique: Montréal tourne la page." 23 August. Online at https://www.lapresse.ca/affaires/economie /immobilier/201208/23/01-4567391-cite-du-commerce-electronique -montreal-tourne-la-page.php, accessed 15 April 2020.

La Presse. 2014. "La ministre Zakaïb créera trois nouvelles grappes industrielles." 21 February. Online at https://www.lapresse.ca/affaires /economie/quebec/201402/21/01-4741322-la-ministre-zakaib-creera-trois -nouvelles-grappes-industrielles.php, accessed 15 April 2020.

Quebec. 2017. Ministère de l'Économie et de l'Innovation. "Stratégie québécoise de la recherche et de l'innovation, 2017–2022." Quebec City. Online at https://www.economie.gouv.qc.ca/objectifs/informer /recherche-et-innovation/strategie-quebecoise-de-la-recherche-et-de -linnovation/, accessed 14 October 2020.

Quebec. 2018. Ministère de l'Éducation et de l'Enseignement supérieur. "Sommaire statistique 2016–2017." Quebec City. Online at https:// synchronex.ca/en/documents/surveys-and-data /statistiques-du-ministere-de-leducation-de-lenseignement-superieur/, accessed 15 April 2020.

Quebec. 2020. Ministère de l'Économie et de l'Innovation. "Sciences de la vie." Quebec City. Online at https://www.economie.gouv.qc.ca/objectifs /informer/par-secteur-dactivite/sciences-de-la-vie/page/strategies-22512/, accessed 11 May 2020.

Quebec. n.d. Ministère de l'Économie et de l'Innovation. "Investments in Artificial Intelligence." Quebec City. Online at https://www.economie. gouv.qc.ca/fr/bibliotheques/secteurs/technologies-de-linformation-et -des-communications/intelligence-artificielle/les-investissements-en -intelligence-artificielle/, accessed 15 April 2020.

Rettino-Parazelli, K. 2019. "Nouveaux bureaux, nouveaux besoins pour MILA." *Le Devoir*, 29 January. Online at https://www.ledevoir.com/ economie/546567/nouveaux-bureaux-nouveaux-besoins, accessed 15 April 2020.

Service, R. 2019. "U.S. cancer institute cancels nanotech research centers." *Science*, 17 May. Online at https://www.sciencemag.org/news/2019/05/us-cancer-institute-cancels-nanotech-research-centers, accessed 15 April 2020.

Silcoff, S. 2019. "Canada's AI dream: Montreal-based innovator Element AI has impressive backers and a hefty bankroll, but can it deliver what it promises?" *Globe and Mail*, 20 July.

Statistics Canada. 2018. *Canada at a Glance 2018*. Online at https://www150.statcan.gc.ca/n1/pub/12-581-x/2018000/pop-eng.htm, accessed 15 April 2020.

TVA Nouvelles. 2000. "Création de la Cité du commerce électronique à Montréal." 11 May. Online at https://www.tvanouvelles.ca/2000/05/11/creation-de-la-cite-du-commerce-electronique-a-montreal, accessed 15 April 2020.

10 Ontario: Heartland Canada

MICHELE MASTROENI

Context and Innovation Architecture

Ontario is the industrial heartland of Canada and the anchor for both the national research and innovation systems. With 37 per cent of Canada's gross domestic product (GDP) and 45 per cent of the country's manufacturing activity, Ontario's economy is twice the size of that of the next largest provincial economy. Ontario has had the luxury, or perhaps the challenge, of being the prime target of federal efforts, so that in many ways the success and recent failures in the automotive and telecommunications sectors reflect less on provincial policy and more on federal policy. For example, both the automotive and the telecom sector are key to Ontario's economy, but while the province had to cope with the effects of restructuring in the auto sector, the collapse of Nortel and the sharp reversal of Blackberry, most of the policy effort was undertaken in Ottawa. Every provincial budget has mentioned the performance of the auto sector, especially parts, but only one major provincial program has been aimed directly at it: the 2004 Automotive Investment Strategy, a $500 million plan for building skills in the sector and to attract investment. All other direct programs have been federal (Holmes, Rutherford, and Carey 2017; Sorbara 2004). In telecoms, especially when Nortel was the jewel in the Canadian information and telecommunications crown, the federal National Research Council and the Communications Research Centre were given most of the credit for supporting research and development (R&D) and being a source of spin-offs for the sector (Huggins 2008).

Taken as a whole, Ontario has the largest R&D effort in Canada, with more than $13 billion invested annually, with a differentially large effort by business, strong higher education, and a significant federal footprint (Table 10.1).

Table 10.1. Gross Expenditure on Research and Development by Performing Sector, average $ millions, Ontario, 2013–17

		Performers					
		Government		Provincial Research	Business	Higher	Private Non-
Funders	Total	Federal	Provincial	Organizations	Enterprise	Education	profit
Total sectors	13,210	1,346	49	–	7,030	4,787	–
Federal government	2,615	1,323	–	–	157	1,135	–
Provincial government	431	–	49	–	80	303	–
Business enterprise	5,813	22	–	–	5,391	400	–
Higher education	2,380	–	–	–	–	2,380	–
Private non-profit	576	–	–	–	70	524	–
Foreign	1,396	–	–	–	1,351	45	–

Note: Columns and rows may not sum due to rounding.

Source: Statistics Canada, table 27-10-0273-01, "Gross domestic expenditures on research and development, by science type and by funder and performer sector (x 1,000,000)."

The provincial government has worked to take these assets and stake out an innovation policy agenda that is not intertwined with that of the federal government. Ontario's innovation ecosystem has been shaped by four successive governments seeking to move the provincial economy to higher-value-added production, with three of the four directly inspired by cluster theory. The result has been a focus on supporting research centres, mostly in an applied field or representing an economic sector, leveraging private and federal funds to support research centres, a focus on skills development, and supporting entrepreneurial start-ups and expansion. While each political party might have had preferred interactions with different stakeholders, post-secondary institutions have always been key participants in or beneficiaries of innovation policy. The bridging between the private sector and post-secondary research has also been a primary objective. Whether the current (2021) Ford government reverses this trend in policy, as seems to be the case, or decides to continue these efforts, remains to be seen.

The Policy Efforts

The evolution of innovation policy from 1985 to the present includes some important adjustments for Ontario, beginning with the break from the forty-two-year hold on government by the Progressive Conservative (PC) Party, the Canada-US Free Trade Agreement in 1988, and a policy shift towards openly supporting the knowledge economy. As in many provinces, the relevant policies in Ontario might not always have been directly innovation related, but many have had an impact on the human capital, infrastructure, and industrial variables that are important to a functioning innovation system.

Each of the governments in this period is notable for some major effort. In the 1985–90 Liberal era under David Peterson, the Premier's Council is credited with creating a policy framework to respond to the Canada-US Free Trade Agreement in the report *Competing in the New Global Economy* (1988). The Bob Rae New Democratic Party (NDP) government, from 1990 to 1995, shifted towards a sector-based strategy, further focusing on the knowledge economy as a reaction to a more globalized Canadian economy. PC Mike Harris's "Common Sense Revolution" from 1995 to 2003 was characterized by fiscal retrenchment, albeit with a turn to cluster policy for innovation. The Liberal government from 2003 to 2018, first under Dalton McGuinty and then Kathleen Wynne, followed an explicit cluster-based and innovation-focused policy program, with government actively partnering to improve both knowledge capabilities and industrial and business capabilities within the province. Since 2018, under the Doug Ford PC government, research funding for high-technology sectors has been cut, university tuition rates have been lowered without providing alternative funding mechanisms for universities, and innovation has been treated as something to be attracted through potential investors.

In the case of Ontario, politics seems to matter. The ideas, institutions, and interests show some clear differences for each political party – particularly the ideas that ground policy action. Nevertheless, a common thread ran through innovation policy from 1985 to at least 2018 whereby each government worked to increase or maintain commercializable knowledge creation and enhance the skills necessary to compete in the knowledge economy.

The Liberal Government under David Peterson

Although the focus of this book is on innovation policy from the 1990s onwards, the Liberal government under David Peterson (1985–90) introduced innovation policy and paid attention to value-added economic activity, explicitly addressing the innovation ecosystem. Peterson's government removed the Ontario PCs from power after forty-two years, pitching its campaign more to an urban centrist constituency, rather than to its traditional rural base (Bradburn 2018b). In response, the PCs refocused on a more northern, small-town, and rural constituent base. These changes have had a knock-on effect on policy choices ever since, explaining some of the policy emphases and spending for each party.

In the first two years in power, the Liberals served in a coalition with the NDP, the first such government in Ontario history. The coalition accord helped drive the innovation agenda, especially the formation in 1986 of the Premier's Council, made up of twenty-eight people from business, labour, and academia. The Council released *Competing in the Global Economy* in 1988 (Bradford 1998), a statement that introduced into the policy conversation the concept of "value added," in contrast to price competition, as the basis for competitiveness in an export-oriented economy. The report stated that the government should: encourage all industry to move to competitive, higher-value-added-per-employee activities that can contribute to greater provincial wealth; focus industrial assistance on businesses and industries in internationally traded sectors; emphasize the growth of major indigenous Ontario companies to world scale in their sectors; create an entrepreneurial risk-taking culture that fosters an above-average number of successful start-ups in internationally traded sectors; build a strong science and technology infrastructure that can support the technological needs of Ontario industries; improve the education, training, and labour adjustment infrastructure to sustain the province's industrial competitiveness and help workers weather the technological change and disruptions from moving to higher-value-added-per-employee activities; and follow a consensus approach, like that embodied in the Premier's Council, to create economic strategies and specific programs and to mobilize public support for new directions (Hall 1998, vii). These recommendations established what later can be termed cluster policies, influencing the shape of future decisions and related policy debates.

While the Council was deliberating, the government created seven Ontario Centres of Excellence in 1987 with $204 million initially committed over five years. The intent of the Centres was to create greater interaction between industry and university scientists to generate greater technology transfer (Bell 1996). The call for proposals, issued in early 1987, requested ideas with potential economic impact and benefits to Ontario and linkages with industry and small high-technology firms. Seven were chosen: (i) the Ontario Laser and Lightwave Research

Centre; (ii) the Institute for Space and Terrestrial Science; (iii) the Manufacturing Research Corporation of Ontario; (iv) the Waterloo Centre for Groundwater Research; (v) the Information Technology Research Centre; (vi) the Ontario Centre for Materials Research; (vii) and the Telecommunications Research Institute of Ontario (Bell 1996, 328). The creation of the Centres of Excellence established an institutional bedrock that all subsequent Ontario governments would use in their efforts to support R&D and knowledge transfer.

The Liberals' attention to innovation was also evident in early budgets. The 1986 budget initiated three measures. First, it offered "a series of concrete incentives to innovation and entrepreneurship" (Nixon 1986, 1) that would: promote technological innovation by strengthening the links between the private sector and Ontario's universities; support new and growing companies that generate most of the new jobs; encourage better training and retraining to build tomorrow's skills in today's workplace; and promote excellence in schools, colleges, and universities. Second, it announced plans to invest $1 billion in a technology fund for the next decade, in order to compete with "sophisticated new players" such as South Korea, Singapore, and Hong Kong. Third, it introduced a New Ventures program to support entrepreneurship in the province. It is significant that the push for higher-value-added activity and improved technological and innovative activity came *before* the Canada-US Free Trade Agreement was completed (it was then being negotiated), and before any actual effects of the Agreement or the subsequent North American Free Trade Agreement (NAFTA) could be felt. Global competitiveness had come of age for a variety of reasons, not just as a response to policy changes.

In 1988, the Liberal government then created the R&D Super Allowance Tax Credit, providing deductions of 25 per cent for large firms and 35 per cent for small firms for R&D activities in Ontario. It also announced $38 million for a Technology Personnel program to help smaller firms hire qualified people, and $25 million for a Strategic Procurement program to enable the Ontario government to better support innovation by acting as a client of technologies (Nixon 1988).

The Peterson government thereby effectively seeded the innovation policy terrain with the notion of value-added competitiveness.

The Peterson Liberals, in the introduction of their final budget of 1990 (Nixon 1990), offered a range of objectives and actions that directly supported innovation. Paraphrasing from the budget at multiple points, these included:

• Ontario's advantage lies in developing its technologically advanced economy, relying upon innovation and its highly skilled labour force.

- Maintaining competitiveness requires a healthy, well-educated, and adaptable work force.
- The government supported the view of the Premier's Council on Technology that labour and businesses, working together, have a key role in addressing the training and adjustment requirements of the labour market (the Ontario Training and Adjustment Board emerged from this recommendation in 1993 under the NDP).
- Innovation requires continued development of the province's infrastructure.
- Business must have the opportunity to operate at a reasonable cost, within a competitive tax structure and a stable and predictable fiscal climate.
- Demographic, technological and economic changes are creating both competitive challenges and opportunities for Ontario.

In 1990, the Peterson government went to the polls and was defeated. This set of laudable ideas was shelved, and only recently has it resurfaced and been reintroduced into the policy debate.

The NDP Government under Bob Rae

The new NDP government in 1990 actively acknowledged the need to pursue a knowledge-based economy, but tried to do so in a more collaborative, corporatist manner by bringing to the table new stakeholders, including labour groups, anti-poverty groups, and environmental activists (Bradford 2002). The new government was challenged to deliver on its expansive agenda, at least in part because it began its term at the beginning of a national recession. Budgets released from 1991 to 1995 largely reflect the needs of the struggling economy.

Clarkson (1999) notes that, with the advent of NAFTA, the NDP's goal was to make the Ontario economy more competitive, in part through high-value job creation (see also Gertler and Wolfe 2002). The emphasis was to invest in developing higher skills, education, and smart infrastructure to support high-tech clusters connected to post-secondary institutions. To do this, the Rae government sought to create a social partnership between business, labour, academia, and government, moving beyond the initial, and prematurely ended, collaboration efforts of the previous Liberal government. The aim was to encourage cooperation and competition simultaneously through facilitated social learning and multiparty decision making, rather than by picking winners (Bradford 2002). The Centres of Excellence and the Premier's Council established under the previous government continued, though perhaps with less influence (Clarkson 1999). After three years of consultation, the NDP launched the Ontario Training and Adjustment Board (OTAB), first proposed by the Premier's Council in 1990. OTAB was tasked with directing $442 million of public spending on skills training in its first year (Gertler, Wolfe, and Garkut 1998). The Board, representing multiple stakeholders, was intended to move beyond simply training to satisfy industry's demands for skilled labour to enabling new entrants – the disabled, visible minorities, and a wider range of people – into the labour market (Bradford 2002).

The Rae government's Industrial Policy Framework, released in 1992, had three main elements: changing the way government invests, superficially enhancing the infrastructure of the Centres of Excellence and renewing their funding for another five years; changing how government works with companies through strategies with firms *and* unions; and changing how government reacts to economic change, which involved support for green industries and organizational change in firms (Wolfe and Gertler 2001, 19).

According to Wolfe and Gertler (2001), the most significant effort by the NDP was the establishment of the Sector Partnership Fund in 1992. Starting with $150 million, the multiyear investment was designed to motivate groups of Ontario firms to self-identify as a sector and put forward proposals for government funding that demonstrate commercial viability, as measured by private sector co-investment. Sectoral groups had to involve both business and labour, as well as other stakeholders that might be relevant to the sector goals (Bradford 2002; Clarkson 1999; Gertler and Wolfe 2002; Wolfe and Gertler 2001). Projects, capped at $500,000, had to include a review of the external environment, including threats and opportunities; analysis of the sector's internal strengths and weaknesses, and its ability to respond to external pressures; futures scenarios for the sector; and a plan with clear objectives to move the sector to higher-value-added competitiveness (Gertler and Wolfe 2002). Demand for the program was high and many applications emerged, but the budget was underspent, at least partly because applicants found it difficult to leverage industry funding (Gertler and Wolfe 2002). Bradford (2003, 1016) suggests this might have reflected "stakeholder indifference, or at least an unwillingness to commit the necessary resources to join with the state in translating plans to action." Industry and the NDP had not historically been mutually supportive. The government also offered the Ontario Innovation and Productivity Service, a program to help small and medium-sized enterprises put together strategies, fund strategic projects, and access provincial programs (Wolfe and Gertler 2001).

Budgets from 1991 to 1995 for the most part emphasized macroeconomic stabilization at the expense of targeted investments in innovation. The 1991 budget spoke of recession and the economic adjustments occurring in the global economy. The statement highlighted the need for economic growth that is environmentally and socially sustainable, while acknowledging the importance of the knowledge economy and the shift in jobs to that sector. The budget committed $131 million for fiscal year 1991/92 to an Ontario Technology Fund to support research and commercialization activities, including supporting the new R&D Super Allowance for firms, and $21 million to the Innovation Ontario Corporation (Laughren 1991). In 1992, these programs continued, although with little fanfare. Two new investments were announced: a three-year Sectoral Partnership Fund (SPF), with $150 million, and a Jobs Ontario Capital Fund for investment in infrastructure for a "changing economy," with $2.3 billion over five years ($500 million in the first year) (Laughren 1992). In 1993, the budget reported that the provincial operating budget was declining and jobs were the priority. The only relevant innovation investment was to extend the SPF budget from three to five years, the statement explaining that the government's goals had been overly ambitious when the fund was first announced, but the extension likely also reflected changing government concerns (Laughren 1993). The 1994 and 1995 budgets made only one change in the innovation portfolio, announcing the Ontario Innovation Tax Credit, to cost $35 million each year. The focus on tough times and budget woes dominated (Laughren 1994, 1995).

The NDP government had come into power convinced that the knowledge economy was important, especially given the changing economic environment and impact of the free trade agreements on Ontario's manufacturing economy. This went deeper than the previous government's acknowledgement of the knowledge economy. The NDP government was especially influenced by Michael Porter's work on clusters (1990), which was being popularized at the time, and by a group of Toronto-based academic advisors promoting this model for innovation-based competitiveness (Bradford 2002; Clarkson 1999). Clusters were attractive for a number of reasons. First, they would allow the province to step out of policy spaces that duplicated federal activities and concentrate on areas where federal support had dropped off (Clarkson 1999). Second, fundamentals of agglomeration, combining both collaboration and healthy competition, aligned well with the

NDP's social partnership agenda. The challenge was that the institutional structures, practices, and norms in Ontario were not aligned well for this. The NDP faced further challenges in shifting Ontario to a knowledge economy through social partnership, as different stakeholder groups resisted what they interpreted was a corporatist contract.

Institutionally, the norms and practices of social cooperation were not well established in Ontario. Stakeholder interest groups worked to put forward their own interests, but there was no social capital that would overcome conflicts between stakeholders. This impeded collaborative work and the knowledge spillovers that the cluster concept asserts facilitate innovation. Some social capital was established by stakeholders collaborating to secure SPF funding, but Wolfe (2002) asserts that some participants viewed the efforts to promote dialogue as a quirk of the government of the day, while others accepted the benefit of generating coherent visions for their respective sectors. Possibly because of the narrower focus and understanding of sector concerns generated by the government-required reports for the SPF, some progress was made by intergroup coalitions moving on SPF proposals.

Bradford (2002, 2003) suggests that there were even more difficulties of collaboration with OTAB, which was tasked with allocating a fixed amount of funding for training. Clarkson (1999) notes that the private sector, while interested in government support, resisted the call to work collaboratively with labour representatives. Bradford (2002) observes that each group brought very different discourses to the table, with businesses emphasizing competitiveness and believing that policy instruments should be narrowly targeting their economic needs, whereas both government and labour believed policy instruments should have broader remit to include social goals. The trust and dialogue needed to form the social partnership was stunted by groups "caucusing amongst themselves" before approaching the plenary table; disagreements frequently arose about how discussions should be governed and programs focused (Bradford 2002). Over time, these disagreements and the increasing limitation of government resources created ruptures that made collaborative work difficult.

Both might have worked, but they needed more time to become normal practice. With growing concerns about the deficit and recession, this institutional development was cut short.

The PC Governments under Mike Harris and Ernie Eves

At first glance, the Mike Harris Progressive Conservative government, elected in 1995, might seem to have moved away from the construction of Ontario's innovation system. The PCs' latter "discovery" of city-based clusters – based on clusters' perceived complementarity with decentralized government and competitive business – stayed true, even with the government's adjustment of the university funding and tuition model, to the provincial narrative of cluster building and innovation support.

The Harris government rejected the NDP's moves towards social partnership (Bradburn 2018a), instead introducing a "common sense revolution" that focused on cutting spending, making government smaller, and relying more on market forces (Bradford 2003; Wolfe and Gertler 2001). The weak economy undoubtedly was part of the impetus, but the revolution was also influenced by a more neoliberal form of conservatism then making its appearance in Canada. In terms of policy, this meant cutting. By the end of the first year, the Premier's Council, the SPF, and OTAB were eliminated (Bradford 2003). Only the Ontario Centres of Excellence were kept, but these were reduced from seven to four and tied more closely to industry and their ability to access university-based R&D (Wolfe and Gertler 2001). The effort to shrink government involved cutting ministerial budgets, centralizing policy decision making, and offloading program and financial administration to local municipal actors (Bradford 2002, 2003).

The Harris government had a very focused narrative in its budget statements in 1996 and 1997, mostly directed to cutting taxes and reducing the government footprint (Eves 1996, 1997). In 1998, "a good news" message regarding economic growth and competitiveness emerged, tying the "invigoration" of the economy to government tax cuts and the prevailing low interest rates (Eves 1998). The last deficit was in 1999 (Eves 1999). From 2000, the messaging became more about the strong economic environment and a balanced budget, which in fiscal year 2002–03 was credited with weathering the economic uncertainty in global markets (Eves 2000). All these budget statements aligned for the most part with the Harris government's dominant attitude towards industrial policy: that lower taxes and reduced red tape enhance competitiveness, while government is not well suited to selecting who should receive grants or funds (see Clarkson 1999).

Innovation policy and regional clusters became more of a priority in 1997 as the focus shifted to "Creating Jobs for the Future" through R&D that supports industry competitiveness (Eves 1997), building on the philosophy that tax credits are the best way to lower the burden of doing business and to spur industry. The key measure in the 1997 budget was a new, ten-year, $3 billion R&D Challenge Fund; $500 million would be contributed directly by the province, which would require matches by the private sector, universities, and federal sources. Proposals to access the fund would need to pass a "market test linked directly to future economic growth and job creation, in the form of a one third contribution from the private sector" (Eves 1997, 4), similar in concept to funding conditions under the NDP government. Paper "E" of the 1997 budget laid out the benefits of innovation, highlighted the importance of R&D, noted Ontario's strengths in high technology, and acknowledged the need to invest in both capital and "soft assets" such as R&D and intellectual capital. The budget asserted that the Challenge Fund and tax credits would spur investment by increasing R&D and innovative activity, but also by creating an attractive environment for top research talent. The budget then provided a range of measures, including: an Ontario Business-Research Institute Tax Credit (20 per cent credit for firms investing in eligible research institutes, with the credit rising to 30 per cent for small and medium-sized enterprises); an extension of the sales tax exemption for R&D equipment purchases by non-profit medical facilities; removal of barriers for those seeking R&D tax credits; and a new Ontario Technology Tax Incentive to provide tax credits on acquired intellectual property. Other sectors, particularly film and computer animation, had grants cut and replaced with tax credit schemes (Eves 1997).

Clarkson (1999) and Bradford (2002, 2003) note that the 1997 budget was a departure from the initial push of the "common sense revolution." They attribute it to Premier Harris's above-mentioned discovery, through trade visits, of the importance of city-hub clusters of innovation to economic growth and development. Serendipitously, this aligned with the government's goals of offloading program responsibilities onto the municipalities.

The emphasis on cities to build a competitive environment for innovation was furthered in 1998 by the introduction of the Access to Opportunities Program ($150 million over three years), which worked to open new spaces in university engineering and computer science programs (Eves 1998). A newly constituted advisory body, the Ontario Jobs and Investment Board, was also tasked by the premier to develop an economic vision and plan for the province. The Board's report, *The Road to Prosperity*, released in 1999, affirmed the emphasis on fiscal responsibility and tax credits, while advocating building stronger city hubs. To do that, it promoted strengthening both universities' research capacity and the labour force by attracting new talent and promoting talent already in the province.

To provide the infrastructure to travel down the road to prosperity, the Harris government in 1999 announced the SuperBuild Growth

Fund, a somewhat new $2.9 billion allocation. Universities were a prime target, with $742 million for improving classrooms, facilities, and equipment and to accommodate growing student numbers (Eves 1999; Piché 2015). In 2000, the budget added an additional $500 million to the Ontario Innovation Trust for research infrastructure (on top of the initial endowment of $250 million in fiscal year 1998/99) (Eves 2000) and, in 2001, the new University of Ontario Institute of Technology was founded in Oshawa with a $60 million investment by the province (Flaherty 2001). Under new premier Ernie Eves, the province cut corporate tax rates further, and introduced new tax rebates for wind, micro-hydroelectric, and geothermal energy as well as alternative fuel vehicles, while also investing in the establishment of the Northern Medical School (Ecker 2003). Cluster policies were very much in effect, with the emphasis on applied research and applied training programs to make the province competitive in the knowledge economy. The Eves government's realignment of resources for post-secondary institutions, while problematic for smaller universities, favoured programs that were seen as directly contributing to Ontario's capabilities in the knowledge economy.

The funding programs of fiscal year 1999/2000 for universities were part of a larger realignment of resources. The 1996/97 budget had cut university operating grants by 15 per cent (Jones 2004), at which time universities were allowed more latitude to set their own tuition rates to make up for shortfalls. Some universities, especially the University of Toronto, had lobbied heavily for this change in policy. This realignment mostly benefited those universities offering professional programs (for example, in business, medicine, law, dentistry, and veterinary medicine). Not all of the new tuition money went to the bottom line – all universities had to set aside some of the new revenues for student aid, which otherwise would have been provided through government funds (Jones 2004; Rexe 2015). The government continued to provide matching funds for student financial assistance, which benefited those universities best able to attract private donations. These measures worked to create a greater sense of competition and differentiation among universities (Jones 2004), which complemented the rules to access new federal funding for chairs and infrastructure (Doern, Phillips, and Castle 2016). A particular concern for some universities was that the continued matching funds, such as the Access to Opportunities Program, favoured programs such as information technology, rather than allowing universities to allocate according to their need (Jones 2004). Arguably, these changes created a two-tiered system in Ontario's post-secondary institutions. The larger, more research-intensive universities that could mobilize and attract private sector research funding and donations were able to attract the matching provincial funds provided under the Harris and Eves governments; less endowed universities were doubly challenged to undertake their core activities.

Clarkson (1999) asserts that the Harris government had a consistent reasoning for the dismantling of previous industrial policy structures: "the market knows best." The view was that government could not be expected to evaluate investment projects better than the market does, and if it offered businesses support, it likely would unfairly support some firms over others. Interestingly, while the Harris government was clearly a business-leaning, non-urban government, Harris came to be a strong proponent of city-clusters for economic competitiveness. His government's fiscal conservatism, however, led to conflicts with labour and social groups and a mixed relationship with the academic sector.

The Liberal Governments under Dalton McGuinty and Kathleen Wynne

Influenced by cluster theory, new Liberal premier Dalton McGuinty saw the province's role as helping industry transition from traditional manufacturing to higher-value-added production (Forsyth 2007). Cluster theory, supplemented with the emerging concept of regional innovation systems and the triple helix of industry, government, and the entrepreneurial university, gained traction with this government. The implicit assumption underlying policy in this era was that innovation occurs when industry, government, and the academic sector work in tandem to produce knowledge and translate it for commercial benefit.

The election of the Liberal Party in 2003 put a special focus on innovation in the province. The McGinty government introduced a complex set of programs to develop and support the innovation environment in Ontario. Much like those of previous governments, the Liberals' policies can be broken down into three general categories: support for industry and entrepreneurs; research support; and network building to translate knowledge from research institutes to industry.

The McGuinty government considered innovation a source of economic growth and itself as having a key role in supporting innovation and enhancing the province's innovative capacity. The government undertook a concerted, large-scale, long-term effort to expand networks of innovation and to promote and entrench innovation values. It sought to create greater links between communities and industry – in particular, in high-growth sectors such as biotechnology and artificial intelligence (AI).

In 2005, the Ministry of Research and Innovation (MRI) was established to implement a wide array of innovation programs and to improve networks and partnerships with industry and other levels of government (Hepburn 2013; Tamtik 2016). The system that evolved was quite complex. MRI took the lead, with support from other ministries, such as the Ministry of Agriculture, Food and Rural Affairs (Bramwell, Hepburn, and Wolfe 2012). The government also set up the Ontario Research and Innovation Council (ORIC), an advisory body reporting to the premier, with representatives from academia and industry, to guide MRI and its strategy (Ontario 2006). MRI's 2006 Strategic Plan, based on ORIC recommendations, committed to focus government investments in R&D and training initiatives; complement R&D with investments to enhance commercial competence; focus skills formation more on commercial know-how, experiential learning and tech and science training; expand regional centres of "innovation convergence" and link them with researchers, entrepreneurs, and investors; increase access to capital at all stages of the innovation process; develop a communication strategy to promote a culture of innovation and commerce, especially aimed at youth; promote an intellectual property regime that better moves knowledge from universities to market; and establish metrics to track the outcome of innovation policies and programs (Ontario 2006). These recommendations resulted in MRI's committing to a set of "actions" that were effectively more fine-grained versions of the recommendations.

In 2008, ORIC released an Ontario Innovation Agenda to use "close to $3 billion in spending over eight years" to advance five explicit goals: extract more value from all provincial investments in research and innovation; attract the best and brightest innovators and entrepreneurs from around the world and retain homegrown talent; invest in, generate, and attract a workforce with first-rate skills in science, engineering, creative arts, business, and entrepreneurship; stimulate increased private sector investment in knowledge-based companies and capital that boosts productivity; and become globally recognized as a commerce-friendly jurisdiction that supports the growth of innovative companies and activities (Ontario 2008, 4).

MRI established a variety of research funding programs, grew horizontal relationships with different ministries (such as Energy, Agriculture, and Economic Development and Trade) to better deliver the innovation agenda, and enhanced contact with the private sector (Sharaput 2012). The programs that grew under the McGuinty Liberals spanned the spectrum from research to markets, creating links to all parts of the system (Dupuy 2010).

At the core of the system was the discovery and knowledge-transfer effort, with the Ontario Research Fund Research Infrastructure and Research Excellence programs, initially announced in 2005 to attract matching funding from the federal government, private partners, or universities. The universities, colleges, and specific research networks, such as the Ontario Institute for Cancer Research, continued to receive direct support beyond the innovation portfolio, while the Research Talent Programs – including Early Researcher Awards and the Premier's Catalyst, Discovery and Summit Awards – were designed to train, attract, and retain research talent (Hepburn 2013).

Technology and product development were anchored by the Ontario Centres of Excellence program, carried over from 1987 and the Peterson Liberal government. The McGuinty Liberals expanded and built upon the Centres as part of a wider network of support for commercialization and university-industry collaboration. In 2003, in response to the auditor's report, the government established OCE Inc., which unified the management of the remaining Centres (Hepburn 2014). Expansion was linked to business acceleration and market development with the announcement in 2005 of the Regional Innovation Network (RIN), local hubs that would act as multistakeholder, not-for-profit organizations, driven by the private sector, to provide a single access point to commercialization programs and other services for small firms, researchers, and entrepreneurs. This included access to the Ontario Centres of Excellence, the private charity program MaRS, and university tech transfer offices. Collectively this became known as the Ontario Commercialization Network (OCN) (Hepburn 2014), expanded in 2007 to include Provincial Innovation Networks, with MaRS as an anchor, Sector Innovation Networks, and Incubators, all designed to guide clients to provincial programs and a wider set of resources.

The OCN was reviewed by the ministry in 2008 in an effort to tighten governance and delivery of services. From this, the OCN was changed to the Ontario Networks of Excellence (ONE), made up of Regional Innovation Centres (RICs), Provincial Innovation Centres (PICs), and Sectoral Innovation Centres (SICs). The PICs, specifically the Centres of Excellence and MaRS Discovery District, were tasked with funnelling governments funds to clients of the ONE as well as to disburse provincial support to the regions through RICs (Bramwell, Hepburn, and Wolfe 2012; Hepburn 2013). MaRS was the only PIC that also was a RIC. Much like the Provincial Innovation Networks they replaced, RICs delivered services to local entrepreneurs but were meant to be more tightly coordinated and complementary. The ONE, by then rebranded as the Ontario Network of Entrepreneurs, was reviewed again in 2017.

While this system was meant to be more complementary, some of the overlap of roles (such as at MaRS) created confusion and a sense of possible conflict of interest amongst the RICs (ONE 2017).

It should be noted that, throughout this account, the MaRS Discovery District captivated attention. Started in 2000 and located adjacent to the University of Toronto St. George Campus and the main hospital district, MaRS began as a landlord and facilitator for scientists, entrepreneurs, firms, and funders to accelerate innovation in the medical and related sciences. Funded from a mix of provincial, federal, and private sources, the MaRS complex was for a time seen as a potential "white elephant," although it made progress in filling its space with tenants using technologies beyond the medical and health sphere (McIntyre 2018).

A portfolio of directed funds and tax credits in support of commercialization emerged. In 2004, the first McGuinty budget made an initial commitment of $27 million to create the Ontario Research Commercialization Program to support proof-of-principle investments, allocated $36 million for the Ontario Commercialization Investment Funds program to provide seed capital, and relaxed R&D tax credit rules (Sorbara 2004). From 2008 onwards, the budgets focused more on securing economic benefits (Hepburn 2014), which translated into a range of new commercialization support programs.

Much of Ontario's current innovation support infrastructure can be credited to the McGuinty government, although the seeds were sown earlier. The impact of these efforts, however, is hard to evaluate. The Council of Canadian Academies, tasked by the Ontario government to determine the impact of its policies, was able to document inputs and direct outputs of Ontario's efforts and compare them with those of other provinces and some international jurisdictions. The Council's report concluded, however, that more program impact data and more firm-based data were needed for a thorough assessment, as well as a host of indirect impacts on the entire innovation ecosystem that were not currently tracked (Aho et al. 2013).

After Kathleen Wynne took over the leadership of the Liberal Party and became premier in 2013, budgets increasingly highlighted concern around deficit reduction and recovery from the global financial crisis of 2008 – the Ontario economy slumped so much that it received equalization payments from the federal government from fiscal years 2009/10 to 2018/19. Nevertheless, significant investments in the innovation system during the period continued to show the provincial emphasis on applied R&D and skills development. These included: renewal in 2014 of the Ontario Research Fund, with $250 million over three years; an Ontario Youth Jobs Strategy in 2015, with $250 million over two years to support skills and entrepreneurial development; several proof-of-concept and applied research projects in 2016; a New Economy Fund in 2018 with $500 million over ten years to support sector-specific innovation and job creation; and a $700 million, ten-year commitment to the University of Guelph's agri-food research and education programs. There was also an increase in the number of investments in specific institutions in 2015 and 2016 for applied R&D and some changes to the tax system in 2016 to increase government revenue to offset the institutional commitments made during those years. The Liberals' last budget, in 2018, showed large investments in a few sector-specific areas and support for the creation of high-value jobs, but these were never implemented (Sousa 2018).

The PC Government under Doug Ford

The Progressive Conservative party under Doug Ford was elected to a majority on 7 June 2018, removing the Liberals after fifteen years in power. Running a populist-style campaign without any specific policies described in the platform, the party capitalized on public dissatisfaction with the Wynne government. It was suspected, and became apparent within the first year, that industrial and innovation policies were not going to be strong priorities for the Ford government, which was a major change from previous governments.

The changes began right away. In July 2018, approximately one month after the election, Ontario's first chief scientific officer, appointed by Wynne, was dismissed after only six months on the job. While the Ford government said it would find a replacement, the post was still vacant in early 2021 (Rieti 2018). In October 2018, the government cancelled the expansion of three suburban campuses for Toronto-based post-secondary institutions (Westoll 2018), and in May 2019 the government cut $5 million in annual funding from the Ontario Institute for Regenerative Medicine. It also cut $24 million from two institutes working on AI, the Vector Institute and the Canadian Institute for Advanced Research (Canadian Press 2019; Crawley 2019a). Other cancellations included the Water Technology Acceleration Project, a Toronto-based R&D initiative that had provided commercialization and business support to over three hundred companies (Research Money 2019).

The 2019 budget stated the government's top priority was to work "tirelessly to put money back in people's pockets, clean up the hydro mess, create and protect jobs, and end hallway health care and restore trust, transparency and accountability in government," which was contrasted to the previous government's "reckless" spending (Fedeli 2019, ix).

The goal was to resolve a projected $15 billion deficit, although the September 2019 public accounts showed the deficit was less than half that size (Crawley 2019b).

The budget asserted that lower corporate taxes and expenses would generate private sector innovation (Fedeli 2019). There were only three brief mentions of any type of government action or involvement related to innovation. The first was the Driving Prosperity Plan, with three pillars of activity: a competitive business climate, innovation, and talent. The first and third pillars appeared simply to involve marketing Ontario as a location for investment, while the innovation pillar involved sustaining (but not enhancing) support for the OCE's Autonomous Vehicles Innovation Network, established under the previous Wynne Liberal government. Part of the Plan was the launch of the Ontario Automotive Modernization Program, a technology adoption grant for small businesses in the motor vehicle sector (Driving Prosperity 2019). Second, the budget established an expert panel to review Ontario's intellectual property regime to identify ways to spur greater commercialization opportunities. Third, the budget announced a review of the Ontario Innovation Tax Credit, and committed to consulting with business on how to improve it, but with no actual changes proposed or promised (Fedeli 2019, 174).

While not directly related to innovation, the Ford government began a process – whether intentional or not – of dismantling institutional structures that previous governments had built and valued that might affect the innovation system. The most notable change was the decision to break contracts previous governments had made with the private sector. Green energy contracts and agreements with multinational companies tied to the Liquor Control Board of Ontario and beer stores were scrapped to deliver on campaign promises. Critics, including the Ontario Chamber of Commerce, pointed out that these arbitrary actions sent the wrong message to private sector investors and businesses, and could have an impact on future collaborations with government (Walsh 2019).

The relationship between the provincial government and the cities also became problematic after sudden cuts to city budgets were announced, without consultation. The cuts to Toronto city council were viewed as particularly punitive: while done in the name of efficiency, critics saw them as part of a political agenda by the premier against a city government in which he had previously been a councillor (Boisvert 2019; Gurney 2019). While public opposition led the government to reverse many of the cuts, the province remains committed to smaller municipal government.

One big unknown at time of writing is how innovation policy in Ontario will evolve. One observation is that the Ford government, in its first year, showed that it would bow to strong interest group pressure and reverse unpopular decisions (Gurney 2019). What is not clear is whether those most interested in government spending on innovation — particularly firms, scientists, post-secondary institutions, and sectoral associations — will engage in ways to forestall peremptory cuts or to nurture key parts of the innovation architecture. For example, despite limited policy discussion, the Ford government began carrying out changes to the post-secondary system – in particular, cutting tuition rates by 10 per cent without increasing the amount of government funding to post-secondary institutions. In addition, the government pledged to implement an "outcomes-based" funding system for post-secondary institutions, whereby each institution would need to reach performance metrics to sustain funding (Fedeli 2019, 187). Resource constraints began affecting teaching and training offerings in 2019, but the impact on R&D capability is not yet evident.

In early 2020, the Ford government announced that, due to the COVID-19 pandemic, the outcomes-based funding system would be delayed by at least a year. Perhaps more important, concerning Ontario's innovation ecosystem, are the unknown impacts of the pandemic on university income through, for example, lower tuition revenues due to fewer students attending university; fewer foreign students arriving in Ontario and remaining as immigrants, potentially reducing an avenue for skilled labour growth; the impact of institutions switching to online learning during the pandemic and possibly beyond; and related investments in information and communications technology and training to facilitate virtual classrooms and research centres.

Conclusions and Lessons

Innovation-related industrial policy began in Ontario in 1985, spurred by the changing global economy and Canada's evolving political landscape. Free trade agreements and greater competition from offshore manufacturers pushed policy makers to focus more on the knowledge economy and increasing value added in Ontario industry.

Each government brought different ideas to the administration of the province: from collaborative social partnerships to neoliberal "common sense" to cluster-based innovation to populist conservatism. From 1985 to 2018, governments adhered to the idea that competitiveness in the knowledge economy was key, and that it was the province's role to support innovative clusters. Institutional systems were correspondingly constructed and adapted. Requiring private and academic research partnerships, and creating the funding bodies and support networks to encourage such partnerships, were consistent parts of provincial institution building during this time. While different interest groups saw more or less influence under different specific governments, sometimes promoting change and sometimes resisting change – for example, to the Rae NDP government's social partnership – for the most part, post-secondary institutions in Ontario have had a privileged place at the table as key recipients of R&D and commercialization investments, as anchors to innovation clusters, and as both home to and source of skilled labour. Regardless of the government in power, universities play a major role in innovation policy. Universities are generally seen as prime provincial agents for advancing knowledge creation and R&D, and provincial support structures have emphasized applied R&D and skills development. Nevertheless, the pressure continues for improved commercialization of local knowledge.

Ontario's innovation policy has been distinct from that of the federal government, although it does leverage federal funding for some of its own funding programs. The province built institutional structures to support innovation and knowledge translation in the form of the OCE, and created funding structures operating with a fairly consistent focus over the period from 1985 to 2018. The impact of the various policies is difficult to determine, as the necessary measures and corresponding data have not been collected (Aho et al. 2013). Despite the long timeline of effort, there is a continuing sense that not enough knowledge commercialization is carried out at home. The Ontario economy remains vulnerable due to its entrepôt status in some sectors, such as the automotive (see Rutherford and Holmes 2008; Warrian and Mulhern 2005), and while post-secondary institutions are seen as valuable sites of knowledge creation and skills development, this has not immunized them from the vagaries of the provincial fiscal cycle.

References

Aho, E., et al. 2013. *Innovation Impacts: Measurement and Assessment*. Ottawa: Expert Panel on the Socioeconomic Impacts of Innovation Investments, Council of Canadian Academies.
Bell, S. 1996. "University-Industry Interaction in the Ontario Centres of Excellence." *Journal of Higher Education* 67 (3): 322–48. https://doi.org/10.1080/00221546.1996.11780263.
Boisvert, N. 2019. "Doug Ford reverses retroactive funding cuts amid fierce pressure from Toronto." *CBC News*, 27 May.

Bradburn, J. 2018a. "In the mood for cuts: How the 'Common Sense Revolution' swept Ontario in 1995." *TV Ontario*, 6 June.

Bradburn, J. 2018b. "The year the Tories' 'Big Blue Machine' came sputtering to a stop." *TV Ontario*, 24 May.

Bradford, N. 1998. "Prospects for Associative Governance: Lessons from Ontario, Canada." *Politics & Society* 26 (4): 539–73. https://doi.org/10.1177%2F0032329298026004005.

Bradford, N. 2002. "Sectors, Cities and Social Capital: Social Democratic and Neo-Liberal Innovation Strategies in Ontario, 1990–2000." In *Knowledge, Clusters and Regional Innovation: Economic Development in Canada*, ed. A. Holbrook and D. Wolfe, 219–58. Montreal; Kingston, ON: McGill-Queen's University Press.

Bradford, N. 2003. "Public-Private Partnership? Shifting Paradigms of Economic Governance in Ontario." *Canadian Journal of Political Science* 36 (5): 1005–33. https://doi.org/10.1017/S0008423903778949.

Bramwell, A., N. Hepburn, and D. Wolfe. 2012. *Growing Innovation Ecosystems: University-Industry Knowledge Transfer and Regional Economic Development in Canada*. Toronto: University of Toronto, Munk School of Global Affairs, Program on Globalization and Regional Innovation Systems.

Canadian Press. 2019. "Ontario government cuts $24 Million in AI research funding," *CBC News*, 21 May.

Clarkson, S. 1999. "Paradigm Shift or Political Correction? Putting Ontario's 'Common Sense Revolution' in a Global Context." *Regional & Federal Studies* 9 (3): 81–106. https://doi.org/10.1080/13597569908421098.

Crawley, M. 2019a. "Ford government scraps funding for stem cell research." *CBC News*, 16 May.

Crawley, M. 2019b. "Ontario's deficit was $7.4B last year – far lower than the Ford government claimed it was." *CBC News*, 13 September.

Doern, D.B, P. Phillips., and D. Castle. 2016. *Canadian Science, Technology and Innovation Policy: The Innovation Economy and Society Nexus*. Montreal; Kingston, ON: McGill-Queen's University Press.

Driving Prosperity. 2019. *Driving Prosperity: The Future of Ontario's Automotive Sector*. Toronto: Ministry of Economic Development, Job Creation and Trade.

Dupuy, D. 2010. "Strengthening Ontario's Innovation System: The Role of Ontario's Innovation Agenda." Presentation at Innovation Systems Research Network, Toronto, 5 May.

Ecker. J., 2003. *Ontario Budget*. Toronto: Queen's Park.

Eves, E. 1996, 1997, 1998, 1999, 2000. *Ontario Budget*. Toronto: Queen's Park.

Fedeli, V. 2019 *Ontario Budget*. Toronto: Queen's Park.

Flaherty, J. 2001. *Ontario Budget*. Toronto: Queen's Park.

Forsyth, P. 2007. "Mr. Innovation." *Niagara This Week*. 16 February.

Gertler, M., and D. Wolfe, eds. 2002. *Innovation and Social Learning: Institutional Adaptation in an Era of Technological Change.* London: Palgrave Macmillan.

Gertler, M., D. Wolfe, and D. Garkut. 1998. "The Dynamics of Regional Innovation in Ontario." In *Local and Regional Systems of Innovation,* ed. J. de la Mothe and G. Paquet, 211–38. Boston: Springer.

Gurney, M. 2019. "Doug Ford needs to start making decisions he can stick to." *National Post,* 30 May.

Hall, D. 1998. "An Evaluation of Ontario's Industrial Policy Efforts." PhD diss., Queen's University Kingston.

Hepburn, N. 2013. "The Impact of Policy Networks on Ontario's Research and Innovation Infrastructure: Explaining the Development of the Ontario Network of Excellence." Conference Paper, Annual Meeting of the Canadian Political Science Association, 4–6 June.

Hepburn, N. 2014. "Minding the Gap between Promise and Performance: The Ontario Liberal Government's Research and Innovation Policy, 2003–2011." PhD diss., University of Toronto.

Holmes, J., T. Rutherford, and J. Carey. 2017. "Challenges Confronting the Canadian Automotive Parts Industry: What Role for Public Policy?" *Canadian Public Policy* 43 (S1): S75-S89. http://doi.org/10.3138/cpp.2016-030.

Huggins, R. 2008. "The Evolution of Knowledge Clusters: Progress and Policy." *Economic Development Quarterly* 22 (4): 277–89. https://doi.org/10.1177%2F0891242408323196.

Jones, G.A. 2004. "Ontario Higher Education Reform, 1995–2003: From Modest Modifications to Policy Reform." *Canadian Journal of Higher Education* 34 (3): 39–54. http://dx.doi.org/10.47678/cjhe.v34i3.183466.

Laughren, F. 1991, 1992, 1993, 1994, 1995. *Ontario Budget.* Toronto: Queen's Park.

McIntyre, C. 2018. "Discovering MaRS: The Untold Story of Canada's Largest and Most Controversial Innovation Hub." *Logic,* July.

Nixon, R. 1986, 1988, 1990. *Ontario Budget.* Toronto: Queen's Park.

ONE (Ontario Networks of Entrepreneurship). 2017. *Building Global Winners: Expert Panel Report on the Ontario Network of Entrepreneurs.* Toronto.

Ontario. 2006. Ministry of Research and Innovation. *Strategic Plan.* Toronto: Queen's Park.

Ontario. 2008. Ministry of Research and Innovation. *Seizing Global Opportunities: Ontario's Innovation Agenda.* Toronto: Queen's Park.

Ontario Jobs and Investment Board. 1999. *Roadmap to Prosperity.* Toronto: Ontario Jobs and Investment Board.

Piché, P. 2015. "Institutional Diversity and Funding Universities in Ontario: Is There a Link?" *Journal of Higher Education Policy and Management* 37 (1): 52–68. https://doi.org/10.1080/1360080X.2014.991537.

Porter, M. 1990. *The Competitive Advantage of Nations*. New York: Free Press.

Research Money. 2019. "The Short Report. " 26 June.

Rexe, D. 2015. "Anatomy of a Tuition Freeze: The Case of Ontario." *Canadian Journal of Higher Education* 45 (2): 41–59. https://doi.org/10.47678/cjhe .v45i2.184344.

Rieti, J. 2018. "Science is not political, says Ontario's 1st Chief Scientist after being fired by Doug Ford." *CBC News*, 5 July.

Rutherford, T., and J. Holmes. 2008. "'The flea on the tail of the dog': Power in Global Production Networks and the Restructuring of Canadian Automotive Clusters." *Journal of Economic Geography* 8 (4): 519–44. https:// doi.org/10.1093/jeg/lbn014.

Sharaput, M. 2012. "The Limits of Learning: Policy Evaluation and the Ontario Ministry of Research and Innovation." *Canadian Public Administration* 55 (2): 247–68. https://doi.org/10.1111/j.1754-7121.2012.00216.x.

Sorbara, G. 2004. *Ontario Budget*. Toronto: Queen's Park.

Sousa, C. 2018. *Ontario Budget*. Toronto: Queen's Park.

Tamtik, M. 2016. "Policy Coordination Challenges in Governments' Innovation Policy: The Case of Ontario, Canada." *Science and Public Policy* 44 (3): 417–27. https://doi.org/10.1093/scipol/scw074.

Walsh, M. 2019. "Ford's plan to cancel Beer Store contract alarming, says business." *iPolitics*, 4 June.

Warrian, P., and C. Mulhern. 2005. "Knowledge and Innovation in the Interface between the Steel and Automotive Industries: The Case of Dofasco." *Regional Studies* 39 (2): 161–70. https://doi.org/10.1080 /003434005200059934.

Westoll, N. 2018. "Doug Ford government cancels funding for post-secondary campus expansions for Brampton, Milton, Markham." *Global News*, 23 October.

Wolfe, D. 2002. "Negotiating Order: Sectoral Policies and Social Learning in Ontario." In *Innovation and Social Learning*, ed. M. Gertler and D. Wolfe, 227–50. London: Palgrave Macmillan.

Wolfe, D., and M. Gertler. 2001. "Globalization and Economic Restructuring in Ontario: From Industrial Heartland to Learning Region?" *European Planning Studies* 9 (5): 575–92. https://doi.org/10.1080/09654310124479.

11 Manitoba: The Challenge of Being Average

DEREK BREWIN, ANNE BALLANTYNE,
AND PETER W.B. PHILLIPS

Manitoba exemplifies the challenge for smaller jurisdictions seeking to contribute positively to the innovation effort. The province has invested in all the right things that theory and experience elsewhere suggest are needed for success, but outside agriculture it has failed to align efforts in any way that generates notable change. Universities, firms, and governments have not found a way to work together to advance innovation. Instead, stability is the watchword, with most actors engaged and investing, but not visibly going out of their comfort zone to destabilize what are otherwise comfortable markets and relationships. Creativity is evident, but the necessary attendant destructive stage of adapting and adopting transformative technologies is muted. The province is muddling along, doing better than some and worse than others in terms of its efforts, but with little to show by way of commercial success or measurable improvements in jobs, incomes, or productivity. Agriculture is the one outlier. The gross domestic product (GDP) of the agricultural sector, which has a larger share of Manitoba's economy than in all other provinces except Saskatchewan and Prince Edward Island, grew faster from 1997 to 2018 than in any other province. Moreover, even some of Manitoba's more prominent recent technology start-ups serve the agriculture sector.

Context

Manitoba is often lumped in with the Prairie provinces, along with Saskatchewan and Alberta, but its history, geography, and people are significantly different than those of its two western neighbours. Whereas the economies of Saskatchewan and Alberta have been characterized by booms and busts, Manitoba's has sailed along on a slow but steady course, serving its resource-rich neighbours but neither suffering from major downturns nor reaping the rewards of commodity booms or disruptive developments. Stability is order of the day. While some might think this stability would provide a sound base for innovation, in practice the province has lagged in motivating or capturing the benefits of innovative ventures.

When Manitoba joined Confederation in 1870, the province was just 14,000 square miles, giving rise to the name "the postage stamp province." There was a reason Manitobans chose that space: the region had been a transportation and trading hub for thousands of years before European contact. During the recent excavation of lands for the foundation of the Canadian Museum for Human Rights at the Forks of the Assiniboine and Red River in the heart of Winnipeg, diggers found evidence of concentrated co-habitation of the area back to the Stone Age (CMHR n.d.). The current transportation, warehousing, and commodity handling that make up much Winnipeg's reason for being have been an economic focus of the area for millennia.

The modern history of the province begins in the 1730s and La Vérendrye's exploration of the area for fur trading for the North West Company. The French-English partnership that galvanized Canada in 1867 had already happened in Winnipeg with the 1821 merger of the Métis-supported North West Company and the Hudson's Bay Company aligned with Lord Selkirk's colony (Taylor and Baskerville 1994). The Métis colony led by Louis Riel during the Red River Rebellion of 1869–70 formed its own provisional government, which entered Confederation in 1870 as the province of Manitoba, albeit governing only about one-eighteenth of the territory that now forms the province.

Although vast western and northern territories were added to the province in 1889 and 1912, Winnipeg has dominated Manitoba's population, politics, and economy for over 150 years. This overwhelming dominance differentiates Manitoba from other Prairie provinces. Both Alberta and Saskatchewan have two major cities and a larger proportion of their populations in smaller cities, towns, and rural areas. In contrast, Winnipeg is the de facto hub of most of Manitoba's economic output and employment, with strengths in food manufacturing, equipment manufacturing, aerospace, agribusiness, financial services, life sciences, and transportation and distribution (Economic Development Winnipeg 2020). Spencer (2014) reports that, in 2011, Manitoba had five statistically significant clustered sectors, compared with six in Saskatchewan and thirty in Alberta. In addition to agriculture, life sciences and aerospace, which are evident in the statistics, textiles and mining also had small regional clusters. Less than 3 per cent of the jobs in Manitoba were clustered, compared with 7 per cent in Saskatchewan and almost one-quarter in Alberta. Perhaps most challenging is that the clustered sectors in Manitoba were adding less than 1 per cent of new jobs annually, while clusters in Alberta and Saskatchewan were adding on average about 5 per cent each year.

Manitoba does have significant endowments of resources spread across its geography, but these are sparse in scope relative to the diverse economy in and around Winnipeg. In 2016, Winnipeg's metro area generated $41.4 billion of Manitoba's $62.3 billion in GDP. Winnipeg's 66 per cent share was larger than any other metro area's share of GDP in any other province in Canada; in contrast, although larger than most provincial GDPs, metro Toronto's $386 billion GDP in 2016 was only 53 per cent of Ontario's total GDP (Statistics Canada n.d.b).

Winnipeg's diverse economy is part of the reason the province has had relatively few booms or busts. The fact that this large urban economy is so dominant has influenced the nature of the provincial economy. In many ways, Manitoba is the quintessentially Canadian province: at the geographic centre of the country and with an industrial structure that is for the most part a mirror image of national averages, with 30 per cent of GDP from goods production and the rest from services activities. The two outliers in terms of share of GDP are agriculture and transportation, which in Manitoba represent a significantly larger share of the economy than they do for Canada as a whole. The overall long-term rate of economic growth also converges on the national performance. Most studies of and reports on the provincial economy emphasize its stability. But given the unevenness of averages, this has translated into weaker employment growth and lower average per capita incomes, leaving the province in perennial "have-not" status and a perpetual recipient of equalization payments.

Geography, once the singular reason for Winnipeg's advantage as a wholesale and transportation hub, continues to contribute to its prosperity even though the city is one of the coldest in the world (Byrne 2019). Nevertheless, the rail branches from the west that converge on Winnipeg still support its position in the grain market and as a major branch office centre for all forms of transportation and services. Canada's two major railways, Canadian Pacific and Canadian National, are key employers, as is the grain-handling sector, which is anchored by some very successful, and increasingly philanthropic, families (exemplified by the Richardsons). Their old money, mostly invested in traditional ventures, is increasingly directed as venture capital or shared with universities and various non-profit projects. This type of philanthropy has been found to be supportive to innovation (Gibson, Barrett, and Parmiter 2013).

Manitoba's overall economy is absolutely smaller than Saskatchewan's, despite Manitoba's larger population and the Winnipeg labour hub. Saskatchewan gets a large share of its income and jobs from exploiting rich resource deposits, while Manitoba gets the bulk of its income and jobs from processing and servicing activities, which generally operate at lower gross margins. Similarly, Manitoba's average annual growth rate of GDP from 1988 to 2018 was 2.1 per cent, just a bit lower than the 2.2 per cent Canadian average, but much less than Alberta's 3.0 per cent (Statistics Canada n.d.a).

Beyond geography, and perhaps agriculture, it is hard to find a distinct comparative advantage for Manitoba. Having fewer busts than booms should be something to cheer about, but the absence of booms means that the province is a perpetual "have-not," with all the attendant negative implications, including low investment in infrastructure, poor ability to attract talent, and fewer opportunities for strategic partnerships and growth. While the city of Winnipeg is growing, it is doing so more slowly than other urban centres in the West, especially Edmonton, Calgary, and Saskatoon. The city's economics and politics run through all of the main innovation stories in the province, even those about supplying services to remote farm communities.

Innovation Architecture

A frontier-style of co-operative entrepreneurism in Winnipeg and the rest of Manitoba still drives business choices, tempered with community pride. Business leaders are local heroes. Beyond this celebration of entrepreneurism, it is difficult to identify much interest in or focus on Manitoba's science and innovation. While Premiers Duff Roblin and Ed Schreyer were early innovative politicians who invested in science and infrastructure (especially Manitoba Hydro), both lived within the limits of interests and institutions that were well entrenched before they came to power. Neither was able to change the ongoing trajectory of slow and steady growth untroubled by disruptive innovation.

Supported by federal investments – especially related to the grain and health sectors – Manitoba has tried to foster clusters. The province is a recent promoter and partner of the protein supercluster anchored in Saskatchewan but partnered with the Canola Council of Canada and several major firms located in Winnipeg (Manitoba 2020). In terms of GDP, both agriculture and health have grown faster in Manitoba than the national average over the past two decades, but this has not been enough to pull the whole population out of the doldrums. Historically, Manitoba politicians have lamented the lack of capital investment in the province, and many, especially Premier Roblin, used this as an excuse for significant public capital projects (supported by tax increases), albeit with a focus on education, health, and infrastructure (Neville 2010).

Beyond the creation of the universities and the early presence of federal labs in Winnipeg, Manitoba's current innovation policy saw its beginnings in 1963 with the creation of the Manitoba Research Council (MRC) by the Roblin government. The MRC provided research grants to support industry and university scientists, and advised the government on the allocation of funds for scientific research, but unlike comparable provincial research organizations, it did no in-house research (McNicholl 2015). Eventually, the MRC helped start the Food Development Centre in Portage la Prairie and the Industrial Technology Centre in Winnipeg, both of which have offered significant support to firms for industrial research and development (R&D). The MRC was a regular focus in the Throne Speeches of Premier Gary Filmon in the late 1980s and 1990s. In 2014, the MRC was folded into Research Manitoba, along with the Manitoba Research and Innovation Fund, the Health Research Initiative, the Manitoba Centres of Excellence Fund, and the Manitoba Health Research Council. This amalgamation might have allowed researchers more flexibility, but its impact has yet to be measured. The provincial councils contributed on average a total of $27 million per year from 2013 to 2017 (Statistics Canada n.d.c).

Winnipeg has a diverse labour pool, a significant presence of angel investors, and the occasional emerging business leader. In the 1980s and 1990s, Izzy Asper with CanWest Global anchored economic and community development, championing the Canadian Museum for Human Rights. The Richardson family in 2005–12 responded to the winding down of farmer-owned grain co-operatives by consolidating a significant share of the industry in their family-owned firm. Most recently, Mark Chipman, a successful local businessman and property developer and owner of True North Sports and Entertainment, has been a major investor in downtown Winnipeg, and is a local hero for his efforts since 2011 in bringing back the Winnipeg Jets NHL hockey franchise.

The University of Manitoba, with two campuses in Winnipeg, is a U-15 research-intensive university with significant leadership in agriculture, physics, Arctic research, and health sciences (University of Manitoba n.d.b). The focus on the Arctic is partly due to the northern access to Hudson Bay and ongoing questions about what to do with the Port of Churchill. Arctic research is supported by a Canada Excellence Research Chair in Arctic Geomicrobiology and Climate Change, the research vessel *Amundsen*, the Sea-Ice Environmental Research Facility, co-leadership in the ArcticNet Networks of Centres of Excellence, and the Arctic Science Partnership. Health sciences are supported by the Institute of Musculoskeletal Health and Arthritis, the National Microbiology Laboratory, the Centre for Global Public Health, and the Manitoba Centre for Health Policy. Agricultural and food sciences are supported by the National Centre for Livestock and the Environment, the Canadian Wheat Board Centre for Grain Storage Research, the Richardson Centre for Functional Foods and Nutraceuticals, and the Canadian Centre for Agri-Food Research in Health and Medicine.

Winnipeg is also home to the University of Winnipeg, the Canadian Mennonite University, and Red River College, a major trade college with some research capacity. There are also smaller universities at Brandon and The Pas, and a range of colleges in smaller centres across the province.

Federal facilities have been a vital part of Manitoba's innovation capacity since the arrival of the first agricultural research stations in Morden (1915) and Winnipeg (1924). As of 2020, Agriculture and Agri-Food Canada continues to operate research stations at Morden and Brandon, Atomic Energy Canada manages Whiteshell Laboratories in Pinawa, and the University of Manitoba's Fort Gary campus is home to the Fresh Water Institute, a Department of Fisheries and Oceans lab. Winnipeg is also a major centre for health research, with downtown housing the Canadian Centre for Human and Animal Health (which hosts the Canadian Food Inspection Agency's National Centre for Foreign Animal Disease), Public Health Agency of Canada's National Microbiology Laboratory, and JC Wilt Infectious Diseases Research Centre (Canada 2020). In total in 2018–19, Manitoba was home to 1,513 federal scientists compared with to 651 and 1,463 in Saskatchewan and Alberta, respectively (Statistics Canada 2020).

Provincial gross expenditure on R&D as a percentage of GDP was 1.2 per cent as of 2016 – approximately 50 per cent higher than in Saskatchewan and 30 per cent higher than Alberta. The federal government is a significant funder. Beyond the federal labs in Manitoba, federal support for higher education R&D averaged $172 million per year from 2013 to 2017 (Table 11.1). Business outlays on R&D, at about $220 million, or 0.48 per cent of GDP in 2016, were relatively higher than in Alberta and Saskatchewan, but well below the peak of 1.3 per cent of GDP in Quebec. Business performed only about 31 per cent of all research in the province over the 2013–17 period. Only two firms, Monsanto Canada and Winpak Ltd., a packaging products firm in Winnipeg, spend more than $10 million annually on R&D, which is what is needed to break into the top 100 corporate R&D investors in Canada.

Table 11.1. Gross Expenditure on Research and Development by Performing Sector, average $ millions, Manitoba, 2013–17

		Performers					
		Government		Provincial Research	Business	Higher	Private Non-
Funders	Total	Federal	Provincial	Organizations	Enterprise	Education	profit
Total sectors	691	95	7	–	242	348	–
Federal government	172	95	–	–	8	69	–
Provincial government	27	–	7	–	2	19	–
Business enterprise	220	–	–	–	207	13	–
Higher education	191	–	–	–	–	191	–
Private non-profit	50	–	–	–	5	48	–
Foreign	28	–	–	–	23	10	–

Note: Columns and rows may not sum due to rounding.

Source: Statistics Canada, table 27-10-0273-01, "Gross domestic expenditures on research and development, by science type and by funder and performer sector (x 1,000,000)."

While far from major funders or performers, private sector firms are key in framing and motivating provincial innovation policy. Winnipeg held an early advantage in wholesale and commodity trading with its location at the eastern point of the triangle of arable land in the Prairies, leading both Canadian National and Canadian Pacific to choose the city to coordinate their final move of cars to ports in Thunder Bay and Quebec City for shipment to Europe. That led to the early location of major grain-handling firms in Winnipeg, and then the formation of the Winnipeg Commodity Exchange and the Canadian Wheat Board. Early agricultural equipment manufacturing and wholesale goods and distribution also co-located. More recently, grain handling has changed markedly, with the exit of the large integrated co-ops and the wind-down of federal single-desk selling. Nevertheless, the industry left a legacy of a number of large, long-term, family-owned firms such as Richardson Pioneer, Parrish & Heimbecker, and Paterson Grain, all of which have headquarters in downtown Winnipeg. This is undoubtedly part of the reason Winnipeg hosts the Canadian branch offices for Cargill and Monsanto, two global agricultural companies, and why the city is home to troops of federal grain regulatory personnel, including the main office of the Canadian Grain Commission. As a result, numerous national agricultural commodity non-governmental organizations, such as the Canada Grains Council, Pulse Canada, Cereals Canada, Canadian Canola Growers, and Canola Council of Canada, have located in the city; in aggregate they manage significant private resources for R&D on behalf of their farmer members.

Winnipeg's useful distribution location and historical investment in equipment manufacturing have led to a healthy equipment manufacturing sector in Manitoba, with firms producing agricultural equipment (MacDon, Buhler), buses (New Flyer) and aerospace equipment (Magellan, Winnipeg Aero Space, Boeing Canada). The aerospace sector has grown to be Canada's third-largest agglomeration, producing world-class products for customers on six continents. From modest roots in small bush plane repair in the 1930s, the industry has grown to include design, manufacturing, servicing, testing, certification, and research and development capabilities. The province has Canada's largest aerospace composite manufacturing centre, as well as the world's largest independent gas turbine engine repair and overhaul company, drawing on capacity from the Composites Innovation Centre and advanced aircraft engine testing and certification centres developed by Rolls Royce, Pratt & Whitney, and GE Aviation. A network of small and medium-sized enterprises is growing to supply the sector, strengthened through the provincial Competitive Edge Supplier Development initiative to support supplier and supply chain development. Aerospace has more than 30 companies and more than 5,300 employees.

Technology-focused trade papers suggest Winnipeg is particularly well placed to host technology start-ups. The traditional pitch is that the province offers generous tax credits, a low cost of living, and what the Filmon government in 1997 called "The Manitoba Advantage," a package of lower energy prices, fibre optic connectivity, modest office rental costs, and a publicly funded health sciences cluster. The province also offers fast-track visas for tech developers through the Provincial Nominee Immigration Program. One relevant measure was the 58.5 per cent growth in tech jobs over the 2013–18 period, with Winnipeg outpacing all other major urban centres in Canada (Brotzky 2018). Florida, Mellander, and Stolarick (2010) suggest that Winnipeg's cultural assets might be more important for attracting the creative class and for the success of tech firms such as Skip the Dishes, Farmers Edge, and Sightline Innovation than general economic conditions, place-based assets of clusters, or the dynamics of the local innovation system. The Manitoba Advantage pitch highlights that Winnipeg's per capita ticket revenues from the arts, numerous festivals, and cultural organizations are the highest in North America.

Like much else in the province, politics is dominated by what happens in Winnipeg, the provincial capital, if for no other reason than that the Winnipeg metro area represents forty-eight of the fifty-seven seats in the legislative assembly. Since the 1960s, Manitoba's provincial governments have been mostly centrist, shifting moderately to the left or right as governments change. A conservative base is well established in agriculturally focused communities and in the smaller cities, but Winnipeg and northern Manitoba have been swing regions in both provincial and federal elections for at least sixty years. Liberals, Conservatives, and New Democrats have all been elected in Winnipeg's downtown core over the past twenty years. The importance of the city has led perhaps to uneven power in the hands of large unions within the city of Winnipeg and with general municipal interests. They have imposed their will on electoral politics at times. The election of Premier Brian Pallister and his Progressive Conservative (PC) government in 2016 marked a bit of a departure, with his government staking out a more robust, right-of-centre package of priorities, including funding for business innovations. Despite Pallister's departure as premier in 2021, the governing PCs continue with their policies.

The Policy Effort

After 1988, Manitoba's provincial policy was dominated by two premiers, PC Gary Filmon from 1988 to 1999, and New Democrat Gary Doer from 1999 to 2009, after which Doer was followed by Greg Selinger (Doer's finance minister). From 2016 to 2021, the Manitoba government was led by PC Brian Pallister. In reviewing Hansard, we can see that, in Throne Speeches, Filmon regularly mentioned science, innovation and the MRC as part of his strategy to grow the economy of Manitoba. In his government, the MRC was controlled by the Minister of Industry, Trade and Tourism. In 1999 alone, $2.5 million in support was provided by this ministry as grants through the Innovation and Technology Fund, and another $7.3 million was given to the Manitoba Health Research Council, the Health Research Initiative, and Agri-Food Research and Development Initiative.

Unlike Filmon, Doer seldom mentioned science or innovation in Throne Speeches. Science was usually contextualized to training and education, and if innovation was mentioned, it usually was related to the civil service delivering better services matched more systematically to community needs. Nevertheless, financial support for basic science and innovation programming stayed steady throughout Doer's government and in most of the budgets of his successor, Greg Selinger, although one could detect over time a shift of resources towards health research. In Doer's last year, 2009, a revamped MRC called the Manitoba Research and Innovation Fund had a budget of $12.6 million. In contrast, the Agri-Food Research and Development Initiative dropped to $750,000, a reduction of over 70 per cent from 1999, while the Manitoba Health Research Council's budget increased to $6 million. Jumping ahead another decade, in 2019, Research Manitoba – which had replaced the Manitoba Health Research Council, the Manitoba Research and Innovation Fund, and the Health Research Initiative – was limited to a combined budget of only $12 million, the equivalent of a 35 per cent cut from 2009 (Research Manitoba n.d.).

Provincial support for the universities has been consistent but modest. When forming his first government, Filmon asked former premier Duff Roblin to review the mandates of higher education in Manitoba; this led to several years of increased direct support. In the early 1990s, however, Filmon lowered provincial support and allowed the universities to make up the difference by increasing student fees. New Democrat governments, under both Doer and Selinger, then froze student fees without offering much in the way of additional support. One result is that the University of Manitoba has among the lowest-paid professors of any research-intensive university in the country (UMFA 2020).

As everywhere, Manitoba has rising expectations that the university sector will engage more in economic development. There is some evidence of the entrepreneurial university mission taking hold, especially at the University of Manitoba under President Emőke Szathmáry (1996–2008) and at the University of Winnipeg under President Lloyd Axworthy (2004–14). Szathmáry presided over the creation of the University of Manitoba's 100-acre Smartpark Research and Technology Park, and worked to attract key investments for the park from the National Research Council (NRC), Cangene, Monsanto, and the Richardson family. Smartpark was modelled after the University of Saskatchewan's successful Innovation Place in Saskatoon. As of 2020, Smartpark had 18 tenants employing around 1,200 people in 9 buildings with 415,000 square feet of research space (University of Manitoba n.d. a).

Both the University of Manitoba and the University of Winnipeg have played roles in a number of major innovation developments, but a general lack of faith in these institutions suggests public scepticism about the function and impact of the modern university. This was clearly stated in the Roblin report, and one can hear echoes of this even today:

> Research is an essential university function in which the wider community has a vital interest. A more effective link between universities and the community must be achieved. We estimate that, in 1992/1993, in addition to externally sponsored research, the University of Manitoba devoted about $60 million, mostly publicly funded, to internal unsponsored self-directed research including graduate studies. Over time, this represents a large investment by Manitobans. As far as we could ascertain from the information available to us, this self-directed research is only tenuously linked to Manitoba's social, cultural and economic interests. There is little policy pointing the direction of research to these areas. Technology transfer is underdeveloped. This need not be so. The success of the University of Manitoba Faculty of Agriculture in undertaking outreach to its provincial constituency while gaining scholarly recognition internationally is a case in point. We recommend that better links be formed both by policy and infrastructure to connect internally self-directed university research to Manitoba's social, cultural and economic interests. To assist the process, we recommend that the Provincial Government, through the Economic Innovation and Technology Council, convene regular meetings of interested parties, especially from the small business sector, to highlight the issues and promote practical interconnections. (Roblin 1993, 1)

Despite these perceived weaknesses, the university system anchors two nationally competitive research-intensive clusters: agri-food R&D and biomedicine.

Agri-food Research and Development

The University of Manitoba is home to one of Canada's major agricultural colleges, which has made major contributions to plant breeding and agronomy. The development of canola, Canada's first domestic edible oilseed, was a collaboration (sometimes competition) between Agriculture and Agri-Food Canada and NRC research staff in Saskatoon and university faculty at the University of Manitoba. Dr Baldur Stefansson, a University of Manitoba plant scientist, was one of the "fathers" of this Cinderella of crops, which now supports an industrial effort that generates more than $27 billion of activity annually in Canada (ILMC International 2016). There have been rapeseed and canola breeders at the University of Manitoba since the 1960s; investments to support the emerging bioscience related to new traits in canola have led to a significant investment in plant breeding in Winnipeg since the mid-1990s. Monsanto invested in a major breeding operation in Winnipeg in 2009; the laboratory remained in Winnipeg even after the company's merger with Bayer in 2019 (Dawson 2019). Agriculture remains one of Manitoba's success stories. Driven by the widespread adoption of canola and shorter season varieties of corn and soybeans, Manitoba's agricultural GDP grew 147 per cent from 1997 to 2018, the largest growth in that sector of any province over that period.

Food processing, nutraceuticals, and agronomy illustrate the nature of the challenges of innovating in smaller provinces. Although Manitoba is more diversified than Alberta and Saskatchewan, there historically has been concern that too much of its production is exported as low-value commodities. Most provincial governments in Manitoba have offered some form of support to add value to agricultural output. One of the creations of the MRC (in collaboration with federal labs) was the Food Development Centre (FDC) in Portage la Prairie, created in 1978 to carry out R&D for small food manufacturing firms (FDC n.d.). In fiscal year 2017/18 alone, the FDC reported it had helped develop 28 new food product prototypes, launched 8 new food products, answered 324 technical requests for 230 clients, created 271 food labels for 134 clients, and developed 63 US nutrition facts tables for 20 Canadian companies and 5 Canadian nutrition facts tables for 3 US clients, which generated $1.25 million in new retail sales (FDC n.d.). Provincial, federal, and private funds have also been used to support development of nutraceuticals thorough the Richardson Centre for Functional Foods and Nutraceuticals (RCFFN). The current provincial government points to the FDC, RCFFN, Canadian Centre for Agri-food Research in Health and Medicine, and related science-based departments at the University of Manitoba as forming a cluster of food science excellence in Winnipeg. This cluster has been credited with attracting recent investment in R&D-intensive food- and nutrient-focused firms, such as the $400 million Roquette pea-processing plant at Portage la Prairie and the $65 million Merit Functional Foods plant in Centreport, the world's first commercial canola-protein manufacturing plant.

One part of the acknowledged success in agri-food research is the linkage between the research system and users. Proactive extension programs run by the provincial government, the University of Manitoba Faculty of Agriculture and Food Sciences (and former Manitoba

College of Agriculture), and some of the commodity associations have a long history of taking the latest agronomic knowledge into the farm community, which has been a strong impetuous for the uptake and use of new technologies and new seeds. In the late 1990s, Manitoba reduced its agricultural extension service (as did Saskatchewan and Alberta). Alston et al. (2000) estimate that the average rate of return for public extension investments was as high as 80 per cent, which strongly suggests that more, not less, extension would have been justified. Despite this evidence, government funds were cut. There is no clear evidence of whether Manitoba's divestment was strategic or simply an unintended victim of Filmon's austerity-focused government. Some extension work continued, but undoubtedly at suboptimal levels. Meanwhile, there is significant continuing capacity to support knowledge translation from research to practice at the University of Manitoba, which offers a two-year diploma within its Agricultural Faculty to train future farmers.

While farm production has not suffered from the extension divestment, it is unclear what industrial productivity might have been forgone. Crop yields have jumped significantly in recent years, partly because higher world prices have supported higher levels of inputs. The private sector – especially farm input providers and grain-handling firms with an interest in large volumes of grain – has taken on some of this extension role. This service has evolved into a new line of business for many firms, generates good returns for both farmers and the handling companies, and is one asset some are hoping will provide a base for exploiting new automated sensing and digitally assisted decision making.

The Protein Industries supercluster, of which Manitoba is a partner, is one venture that hopes to tap into the big data generated by new technology embedded in farm equipment to improve agronomy. One of Manitoba's leaders in this venture is Farmers Edge, which started in 2005 as a new type of agronomy consulting firm and is a leading innovator generating fees from farmers for data-driven advice to maximize returns (Phillips et al. 2019). Farmers Edge has partnered with Sightline Innovation, a Manitoba-based firm applying artificial intelligence, to scale up its information-technology-based advice apps to a worldwide presence (Farmers Edge n.d.).

Biomedicine and Medical Devices

Manitoba also hosts a life sciences cluster anchored on biomedicine and medical devices. Twenty years ago, the Winnipeg biomedical cluster did not exist. The entire biomedical community numbered about nine hundred individuals working in universities and hospital research laboratories. Although Winnipeg was home to leading research in the life sciences, especially infectious diseases, this had not translated into economic development or the creation and growth of innovative firms. Since then, the Winnipeg biomedical community has developed a growing cluster from its strong research foundation, now home to 8 per cent of Canada's biotech activity (Economic Development Winnipeg n.d.). The cluster has five main components: diagnostic techniques and methods; imaging software and technologies; medical manufacturing; telecommunications, software, and hardware (for the distant communication of medical images and linking devices, and services); and expertise in health systems (health economics and how devices and technologies are integrated into health institutions and systems).

A big part of the biomedical cluster's success is the federal and provincial research facilities located in and around Winnipeg that partner with the University of Manitoba, a leading medical-doctoral institution. The city hosts the Public Health Agency of Canada National Microbiology Laboratory, the I.H. Asper Clinical Research Institute, Biovail's Steinbach drug manufacturing facility, the Winnipeg-based Canadian Science Centre for Human and Animal Health (a biosafety Level 4 lab that is exploring upgrading to Level 5), the NRC Medical Devices Research Centre (formerly NRC-Institute for Biodiagnostics), the University of Manitoba Faculty of Medicine, the St. Boniface Hospital & Research Foundation, CancerCare, the University of Manitoba's Biomedical Engineering program, Red River College's Medical Radiologic Technician program, and a new partnership and investment between Siemens Healthcare and the Institute for Advanced Medicine at the Health Sciences Centre.

The cluster contributes almost 8 per cent of the province's GDP, and more than twenty-five viable biomedical firms employ more than four thousand highly skilled personnel (Economic Development Winnipeg n.d.). There is a healthy pipeline of start-ups and early-stage firms, and a growing commercial sector and network of support services in both the private and public sectors. The local supply chain, while not yet fully developed, is becoming more extensive and robust. Key commercial actors, many spun out of local research, include Cangene Corporation, Biovail Corporation, Intelligent Hospital Systems, Apotex Fermentation Inc., Younes Respiratory Tech, Monteris Medical, and Koven Technology Canada.

The Winnipeg biomedical cluster links the local community with industry and research linkages across Canada through satellite institutes of the NRC Medical Devices Research Centre in Halifax and Calgary and a series of international connections. The cluster also has strong linkages with the Life Science Alley biomedical cluster in Minneapolis–St. Paul, Minnesota, helping to integrate Winnipeg companies into the supply chain there, as well as using it as a gateway to the US market. The Bioscience Association of Manitoba and Life Science Alley industry association in Minneapolis are working to strengthen that relationship and align it with Manitoba's Mid-continent Trade Corridor marketing strategy (NRC 1979). The cluster also has links to the larger North American and European markets through Siemens (Germany), Medtronic (United States), and Sentinelle Medical (Toronto).

That Winnipeg has managed to secure a foothold in the biomedical industry is, however, much more a story of local and established strengths, especially in the areas of leadership, entrepreneurship, and research. Fittingly, much of the biomedical cluster's industrial strength and export performance come from manufacturing, an area in which Winnipeg traditionally has been strong: since early on in its economic history, manufacturing has figured prominently in Winnipeg's industry structure. As in other sectors and provinces, local entrepreneurs and leaders have leveraged research from federal labs and university and health research facilities, and merged with local capacity – in this case, including some highly skilled personnel recruited from the aerospace sector – to exploit market opportunities locally and globally.

Conclusion and Lessons

One commentator has noted that Manitoba's innovation history lays out the set for what could an innovation play, but there is no obvious script or plot. In the context of the "3 Is" of innovation discussed in this book – ideas, interests, and institutions – Manitoba is aware of the many new ideas about innovation, mostly through interactions with federal programs and initiatives, but has seldom been driven to be an early adopter. There is a full cast of actors, but the motivations are subtle at best.

Many agents in Manitoba's innovation space have made many of the right choices, but there appears to be a failure to launch. This might be due to the very stability and diversification that Winnipeg brings to Manitoba's economy. There is an absence of economic busts and hard times that in other regions might have led to greater incentive for innovation. Busts generate their own form of destruction, which motivates firms and sectors to make the hard decisions to change what they do; in some sectors, booms are motivating, but in the absence of any willingness to creatively destroy some of the built capital and markets, they do not transform the sector.

In the one sector where there has been some success, agriculture, weak returns in the 1980s contributed to efforts by the players in that space to innovate. The massive restructuring of the wholesale grain-handling business in the 2005–12 period, centred largely in Winnipeg, gave an added boost to new ideas and new approaches. The significant and relatively strong growth in agriculture in Manitoba suggests that the tonic helped. The industry faces a new set of challenges from the digitization of the market and industrial system, and the Manitoba sector seems to have responded in real time. Recent technological innovations, such as the agronomy services of Farmers Edge or the protein processing at the Roquette and Merit Functional Foods plants, are too recent to be evaluated or validated. But they might soon affirm Hawkins' (2012) assertion that the key to Canadian innovation is the history and market dynamics of the natural endowments of our regions. The successful firms innovating in Manitoba are rooted in the provincial agricultural sector, drawing on the endowments in the grain companies, the capacity generated through the effort to develop such key successes as canola, and the entrepreneurial efforts to exploit cutting-edge breeding technologies and data science.

Manitoba now has an opportunity to generalize its successes in agriculture, and a start has been made in the aerospace and biomedical sectors. The Roblin (1993) review of the universities pointed the way, but so far most industries and institutions have been profitable enough being average. As industries digitize around the world, however, we are seeing that few firms or regions thrive in the middle: the gains from production and innovation are concentrating in the hands of first movers and dominant market players. Manitoba will need to come to grips with this risk in the not-so-distant future.

References

Brotzky, I. 2018. "Canada's Fastest Growing Tech Hub: Winnipeg and Saskatoon." *VanHack*, 1 February. Online at https://vanhack.com/blog/winnipeg-tech-jobs/, accessed 20 April 2020.

Alston, J.M., M.C. Marra, P.G. Pardey, and T.J. Wyatt. 2000. *A Meta Analysis of Rates of Return to Agricultural R&D: ex pede Herculem?* IFPRI Research Report 113. Washington, DC: International Food Policy Research Institute.

Byrne, K. 2019. "Five of the Coldest Cities in the World." AccuWeather. Online at https://www.accuweather.com/en/weather-news/5-of-the-coldest-cities-in-the-world/434260, accessed 20 April 2020.

Canada. 2020. "Facilities: Manitoba." Online at https://profils-profiles.science.gc.ca/en/facilities, Accessed 20 April 2020.

CMHR (Canadian Museum for Human Rights). n.d. "CMHR releases important archaeology findings: New light cast on historic role of The Forks." Online at https://humanrights.ca/news/cmhr-releases-important-archaeology-findings-new-light-cast-on-historic-role-of-the-forks, accessed 20 April 2020.

Dawson, A. 2019. "Monsanto Canada's Winnipeg office closing, Sept. 1, 2019." *Manitoba Co-operator*. Online at https://www.manitobacooperator.ca/news-opinion/news/monsanto-canadas-winnipeg-office-closing-sept-1-2019/, accessed 20 April 2020.

Economic Development Winnipeg. 2020. "Key Industries." Online at https://www.economicdevelopmentwinnipeg.com/, accessed 20 April 2020.

Economic Development Winnipeg. n.d. "Winnipeg's Life Sciences Industry Sector Overview." Online at https://www.economicdevelopmentwinnipeg.com/, accessed 20 December 2020.

Farmers Edge. n.d. "About Us." Online at https://www.farmersedge.ca/about-us/, accessed 20 April 2020.

FDC (Food Development Centre). n.d. "About Us." Online at https://www.gov.mb.ca/agriculture/food-and-ag-processing/starting-a-food-business/food-development-centre/about-us.html, accessed 20 April 2020.

Florida, R., C. Mellander, and K. Stolarick. 2010. "Talent, Technology and Tolerance in Canadian Regional Development." *Canadian Geographer* 54 (3): 277–304. https://doi.org/10.1111/j.1541-0064.2009.00293.x.

Gibson, R., J. Barrett, and S. Parmiter. 2013. *Philanthropy as a Vehicle for Regional Development*. St. John's: Memorial University of Newfoundland, Harris Centre.

Hawkins, R. 2012. "Looking at Innovation from a Uniquely Canadian Perspective." Discussion Paper for the Institute for Science, Society and Policy, University of Ottawa.

LMC International. 2016. *The Economic Impact of Canola on the Canadian Economy. A Report for the Canola Council of Canada*. Online at https://www.canolacouncil.org/download/215/pages/5255/lmc_canola_10-year_impact_study_-_canada_final_dec_2016, accessed 20 April 2020.

Manitoba. 2020. "Province creates new protein consortium to further Manitoba's protein advantage strategy." News release, 21 January. Online at https://news.gov.mb.ca/news/index.html?item=46740, accessed 20 April 2020.

McNicholl, M.K. 2015. "Manitoba Research Council." *Canadian Encyclopedia*. Online at https://www.thecanadianencyclopedia.ca/en/article/manitoba-research-council, accessed 20 April 2020.

Neville, W.F.W. 2010. "Duff Roblin, 1958–1967." In *Manitoba Premiers of the 19th and 20th Centuries*, ed. B. Ferguson and R. Wardhaugh. Regina: Canadian Plains Research Centre.

NRC (National Research Council). 1979. *Portfolio Evaluation of the NRC Technology Cluster Initiatives, Final Report*. Ottawa: NRC, Corporate Services.

Phillips, P., J. Relf-Eckstein, G. Jobe, and B. Wixted. 2019. "Configuring the New Digital Landscape in Western Canadian Agriculture." *NJAS-Wageningen Journal of Life Sciences* 90–91, 100295. https://doi.org/10.1016/j.njas.2019.04.001

Research Manitoba. n.d. "About Us." Online at https://researchmanitoba.ca/about/about-us/.

Roblin, D. 1993. *Post-secondary Education in Manitoba: Doing Things Differently, Executive Summary.* Report of the University Education Review Commission. Online at https://www.gov.mb.ca/educate/postsec/roblin/rexecsum/rexecsum.html, accessed 20 April 2020.

Spencer, G. 2014. *Cluster Atlas of Canada.* Toronto: University of Toronto, Munk School of Global Affairs.

Statistics Canada. 2020. "Federal personnel engaged in science and technology by geography." Table 27-10-0011-01. Online at https://www150.statcan.gc.ca/t1/tbl1/en/cv.action?pid=2710001101#timeframe, accessed 20 April 2020.

Statistics Canada. n.d.a. "GDP at basic prices." Tables 3610040201 and 3610022201. Online at https://www150.statcan.gc.ca/t1/tbl1/en/cv.action?pid=3610022201#timeframe, and https://www150.statcan.gc.ca/t1/tbl1/en/tv.action?pid=3610040201, accessed 20 April 2020.

Statistics Canada. n.d.b. "GDP for metro areas and provinces." Table 361 0046801. Online at https://www150.statcan.gc.ca/t1/tbl1/en/tv.action?pid=3610046801, accessed 20 April 2020.

Taylor, G., and P. Baskerville. 1994. *Concise History of Business in Canada.* Oxford: Oxford University Press.

UMFA (University of Manitoba Faculty Association). 2016. "2016 UMFA Salary Information." Online at https://umanitoba.ca/admin/human_resources/staff_relations/bargaining/6127.html, accessed 20 April 2020.

University of Manitoba. n.d.a. "About Smartpark Research Park." Online at http://umanitoba.ca/admin/vp_admin/smartpark/history/about.html, accessed 20 April 2020.

University of Manitoba. n.d.b. "The University of Manitoba – Strategic Research Plan 2015–2020." Online at https://umanitoba.ca/research/media/Strategic_Research_Plan.pdf, accessed 20 April 2020.

12 Saskatchewan: Where Innovation Is a Contact Sport

PETER W.B. PHILLIPS AND ANNE BALLANTYNE

Given its rural base and natural resource dependence, Saskatchewan is an unlikely participant in the innovation policy space. Few in Canadian policy circles call out the province as a key player. Admittedly the province has had difficulty framing a compelling policy rhetoric or set of enduring institutions and mechanisms, yet some sectors have exhibited sustained innovation. Despite a relatively poor natural endowment, climate, and location, the agri-food sector is world competitive, almost exclusively due to sustained innovative efforts. Other sectors have followed suit, with many of the export-dependent industries generating or using world-leading technologies. For the most part, Saskatchewan has realized success by pursuing a mixture of public, private, university, and producer partnerships that exploit the endowments of clustered communities and tap into the pipelines of related innovation systems. While not universally transferrable, Saskatchewan's experience offers some lessons for other, similarly endowed smaller provinces.

Context

The innovation treadmill is one dominant narrative in Saskatchewan. As a resource and trade dependent economy, the province has to run quickly to sustain relative income levels. Most of Saskatchewan's products trade in volatile export markets. Over the past century of development, the province has gone through a sequence of booms and busts, with the terms of trade and markets gyrating in response to volatile global supply and uncertain demand. Provincially, demographics have tracked the volatile economy, with large inflows of skilled and semi-skilled workers during booms and equally large and rapid outflows during contractions (Phillips 1999).

From 2015 to 2020, more than half of Saskatchewan's gross domestic product (GDP) was generated through goods production, most of it exported; services-producing industries contributed less in Saskatchewan than in any other province. Resource depletion works to depress multifactor productivity in many of these sectors, making research and innovation all the more important. Saskatchewan has had significant success in gaining first-mover and early-adopter returns from developing and exploiting improvements in production systems and supply chains, but its global competitors almost as quickly adapt and adopt anything we use. The net result is that every improvement generates only temporary gains: rising global productivity drives real prices lower over the long term, necessitating further innovation. This treadmill metaphor describes almost every sector and every firm in the province.

Multinational firms have been major economic players in the development of Saskatchewan, but at times have been fair-weather friends, taking downturns as reason to retreat or exit to other, more stable and profitable markets. This has frustrated citizens, producers, communities, and governments alike. In response, the province has been a hotbed of organizational innovation to supplement or replace weak for-profit performance (Phillips and Webb 2014a). From the early days, farmers imported and adapted the co-operative model from the United Kingdom and United States, forming marketing co-operatives and then an extensive network of processing, wholesale, and retail co-ops and credit unions. These enterprises dominated in the agri-food sector and in rural Saskatchewan, controlling at their peak in the 1990s the bulk of the farm input, processing, and marketing assets and business, owning and managing the only oil refinery, and managing a plurality of the province's financial intermediation. Governments have also been more engaged in the economy than in many other provinces. After 1944, a new social democratic government – the first in North America – moved to develop tools for expanding the role of government, including creating the first planning and budget bureaus in the Commonwealth and expanding the use of Crown-owned enterprises in the economy. At its peak in the early 1980s, the Crown sector both directly owned and operated all of the utility companies in the province and had a stake in virtually every firm of any significance, except in the primary farm sector, which was dominated by co-operatives. That included at least a minority stake in every oil, gas, and mining development, majority control of potash and uranium, and equity in most larger manufacturing firms. While the contribution of both co-ops and Crowns to provincial GDP has dropped by about half since 1980,

Saskatchewan remains differentially dependent on those two extra-market organizational systems.

Against this background, Saskatchewan faces three long-term challenges. First, wide gyrations in resource prices have caused the province to swing between "have" and "have-not" status, one of the few provinces to do so (Phillips 1998). Extended periods of dependence on equalization payments worked to create a welfare-trap mentality in the provincial corridors of power, as new development was expected at best simply to reduce equalization payments and at worst to cause net losses. This was a bigger problem than in other provinces, as the provincial treasury board and cabinet had such wide powers and reach through their Crown holdings that their decisions often worked to suppress overall investment in research and development (R&D) and productivity growth (Phillips and Webb 2014a). Conservation of capital dominated thinking, at least until the commodity supercycle that started in 1996 and peaked in 2011 (Büyükşahin, Kun, and Zmitrowicz 2016) hoisted the province unambiguously into the "have" category. A concomitant problem that has diminished in recent years is that global price signals often were weak, as state ownership, supply management, and various public interventions in the resources market – including the Canadian Wheat Board's single-desk-selling function, various energy programs, and the Canpotex global marketing effort – dampened the effects of global price changes on firm-level investment decisions.

Second, most of the goods in which Saskatchewan has a comparative advantage are globally controversial. The province is the world's top producer of uranium, which has generated pushback locally and globally since its development. Now, with the focus on greenhouse gas emissions, the large carbon footprints of food and natural resources sectors (farming, coal, oil, gas, power generation, mining, and transportation) create concern about carbon management policies. This adds to the angst in the crops-based sector, which has faced significant market disruption following its development and adoption of some of the world's first and most competitive transgenically modified crop varieties.

Third, the province has one of the largest percentages of Indigenous peoples in Canada, with more than 16 per cent of residents recording First Nations or Métis backgrounds in the 2016 census, lower than the Territories and Manitoba but more than three times the national average. Although all First Nations in the province have treaties, many of those were not fully met in the past. First Nations and Métis peoples historically have been isolated from the market economy, but that is changing. In recent years, more than half of the people entering the provincial labour force have been young Indigenous workers, many with tertiary education and skills training. Effectively, efficiently, and equitably engaging First Nations in the economy is a generational challenge, somewhat complicated when industries are innovating and investing to reduce their labour requirements and operational costs.

Innovation Architecture

Interests and institutions have been more influential than ideas in the evolution of provincial strategy in Saskatchewan. Ideas have been more justifications for, rather than drivers of, action. Governments in Saskatchewan, like many other governments, have wish lists for their citizens: more employment; larger incomes; more wealth; higher standards of living; and, implicitly, sustainability of their populations. During the past half-century, Saskatchewan governments have tried the whole range of policies in pursuit of these goals. Before innovation became a focus in the late 1980s, provincial policy was mostly targeted at stabilizing the macroeconomy, promoting export growth (sometimes import substitution), and attracting turnkey foreign investment in industrial plants (Phillips 1999). But the open structure of the provincial economy (and one of the lowest provincial economic multipliers) neutralized the benefits of most of these strategies. Tax cuts, subsidies, and other discretionary spending usually had little lasting impact on the economy.

While research and innovation has been important since the beginning of the province, and specific stories of key breakthroughs can be found in each sector, the first evidence that the province was taking proactive measures in this policy file emerged in the late 1980s, when Grant Devine's Progressive Conservative (PC) government created the first provincial department of Science and Technology. Since then, the province has promoted clusters, worked with innovation systems, and toyed with the creative-class hypothesis. Which set of ideas dominated can be traced to which political party had power and how it interacted with the industrial opportunities in the economy.

Saskatchewan has an aggressive left-right political discourse – although Eager (1980) argues this is more style than substance. The rhetoric suggests quite divergent aspirations: the Allan Blakeney New Democratic Party (NDP) government (1972–81) created "the family of Crown corporations" to drive the economy; the Devine PC government (1982–91) announced it was "open for business," and pursued "public participation" to rebalance the economy, with new joint-stock companies controlling the resource economy; the Romanow NDP government (1991–2001) created "partnership" plans to drive fiscal renewal and growth; the Calvert NDP administration (2001–07) advocated "balanced" growth with a modest focus on the economy; and the Wall and Moe Saskatchewan Party governments (since 2007), elected on the upswing of the commodity supercycle, shifted the focus towards a host of special ventures to grow industry.

While the rhetoric sounds divergent, the specific actions were quite similar. In most cases, governments worked with available resources and opportunities and those willing to develop them. In earlier years, that entailed one-off industrial joint ventures, often with out-of-province investors, such as in the wood and pulp sector (PAPCO, Millar Western), steel (IPSCO), meat processing (Intercontinental Packers and Maple Leaf), heavy oil (Husky and Federated Co-op Refinery), and fertilizers (Saskferco). The focus was almost exclusively on "the deal," rather than on creating the conditions for more widespread industrial development or innovation.

As provincial governments gained experience with firms and sectors, they learned that the broader operating context for specific projects was as or more important for long-term success than any terms of the deal. The clusters model was introduced to the province in the late 1980s as graduates from Harvard were recruited to the civil service. The model resonated with firms and government officials – most recognized that enterprises locating in places with competing and collaborating firms that generate thick labour markets and extensive forward and backward linkages were doing better than firms in greenfield sites. The clusters idea was first formally embodied in the Partnership for Renewal provincial strategy in 1992, and has continued, albeit often unacknowledged, ever since.

In the late 1990s and early 2000s, the province also accepted the need for more capital for universities to anchor local nodes in the global innovation systems of particular interest to provincial industry. The agricultural biosciences are one example of sustained public, private, university, and producer engagement, with substantial success (Boland, Phillips, and Ryan 2010; Boland et al. 2012; Phillips and Khachatourians 2001). Both funding for and leadership of this effort shifted to the universities. The University of Saskatchewan, in particular, has had significant success leveraging federal funding to secure new science infrastructure – for example, Canadian Light Source and VIDO-InterVac – and large-scale research projects – for example, two $20-million-plus Canada Excellence Research Chairs (CERCs) and two Canada First Research Excellence Fund (CFREF) projects together worth more than $100 million. All these ventures were premised on the concepts embodied in the innovation systems literature, and especially the entrepreneurial university model espoused as part of the triple-helix theory. The province has assisted university efforts to attract world-class researchers through matching grants for Canada Research Chairs (CRCs), CERCs, and various research institutes, while the Saskatoon municipal government has worked to promote itself as "Paris of the Prairies," a "creative capital," and "science city" in an effort to overcome the city's image as relatively small, physical isolated, climatically challenged, and culturally homogenous. There is some evidence that the city has some pull: surveys show that those who come to the city and stay are attracted by many of its cluster and innovation system attributes (Phillips and Webb 2016).

Translating interests and institutions into measurable effort, we observe gross expenditure on R&D (GERD) in Saskatchewan has averaged only about 0.85 per cent, which is among the lowest in Canada. The array of institutions engaged in the research and innovation policy space is large, but the number of institutions actually undertaking significant R&D is smaller than in larger provinces (Table 12.1).

The public sector funds the lion's share of the province's R&D. The federal government is the key player, investing more than $140 million annually, about half of which is performed inside federal labs, including the NRC, Agriculture and Agri-food Canada, the Canadian Food Inspection Agency, and Environment and Climate Change Canada. Most of the rest of federal support and much of the provincial funding flow through the universities. Provincial funds come from two sources: the Ministry of Agriculture, which has always allocated funds to support R&D in the farm sector, and, initially, the Ministry of Advanced Education, but now Innovation Saskatchewan, a special operating agency that supports six institutions and foundations in the life and physical sciences. Provincial allocations are targeted to leverage federal money in areas of provincial interest. The Saskatchewan Research Council (SRC), founded as a Crown corporation in 1947 to facilitate R&D in the province, is one of the few remaining traditional provincial research organizations undertaking research. When it opened its own laboratories in 1958, they were aligned with academic disciplines, but in 1972 the SRC refocused work to support industry sectors (such as agriculture/biotechnology, energy, the environment, and mining). Cities are also active players: the provincial Regional Economic Development Authority (REDA) program and the federal Community Futures program in the 1980s encouraged urban and rural communities to collaborate to form larger development authorities. There is now a range of community and regional authorities across the province, with the two centred on Regina and Saskatoon the most aggressively engaged in the innovation file, albeit in a modest way.

Table 12.1. Gross Expenditure on Research and Development by Performing Sector, average $ millions, Saskatchewan, 2013–17

Funders	Total	Government Federal	Government Provincial	Provincial Research Organizations	Business Enterprise	Higher Education	Private Non-profit
Total sectors	638	71	4	15	264	285	–
Federal government	142	71	–	–	10	61	–
Provincial government	37	–	4	3	5	26	–
Business enterprise	254	–	–	6	233	15	–
Higher education	162	–	–	–	–	162	–
Private non-profit	23	–	–	–	2	21	–
Foreign	17	–	–	1	16	1	–

Note: Columns and rows may not sum due to rounding.

Source: Statistics Canada, table 27-10-0273-01, "Gross domestic expenditures on research and development, by science type and by funder and performer sector (x 1,000,000)."

Firms fund a bit over 40 per cent and perform about 35 per cent of total R&D in the province, but no firm in Saskatchewan cracks the "top 100 industry performers in Canada," which means no firm invests more than $10 million annually. The biggest investors are farm commodity groups such as the Western Grains Research Foundation, SaskCanola, Saskatchewan Pulse Growers, and the Saskatchewan Wheat Commission, which levy fees on sales for collective action (usually called "check-offs"). Commodity groups generate significant resources, which they use to fund industrial research and market development, usually in collaboration with firms, public labs, and university researchers.

Universities are the second-biggest player. Saskatchewan's higher education R&D is differentially supported by provincial operating grants and industrial funds, with weak performance in the standard grant processes run by the federal Tri-Council, especially the Canadian Institutes of Health Research. Saskatchewan's main success is in strategic research ventures: two of eighteen Canada First Excellence Research Excellence Fund grants, two of thirty-five Canada Excellence Research Chairs, one of twenty-four Canada 150 Research Chairs, and a disproportionate share of Genome Canada–funded research grants. The province has also benefited from Canada Foundation for Innovation–funded infrastructure competitions. Apart from the Saskatchewan Health Research Foundation, a small provincially funded grant program, the province has no local health research foundations of any size directly funding health-related research.

Somewhat surprisingly, given this set of circumstances, Saskatchewan has delivered some world-first innovations, and its foundational biosciences cluster is globally recognized (Phillips et al. 2015). For the most part, R&D seems less important for innovation in sectors dominant in Saskatchewan. Specific stories about the policy effort help to explain that apparent contradiction.

The Policy Efforts

Saskatchewan's efforts to incentivize science and technology development have ebbed and flowed between strategic and tactical engagements at the local and global levels. Four key stories reveal the dynamics and circumstances underlying success, failure, and the future.

The Biosciences Success Story

In many ways, the biosciences success in Saskatchewan appears both inevitable and exemplary. Agricultural research has been sited in Saskatoon on the university campus for more than a century, with federal labs and university academics variously taking the lead (Phillips et al. 2004). The largely public research system delivered Marquis wheat in the 1920s, an early maturing variety credited with opening western Canadian agriculture, the rust-resistant Selkirk wheat variety in the 1950s, double-zero rapeseed (canola) in the 1970s (Phillips and Khachatourians 2001), and in the 2010s a series of world firsts in lentil breeding. Each advance overcame technical hurdles and met economic needs. Most of this work would not be classed as much more than fee-for-service research, with small teams bootstrapping their research efforts in pursuit of a specific goal.

Nevertheless, these ventures laid the foundation for long-term sustained biosciences research effort in Canada, centred in Saskatoon (Phillips and Khachatourians 2001; Phillips et al. 2012). Since the 1980s, the local effort has been an all-hands-on-deck venture. All three levels of government, the producers themselves through their commodity groups, the university, the co-ops, and a number of multinational companies have put Canada on the map as a centre that can apply new biosciences, develop new technologies, reduce those technologies to practice, apply them to create new products, scale them up, and deliver real value to farmers, consumers, industry, and the broader economy. Concerted effort to build capacity jointly between federal labs, targeted provincial funding, and the university's focus on plant-breeding innovations have delivered a number of world firsts, including virtually every major innovation in rapeseed/canola, some of the best malting barley in the world, the world's first transgenic flax, and advanced lentil varieties.

Many institutions can claim credit for the success. The federal government, as an early and sustained performer of foundational R&D, including with biotechnology, provided a strong base for others to apply that work to specific targets. The federal labs, federal peer-reviewed grants, and a suite of new granting agencies (especially Genome Canada and the Canada Foundation for Innovation) all contributed to local capacity. The province meanwhile has been a major long-term investor in R&D, mostly through the College of Agriculture on the University of Saskatchewan campus. Federal and provincial legislation also has created a dense network of commodity groups that organize producer levies, or check-offs, that are invested in agronomic research. In 2019, more than twenty provincially based groups raised over $60 million annually for research and market development.

The University of Saskatchewan is the anchor of the biosciences research system. To its credit, the university worked to build something greater than the sum of the grants received. Agriculture is one of the founding colleges, created in 1907, and was viewed as the "sheet anchor" of what was intended as a land-grant-style university (Hayden 1983, 20). Over the years, a range of ancillary and spin-off units was created. In 1971, the Crop Development Centre was developed to focus on and accelerate crop-breeding efforts and to maintain a direct relationship with farmers and the broader industry; it has since delivered more than five hundred commercial varieties of spring wheat, durum, canary seed, barley, oat, flax, field pea, lentil, chickpea, faba bean, and dry bean. In the 1990s, the university made a strategic decision to engage in new transformative technologies in agriculture, and has engaged in waves of effort to adapt and use transgenic technologies, genomics, molecular breeding, and now digital innovations in the breeding and production system. Each technology wave has been taken up by faculty in a variety of colleges and supported by senior administration with a bundle of new funding and institutional innovations, including the Veterinary and Infectious Disease Organization, the virtual College of Biotechnology, the Swine Centre, the Feeds Centre, and the Global Institute for Food Security. While other farm programs at universities in Canada and the United States have tended to move towards the study of food, the environment, or natural resources, the University of Saskatchewan has remained steadfastly focused on crops and related research.

Ag-West Bio Inc., a non-profit industry association created by the Devine government in 1989, is a key facilitator in the biosciences ecosystem (Ryan and Smyth 2010). Largely funded by the provincial Ministry of Agriculture but operating under the direction of an independent board of directors, the venture is tasked with initiating, promoting, and supporting the growth of Saskatchewan's agricultural biotechnology sector and the commercialization of related food and non-food technologies. Over the past thirty years, Ag-West Bio has absorbed the International Centre for Agricultural Science & Technology investment portfolio, and merged with Bio-Products Saskatchewan and the Saskatchewan Nutraceutical Network, all provincial ventures that lost steam. The main benefit of this arm's-length institution has been its ability to sustain effort even when various administrations and ministries lost enthusiasm for or interest in agri-food innovation. At the same time, the renewable nature of the government partnership has ensured that the entity has not strayed far from the interests of the province. It has been host, sounding board, leader, and catalyst of most of the large-scale biosciences ventures in Saskatoon and the province, including the early location of biotech research, the emergence of the medicinal cannabis industry, and the creation of the local supercluster.

Both entrepreneurial start-ups and multinational corporations have worked with this platform of public, collective, and university capacity. Beginning in the early 1990s, Ag-West Bio and the province began to subsidize private investment directly in the biosciences. Over the intervening period, more than a hundred firms – including start-ups such as BioOriginal and Prairie Plant Systems and multinationals such as Plant Genetic Resources and Agrevo – have received some direct support, first in the biotechnology space and now in a range of new technology and crop spaces. Collective action ventures (for example, POS Pilot Plant and Saskatchewan Food Development Centre) have filled some of the gaps. In early years, Ag-West Bio had adequate funds in its investment pool to finance projects; now, it collaborates with the Saskatchewan Angels Investors Network and a number of local venture capital firms, such as PIC Investments and various local labour-sponsored venture capital pools, to advance commercial development.

While the story is often told in the context of technology, Phillips and Webb (2016) conclude that the Saskatoon story can be generalized as one of codified knowledge, often in the forms of published academic research and patented technologies, flowing through global pipelines, while contextual, intangible knowledge is embedded in relatively self-contained, sector-specific local labour and knowledge markets. The local innovation system has been characterized as an entrepot, drawing on global pipelines and exploiting local buzz (Bathelt, Malmberg, and Maskell 2004; Phillips 2002). In this context, the local cluster is far from self-contained; rather, it draws critical inputs from other markets, especially knowledge and money, and uses those to craft differentiated products and services that are then marketed to the world, often in a primary or semi-finished form. These pipelines need to be refilled regularly; they are not self-sustaining.

In Saskatoon, it appears that a large proportion of the collaboration and cooperation among firms and other organizations in the local economy occurs informally through personal contacts and loosely structured networks (Phillips and Webb 2014b, 2014c). In general, Saskatoon entrepreneurs and business leaders appear open to exchanging information whenever this is not a direct threat to their company. Sharing is the natural order of things. Some local leaders assert that Saskatoon's environment of informal connections based on social norms appears to facilitate greater knowledge transfer and willingness to assist other firms and individuals than if payment were the norm. Where social norms predominate, reputation is critical: Saskatoon's small size likely allows for easier tracking of reputational factors.

A side story that shows a lighter touch but significant success is the short-line agricultural machinery manufacturing sector, which delivers farm equipment pulled by a tractor. The emergence of the industry in the province can be traced to the settlement around Humboldt of a community of German immigrants in the inter-war period. As latecomers, they settled on land that was burdened with rocks, poor soil, and weeds, but used their apprenticed skills to tinker with machinery to produce locally viable solutions. Starting from making lowly rock pickers, these entrepreneurs created a world-class farm machinery industry that produces cutting-edge tillage technologies and digital applications. The industry, aided by a publicly supported industry association and testing facility in Humboldt, now has ten thousand workers and more than three hundred companies, many with global product mandates. This industry evolved mostly out of the limelight, but with a liberal dose of cluster strategies – such as training to thicken the labour pool, cut-throat competition, and development of forward and backward linkages – combined with the social capital nurtured in a close-knit immigrant community. In many ways, Saskatchewan's highly publicized successes in the biosciences have depended on the less sexy but foundational improvements in machinery (see Awada, Gray, and Nagy 2016).

In 2018, Saskatchewan, with partners in Alberta and Manitoba, won $153 million from the federal Innovation Superclusters Program to deliver Protein Industries Canada, a venture to translate the flow of science and technology from universities across the West into new production and processing in order to expand value-added exports. Ag-West Bio held the pen and led the aggressive public-private-producer team that won this application, but the operations have been handed over to commercial management. If and how it delivers on the vision might determine where this sector goes in the next while; by fiscal year 2020/21, PIC Investments put $352 million into twenty-two projects in the plant protein industry across the Prairies.

Just-in-Time Innovation in Mining and Energy

Saskatchewan's resource industry has always underperformed in terms of expenditures on research, but for the most part has brought new technologies and innovations to the industry just in time to realize economic opportunities or to avoid existential threats. The province actually was the first in Canada in which significant deposits of oil, uranium, and potash were found, but it was relatively slow to exploit them. By 2010, Saskatoon and Regina hosted modest-sized mining clusters, two of the sixteen in Canada, while Regina had one of Canada's thirteen oil and gas clusters (Spencer 2014). Innovation underpins each sector, but in a self-limiting way.

Uranium was first mined in the 1930s under federal management; that early development offered an opportunity for some engineers to learn-by-doing – skills that transferred to the potash sector. Potash was first discovered in 1943 in the process of drilling for oil (Burton 2006). The Prairie Evaporite Deposit – the largest in the world – extends from central to south-central Saskatchewan, south into North Dakota, and just into western Manitoba. Active exploration began in 1951, and in 1958 Potash Company of America, incentivized by provincial subsidies, started drilling. When the shaft pierced the Blairmore underground reservoir, a two-hundred-foot geological sand-and-clay layer filled with compressed salty water, the mine flooded. It took years of experiments with freezing technologies and adaptation of metal mining rings imported from Germany (known now as Blairmore rings) to stabilize the shaft and allow drilling into the rich deposits below. Kalium Potash adapted other technology to develop a solution system to exploit another part of the deposit. Over time, Saskatchewan expanded capacity to the point it dominated the global market, leading to price declines. The government responded over the years with compulsory market management through Canpotex (1969), nationalization of the majority of the sector, then expansion through Potash Corporation of Saskatchewan as a Crown corporation (1975–82), and its privatization (1982). The renamed Potash Corp invested heavily in all three components of fertilizer (nitrogen, phosphorus, and potassium), and over time built a host of assets outside the province; innovation in mining in Saskatchewan lost traction as expansion moved abroad. Higher world prices and a new royalty regime in the past decade spurred Germany's K&S to build a new solution mine and Australia's BHP to invest heavily in what could be the largest potash mine in the world; both ventures added to industrial R&D as they worked to resolve challenges in their projects. Since 2018, the industry has hit turbulence, and investment in research has taken a back seat to other developments. After seeing off an attempted hostile takeover by BHP, Potash Corp (with five mines) merged with Agrium (which owned a large mine near Saskatoon) to form Nutrien; most head office functions have now moved to Calgary. As world prices have fallen in recent years, K&S has solicited bids on its new mine, and BHP has slowed development for the foreseeable future.

Oil and gas similarly had to adapt technologies from elsewhere to exploit both the light sour crude deposits in the south, the heavy crudes in the northwest and locked-in oil in the south east of the province. Each required innovation. The early drilling in the southeast produced modest flows that tapered off over time. In the 1990s, the industry, incentivized with a new royalty regime, imported and adapted horizontal drilling to extend the life of these deposits. Meanwhile, heavy crude in the northeast had a very limited market. The Devine government went into partnership with Husky Oil to develop the technology and build a heavy oil upgrader at Lloydminster, on the Alberta-Saskatchewan border; this was followed soon after by a government-co-operative partnership to develop capacity to refine heavy oil to finished product in Regina at the Federated refinery. In the past decade, fracking has been adapted and adopted to the Saskatchewan part of the Bakken field.

Modest federal and provincial government–owned uranium mining and processing ventures were merged into Cameco in the 1980s and gradually privatized. Facing declining productivity of its deposits in the 1990s, Cameco and its partners moved to open new deposits. An innovative and successful joint federal-provincial environmental impact assessment process approved seven developments, including the Cigar Lake mine, which needed new technology to get 14 per cent grade ore out of the ground without any human contact (the average mine has less than 1 per cent grade ore). Eventually a fully automated mine and mill were developed, a world first.

Project-focused innovation continues to dominate in the industry to this day. While Saskatoon hosts a mining cluster and Regina an oil cluster, they are small and have limited synergies. Most enterprises are more focused on their global innovation and value chains, and few firms are investing much in the next generation of resource extraction in the province – they await the next existential threat or economic opportunity to trigger action.

Universities and Strategic Growth

Saskatchewan's two universities have filled some important roles in the province's innovation system since the 1990s. Florida's (2002) creative class theory and the entrepreneurial university espoused by Etzkowitz and Leydesdorff (1995) in their triple-helix framing of innovation systems caught the attention of administrators and scholars alike at both universities.

The University of Saskatchewan in Saskatoon has always been host and hub for the science part of the innovation system, and is the only university in the province that is a member of the U15 Group of Canadian Research Universities, with all six core life science colleges, as well as the full array of natural sciences, social sciences, humanities, fine arts, and professional colleges. From the beginning, the campus hosted both the Agriculture Canada research effort and then invited in the NRC, the Canadian Food Inspection Agency, and Environment and Climate Change Canada. The university also hosts a research park. In the 1970s, the province leased university land north of the campus and began construction of Innovation Place, intending to create "Silicon Valley North," but found more traction in the agricultural and resource sectors. By 2019 Innovation Place was home to more than 110 firms with 2,600 employees undertaking agri-food, mining, energy, and digital research.

The University of Regina, a comprehensive school, waited until 2000 to partner with the province to create its own Innovation Place, just south of the campus. It now is home to thirty companies with a thousand employees working on digital, energy and environmental research. Both universities see partnership with their research parks as key to their role as entrepreneurial universities.

The University of Saskatchewan was the first and most aggressive in using its assets to leverage resources from government and industry to create new large-scale infrastructure and strategic research capacity. Early successes with the Crop Development Centre and VIDO offered a model that has been generalized and applied more widely: academic ownership, with a blend of scholars and contract researchers using public, private, and producer funds to undertake basic and applied research directed to real-world application. A range of initiatives emerged. The Feeds Centre, Swine Centre, Toxicology Research Centre, Centre for the Study of Co-operatives, Virtual College of Biotechnology, and graduate schools for the environment, health, and public policy, among others, were attempts to build interdisciplinary programs and ventures to sharpen the focus and impact of the university. In addition, the University of Saskatchewan technology transfer office had some success in generating positive cash flow from its intellectual property portfolio. The university's vice president research also has worked to support large-scale research infrastructure (such as Canadian Light Source, InterVac, and the Canadian Hub for Applied and Social Research) and strategic research programs (including two CFREFS, two CERCS, and a multitude of large-scale Genome Canada projects). All of these have been adjudicated through some sort of merit-based system, where research quality is balanced against partnerships, economic impact, and the capacity to leverage industry support (Doern, Phillips, and Castle 2016). While the university underperforms on standard peer-reviewed grants, it has gained more than 10 per cent of the funds in many of these strategic and networked programming spaces, three times its expected allocation based on the size of the province. To complement these large-scale investments, the university has created global institutes for water and food security as external-facing centres to connect scholarship with potential users. The University of Regina, which has doubled its student population in the past decade, has followed suit and developed its own strategic research effort, targeting, among others, computer systems (to leverage its proximity to IBM's subsidiary ISM Canada), sustainable community infrastructure, petroleum technologies, and clean coal and carbon capture.

Canadian Light Source is among the largest university-led science infrastructure projects in Canada. Located at the University of Saskatchewan, building upon a pre-existing linear accelerator, this facility was designed to increase Canadian-based scientific research in order to enhance global competitiveness. The project started with an initial capital cost of $173 million for the energy ring and seven beam lines, and has since expanded to eighteen lines with a minimum cost of $10 million per additional line. Canadian Light Source was one of the first and largest investments by the Canada Foundation for Innovation, leveraging contributions from the two federal agencies, the provinces of British Columbia, Alberta, Saskatchewan, Manitoba, Ontario, and Quebec, the local municipality (which contributed about $10 per capita), a number of research-intensive universities outside the province, a range of health research funders, and industry. Funding ongoing operations of this major science initiative has been a major challenge, as initially the host university and province were responsible for all ongoing costs. This put a disproportionate burden on Saskatchewan, as it needed to contribute almost $30 per capita per year to meet the $35 million operating costs; if located in Ontario, the per capita cost would be below $2.40 per year. In response, the federal government developed and implemented a new operational funding stream for major science initiatives across Canada, which provided more stable funding.

The local pitch for getting this large-scale science facility for Saskatoon was that it would enhance university research and generate significant research and commercial spinoffs. The evidence for both is mixed. Undoubtedly, high-quality research is being done in the facility, but the impact on the university is less than planned, as much of the research is done by non-resident researchers with limited links to the University of Saskatchewan (Ryan, St. Louis, and Phillips 2014). Moreover, while some of the work has been highly useful for some existing firms, such as studies on uranium tailings ponds that were used in regulatory assessments, there has been little or no direct industrial spin-off activity in Saskatoon. Part of the problem is that, initially, the faculty pitched itself as open to studies in all fields. In recent years, however, the operation has refocused on agriculture, advanced materials, the environment, and health to link to local industrial capacity, which might improve the local impact in coming years.

One enduring concern at the University of Saskatchewan is its historically relatively weak health research capacity. As a U15 medical-doctoral campus, it should generate more than $200,000 per faculty annually in research grants, but until recently realized less than $58,000 per faculty. One explanation is that, when the province made cuts to the medical system in the 1990s, the medical faculty and University Hospital moved to fill the gap, which diverted attention from research to service. This weakened the training program, jeopardized college accreditation, and diverted both university and provincial attention away from exploiting research opportunities with economic and commercial potential. Recent changes in the college and faculty complement and significant new investments have started what looks to be a long recovery. Early results are promising.

The Digital Future

Saskatchewan's future might be determined by how it responds to the Internet of Things (IoT). The province was an early participant in building the infrastructure for the digital revolution, as the home to SED Systems, with produces and operates satellite control systems, and SaskTel, the Crown telco that in the 1980s invested heavily in fibreoptics and switching infrastructure. As the last remaining publicly owned telco in North America, SaskTel offers a potentially useful window into this critical sector, while the presence of ISM, which started as the government computer agency, provides a gateway to IBM and its global capacity.

There is substantial debate about if or how digital transformation will change our economy and society. Agriculture is heavily engaged with the digital opportunity: the University of Saskatchewan is applying digital tools and sensing technology to breeding and farming; industry is developing a host of digital apps, sensors, and platforms; and governments are supporting both upstream research and downstream ventures such as the Co-Labs incubator and the PIC Supercluster (Phillips et al. 2019). Mining, in contrast, is further behind and still sorting out how and when to adapt and adopt digital systems (Wixted 2019). Other sectors are somewhere in-between, testing the value and impact of the digital platforms and tools that underlie the IoT. Given the province's long and variable global supply chains, there is particular interest in distributed-ledger technologies and how they might address some of the provenance questions that dog its products in global markets. All of this is forward looking, but definitely focusing attention throughout the local innovation system.

Conclusions and Lessons

Saskatchewan's innovation experience offers a few lessons. First, outcomes can be traced back to the new ideas that motivate institutions individually and through partnerships to pursue specific innovation goals. In earlier eras, the overriding idea was that science would overcome development barriers, which engaged universities, key industrial actors (including industrial co-operatives), and governments, both indirectly through subsidies and programs and directly through Crown corporations. The wheat, canola, and mining stories illustrate the power of coordinated and sustained development. More recently, there has been effort to build resource development, but this has proved more difficult, as there are few industrial partners or champions for new activities.

Saskatchewan governments and industry have been particularly engaged in cluster-based efforts, primarily focused on agriculture and mining. As early as 1990, the province articulated a clusters-based economic plan. A few administrations have tried to walk back active engagement with industry, but the inexorable pull of the dominant resource industries has kept them engaged. The evidence suggests that the few truly clustered efforts are focused on the two globally competitive resource-based sectors, and that clustering and networking are core to their enduring success. Governments, universities, and their specially created partnerships have been vital to this success. They, not multinational enterprises, anchor the local clusters and innovation systems – over time, if not for every specific innovation. A corollary is that one-off, one-firm ventures that are disconnected from these systems have a hard time surviving or thriving.

Universities have been willing to engage with clusters, but they are far more attracted by the innovation systems and triple-helix approaches. Senior administrators have styled themselves in the manner of the "entrepreneurial university," using grant money to build capacity and leverage government and industry support for higher education. The University of Saskatchewan has also had some modest success in translating its research and generating positive cash flows in its tech transfer unit. While industry and municipal leaders in Saskatoon have tried to promote the city as an oasis of creativity and bohemianism, oft-cited draws for the creative class, the little evidence we have suggests the city's key attraction is dynamic research and labour markets, not the local quality of life.

Saskatchewan's small and thin markets work to create more local engagement, which theory suggests could enhance creativity, but which practice shows leaves gaps in the capacity to deliver diversified innovation. While governments, universities, and communities, through co-ops and local action, try to make up for the lack of large-scale, locally managed diversified commercial firms, this is a perennial weakness in the provincial system. With no large-scale private R&D, the province depends more than other provinces on entrepreneurial start-ups and small- and medium-sized, often family-owned, firms for innovation. The few successes that can be identified usually involve local specialization (some call it buzz) explicitly linking to global pipelines in ways that emulate the entrepôt model of development.

Looking ahead, the Saskatchewan experience offers some useful insights into how policy might be better aligned to realize profitable and sustainable innovation. First, the formal science and technology effort sponsored by provincial governments has often been disconnected from the actual innovations that generate new markets and new jobs. This is worth keeping in mind for both future policy and for other provinces. The common refrain in the scholarly and policy literature is that we need to accelerate GERD, especially the effort performed by industry, assuming that innovators and firms have a clear pathway to use and impact. While that might be a precondition for innovation, it probably will not be sufficient. Saskatchewan shows that industries such as agriculture and mining have developed and grown without such formal support. As counterpoint, the province also offers many examples of good ideas with funding that failed to advance due to incomplete and disjointed provincial and national supply chains.

Second, the biosciences story shows that none of the contextualized theories uniquely explains what is happening. Each offers a partial perspective on what is a complex, dynamic set of actors and events. If there is a distilled lesson, it is that the most successful ventures have been explicitly targeted to solving near-to-market problems that, once overcome, generate goods and services that can compete in global markets. Most of the theories and many federal and provincial strategies and programs assume basic research is needed to drive innovation, often ignoring the opportunity for Canada to translate best-in-world ideas, regardless of where they originate, to our particular industrial needs. The long-term successes in agricultural bioscience, energy, and mining are the exceptions that make the rule: most of their successful innovations were based on global pipelines that feed local effort.

Third, none of the stories of success in Saskatchewan involves key innovations driven by joint-stock ventures, and there is little discussion of venture capital exits, especially at the scale of the almost-mythical unicorns so popular in global literature. The innovations realized in Saskatchewan have been the result of hard work, and have generated well-earned but modest long-term returns. Innovation in Saskatchewan, as in much of Canada, does not and is unlikely to deliver windfall gains – so innovation policy should not be structured with large gains in mind.

Finally, one big imponderable is whether this model is sustainable in the face of massive digital disruption. For the better part of the past decade, digital tools have been moving into the research system, on-farm, into mines, and into our global supply chains; few have paid off yet, but interest in digital transformation is high. As we recover from

COVID-19, there is an extra push in many sectors to use more digital technology to manage the risk of future disruption. In many ways, the province looks prepared – as an early adopter of digital tools in agriculture – but the winner-take-all results in sectors where digital transformation is most advanced create profound uncertainty and unease about whether this transformation might simply hollow out the provincial and national economy, if created value and associated jobs migrate to other centres.

References

Awada, L., R. Gray, and C. Nagy. 2016. "The Benefits and Costs of Zero Tillage RD&E on the Canadian Prairies." *Canadian Journal of Agricultural Economics* 64 (3): 417–38. https://doi.org/10.1111/cjag.12080.

Bathelt, H., A. Malmberg, and P. Maskell. 2004. "Clusters and Knowledge: Local Buzz, Global Pipelines and the Process of Knowledge." *Progress in Human Geography* 28 (1): 31–56. https://doi.org/10.1191%2F0309132504ph469oa.

Boland, W., P. Phillips, and C. Ryan. 2010. "Centerless Governance and the Management of Global R&D: Public-Private Partnerships and Plant-Genetic Resource Management." Paper presented at VIII Triple Helix Conference, Madrid, 20–22 October.

Boland, W., P. Phillips, C. Ryan, and S. McPhee-Knowles. 2012. "Collaboration and the Generation of New Knowledge in Networked Innovation Systems: A Bibliometric Analysis." *Social and Behavioural Sciences* 52: 15–24. https://doi.org/10.1016/j.sbspro.2012.09.437.

Burton, J. 2006. "Potash industry." In *Encyclopedia of Saskatchewan*. Online at https://esask.uregina.ca/entry/potash_industry.jsp, accessed 20 April 2020.

Büyükşahin, B., M. Kun, and K. Zmitrowicz. 2016. "Commodity Price Supercycles: What Are They and What Lies Ahead?" *Bank of Canada Review* (Autumn), 35–46.

Doern, D., P. Phillips, and D. Castle. 2016. *Canadian Science, Technology, and Innovation Policy: The Innovation Economy and Society Nexus.* Montreal; Kingston, ON: McGill-Queen's University Press.

Eager, E. 1980. *Saskatchewan Government: Politics and Pragmatism.* Saskatoon: Western Producer Prairie Books.

Etzkowitz, H., and L. Leydesdorff. 1995. "The Triple Helix: University-Industry-Government Relations: A Laboratory for Knowledge Based Economic Development." *European Society for the Study of Science and Technology Review* 14 (1): 14–19.

Florida, R. 2002. *The Rise of the Creative Class.* New York: Basic Books.

Hayden, M. 1983. *Seeking a Balance: University of Saskatchewan, 1907–1982.* Vancouver: UBC Press.

Phillips, P. 1998. "Whither Saskatchewan? A Look at Economic Policies 1975–2000." *Canadian Business Economics* 6 (4): 37–49.

Phillips, P. 1999. "The Geography of the Saskatchewan Macro-economy." In *Atlas of Saskatchewan*, ed. J. Richards and K. Fung. Regina: Canadian Plains Research Center.

Phillips, P. 2002. "Regional Systems of Innovation as a Modern R&D Entrepôt: The Case of the Saskatoon Biotechnology Cluster." In *Innovation, Entrepreneurship, Family Business and Economic Development: A Western Canadian Perspective*, ed. J. Chrisman et al., 31–58. Calgary: University of Calgary Press.

Phillips, P., E. Hassanpour, E. Mian, H. Dutta, Lokpriy, N. Sheryar, and N. Carlson. 2015. *Innovation in Saskatchewan: The Theory and Evidence.* Ottawa: Conference Board of Canada.

Phillips, P., and G.G. Khachatourians. 2001. *The Biotechnology Revolution in Global Agriculture: Invention, Innovation and Investment in the Canola Sector.* Wallingford, UK: CABI.

Phillips, P., J. Parchewski, T. Procyshyn, C. Ryan, J. Karwandy, and J. Kihlberg. 2004. *Agricultural and Life-Science Clusters in Canada: An Empirical and Policy Analysis.* Final project report for Agriculture and Agri-food Canada. Saskatoon.

Phillips, P., J. Relf-Eckstein, G. Jobe, and B. Wixted. 2019. "Configuring the New Digital Landscape in Western Canadian Agriculture." *NJAS-Wageningen Journal of Life Sciences* 90–1 (December): 100295. https://doi.org/10.1016/j.njas.2019.04.001.

Phillips, P., and G. Webb. 2014a. "Governance Innovations in Saskatoon: From State and Local Partnerships to Cooperatives." In *Governing Urban Economies: Innovation and Inclusion in Canadian City-Regions*, ed. N. Bradford and A. Bradwell, 229–47. Toronto: University of Toronto Press.

Phillips, P., and G. Webb. 2014b. "Social Dynamics, Diversity and Physical Infrastructure in Creative, Innovative Communities: The Saskatoon Case." In *Innovating in Urban Economies: Economic Transformation in Canadian City-Regions*, ed. D. Wolfe, 269–91. Toronto: University of Toronto Press.

Phillips, P., and G. Webb. 2014c. "Tolerance and Community in Saskatoon." In *Attracting and Retaining Talented and Creative Workers in Canadian Cities: The Social Dynamics of Economic Innovation*, ed. J.L. Grant, 159–77. Toronto: University of Toronto Press.

Phillips, P., and G. Webb. 2016. "Saskatoon: From Small Town to Global Hub." In *Growing Urban Economies: Innovation, Creativity, and Governance in Canadian City-Regions*, ed. D. Wolfe and M. Gertler, 287–310. Toronto: University of Toronto Press.

Phillips, P., G. Webb, J. Karwandy, and C. Ryan. 2012. *Innovation in Agri-food Research Systems: Theory and Case Studies*. Wallingford, UK: CABI.

Ryan, C.D., M. St. Louis, and P.W.B. Phillips. 2014. "Incorporating Network Analysis into Evaluation of 'Big Science' Projects: An Assessment of the Canadian Light Source Synchrotron." *International Journal of Innovation Management* 18 (5). https://doi.org/10.1142/S1363919614500376.

Ryan, C., and S. Smyth. 2010. "Facilitating Innovation in Agricultural Biotechnology: An Examination of the Ag-West Biotech Model, 1989–2004." *AgBioForum* 13 (2): 183–93.

Spencer, G. 2014. *Cluster Atlas of Canada*. Toronto: University of Toronto, Munk School of Global Affairs. Online at https://localideas.files.wordpress.com/2014/05/cluster-atlas.pdf, accessed 20 April 2020.

Wixted, B. 2019. "Innovation, Disruptions and the Second Economy of Mining." *JSGS Policy Brief*. Online at https://www.schoolofpublicpolicy.sk.ca/research/publications/policy-brief/innovation,-disruption-and-the-second-economy-of-mining.php, accessed 20 April 2020.

13 Alberta: A Paradox of Riches

RICHARD HAWKINS AND PETER JOSTY

Alberta presents a conundrum for policy analysts. For decades Alberta has been Canada's wealthiest province. It has enjoyed Canada's highest employment-to-population ratio and has been a major generator of new jobs. It is home to two of Canada's largest and most productive research universities, together boasting one of the highest national graduation rates in the STEM fields. It hosts more head offices per capita than any other province, has become a major financial hub, and has one of the highest per capita concentrations of scientific and engineering talent in the country. It also has the lowest number of government workers per capita and the lowest level of taxation, especially for business. In short, Alberta has all of the economic fundamentals usually associated with encouraging the growth of a vibrant, knowledge-intensive and innovation-driven commercial sector. But it also has a key vulnerability. Most of these fundamentals are linked in some way, often structurally, to the boom-and-bust volatilities of a single industry: oil and gas. Even the development and exploitation of the oil sands, arguably the single most impactful innovation of the past generation for both Alberta and Canada, were largely led and financed by government. Partly with the aim of moderating this dependency, the public sector has been the primary force in encouraging entrepreneurship and innovation across a broader range of economic activities. How and why this occurred is the story of science, technology, and industry policy in Alberta.

Context

Alberta's economic history has evolved primarily in response to the fortunes of a succession of key structural resource commodities. Each era of resource exploitation, from the fur trade through ranching and farming to energy, has been accompanied by the development of a broader base of industrial and service capabilities (Klassen 1999). Links between industrial development, higher education, and scientific research were first established in 1916 when Henry Marshall Tory, the first president of the University of Alberta, set up a Research Department at the university, which over time evolved into the Honorary Advisory Council for Scientific and Industrial Research. In 1921, Tory became chairman of the Alberta Council of Scientific and Industrial Research (the forerunner of the Alberta Research Council), established through a provincial Order-in-Council. These early initiatives were ahead of their time, having the explicit aim of promoting what today we would call research and development (R&D): making discoveries for the express purpose of enabling and enhancing the development of industry. Thus, what we would eventually call science, technology, and innovation (STI) policy in Alberta began virtually with provincehood.

Prophetically, in terms of the subsequent development of such policy, the first Research Chair at the University of Alberta was Karl Clarke, who in 1920 inaugurated research on the possible uses of the oil sands deposits (Chastko 2007). Originally, the oil sands were seen primarily as a source of compounds for civil engineering applications. It took the better part of fifty years and several significant federal and provincial research initiatives before the potential of this resource as a fuel stock was unlocked. In an often-tangled web of direct and indirect ways, the story of this evolution has always been and remains inextricably at the core of the story of STI policy in Alberta.

Currently, the Alberta economy is structured around oil and gas, but this too is a relatively recent development. Exploitation of Alberta's petroleum reserves on any significant scale dates only from the 1940s. By the 1960s, exports of oil and gas from conventional reserves were becoming structurally important to the Alberta economy. But only in the 1990s did exports, increasingly from the heavy oil reserves, begin to become important to the Canadian economy as a whole, most significantly as an attractor of both domestic and foreign investment. And only in the early 2000s did it begin to approach present levels of production (Chastko 2007; Hester and Lawrence 2010).

By 2018, oil exports amounted to just over $100 billion (CAPP 2019), equal to about 22 per cent all Canadian merchandise exports. Oil had become Canada's single largest export, larger by nearly a third than automotive products. In 2018, just over 80 per cent of Canadian oil and about 60 per cent of natural gas originated in Alberta, contributing around 30 per cent of Alberta's gross domestic product (GDP) directly, but undoubtedly much more indirectly (Alberta 2019; CAPP 2019). The other four major industrial GDP contributors – construction, finance, technical services, and manufacturing – contribute about a quarter of provincial GDP collectively, but all have strong and, in many cases, structural links to the energy sector, particularly manufacturing, which is dominated by refining, upgrading, and petrochemicals. Spenser (2014) reports that, in 2011, almost 25 per cent of the jobs in Alberta were generated by one of thirty industrial clusters, ten of which were explicitly centred on oil and gas, with most of the rest dependent on serving that sector. These clusters not only were generating new jobs faster than other parts of the economy; they were also hosting the highest-paid workers in the province.

Many non-energy sectors figure prominently in terms of technology, investment, and employment, but they remain only marginal contributors to provincial GDP and to exports. For example, agricultural and other resource industries, primarily forestry, contribute less than 2 per cent of GDP. Notwithstanding substantial capabilities in advanced manufacturing and technical services, Alberta-sourced high-value capital goods have attained only small shares of global markets overall, although some have been successful in creating or exploiting key export niches (Hawkins et al. 2018). The potential for such sectors to develop and grow is nevertheless positive. Recent data from Calgary Economic Development (2019) indicate that the city has the highest concentration of high-tech workers in Canada, that it hosts nearly eight hundred private high-tech companies, and that nearly 30 per cent of graduates from Calgary's post-secondary institutions have STEM qualifications.

The longer-term issue is that, despite this potential, no sector currently is even close to being able to replace oil and gas as an anchor for the provincial economy. The main challenges arising from this dependency come, of course, from the extreme volatility of petroleum prices, over whose global dynamics Alberta, or indeed Canada, has little to no influence. Moreover, a clear shift is evident globally as economies move away from carbon-intensive fossil fuels and towards lower-carbon alternatives. The issue for forward planning, and particularly for STI policy, is no longer how to compensate for "peak oil," but how to cope with the prospect of "peak market," at least as far as fuel stocks are concerned (Steward 2017).

This situation leaves Alberta with basically three strategic options. The first is to open up new internal and/or export markets for existing products. This is embodied in the pipeline-to-tidewater debate, and is where most provincial political capital is invested. The second is to increase the value of exported products based on oil and gas. This could involve various forms of upgrading, including investing in refining capacity or derivative manufacturing, such as speciality chemicals and compounds. It could also involve neighbouring initiatives, such as environmental mitigation. The third option is to diversify part of the economy out of the petroleum sector altogether. This could take two directions: divert or repurpose knowledge and skills to other industries, including alternative energy ventures, or develop competencies in entirely new sectors that have no historical anchors in the region, whether by supporting new local ventures or by encouraging foreign direct investment.

In terms of linkage to STI policy, the first option is perhaps the most distant. It is also the option that to date has been mostly unsuccessful. As things stand, Alberta's fossil fuel resources remain landlocked, controlled for the most part by foreign companies and exported overwhelmingly to the US market at a substantial discount. It is still very uncertain whether this will change anytime soon. Even if new pipelines are rolled out, it is unclear that other, more profitable export markets will materialize. For example, even if the Trans Mountain Expansion project is completed, California, not Asia, likely will remain the principal receiving port.

The other two strategies have yielded at least a few successes, and still hold out possibilities. Upgrading and refining capabilities in Canada have not increased significantly since the 1990s (National Energy Board 2018), the exception being the new Sturgeon Refinery north of Edmonton, a technologically leading-edge facility brought on line in 2019 to produce mainly ultra-low-sulphur diesel fuels and diluents. By far the major success has been the growth of Alberta's ethylene cluster, now one of the largest in the world. With current exports in the $7 billion range, this is Alberta's largest manufacturing industry, employing about eleven thousand workers in a large cluster of firms, many of them small, but anchored by Nova Chemicals and Dow Canada (Alberta n.d.). Collectively they produce about a third of total manufacturing output in the province, which amounts to just under 30 per cent of Canada's total petrochemical production.

Alternative energy segments – natural gas, wind, and solar – present additional opportunities to diversify the energy sector into neighbouring segments, if to date little significant industrial or export activity has emerged. Perhaps the most accessible new industry in terms of quickly repurposing most of the technical skills already extant in the petroleum sector is geothermal energy, but, as Leitch, Haley, and Hastings-Simon (2019) have noted, the kinds of policy and agency complementarities necessary to achieve this transition in Alberta are absent at this point.

The record on other diversification fronts is much more mixed. There are notable successes in areas such as geomatics, which grew out of initiatives begun by Shell Oil to plot drilling locations more accurately, and in the biomedical fields, which were spurred by targeted provincially funded research and human capital attraction programs. On the other hand, investments in fields such as nanotechnology and artificial intelligence (AI) have yet to yield significant commercial activity. Indeed, most of the provincial effort for advanced technology has always been and remains highly skewed to upstream research, largely in universities, and to supporting start-up companies, rather than to major investments in creating new industries.

Innovation Architecture

To understand the innovation architecture in Alberta and how it evolved, one must first understand that not only is oil and gas Alberta's largest industry, it must also be considered Alberta's most "innovative" industry, when reckoned in terms of total average investment in activities corresponding to the standard input measures as set out in the Oslo Manual (OECD/EUROSTAT 2006). Compared with other industries, the petroleum industry globally is not generally reckoned to be a leading R&D performer, often owing to problems of factor definition and attribution, rather than to actual effort (Cooke 1987; Thurston and Stewart 2005; Ville and Wicken 2012). As Sharpe and Gilbaud (2005) have shown, over the full range of innovation indicators, including R&D investment, the performance of the oil and gas industry in Canada is comparable to that of other large domestic industries, with its relative effort exceeding many of theirs.

Sustaining competitiveness in Alberta's conventional petroleum segment has always required significant locally anchored efforts to pioneer or improve various exploration, drilling, and profiling technologies (Thurston and Stewart 2005). This requirement intensified for the heavy oil reserve, which is more technically difficult and costly to extract and transport. Making and keeping this segment competitive has required continuing large investments in R&D to enable more efficient *in situ* extraction from deep deposits. Indeed, the taxation and royalty regimes for oil sands production was originally predicated on explicit calculations of profit relative to these ongoing costs, among many others (Campbell 2013; Chastko 2007; Steward 2017). In recent years, this R&D effort has also expanded to encompass environmental management and mitigation technologies and methods.

With combined gross expenditures on R&D of about $1.2 billion, Suncor, CNRL, Imperial Oil, and Syncrude are the only Alberta-based companies that break into the top fifty Canadian R&D performers by

Table 13.1. Gross Expenditure on Research and Development by Performing Sector, average $ millions, Alberta, 2013–17

		Performers					
		Government		Provincial Research	Business	Higher	Private Non-
Funders	Total	Federal	Provincial	Organizations	Enterprise	Education	profit
Total sectors	3,167	107	119	–	1,699	1,242	–
Federal government	374	106	–	–	25	240	–
Provincial government	361	–	119	–	13	229	–
Business enterprise	1,682	1	–	–	1,574	108	–
Higher education	554	–	–	–	–	554	–
Private non-profit	113	–	–	–	11	106	–
Foreign	83	–	–	–	77	5	–

Note: Columns and rows may not sum due to rounding.

Source: Statistics Canada, table 27-10-0273-01, "Gross domestic expenditures on research and development, by science type and by funder and performer sector (x 1,000,000)."

expenditure (Research Infosource 2019). They are by far the largest contributors to provincial business expenditure on R&D (BERD). Of the top ten Alberta-based R&D performers, only ResverLogix, a biotech/pharma company, lies outside the petroleum sector. The energy and affiliated industries also maintain extensive and long-standing ties to the university research base, and thus are the most significant corporate correspondents and beneficiaries of higher education R&D (HERD). They also constitute the main locus of Alberta's high concentration of highly qualified technical and scientific workers (Table 13.1).

Since the 1980s, however, the bulk of R&D investment in energy industries globally has focused not on fossil fuels but on alternative energy sources (IEC 2019). To an extent, the Alberta-based energy sector also reflects this trend, with investments in a range of alternatives, including wind and solar. Nevertheless, the bulk of that R&D effort in Alberta is aimed at mitigating the environmental effects of oil sands production, rather than on energy alternatives. These efforts are largely centred in Canada's Oil Sands Innovation Alliance (COSIA), a cost- and intellectual property–sharing venture set up by the major companies active in the oil sands to pool R&D capabilities. In 2017, the COSIA portfolio held three hundred initiatives at a reported value of about $550 million (COSIA 2017), more than double the average annual expenditures over the past few years of the entire cluster of provincially supported research and business development organizations. Owing to its collective and, to some extent, extra-provincial nature, it is unclear how or if the COSIA effort is reflected fully in official R&D statistics. Nevertheless, it must be reckoned as by far the largest industrially sponsored R&D effort in the province.

Notwithstanding substantial private and public investment in energy technology, the specific focus of "innovation" policy in Alberta has been associated with the somewhat counternarrative of economic "diversification" – that is, moving away from, or at least hedging dependency on, fossil fuel exports. Currently, most designated STI policy measures focus on research and technology development and on entrepreneurship, as centred in the technology start-up segment. In this endeavour, Alberta's two major research universities, along with the polytechnics (Southern Alberta Institute of Technology and Northern Alberta Institute of Technology) have played a prominent role, as have linkages to federal programs like NRC-IRAP. Start-up ventures have also accessed a range of fiscal incentives. Federal and provincial Scientific Research and Experimental Development (SR&ED) subsidies for in-house R&D are supplemented by programs such as the Alberta Investor Tax Credit, aimed at attracting venture capital by offering up to 30 per cent in tax rebates for investors in small Alberta firms.

With the election of the new United Conservative Party (UCP) government in 2019, however, the future of most provincial programs of this kind came into question and some seemed destined to be discontinued. This sudden injection of uncertainty was by no means unusual for diversification-oriented policy in Alberta, which has always been convoluted and full of controversy and tension as to whether diversification goals are achievable or even desirable.

Following the first Alberta petroleum crisis of the 1980s, which mainly concerned the conventional oil and gas segment, an influential report by Mansell and Percy (1990) recommended a "shotgun" approach to promoting new industry that was based not on explicit policies for industry, technology development, or higher education, but on promoting a generally conducive (read "low tax") environment for the attraction of new ventures both within and outside the petroleum sector.

This approach was basically a formula for minimalist intervention – getting the prices right and then letting markets decide. It reflected a venerable provincial political mythology that is strong on free enterprise, low taxes, open markets, and individualism – often rolled into the mantra of "the Alberta advantage." In truth, however, with the possible exception of taxes, it is dubious that Alberta has stronger associations with such characteristics than do other provinces. Historically, "low taxes" has been a euphemism for transferring oil income to general revenue in lieu of taxation (Campbell 2013). Data from the Global Entrepreneurship Monitor do indicate that Alberta leads other provinces in "entrepreneurship," very broadly defined, but somewhat counter to prevailing perceptions, those data also indicate that Canada as a whole is an entrepreneurship leader globally (GEM 2019a, 2019b). This makes it difficult to attribute special significance to such findings at the provincial level.

While not discounting the productive efforts of many past and present entrepreneurs, the political narrative that the province grew to its present economic status in Confederation by dint of Alberta-based private entrepreneurship is simply incorrect. The wellspring of Alberta's current wealth was from the beginning the result of a coordinated provincial, interprovincial, and federal effort to exploit the oil sands. This involved foreign direct investment coupled with major strategic investments in R&D from both provincial and federal agencies and at one point also from the province of Ontario (Chastko 2007; Steward 2017).

Policy Effort

In policy terms, the Alberta case exemplifies the perennial debate about the relative economic efficiency of policy measures relative to the presumed technological sophistication of different industries. It has become commonplace for industries to be classified into low-, medium-, and high-technology categories, with resource industries usually classified as low- to medium- technology sectors and, hence, less innovative by definition (Hatzichronoglou 1997). But this can be highly misleading, as the exploration, production, and processing facets of resource production are now highly sophisticated technologically, often with extensive linkage to the science base (Acha and Cusmano 2005; Hirsch-Kreinsen 2008; Mahroum and Al Saleh 2017; Ville and Wicken 2012). This typically leaves policy makers in resource-rich jurisdictions with the dilemma of how to balance continued investments in the technological capabilities of the resource sector, thus prolonging export dependencies, with leveraging these capabilities in transitioning to allied, neighbouring, or entirely new areas of economic activity.

The trajectory of Alberta STI policy from the 1970s to the present has been largely defined by this dilemma, and has gone through roughly three (significantly overlapping) phases. These have involved the rise and fall of literally hundreds of programs and measures. In setting out the story, we have focused only upon a few of the most significant initiatives in terms of investment, impact, and influence on shaping policy as it exists today.

Phase One: Unlocking Alberta's Oil Wealth

The economic objective that spawned Alberta's first and certainly most substantial and impactful STI strategy was to unlock the wealth potential of the oil sands in the first place. A significant obstacle was technological: it was not obvious how to extract the vast bulk of the bitumen reserve that could not be surface mined in a commercially viable way. To solve this problem, the province set up the Alberta Oil Sands Technology and Research Authority (AOSTRA 1990). Between 1974 and 2000, AOSTRA invested about $1 billion in a variety of R&D and allied initiatives, mainly to develop so-called *in situ* extraction methods.

AOSTRA was an audacious industrial policy initiative, undertaken at a time when industry interest and commitment to the oil sands was not certain (Hester and Lawrence 2010). It became not only the single largest Alberta investment in research and industrial development, but also one of the largest in Canadian history. It was also one of the most influential. By effectively de-risking large-scale commercial development of the oil sands, it precipitated an economic boom that persisted until the global price downturn of 2014. It also induced a trajectory of investments that continues today. After 1990, AOSTRA went through several transformations. In 2000, its functions were transferred to the Alberta Energy Research Institute, which in 2010 became Alberta Innovates – Energy and Environment Solutions.

Significantly, the success of AOSTRA had implications for all three diversification options. In itself it was a significant innovation that opened up both a new industry and a new market. But, at least in the beginning, it also sustained and enhanced a pool of public revenue that in principle could be invested in a broader range of industrial development initiatives, including those in key emerging technology sectors. Although AOSTRA was not conceived as a general model for industrial policy or strategy for the province, questions have always percolated as to whether a similar approach, structure, and long-term orientation could provide similar results if applied to other emerging industries (Hastings-Simon 2019).

Phase Two: Leveraging Oil Wealth

From roughly the early 1980s to the mid-2000s, albeit with a significant shift of political emphasis midway through, Alberta STI policy was actively concerned with how to generate a higher social return on the public revenues from oil wealth. The first Lougheed government of the 1970s identified energy revenues early on as sources of investment for economic development and diversification in all regions of the province, as well as for public welfare initiatives – chiefly health and infrastructure. The strategy was contingent originally on reinvesting some of the financial returns in a sovereign wealth fund, the Alberta Heritage Savings Trust Fund, set up in 1976 as a repository for provincial revenues, which came at the time mostly from conventional oil and natural gas (Campbell 2013; Poelzer 2015).

AOSTRA was set up partially with funds from the Heritage Fund, but by 1980, the Fund was drawn upon to establish and support the Alberta Heritage Fund for Medical Research (AHFMR), which blended health delivery goals with research-based initiatives in the universities that were also intended to stimulate a medical technology and services industry in the province. By the mid-1990s, a broad range of research-based initiatives had been set up, eventually coming under the umbrella of the Alberta Science and Research Authority (ASRA), which had as one of its goals to increase the share of Alberta's "innovation economy" from 7 per cent to 25 per cent of the provincial economy by 2020 (ASRA 1998). By 2000, ASRA had established a broad range of competencies, not only in organizing and funding the research system, but also in developing performance monitoring.

Later in the 1990s ASRA proposed a vehicle to consolidate and stimulate research and industrial development in the computing industries. This culminated in the establishment of the Alberta Informatics Circle of Research Excellence (iCORE), a not-for-profit research organization constructed along the lines of AHFMR and likewise mostly situated in the universities. Both AHFMR and iCORE were essentially human capital acquisition strategies aimed at attracting top research talent to the province. To this end, both were highly successful, establishing funded research chairs and new research initiatives in areas nominated to be of strategic importance. Research output in these fields increased significantly, especially from the medical research cluster, which also increased its intake of funding from other sources, including US-based National Institutes of Health grants (Ross 2016). The iCORE mandate was centred mainly in the fields of advanced computing and AI, but also encompassed the application of advanced technologies to fields such as medicine, energy, and environmental management. AHFMR and iCORE programs also provided support for graduate and post-doctoral students, with iCORE also providing top-ups to students already holding grants from the Natural Sciences and Engineering Research Council.

It was also expected, however, that this newly recruited human capital pool would enrich the provincial stocks of commercially viable technologies and spur the growth of new hi-tech commercial ventures. To a limited extent, this expectation was fulfilled, but certainly not to the extent that successful tech start-ups have contributed substantially to counterbalancing, much less supplanting, the resource industries in terms of attracting investment, creating employment, or contributing to provincial GDP.

The original scope of economic strategy in the Lougheed and Getty governments of the 1970s and 1980s was aimed at far more than commercializing research; it was also intended to build up substantial commercial enterprises in a broad range of sectors in each region of the province. The goal was to establish anchor enterprises that would kickstart diversification. These investments were targeted, however, mostly at conventional industries – for example, grain terminals, fertilizer plants, steel mills, and even a waterski company, as well as purchasing Pacific Western Airlines. In terms of medium-term expectations, this part of the strategy was largely unsuccessful. Few of these ventures prospered and many lost significant amounts of public money.

The Lougheed government's strategy is usually described in retrospect as "winner picking," a concept that has become established in the provincial mindset as something to be avoided at all costs. One particular initiative, NovaTel, became something of a poster child for the assumed failure of the Lougheed approach, and it continues to colour political attitudes towards STI policy today. Begun in the late 1980s as a joint venture between Alberta Government Telephones (now Telus) and NOVA Corp. (formerly Alberta Gas Trunk Lines), NovaTel was born out of the burgeoning global enthusiasm to create information technology clusters like Silicon Valley. Unfortunately, its founders miscalculated, and its core business, manufacturing cellphone handsets, was not a high-growth sector. That manufacturing segment globally shifted to low-wage economies, and Alberta lost in the range of $500–600 million in public subsidies.

Many in the province continue to interpret the NovaTel debacle as evidence that attempts to diversify into high-technology industries are futile (see, for example, Morton and McDonald 2015). This, however, is a myopic view that ignores the essentially long-run dynamics of innovation as an economic driver. In fact, NovaTel is still in business, has diversified into much more sophisticated areas of the electronics industries, and has become a significant exporter. Moreover, there is clear evidence that NovaTel and several other similar ventures have had significant positive effects on Alberta's human capital pool. Indeed, Langford, Wood, and Ross (2003) document that they were instrumental in retaining significant amounts of technical and scientific talent following the first major downturn in the conventional energy sector in the 1980s.

Arguably, these new clustering effects also contributed to the generation of subsequent high-technology ventures. For example, SMART Technologies, the Calgary-based company that at its peak in the early 2000s was one of Canada's largest exporters of producer-technology goods, began in this milieu, as did iCORE itself. In 2001, the National Institute for Nanotechnology (now the Nanotechnology Research Centre) was established in Edmonton as a joint venture between the National Research Council, the University of Alberta, and the Alberta government. Although this venture has yet to realize any commercial potential, it remains one of the largest nano-research facilities in the world. Since 2002, both federal and provincial governments have continued to invest in advanced computing and AI research at the University of Alberta and the Alberta Machine Intelligence Institute.

The Klein government, which came to power in 1992 on a populist promise to balance budgets, completely abandoned the industrial development component of the Lougheed-Getty strategy, citing presumed disasters such as NovaTel. Although the Heritage Fund continued to be used in part to invest in high-tech sectors and established research trajectories such as those in medicine and advanced computing continued to be supported, the focus of STI policy overall shifted decisively upstream to commercializing basic research and to providing general, mostly fiscal, business attraction and development measures.

STI policy in the post-Klein era remained tilted decidedly in the direction of keeping government distant from direct involvement with specific firms. The institutional outcome of this philosophy is the current complex of provincial and municipal bodies and programs that self-identify today as the Alberta "innovation system" (Josty 2002). Today this encompasses Alberta Innovates – the main provincially supported cluster of research and business development organizations – along with the universities and polytechnics, various federal research facilities and business development agencies, and an array of municipal technology incubators and their like. Thus, admittedly with many flaws, what started out in the 1970s as a genuinely distinctive and visionary approach to subnational economic development in Canada – one that aimed to leverage diversification with resource wealth and to couple investment in both basic science and R&D with industrial development – has settled into a model that is virtually identical to that pursued in most other subnational jurisdictions in Canada and elsewhere.

Phase Three: In Search of a Way Forward

The third, and current, phase is predominantly concerned with the management and evolution of the ecosystem that emerged from phases one and two. We must admit that we are limited in assessing the performance of policy in this phase in that few formal evaluations or impact assessments appear to have been undertaken of any of the key agencies, or at least never issued publicly. We can, however, underscore some key events to illustrate broadly how the STI ecosystem has evolved and some of the challenges it faces.

Probably the best phrase to describe the policy environment over roughly the past decade would be "constantly in flux." Indeed, in trying to reconstruct the procession of organizational changes and transfers of responsibility as far back as 2005, we found it impossible even to recall many of them, let alone trace their evolution in any coherent way. To give the reader some idea, between February 2011 and the election of 2019, seven different ministers and seven different deputy ministers were handed responsibility for the STI portfolio. Of these ministers, only one – in the New Democratic Party (NDP) government – lasted longer than a year. We leave to the reader's imagination the challenges this fluid state of affairs presented and continues to present to both public servants in this portfolio and to their client communities. Some of the possible consequences can be seen in a recent study by Scott et al. (2020) that documents how one of the main impediments to the development of "precision health" as a new industry in Alberta was not resources or expertise, but the woeful lack of linkage between most of the research and industrial development agencies and programs necessary to achieve this result.

The most visible overall outcome of these changes has been the gradual incorporation of most of the provincially run R&D and technology commercialization agencies into Alberta Innovates. But the structure, mandate, and management of this body has also been fluid, with changes often spurred by frequent shifts in the locus of responsibilities for the STI-related portfolios between ministries. Responsibilities for advanced education and STI sometimes have been combined into a single ministry and sometimes shared between two separate ministries. It is not clear, however, whether constant shifts of responsibilities and of institutional and management structures were ever guided by any coherent vision or strategy. Most of these changes occurred while the same party (the Progressive Conservatives) was in power. For the most part, it would appear that much the same wine was simply poured into different bottles.

Over its single term in office, the NDP government did not depart significantly from this pattern, other than perhaps to articulate more strongly the goal of diversifying the provincial economy and targeting some of the provincial budget more explicitly to defined goals. For example, in 2018, $1.1 billion of fiscal incentives was provided to petrochemical producers to move up the value chain by engaging in the manufacture of plastics, fabrics, and fertilizers. Also, the beginnings of a more coherent diversification strategy were outlined as the Alberta Research and Innovation Framework (Alberta 2017). Apart from perhaps a greater emphasis on non-positional sectors, such as information technology and advanced materials, the goals and approaches in the Framework were not dissimilar to long-standing priorities as set out by previous governments. Indeed, they were much less coherent or visionary than the strategy set out by ASRA in the late 1990s. Targets, for example, were only vaguely described, and little emphasis was given to assessing policy outcomes and impacts. The one significant change was a modest increase in funding for Alberta Innovates, whose allocations rose to over $300 million in 2017 (from a previous average of about $230–$250 million per year), sliding back somewhat in 2018 (Alberta Innovates 2019).

The change of government in 2019 ushered in yet more upheaval. The incoming UCP had pinned virtually all of its political capital during the election on resurrecting the fortunes of the petroleum sector. Accordingly, early indications were that support for programs outside this sector would be relegated to blanket measures aimed only at stimulating the general business environment. Basically, the new government articulated a recovery strategy based on austerity in the Klein-era mode: reducing corporate taxes (already the lowest in Canada), slashing public spending, reducing public sector and employment, and reducing the deficit.

In this framework, nominal responsibility for the STI file was split at first between the Ministry of Advanced Education and the Ministry of Economic Development, Trade and Tourism. This was accompanied by significant cuts in funding and staffing for many relevant agencies. The Alberta Innovates budget was slashed by nearly a third. University budgets were cut also, as was the Health Services budget along with those of numerous technical service agencies – all key players in the innovation system overall. Almost all of the existing small business measures were eliminated, including SR&ED and the Alberta Investor Tax Credit, and funding for the AI initiatives was terminated (Simpson 2019).

The one possibly relevant new initiative to be launched in this early period was the Technology Innovation and Emissions Reduction (TIER) system, which implied some sort of R&D incentive. It was, and remains, unclear, however, whether this venture would be resourced with new money or with money transferred from the budgets of existing agencies. TIER is consistent with the political position of the UCP (and of its Progressive Conservative forebear), that climate change should be managed through investments in new technology, not through carbon taxes – this is despite the rather dubious performance of previous environmental R&D initiatives centred in provincial agencies (see, for example, Adkin 2019)

Over the summer of 2020, however, a more coherent economic recovery plan emerged, and with it a somewhat clearer picture of the government's position on advanced education, research, and innovation (Alberta 2020). Once again, responsibilities were separated. The Advanced Education portfolio became focused mostly on the education and training role of universities and colleges. The Ministry of Economic Development, Trade and Tourism was rebadged as the Ministry of Jobs, Economy and Innovation, and most responsibilities for STI policy appear now to be concentrated there.

Rather curiously, the NDP's 2017 Framework appears to have been carried forward as a source document, but elaborated in a different landscape of institutions and measures. The Alberta Innovates system was preserved virtually intact, albeit supplemented by a range of new programs, mostly focusing on the universities and small and medium-sized enterprises. Also added were two consultative bodies: the Research and Innovation Advisory Committee and the Talent Advisory Council on Technology. On the whole, however, most of the "new" structures remain oriented to exactly the same basic established strategy: first, attracting more research talent; second, investing in upstream technology development; and third, providing various supports for commercialization, primarily through start-ups. The financial picture for these agencies remains murky, and it is not clear that substantial new money has been made available to them.

Thus, in the face of the most volatile economic crisis since the 1920s, the current government appears strongly committed to much the same kinds of measures as have predominated since the 1990s, although yet again distributing responsibility for them among a different set of administrative bodies. In substance, it remains committed to approaches that, while certainly adding significantly to scientific, technological, and even business development capabilities in the province, have nevertheless consistently failed to moderate Alberta's dependency on the oil and gas industry.

Conclusions and Lessons

The story as set out above leaves Alberta with a serious dilemma. The bulk of its very considerable scientific and R&D capabilities has in one way or another been dedicated to or shaped by an underlying economic strategy geared mainly to stimulating growth in what essentially is a sunset industry. The challenges Alberta policy makers face today remain products of this seeming paradox. But it is not beyond resolution.

Attitudes and approaches to STI policy in Alberta continue to be shaped fundamentally by a conflict of ideas as to what role government should play in a modern economy. The popular perception, cultivated by successive conservative governments since the 1950s, is that Alberta is strong economically because government stays away from industry and commerce, except to provide a conducive fiscal and regulatory environment or to mitigate presumed market failures. The reality is that Alberta's public and private sectors have always been as closely intertwined and interdependent as they are in any of the other provinces, and in many respects more so.

Problematically, with the exception of a brief "experiment" during the Lougheed-Getty years, the ideology of STI policy in Alberta has focused firmly on the popular perception, not on the reality. The institutional structure of Alberta STI policy reflects this ideological bias, but as played out against the very real backdrop of three essential if not always harmonious objectives: maintaining and increasing oil sands investment; mitigating fluctuations in government oil revenues; and diversifying the provincial economy beyond structural dependence on resource income.

To this point, the mobilization of science, technology, and skills has been devoted overwhelmingly to the first two goals, which is not unreasonable considering Alberta's immediate economic realities. And it must be acknowledged that innovation in the key oil and gas sector has been significant and has had a powerful impact. Alberta's oil prosperity is not the product of merely possessing this resource – as is the case in a true "petro state" – but of continuous innovation in how it is extracted and processed, most of this originating in Alberta itself. The problem is that innovation in this sphere is no longer sufficient to ensure economic resilience in the longer term, unless capabilities shift towards allied and neighbouring industries.

Attention to the third goal has a checkered history and still an ill-defined future. The ecosystem of educational, research, and business development institutions that exists today is providing Alberta many of the advanced scientific and technological capabilities that could someday transition the province's economy away from resource dependency – or at least move it towards a more forward-looking and perhaps even symbiotic balance between exploiting the resource base and developing new, high-value, knowledge-intensive industries.

The missing piece is recognition and acceptance that accomplishing such a goal requires more than a further proliferation of inputs – more science, R&D, start-ups, and so forth – and far more than a putative levelling of the macroeconomic playing field in the expectation that new industries will grow miraculously. This "immaculate conception" model of economic development has never applied in Alberta, nor anywhere else. In this regard, we are reminded of a comment from noted Harvard economist Dani Rodrick: "[W]hen we look closely at the details of how successful industries are actually generated – how they 'get off the ground' – we find that in almost all such cases public intervention has played a significant role ... [G]rowth strategies are needed to complement the pursuit of macroeconomic stability with a more productive economic strategy that focuses on the needs of the real sector and does not just assume that, once the macro framework is in place, the real sector will take care of itself and will generate the dynamism needed for sustained growth" (Rodrik 2005, 8–9).

In terms of finding a way forward for STI policy in Alberta, the key seems to lie in a more realistic and strategic perception of "real" sectors: how they develop and grow, and what specific functions government must fulfil to develop sustainable and resilient new industries, not just random clusters of new companies. Doubtless this can occur only with a significant, even radical, realignment of interests. The current government orientation remains predominantly tied to the goal of preserving wealth from the oil resource. But the alignment of other interests in the province – the entrepreneurial segment, the universities and colleges, segments of the general public, and segments also of large industry, including the petroleum industry – is far more fluid, dynamic, and oriented to a different future. This future is replete with opportunity provided STI policy becomes firmly and productively aligned with the task of turning their vision into reality.

References

Acha, V., and L. Cusmano. 2005. "Governance and Co-ordination of Distributed Innovation Processes: Patterns of R&D Co-operation in the Upstream Petroleum Industry." *Economics of Innovation and New Technology* 14 (1–2): 1–21. https://doi.org/10.1080/1043859042000228651.

Adkin, L.E. 2019. "Technology Innovation as a Response to Climate Change: The Case of the Climate Change Emissions Management Corporation of Alberta." *Review of Policy Research* 35 (5): 603–34. https://doi.org/10.1111/ropr.12357.

Alberta. 2017. *Alberta Research and Innovation Framework 2017*. Edmonton: Alberta Ministry of Economic Development and Trade.

Alberta. 2019. "Alberta Gross Domestic Product." Province of Alberta, Economic Dashboard. Online at https://economicdashboard.alberta.ca /GrossDomesticProduct, accessed 20 April 2020.

Alberta. 2020. "Alberta's Recovery Plan: An Ambitious Strategy to Create Jobs, Build and Diversify." Online at https://www.alberta.ca/recovery -plan.aspx, accessed 22 September 2021.

Alberta. n.d. "PetroChemicals, InvestAlberta." Online at https://investal berta.ca/industry-profiles/petrochemicals/, accessed 20 April 2020.

Alberta Innovates. 2019. *Innovation in Action: 2018–19 Annual Report*. Edmonton: Alberta Innovates.

AOSTRA. 1990. *AOSTRA: A 15-Year Portfolio of Achievement*. Edmonton: Alberta Oil Sands Technology and Research Authority.

ASRA. 1998. *Sustaining the Alberta Advantage through Science and Research*. Edmonton: Alberta Science and Research Authority.

Calgary Economic Development. 2019. *Calgary in the New Economy*. Online at https://calgaryeconomicdevelopment.com/the-new-economy.

Campbell, B. 2013. *The Petro-Path Not Taken: Comparing Norway with Canada and Alberta's Management of Petroleum Wealth*. Ottawa: Canadian Centre for Policy Alternatives.

CAPP. 2019. "Frequently Used Statistics." Calgary: Canadian Association of Petroleum Producers.

Chastko, P.A. 2007. *Developing Alberta's Oil Sands: From Karl Clark to Kyoto*. Calgary: University of Calgary Press.

Cooke, P. 1987. "Research and Development Networks and Market in a Complex Industry: The Example of Offshore Oil Equipment." In *Industrial Policies and Structural Change*, ed. C. Saunders, 105–17. London: Palgrave Macmillan.

COSIA. 2017. *Improving Environmental Performance through Open Innovation.* Project Portfolio 2017. Calgary: Canada's Oil Sands Innovation Alliance.

GEM. 2019a. *GEM Canada 2018–19 Report.* Calgary: The Centre for Innovation Studies.

GEM. 2019b. *GEM Alberta 2018–19 Report.* Calgary: The Centre for Innovation Studies.

Hastings-Simon, S. 2019. "Industrial Policy in Alberta: Lessons from AOSTRA and the Oil Sands." *SPP Research Papers* 12 (37).

Hatzichronoglou, T. 1997. *Revision of the High-Technology Sector and Product Classification.* Paris: Organisation for Economic Co-operation and Development.

Hawkins, R., C. Saunders, G. Gregson, and P. Josty. 2018. *The Role of Medium-sized Enterprises in the Alberta Industrial Ecosystem.* Report for the Alberta Government (Economic Development and Trade) and the Government of Canada (Western Economic Diversification Canada), The Center for Innovation Studies (THECIS), Calgary, 30 November.

Hester, A., and L. Lawrence. 2010. "A Sub-national Public-Private Strategic Alliance for Innovation and Export Development: The Case of the Canadian Province of Alberta's Oil Sands." Santiago, Chile: Economic Commission for Latin America and the Caribbean.

Hirsch-Kreinsen, H. 2008. "'Low-tech' Innovations." *Industry and Innovation* 15 (1): 19–43. https://doi.org/10.1080/13662710701850691.

IEC (International Energy Commission). 2019. *World Energy Investment 2019.* Paris: International Energy Commission.

Josty, P. 2002. "The Alberta Innovation System: The Main Players and Suggested Research Priorities." In *Innovation and Entrepreneurship in Western Canada. From Family Businesses to Multinationals,* ed. J.J. Chrisman, J.A.D. Holbrook, and J.H. Chua, 77–109. Calgary: University of Calgary Press.

Klassen, H. 1999. *A Business History of Alberta.* Calgary: University of Calgary Press.

Langford, C., J. Wood, and T. Ross. 2003. "Origins and Structure of the Calgary Wireless Cluster." In *Clusters Old and New,* ed. D. Wolfe, 161–85. Montreal; Kingston, ON: McGill-Queen's University Press.

Leitch, A., B. Haley, and S. Hastings-Simon. 2019. "Can the Oil and Gas Sector Enable Geothermal Technologies? Socio-technical Opportunities and Complementarity Failures in Alberta, Canada." *Energy Policy* 125: 384–95.

Mahroum, S., and Y. Al-Saleh, eds. 2017. *Economic Diversification Policies in Natural Resource Rich Economies.* Abingdon, UK: Routledge.

Mansell, R., and M. Percy. 1990. *Strength in Adversity: A Study of the Alberta Economy.* Edmonton: University of Alberta Press.

Morton, T., and M. McDonald. 2015. "The Siren Song of Economic Diversification: Alberta's Legacy of Loss." *SPP Research Papers* 8 (13).

National Energy Board. 2018. *Canadian Refinery Overview*. Ottawa: National
  Energy Board, April.
OECD/Eurostat. 2006. *Oslo Manual*. Paris: OECD Publishing.
Poelzer, G. 2015. *What Crisis? Global Lessons from Norway for Managing Energy-
  Based Economies*. Ottawa: Macdonald-Laurier Institute.
Research Infosource. 2019. "Canada's Top Corporate Spenders List." Online at
  https://researchinfosource.com/top-100-corporate-rd-spenders/2019/list.
Rodrik, D. 2005. "Policies for Economic Diversification." *CEPAL Review* 87
  (December): 7–23.
Ross, T. 2016. "Innovation Agencies in a Resource Based Economy, the Case
  of Alberta: Leadership, Energy and Innovation." PhD diss., University of
  Calgary.
Scott, C., H. Eng, A. Dubkk, and J. Zwicker. 2020. "What Is Holding Back
  Alberta's Precision Health Innovation and Commercialization Ecosystem?"
  SPP Research Papers 13 (5).
Sharpe, A., and O. Guilbaud. 2005. *Indicators of Innovation in Canadian Natural
  Resource Industries*. Ottawa: Centre for the Study of Living Standards.
Simpson, M. 2019. "How Alberta's tech sector is affected by cuts in much
  anticipated 2019 provincial budget." *Betakit: Canadian Startup News*, 24
  October.
Spencer, G. 2014. *Cluster Atlas of Canada*. Toronto: University of Toronto, Munk
  School of Global Affairs. Online at https://localideas.files.wordpress
  .com/2014/05/cluster-atlas.pdf, accessed 20 April 2020.
Steward, G. 2017. *Betting on Bitumen: Alberta's Energy Policies from Lougheed to
  Klein*. Edmonton: Parkland Institute.
Thurston, J.B., and R. Stewart. 2005. "What Drives Innovation in the
  Upstream Hydrocarbon Industry?" *Leading Edge* 24 (11): 1110–16. https://
  doi.org/10.1190/1.2135099.
Ville, S., and O. Wicken. 2012. "The Dynamics of Resource-based Economic
  Development: Evidence from Australia and Norway." *Industrial and
  Corporate Change* 22 (5): 1341–71. https://doi.org/10.1093/icc/dts040.

14 British Columbia: The Pacific Economy

DAVID CASTLE

British Columbia has no overt, consolidated innovation policy – or science or industrial policy for that matter. Nevertheless, the public, private, and voluntary sectors are increasingly engaging on innovation policy issues. The overall context is good for innovation: a healthy economy, increased political stability with the transformation of a New Democratic Party (NDP)-Green coalition government from 2017 to an NDP majority in October 2020, a strong cohort of post-secondary organizations, a growing base of small and medium-sized enterprises, and emerging collaboration between firms in the Cascadia corridor of northwestern provinces and states, spurred by potential for more robust and potentially high-speed transportation linkages between Canada and the United States. British Columbia has an opportunity to nurture and add value to traditional industrial sectors (particularly resource extraction), while developing selective strategies to capitalize on its competencies and capacities in an economy increasingly focused on specialized services and technology (OECD 2004). More overt strategy is actively being sought as new political leadership recognizes and responds to the changing economy and the province's rapidly shifting demographics. Is there enough corporate and political will to pick some focal points, such as digital technologies, for concerted innovation activity?

Context

From the contemporary vantage point, it is easy to view British Columbia as the populous, economically prosperous, and culturally vibrant westernmost Canadian province. It almost never became these things: as the gold rush collapsed in the late 1860s, the economic outlook for British Columbia was dire, and the region stood on the precipice of being annexed by the United States. The nation-building aspirations of Sir John A. MacDonald prevented this from happening. Absolved of its debt, British Columbia became the sixth province of the Dominion of Canada in 1871, following Manitoba in 1870 and predating Alberta and Saskatchewan by thirty-four years. The desire in Ottawa for westward expansion of the Dominion was always economically motivated. When the "last spike" of the Canadian Pacific Railway was pounded in at Craigellachie in November 1885, it ensured access to Pacific trade and the movement of resources and people from the Pacific region and the newly founded city of Vancouver (1886) to Central and Eastern Canada.

From these precarious and humble beginnings, the outlook is markedly different almost 150 years later. Vancouver is now Canada's busiest port, handling more than half the country's container traffic, and the traditionally resource-based economy is becoming increasingly diversified. Yet British Columbia is often perceived (or perceives itself) as an outlier province, associated with untouched natural beauty and indeterminate cultural orientation – at times more Pacific Rim or Cascadia than part of Canada. The Rocky Mountains stand as a metaphorical barrier between British Columbia and the rest of Canada, at once keeping the preoccupations of Central Canada out, while making it harder for British Columbia to feel part of the national innovation conversation.

Apart from the sense of, or perhaps wish to be, isolated from federal politics and the federal policy environment, being the westernmost province in Canada puts British Columbia in an unusual position. This is certainly true of its demographic patterns, both historically and in terms of its contemporary position. It took until 1951, more than seventy years from becoming a province, for British Columbia's population to reach 1.18 million. By 1990, the population had risen to 3.25 million, and by the end of 2019 it was 5.1 million (BC Stats 2020b). Although there is an impression that British Columbia's population has grown mostly because of international immigration, particularly from India and China into the lower mainland, for fifty years the province's population has expanded mostly because of strong interprovincial migration (BC Stats 2020a). The median age in British Columbia is slightly higher (42.2 years) than the Canadian average (40.8 years), partly because of the influx of retirees into some BC communities from elsewhere in Canada (Statista 2019). Although English remains the dominant language in British Columbia, the range of languages spoken is staggering, with approximately one quarter of BC residents reporting one of nearly 250 languages other than English or French as their first language (Statistics Canada 2016). The linguistic diversity is explained by recent international immigration patterns, but also by the remarkable diversity of

First Nations languages – one-third of Canada's First Nations are in British Columbia (Canada 2010).

Between 2018 and 2019, 70,000 people moved to British Columbia, contributing to 2 per cent growth in the Fraser and Okanagan valleys. In absolute terms, the Greater Vancouver Region accounted for more than half of the growth, with an influx of 40,000 people. Some regions slipped, however, including the Northern Rockies, which posted a 4 per cent decline (BC Stats 2020c). Metro Vancouver's population of 2.6 million is roughly half the province's total, and is expected to grow by more than a million by 2050, largely from low but constant intra- and interprovincial movement combined with ongoing growth through immigration (Metrovancouver 2018). If the province reaches a forecast 7 million people by 2050 (Statistics Canada 2019), the Greater Vancouver Region alone could account for nearly two-thirds of the province's population. Following these trends in population growth, it is fair to say that, for the foreseeable future, there are three distinct economic and population groupings in British Columbia: the "lower mainland," the "interior," and the "island."

British Columbia's demographic patterns are rooted in historical precedents and have strong implications for the future of innovation, economic activity, and political economy in the province. For the first century after becoming a province, British Columbia's economy was rural and resource based (fishing, forestry, farming, and mining), with low levels of urbanization and just a few cities. As typical for a "staples-based" economy, British Columbia in the early days was characterized by economic activity in the resource-rich "hinterland," which relied heavily on transportation linkages to move goods from remote areas to markets (Innis 1930, 1933). As major urban centres expanded, supported by a growing services economy, the growing urban population increasingly viewed the staples economy as "rest-of-province" activities. The staples sectors thus confronted a changing political economy in which they were viewed as support for the services sector (Davis and Hutton 1989). Ley and Hutton (1987) commented that these differences likely would give rise to "divergence in the economic evolution" of the two different regions, one based on staples and the other on serving it. By the end of the 1980s, another economic driver had in fact become established in British Columbia. The third distinct sector was the expanded public sector economy, which, in British Columbia as in other provinces, contributed about half of total economic activity by the mid-1990s (Howlett and Brownsey 1996).

A mixture of demographics, political economies, and regions continues loosely to structure present-day British Columbia. South Vancouver

Island, with the provincial capital at Victoria, is dominated by public sector activity – primarily government, post-secondary education, and tourism. The lower mainland, especially the Greater Vancouver area, is services oriented and increasingly invested in digital technology. The "interior," as the hinterland or "rest-of-province" is sometimes called, is dominated by resource industries and tourism. The question for British Columbia as it grapples with policy options about the future of its economy, and the role of innovation in it, is how the choices for future economic activity will be made, given that economic diversification is relatively recent. The challenge for British Columbia is to provide coherence to the diversity of ideas about what the province is (or can be), with both new and old institutions reflecting commitments to different political economies and strongly vested economic, social, and political interests, often anchored in specific sectors and regions.

Innovation Architecture

Over four decades of economic transition, the BC economy has become less insular, less reliant on resource-based activity, and more diversified. Natural resources continue to play a small but significant role in British Columbia's economy, with agriculture, forestry, fishing, and hunting contributing an average of 2.4 per cent of the province's gross domestic product (GDP) and mining, oil, and gas extraction another 3.2 per cent. Construction and manufacturing, particularly in the cleantech sector, contribute 8.3 per cent and 7.0 per cent, respectively, to GDP, and experienced an average 2.5 per cent growth annually from 2014 to 2018. Stronger growth for wholesale and retail trade (3.5 per cent and 3.2 per cent annually) in the same period raised their GDP contributions to 4 per cent and 6 per cent, respectively. Nearly a quarter (23.7 per cent) of the contribution to GDP, however, came from the finance, insurance, real estate, rental, leasing, and management of companies and enterprises, which grew only 0.9 per cent annually from 2014 to 2018. Professional, scientific, and technical services contributed 6.3 per cent to GDP and educational services and health care and social assistance 5.2 per cent and 7.2 per cent, respectively. Accommodation and food services, both critical to the tourism and business travel industries, had good growth, at 2.6 per cent, over the period, and contributed 3.0 per cent to GDP. The information and cultural industries – sometimes colloquially referred to as "Hollywood North" – contributed 3.1 per cent of GDP.

Although evidence shows that British Columbia's economy has become steadily more diversified, there is relatively low gross expenditure on research and development (GERD) in the province. Across the economy as a whole, British Columbia invested on average approximately 1.5 per cent of its GDP on research and development (R&D) from 2013 to 2017 (Table 14.1). Performance tended to be relatively evenly split between the business sector and the higher education sector, which is itself interesting for two reasons. The first relates to a relatively recent "policy fix" during the first Trudeau mandate (2015–19) to address the low level of business expenditure on research and development (BERD). The federal government, during the Conservatives' leadership under Stephen Harper, attempted to make universities better at commercializing research, and examined the potential contribution that stronger intellectual property protection could make to innovation. These measures did not improve Canada's innovation performance, so the new Liberal government turned the focus to BERD. This, in turn, gave rise to the Innovation Superclusters Initiative, essentially a BERD stimulus program. British Columbia was awarded a supercluster in digital technology in an effort to shift what had been an even split between the private and public sector to greater levels of business-led R&D.

The second point to make about the relative split of GERD between business and higher education is that the provincial and federal governments offer good support for R&D in British Columbia, but they themselves are not strong performers of R&D, undertaking only 3.5 per cent of total R&D performed in the province. Corroborating evidence for this observation is that there are relatively few federal laboratories in British Columbia compared with Ontario and Quebec. For example, the National Research Council has only four of its seventy-two large facilities in British Columbia: the Canadian Astronomy Data Centre, the Dominion Astrophysical Laboratory, the Radio Astrophysical Observatory, and the Microgrid Testing and Training Facility. While there is nothing like proportional per capita distribution of federal labs in the province, it is worth noting that the labs present are usefully concentrated in related fields of inquiry.

When one considers the mix of R&D funders and performers in British Columbia, the overall balance looks quite strong, with a total expenditure over $3 billion on average per year. Put into context, in 2017 British Columbia had 13.5 per cent of the Canadian population, but accounted for only 11.6 per cent of national R&D expenditure – which means there is room to grow (Statistics Canada n.d.). This is particularly true of the private sector. While fifteen of the top one hundred Canadian industrial investors in R&D in 2017 were headquartered in British Columbia, the highest ranked was Telus at seventeenth. Each of these fifteen enterprises invested more than $11 million in 2017, but

Table 14.1. Gross Expenditure on Research and Development by Performing Sector, average $ millions, British Columbia, 2013–17

		Performers					
		Government		Provincial			Private
				Research	Business	Higher	Non-
Funders	Total	Federal	Provincial	Organizations	Enterprise	Education	profit
Total sectors	3,148	89	21	–	1,714	1,324	–
Federal government	542	89	–	–	84	366	–
Provincial government	110	–	21	–	12	77	–
Business enterprise	1,294	1	–	–	1,232	62	–
Higher education	657	–	–	–	–	657	–
Private non-profit	170	–	–	–	46	143	–
Foreign	387	–	–	–	368	19	–

Note: Columns and rows may not sum due to rounding.

Source: Statistics Canada, table 27-10-0273-01, "Gross domestic expenditures on research and development, by science type and by funder and performer sector (x 1,000,000)."

many projects were still at the research stage of development, investing multiples of their annual revenues. The mix includes information and communications technology (ITC) enterprises (TELUS, Sierra Wireless, Vecima Networks), biotech and pharmaceutical companies (Arbutus, Novelion), and a variety of new and cleantech companies (Maxar Technologies, Westport Fuel, Ballard Power Systems).

Within British Columbia's higher education sector, there is certainly capacity to increase the level and complexity of the R&D effort. The province has a diverse mixture of twenty-five private and public post-secondary institutions, of which eleven are regional colleges, three are provincially recognized institutes, and eleven are universities. Six universities are considered research intensive, and are represented by the Research Universities' Council of British Columbia (RUCBC). In reality, three universities – University of British Columbia (UBC), Simon Fraser University, and the University of Victoria – account for most of the

$900 million of annual research funding attributable to the six RUCBC members (RUCBC 2020); about another $400 million is absorbed by the other twenty-two universities, colleges, and institutes. Predictably, the research effort tends to be concentrated in the Greater Vancouver Region and the Greater Victoria Region, although Prince George, Kelowna, and Kamloops have significant local presence and increasing research effort.

Many of the major research organizations in British Columbia were started by research universities and their partners, which continue to host most of them on-site as separate legal entities. For example, MITACS (Mathematics of Information Technology and Complex Systems), founded in 1999 as one Canada's Networks of Centres of Excellence, provides programs and supports across Canada and internationally. MITACS has offices in all major cities across Canada, but is primarily sustained on the UBC campus. In a case of true BC leadership for Canada, MITACS has supported more than 33,000 students and 3,600 international collaborations. Another development with national research is the Tri-University Meson Facility, TRIUMF, a five-decade-long initiative of the University of Victoria, UBC, and Simon Fraser University, now with twenty-one member universities across Canada. TRIUMF is Canada's national laboratory for nuclear and particle physics research, supporting over five hundred researchers and nearly a thousand visitors each year, and hosts TRIUMF Innovations, a business development and commercialization unit originally created in 2008 as Advanced Applied Physics Solutions Inc., one of eleven awards under the Centres of Excellence in the Commercialization of Research Program.

Two environmentally oriented major research organizations at the University of Victoria have large R&D footprints. Ocean Networks Canada (ONC), founded in 2012, operates cabled ocean observatories, coastal remote sensing, and earthquake early warning sensors, mostly located in British Columbia, but also in the Arctic and Atlantic Canada. ONC receives substantial funding from the Canada Foundation for Innovation (CFI) as a Major Science Initiative, employs more than 140 people, has strong partnerships with local, national, and international private sector partners, and is a World Data System member out of recognition for its in-house ocean research data platform. A different kind of research institute is the Pacific Institute for Climate Solutions (PICS), created in 2008 with a $90 million endowment from the Gordon Campbell Liberal government. PICS is hosted by the University of Victoria, but works with UBC, Simon Fraser University, and the University of Northern British Columbia to create province-wide support for research into innovative climate change solutions. Over the years, PICS has supported 160 graduate and post-doctoral fellows and 100 interns in industry, government, and the community, contributing an important part of the R&D on which the BC government relies to deliver the Climate Action Plan and CleanBC strategies.

British Columbia has three major health research organizations. The Centre for Drug Research and Development at UBC acts as an intermediary in the innovation system to foster clinical drug development with university, government, and private sector partners, providing both R&D infrastructure and access to partners and investment. Genome BC, part of the network of regional centres coordinated by Genome Canada, has received more than $240 million from the BC government to support leveraged partnerships with universities and private sector partners. Genome BC has invested in 360 projects worth more than $1 billion since 2001. The Michael Smith Foundation for Health Research has funded more than 1,700 individual health researchers and 120 research teams, and is an important part of overall health research coordination in British Columbia, facilitating collaboration among government, health systems and research universities.

Beyond the post-secondary sector and these major research organizations, there is a range of interests associated with R&D and innovation more generally in British Columbia. The provincial government does not undertake a large amount of intramural research itself, but instead makes use of its own secondary research analysis and contract research from universities and colleges to set policy directions and fulfil regulatory mandates. There are six health authorities in the province, with highly variable R&D and innovation capacity – much of their research is conducted with university partners through sponsored research funds. British Columbia's single medical school is based in Vancouver at UBC, but its programs are also offered regionally in Kelowna, Prince George, and Victoria, leading to a distributed approach to parts of health research and innovation. There is also a loose fabric of regional economic development agencies across the province, such as the South Island Prosperity Partnership and the Union of BC Municipalities, which work with the provincial government and Western Economic Diversification Canada – divided in 2021 into a BC specific agency, Pacific Economic Development Canada (PacifiCAn), and Prairies Economic Development Canada (PrairiesCan) – to develop mostly social innovation programs that promote the interest of local partners. Some attempt has been made to measure the impact of this kind of activity because it involves research and socio-economic development, but it tends to be spot analysis rather than sustained across the province (Victoria Foundation 2018).

The Policy Effort

British Columbia has many of the elements one would hope for in a fully functioning innovation system, but the question is whether it is purposefully structured and functioning. As the following discussion suggests, the elements in the system anticipate an emerging innovation agenda in the province, responding to recent evolution of the political and economic landscape. For its first seventy years as a province, British Columbia was dominated by left-of-centre politics that grew out of labour movements in the early to mid-1900s. More recently, right-of-centre parties have governed: the fiscally and socially conservative Social Credit party for thirty-five years after 1952 and the Liberals from 2001 to 2017. The NDP has governed for about twenty years, in three blocks, since the early 1970s. Consistent with expectations of those working in the resources and related industries, worker protection and the right to fair wages and treatment were dominant political issues for many decades, and remain salient today. One of the central election promises that returned the NDP to office in 2017 was making British Columbia more affordable for all residents, a promise reiterated in subsequent NDP budgets. Compared with neighbouring Alberta, the frequent left-right changes in British Columbia's government might seem politically dramatic, but the impact on innovation policy has been mostly negligible.

Two notable changes happened in 2017. The first was that John Horgan became the first premier of British Columbia representing a Vancouver Island constituency since John Hart's premiership from 1941 to 1947. This was an important political shift because it relocated the perspective on BC politics and the economy to a view from the island, and away from the lower mainland. Of the nine premiers since the early 1990s, most were elected from lower mainland or Vancouver ridings, or from the interior in the cases of Christy Clark and W.A.C. Bennett. Second, the BC Liberals had been right-of-centre drivers of diversification of the economy, supporters of domestic and foreign investment, and followers of a more centrist approach to taxing and spending relative to the NDP. By the time the NDP resumed power in 2017, the political-economic narrative of British Columbia as a resource-dependent economy was an attenuated and slightly tired narrative. The BC Liberals had elevated a private sector–oriented and largely metro Vancouver services economy narrative. The Liberals were primarily responsible for breaking free from the staples trap and the public policy it fostered, long described in the literature about British Columbia's political economy (see Watkins 1963). In its return to power, the NDP has attempted to build a bridge between the resource and services sectors, often seeking to exploit linkages between them – for example, in mining and related high-technology services. It has balanced this pro-innovation stance, however, with a sense of urgency of the need to make British Columbia more affordable, diverse, and accessible. In many ways, this represents an important inflexion point in British Columbia's political economy, as the traditionally left-of-centre NDP has moved slightly towards the centre on the economic spectrum, while maintaining and sharing left-spectrum politics and social policy with the Greens, with whom it formed a Confidence and Supply Agreement over the 2017–20 period. The implications of the evolving political and political economic landscape for innovation policy are not yet clear, but one can see that the government needs to shape its policy effort to respond to emerging trends in the economy.

The British Columbia economy's strength in recent decades is shown in part by its growth across increasingly diversified sectors. Relative growth between sectors, however, acts as much as a political as an economic driver. Using North American Industry Classification System (NAICS) Aggregations from 1997 to 2018, one can see some interesting, coarse-grained differences. Overall, the economy doubled. Sectors that showed slower growth include forestry and logging, services related to forestry and agriculture, supports to mining, oil, and gas, clothing, textiles, and paper industries, and the local insurance industry. These sectors reflect the traditional extractive industries and associated regional services, many of which have either closed or been offshored. Many of the sectors that are the core of the new services economy, in contrast, were relatively stable. Sectors that more than doubled output over the period include beverage and tobacco manufacturing, retail trade, rail and truck transportation and related support services, information and cultural industries (especially motion picture and sound recording industries), real estate, and professional and scientific services. Fast-growth sectors, which more than tripled their output over the decade, include oil and gas extraction, construction, electrical equipment, appliance and component manufacturing, air transportation, and the ICT sector, including both manufacturing and related services. This is an interesting mix, for it includes growth in generally high-skilled roles in industries such as liquefied natural gas (LNG) extraction and shipping, as well as the creative and digital sectors.

The policy effort in British Columbia, as in many parts of Canada, continues to pay attention to slower-growth areas of economic activity because they reflect political sensitivities about "traditional" (often rural) economic sectors. The struggling logging industry and the impact that lumber mill closures have on single-industry small towns is an ongoing concern. Between 2001 and 2011, the province's small-town population declined by 3 per cent, whereas the urban population grew by nearly 17 per cent (Strengthening Rural Canada Initiative 2015). At the same time, there are sectors in British Columbia that are clearly higher value added – for example, some life sciences and digital technologies – but any appearance of unequivocal support for these (mostly urban) industries puts political elites offside with the voting public, as it did in 2017. Given that any BC government has a rough ride whenever it appears to be picking winners, the safer bet would be to take a step back from visibly supporting individual firms or sectors and nurturing the broader innovation system. Here the policy effort would be directed towards creating conditions under which innovation can flourish – so called determinants of innovation – in the broader context of the system of "all important economic, social, political, organizational, and other factors that influence the development, diffusion, and use of innovations" (Edquist 1997, 14; 2004). Governments have a legitimate and important role in shaping the institutions and organizations that are conducive to innovation (Edquist and Johnson 1997). In recent years, the provincial government has become increasingly interested in pursuing a policy effort that promotes system coordination, firm growth, and innovation clusters. It is important to note, however, that, while BC-government-sponsored projects, programs, and policy initiatives are liberally sprinkled with the jargon of the day – "innovation," "clusters," "unicorns," "disruptive technology" – the initiatives themselves are not steeped in the recognizable innovation systems thinking that anchors scholarly research and explicitly guides some other jurisdictions' policy efforts.

Purposeful innovation policy effort is relatively new in British Columbia, and is taking time to mature. Currently, three strands of policy effort are visible in the province. First, there are attempts to provide better overall *system coordination* to improve the likelihood that R&D efforts will lead to innovation. Second, there are targeted efforts directed towards *firm growth*, in both number and size. The third, and most recent, policy effort is to create broad *innovation policy cover* for British Columbia through an explicit innovation policy framework by appointing a Commissioner for Innovation and through a new Crown agency specifically focused on inculcating the culture and practices associated with innovation-led economies.

System Coordination

The provincial government's 2016 Corporate Plan, coming at the end of the seventeen-year run of the BC Liberals, had three goals: building internal capacity, improving competitiveness, and enhancing service to citizens.

The Christy Clark Liberals (2011–17) had placed a major bet on LNG expansion, and had tuned much of the provincial system – government reporting entities (GREs), government business entities (GBEs), and Crown corporations – to ensure that the consolidated financial position would earn the province the best possible bond ratings to attract international investment to the LNG project. System tuning had impacts on organizations and institutions associated with the R&D effort and innovation system, many which were not remotely connected to LNG. For example, new performance screens were put into effect for the Michael Smith Foundation for Health Research and for Genome BC, while the entire post-secondary system of universities and colleges was required by Treasury Board to consolidate and balance its books at the discretion of the finance minister, who decreed that henceforth all these institutions would be GREs. The direct effect of these steps was that higher education institutions were no longer able to take on debt (even if self-financed), which curtailed most capital projects, research oriented or otherwise. Moreover, major real estate plays, such as those undertaken by UBC that raised funds to elevate the school into the top ranks of global universities, were now captured by the GRE rules. The immediate effect was stifling for post-secondary institutions and their partners, and put a spotlight on the broader priorities of government.

A good illustration of British Columbia's approach to providing provincial matching funds for innovation infrastructure is the BC Knowledge Development Fund, established in 1998, which provides matching funds for research and development projects funded by the CFI. During the latter years of the Clark government, the Fund remained in the Ministry of Technology and Citizen Services under Minister John Jacobsen's watch. The paymaster for the Fund was (and continues to be) the Ministry of Advanced Education, then overseen by Minister Andrew Wilkinson. Over the years, an impression had developed in the Liberal cabinet that the advanced education system was on a random walk regarding how major research projects were developed and supported, with the government simply expected to step up to support initiatives that succeeded in CFI competitions. In 2016, the two ministries decided to make co-funding appear less random, at least from their perspective, by restricting how the Fund's resources were used (in much the same way as Ontario), requiring new pre-application screens, a focus on technology development and potential for commercialization, and risk ratings for large projects exceeding a dollar threshold. The latter was a particularly interesting administrative development, as the best available risk-rating screens available to the provincial government were those used for major capital projects (such as bridges) by the Ministry of Transportation and Infrastructure.

Earlier in the decade, the Liberals undertook to stimulate innovation in British Columbia by complementing the policy efforts directed at public sector R&D capacity with greater system coordination between public and private sector efforts. With much fanfare, the BC Technology Summit was launched in 2016, and has since been a yearly draw to Vancouver for researchers, entrepreneurs, universities and colleges, private sector firms, and municipal, provincial, and federal government partners. In parallel to the Tech Summit, new Cascadia Corridor initiatives were launched, principally focused on British Columbia, Washington State, and the joint interests of Vancouver and Seattle, with Microsoft playing a founding role in stimulating cross-border initiatives. Cascadia is a long-term policy effort for British Columbia and its partners, with cross-border collaborative R&D still largely the domain of multinational software and services firms, with the higher education sector using federal funds in each country. Following the 2017 election, the NDP needed the support of Andrew Weaver's Green Party. The resulting Confidence and Supply Agreement came at a price: the Greens wanted a new position of Innovation Commissioner for British Columbia, largely because they wanted to see the province commit to a stronger effort related to clean technologies supportive of the BC Climate Action Plan. About the same time, the BC Innovation Council, which was established in 2004 by the Liberals under Gordon Campbell, morphed into Innovate BC, with a new strategy, leadership, and board, described in greater detail below.

In 2017, the BC Knowledge Development Fund moved into the Ministry of Jobs, Trade and Technology under Minister Bruce Ralston, who was widely viewed as engaged and supportive of greater provincial research and innovation efforts. One of the ministry's first tasks was to support British Columbia's proposal to the federal government's Innovation Supercluster Initiative. The Canadian Digital Technology Supercluster now has projects funded and running, although its impact on the BC and Canadian economies will take time to assess. In parallel, a Quantum Algorithms Institute is being developed to take advantage of previous investments in British Columbia quantum infrastructure under the Canada First Research Excellence Fund and the presence of private sector interests in firms such as D-Wave Systems, 1QBit, IBM, and Fujitsu (British Columbia 2020). In contrast to these significant but relatively niche investments, the broad brushstrokes of the government's 2019 budget presented a more well-rounded conception of public policy, albeit focused on delivering an improved mix of social services. Again, the policy effort on innovation was selective in its approach and supportive of new economy initiatives, without abandoning centre-left social policy. Growing the economy in this way is how the current provincial government hopes to make life more affordable, deliver better services, and invest in a sustainable economy (BC Stats 2019).

For much of 2019 and the first months of 2020, investments in a sustainable economy were guided by the 2019 budget, and influenced by provincial innovation policy. It was generally anticipated that the policy context would stay motivated by these ideas and interests, presumably all the way until the end of the Confidence and Supply Agreement in 2021. Despite an early election in 2020, the six pillars remained intact: the CleanBC Strategy (British Columbia 2019a), a priority on talent, modernizing infrastructure, strengthening resource industries, fuelling job and industry growth, and protecting people and places. As a set of goals, they can either be criticized for attempting to square the circle between British Columbia's current resource-intensive economic activities and a future based on clean technology or they can be positioned as required balance that can lead to energy transitions. For example, the CleanBC Strategy, partly through the Foresight Cleantech Accelerator Cluster created in 2019 in the Greater Vancouver area, supports lower emissions, lower energy use overall, the circular economy, and waste-to-resource strategies. At the same time, the less climate-friendly LNG industry continues to develop. Interestingly, and perhaps an important historical pivot for British Columbia and the NDP, the forest sector was specifically referenced in the 2020 budget, but notably not for further investment in old approaches to the sector, but rather for investment to transition to "engineered wood products," "revitalization within the forest sector," and, where appropriate, supports to workers for early retirement (BC Stats 2020b).

Firm Growth

Following overall system coordination, the second policy effort directed towards improving British Columbia's innovation performance has concentrated on firm growth, in terms of both numbers of firms and the development of more medium-sized and large enterprises. In Canada, most businesses are small or medium-sized enterprises (SMEs). As of December 2017, the Canadian economy had 1.18 million firms, of which 97.9 per cent (1.15 million) were small (1–99 paid employees), 1.9 per cent were medium (100 to 499 paid employees), and 0.2 per cent were large (500 or more paid employees) (Canada 2019). In British Columbia, about 75 per cent of the private sector labour force is employed by small businesses, compared with the national average of 69.7 per cent; consequently, fewer jobs are in medium-sized business (18.7 per cent in British Columbia, 19.9 per cent for Canada) and large enterprises (6.5 per cent in British Columbia, 10.4 per cent for Canada) (Canada 2019).

Compared with other provinces, British Columbia has performed well in terms of new job creation in small businesses, where the average annual growth rate of 1.8 per cent from 2013 to 2017 (compared with 1.1 per cent for Canada) yielded 103,500 new jobs. Although the average annual growth rates for medium businesses (3.3 per cent in British Columbia, 1.0 per cent for Canada) and large businesses (2.9 per cent in British Columbia, 1.6 per cent for Canada) give the impression of strong growth across all business sizes, the relatively small base of employment in these firms yields small absolute net employment growth in medium (44,300 jobs) and large businesses (8,300 jobs) (Canada 2019). Most medium and large businesses in British Columbia are also not typically "home grown," which in part explains the province's policy effort to reshape the SME landscape; there is perennial concern that British Columbia's talent pool can be siphoned off (or enticed away) by BC-based subsidiaries of large multinationals, such as Microsoft, which is headquartered just south of Vancouver in Redmond, Washington.

British Columbia is capable of generating many new small businesses, each with small numbers of employees. Data from 2018 show that 83 per cent of business in British Columbia had five or fewer employees (BC Stats 2019). This is a direct product of the system architecture, which supports smaller, home-grown ventures with relatively easy technology transfer from universities, extensive co-op education and placement opportunities for students, access to supporting programs through Mitacs and the Creative Destruction Laboratories, ease of registering new businesses, and the gearing of public and private supports (accelerators, incubators, angel and venture capital). The system goal has been to encourage entrepreneurship, but arguably at the entry level of investment and risk; consequently, there are not that many large firms or big economic plays in British Columbia. Recognizing and addressing this gap has motivated both the BC Liberals and the NDP. In 2016, the Liberals established a $100 million BC Technology Fund and initiated development work on the Supercluster, which was continued by the NDP and coordinated through the new position of innovation commissioner. These policy efforts clearly demonstrate an interest in growing more firms with scale in British Columbia.

Firm size matters to governments because larger domestic firms offer employees better professional growth trajectories, are more likely to have sustained R&D interactions with local universities and government partners, support serial entrepreneurship, and are more likely to have commercialized products and services that can be licensed and exported. The small number of medium-sized and large businesses has given rise to some other peculiarities in British Columbia. For example, in a departure from international conventions, as well as those of Innovation, Science and Economic Development Canada and Statistics Canada, British Columbia reports large business in the province as those having more than 50 paid employees, rather than the customary 500+ benchmark. The idiosyncratic threshold enabled the province to report a growth rate in large businesses of 10.2 per cent between 2014 and 2018, which would be an extraordinary number if the more conventional threshold for large firms had been used. In reality, however, it portrays an overoptimistic picture, since the British Columbia numbers reflect an overall increase of 800 businesses of only 50 employees or more. Accelerate Okanagan, for example, claims that nearly 693 technology firms with 12,474 employees are driving $1.67 billion in annual impact in the valley, at the same time as the Okanagan Chamber of Commerce's reports that Kelowna, compared with sixteen cities across the world, is below par, earning D grades in GDP and disposable income per capita (Kelowna Chamber of Commerce 2019; Okanagan Edge 2019). Focusing attention on real progress is complicated by these kinds of legerdemain.

Innovation Policy Cover

To give some systemwide coherence to innovation in British Columbia, and to tackle some of the issues and challenges related to firm growth and R&D performance, in 2019 the province released its *Technology Policy and Innovation Framework* (British Columbia 2019b), arguably the first ever explicitly innovation-focused publicly accessible policy document. The Framework was created to guide investments in the British Columbia innovation system, perhaps not explicitly in the language of the "determinants of innovation," but certainly in its spirit. The province had come to recognize a talent gap, especially in high-demand digital industries, and the need to: develop better *in situ* training to address specific company requirements; improve internet connectivity, particularly for rural and remote areas; tackle the firm scale-up issue; improve venture capital access through the BC Tech Fund; develop a more comprehensive procurement strategy; and help small communities to thrive. The policy effort was fourfold: grow globally competitive industry clusters; increase access and diversity to the innovation economy; help companies scale and stay anchored in the province; and grow the talent pool and attract investment through Trade and Invest British Columbia.

One might describe the Framework narrowly as an economic policy to support British Columbia's emerging digital technology sector, since much of it is geared to the Digital Supercluster and the new Quantum Algorithms Institute. Certainly, the impetus for developing the Framework was in part to answer calls for a "Silicon Valley North" strategy in the province. Aspects of the Framework, however, are more akin to a comprehensive innovation policy that would fit many of the high-growth NCAIS sectors discussed earlier. Although the strategy is somewhat dated, identifying actual or potential sectors of strength to encourage clusters – along with scaling, training, and retaining talent and attracting investment – is a well-known regional innovation strategy that has yielded results in other jurisdictions, such as North Carolina's Research Triangle (Etzkowitz 2012). British Columbia implicitly has pursued clustering methodology to locate or assemble concentrations of capabilities and to grow firms, but since the launch of the Framework, it is fair to say that little overt progress has been made or reported. The Framework can be usefully thought of as a signal to British Columbia and the federal government, offering a wish list and a map of the province's strategic direction. Two particular actions by the province have meant to turn aspiration into action.

First, in 2018, Alan Winter, former president and chief executive officer of Genome BC, was appointed innovation commissioner for a two-year term. Winter is something of a fixture in British Columbia science and technology R&D circles, having engaged for years in industry and policy ventures. He was assigned six areas of focus: strategic partnerships with the federal government, advocating for federal innovation funding, championing British Columbia's technology sector, attracting inward investment, linking companies with partners domestically and abroad, and supporting the implementation of government innovation and technology mandates (British Columbia 2018). At the same time, the former British Columbia Innovation Council was upcycled as Innovate BC, a Crown corporation with the mandate to develop programs to support science-and-technology-enabled R&D, business opportunities and partnerships, to support entrepreneurs, capacity building, market access, policy development, and implementation, and to spur post-secondary and regional engagement. Innovate BC continues to manage the BC Tech Summit, which remains a technology showcase and convening point for academe, business, and government with a focus on British Columbia and province's place in the Cascadia innovation corridor.

Conclusions and Lessons

The year 2016 marked the tenth anniversary since the British Columbia government implemented annual service plans for the civil service. In the conclusion of the 2016 plan, *Where Ideas Work*, it asserts that "[t]here is an inherent tension between our traditional responsibilities and the need for innovation" (British Columbia 2016, 22), which suggests recognition that the public service has to be responsive to new socio-economic realities, demands for new services, increased pressure for digital services to complement traditional provision, and so forth. On its own, it is a cogent recognition of where British Columbia stands, and it conveys the sense that the province is shifting focus. In this respect, new ideas about British Columbia's future are generating new political and economic interests in the province as demographic patterns and the composition of the economy continue to shift.

At the same time, however, the impact of newer thinking and different motivations is limited by clear conceptions about how to design and implement institutions that will carry these ideas and interests forward to some tangible impact. The 2016 plan failed to expound on what that movement might be or on where there was a need for fresh thinking, experimentation, monitoring, and evaluation of new initiatives, programs, and experiments with institutional design – such as the potential for impact on the core of government that the BC Behavioural Insights Group could make. Instead, the plan noted: "But our integrity is not at odds with innovation. Our integrity is what compels us to innovate."

These baffling statements can be usefully compared with the much more focused and directional statements of Minister Ralston at the beginning of the 2019 *Technology and Innovation Policy Framework*:

> The B.C. government is focused on championing technology and innovation because it creates good-paying jobs for British Columbians. It also supports economic development and growth across all regions of the province and helps address shared priorities, like meeting CleanBC targets. We have made technology and innovation a priority for economic growth recognizing how critical it is to increase our competitiveness in every sector of the economy, from creating cleaner and greener products, to maximizing the value that is obtained from our wealth of natural resources. (British Columbia 2019b, 2)

In the four years between the two sets of statements about innovation, it appears that British Columbia is starting to develop a more mature policy stance in which ideas, interests, and institutions will have clearer articulation and integration.

But where will it go? At the moment, British Columbia is in a good position to promote research and development and to broaden and deepen nascent innovation policy. With an enviable geography and good quality of life in its cities and rural regions, the province maintains a competitive advantage for recruiting talent into post-secondary institutions, the provincial government, and the private sector. As with all jurisdictions, there are headwinds, and for British Columbia they include the continued dominance of very small business with low growth potential. At the moment, the private sector is not leading the province towards greater innovative capacity or wealth creation – it is still very much a provincial government policy push. The *Framework*, revamping the Council into Innovate BC, and the appointment of Gerri Sinclair as the second innovation commissioner are attempts to broaden the effort. Innovate BC has been working to identify natural clusters for targeted investment to scale R&D and commercialization activity as a lead-in to the creation of medium and large firms in British Columbia. All the while, the challenge for the province will be to balance investment and support for old and new sectors, adapt to rapidly changing demographics, and cope with the long-standing socio-economic, political, and cultural divisions between urban and rural regions.

By March 2020, the analysis of British Columbia's historical footing, demographic patterns, the mapping of different phases in the province's political economy to regions and to political shifts, and the selection of the key factors influencing the nascent science, technology, and innovation policy, had been completed. On 11 March that year, the World Health Organization declared the first pandemic caused by a coronavirus. As COVID-19 became even more disruptive by the fall of 2020, the NDP, knowing it had been polling better than the Liberals even before the pandemic, saw an opportunity to break the Confidence and Supply Agreement with the Greens, end their coalition government, call a snap election off-cycle with a fixed election date of 24 October. The NDP won a solid majority (fifty-seven of eighty-seven seats), and now has to face the vestiges of both its 2017 platform and a pandemic.

Although the toll the pandemic will put on the economy and the long-term stresses and setbacks to British Columbians remain guesswork, the answer could lie in the uneasy, or perhaps creative, tension in the NDP platform (NDP 2020). That platform describes both working "towards full recovery," which has undertones of going back to the way things were pre-pandemic, and working "to move BC forward," which has overtones of making British Columbia more affordable, prosperous, and sustainable. The NDP government has articulated fully a progressive socio-economic agenda (on the table since 2017). Some of it can be leveraged by the pandemic to fast-track some initiatives, such as affordable housing that meets the twin objectives of helping ease homelessness and attending to public health objectives. In other cases, COVID-19 could work against the policy, by, for example, undermining accessible post-secondary education. There will be some hard policy choices to make about the role of science, technology, and innovation in post-COVID British Columbia because "full recovery" and "going forward" are neither binary nor mutually exclusive. We will be able to look back, some years along, to examine whether or not the terrible misfortune of the pandemic helped advance the innovation agenda.

References

BC Stats. 2019. "Small Business Profile." Victoria. Online at https://www2 .gov.bc.ca/assets/gov/employment-business-and-economic-development /business-management/small-business/sb_profile.pdf, accessed 20 April 2020.

BC Stats. 2020a. "Data Catalogue: Inter-provincial and International Migration." Victoria. Online at https://catalogue.data.gov.bc.ca/dataset /inter-provincial-and-international-migration, accessed 20 April 2020.

BC Stats. 2020b. Population and Demographic Statistics Section. "Quarterly Population 1951–2019." Victoria. Online at https://www2.gov.bc.ca/gov /content/data/statistics/people-population-community/population /population-estimates, accessed 20 April 2020.

BC Stats. 2020c. "2019 Sub-Provincial Population Estimates – Highlights." Victoria. Online at https://www2.gov.bc.ca/assets/gov/data/statistics /people-population-community/population/pop_sub-provincial _population_highlights.pdf, accessed 20 April 2020.

British Columbia. 2016. *Where Ideas Work: A Corporate Plan for the BC Public Service.* Victoria. Online at https://www2.gov.bc.ca/gov/content /governments/services-for-government/service-experience-digital -delivery/service-design/service-design-in-the-bc-public-service/service -design-and-our-corporate-vision, accessed 20 April 2020.

British Columbia. 2018. "Innovation Commissioner." Victoria. Online at https://www2.gov.bc.ca/gov/content/governments/about-the-bc

-government/technology-innovation/innovation-commissioner#bio, accessed 20 April 2020.

British Columbia. 2019a. "CleanBC." Victoria. Online at https://blog.gov. bc.ca/app/uploads/sites/436/2019/02/CleanBC_Full_Report_Updated _Mar2019.pdf, accessed 20 April 2020.

British Columbia. 2019b. *Technology and Innovation Policy Framework*. Victoria. Online at https://www2.gov.bc.ca/assets/gov/british-columbians -our-governments/initiatives-plans-strategies/technology-industry /technology_and_innovation_policy_framework.pdf, accessed 20 April 2020.

British Columbia. 2020. "New Quantum Algorithms Institute positions B.C. as hub for quantum computing." Victoria. Online at https://www .britishcolumbia.ca/global/trade-and-investment-british-columbia-blog /october-2019/new-quantum-algorithms-institute-positions-b-c-as-/, accessed 20 April 2020.

Canada. 2010. Indigenous and Northern Affairs Canada. "About British Columbia First Nations." Ottawa. Online at https://www.aadnc-aandc. gc.ca/eng/1100100021009/1314809450456, accessed 22 September 2021.

Canada. 2019. Innovation, Science and Economic Development Canada. "Key Small Business Statistics." Ottawa. Online at www.ic.gc.ca /sbstatistics, accessed 20 April 2020.

Davis, H.C., and T. Hutton. 1989. "The Two Economies of British Columbia." *BC Studies* 82 (Summer): 3–15. https://doi.org/10.14288/bcs.v0i82.1320.

Edquist, C. 1997. "Systems of Innovation Approaches – Their Emergence and Characteristics." In *Systems of Innovation: Technologies, Institutions and Organizations*, ed. C. Edquist, 3–37. London: Pinter/Cassell Academic.

Edquist, C. 2004. "Reflections on the Systems of Innovation Approach." *Science and Public Policy* 31 (6): 485–9. http://doi.org/10.3152/14715 4304781779741.

Edquist, C., and B. Johnson. 1997. "Institutions and Organisations in Systems of Innovation." In *Systems of Innovation: Technologies, Institutions and Organizations*, ed. C. Edquist, 41–63. London: Pinter/Cassell Academic.

Etzkowitz, H. 2012. "Triple Helix Clusters: Boundary Permeability at University-Industry-Government Interfaces as a Regional Innovation Strategy." *Environment and Planning C: Government and Policy* 30 (5): 766–79. http://doi.org/10.1068/c1182.

Howlett, M., and K. Brownsey. 1996. "From Timber to Tourism: The Political Economy of British Columbia." In *Politics, Policy, and Government in British Columbia*, ed. R.K. Carty, 18–31. Vancouver: UBC Press.

Innis, H.A. 1930. *The Fur Trade in Canada*. Toronto: University of Toronto Press.

Innis, H.A. 1933. *Problems of Staple Production in Canada*. Toronto: Ryerson Press.

Kelowna Chamber of Commerce. 2019. "Kelowna Economic Scorecard."
    Online at https://www.kelownachamber.org/files/COK18-041_Economic%
    20Score%20Card_ Single_web.pdf, accessed 20 April 2020.

Ley, D., and T. Hutton. 1987. "Vancouver's Corporate Complex and Producer
    Services Sector: Linkages and Divergence within a Provincial Staples
    Economy." *Journal of Regional Studies* 21 (5): 413–24. https://doi.org/10.1080
    /00343408712331344578.

Metrovancouver. 2018. "Metro Vancouver Growth Projections – A
    Backgrounder." Online at http://www.metrovancouver.org/services
    /regional-planning/PlanningPublications/OverviewofMetro
    VancouversMethodsinProjectingRegionalGrowth.pdf, accessed
    20 April 2020.

NDP (New Democratic Party). 2020. "Working for You: John Horgan's
    Commitments to BC." Online at https://www.bcndp.ca/platform.

OECD (Organisation for Economic Co-operation and Development). 2004.
    "New Economy Definition." *OECD Glossary of Statistical Terms*, 26 August.
    Paris. Online at https://stats.oecd.org/glossary/detail.asp?ID=6267.

Okanagan Edge. 2019. "Kelowna Has Work to Do." Online at https://
    okanaganedge.net/2019/02/11/kelowna-has-work-to-do/, accessed
    20 April 2020.

RUCBC (Research Universities' Council of British Columbia). 2020. "British
    Columbia Research Universities by the Numbers." Online at https://rucbc
    .ca/?page_id=816, accessed 22 April 2021.

Statista. 2019. "Median Age of the Resident Population of Canada in 2019, by
    Province." Online at https://www.statista.com/statistics/444816/canada
    -median-age-of-resident-population-by-province/, accessed 20 April 2020.

Statistics Canada. 2016. "British Columbia Census Profile." Ottawa.
    Online *at* https://www12.statcan.gc.ca/census-recensement/2016
    /dp-pd/prof/details/page.
    cfm?Lang=E&Geo1=PR&Code1 = 59&Geo2=PR&Code2 = 01&Search
    Text=Canada&SearchType=Begins&SearchPR=01&B1=All&type=0,
    accessed 222 September 2021.

Statistics Canada. 2019. "Population Projections for Canada (2018 to 2068),
    Provinces and Territories (2018 to 2043): Technical Report on Methodology
    and Assumptions." Ottawa. Online at https://www150.statcan.gc.ca/n1
    /pub/91-620-x/91-620-x2019001-eng.htm, accessed 20 April 2020.

Strengthening Rural Canada Initiative. 2015. *Fewer & Older: The Population
    and Demographic Dilemma in Rural British Columbia.* Online at http://
    strengtheningruralcanada.ca/file/Fewer-Older-The-Population-and
    -Demographic-Dilemma-in-Rural-British-Columbia1.pdf, accessed
    20 April 2020.

Victoria Foundation. 2018. "Civil Society Impact: Measuring Economic and Social Activity in the Victoria Capital Region." Online at https://victoriafoundation.bc.ca/wp-content/uploads/2018/11/21204-Charity-Impact-Report-FINAL_Low-res2.pdf, accessed 20 April 2020.

Watkins, M. 1963. "A Staple Theory of Economic Growth." *Canadian Journal of Economics and Political Science* 29 (2): 141–58. https://doi.org/10.2307/139461.

15 The Territories: Inverting Innovation for Canada's North

KEN COATES AND SARA MCPHEE-KNOWLES

Governments across Canada share a common belief that engagement with the "new" economy, meaning one based on intensively using new or innovative technologies to produce, sell, and distribute goods and services (OECD 2004), is central to long-term prosperity and economic sustainability. At the federal, provincial, territorial, Indigenous, and municipal levels, governments pursue a variety of strategies, investments, and programs designed to encourage the commercialization of science and technology, the incubation of start-up companies, and the creation of a competitive, globally engaged, and innovative commercial environment. This shared commitment to innovation poses particular challenges for the North.

Canada's three northern territories are heavily subsidized by the federal government, but access to substantial national support has not addressed the fundamental challenges and realities of the "new economy" in this remote and relatively sparsely populated area. The territories are a unique combination of a well-supported, mostly non-Indigenous population living in the main centres, and economically marginalized, mostly Indigenous people living in small remote communities. The core requirements of twenty-first-century competitiveness – high-speed internet connectivity, a highly trained workforce, ready access to investment capital, and a strong entrepreneurial environment – are noticeably weak in much of the North. The challenges facing the territories – cyclical booms and busts in the resources economy, major climate change effects, and lack of many of the fundamental elements of competitiveness – are formidable. Governments and the private sector are struggling to catch up, let alone get ahead, in what has become a truly global effort to reinvent work, commerce, and the foundations of prosperity. Without thoughtful consideration to innovation policy, the territories are at risk of dislocation from innovation and being cut off from a major driver of economic growth.

Context

The territorial North, consisting of the Yukon, Northwest Territories (NWT), and Nunavut, is characterized by economic extremes: heavy reliance on government spending as the foundation of the region's economy; modern treaties that are reinventing and reimagining governance structures; and substantial new investment capital in the hands of Indigenous governments and their development corporations. The North also has cold, long, and dark winters, a volatile and underperforming resource economy, territories bigger than most provinces with populations comparable to the size of medium towns, widely dispersed and small communities, and proportionately larger Indigenous populations than the rest of the country (Table 15.1).

The northern economies appear strong from a high-level statistical perspective, but the underlying reality is a reliance on government transfers to the territorial governments, to First Nations and Inuit communities, and to individuals. Many of the workers in the territorial North are government employees. To provide but one sign of the reliance on government, federal transfers per capita for fiscal year 2019/20 were $43,790 in Nunavut, $30,704 in NWT, and $25,560 in Yukon, as compared with $1,464 in Ontario, Alberta, Saskatchewan, and British Columbia (Canada 2019). The resources sector is episodically strong, sustained at present by mining across the North, although the distance and cost of transporting resources to market mean that mines only operate when demand is strong and resource prices are high. Investments in major infrastructure projects, such as hydroelectric and transportation, at times drive employment in the region.

The northern economy and workforce exhibit considerable unevenness. Most of the region suffers from infrastructure deficiencies, ranging from such basic elements as proper roads and water supplies to economically critical electricity, internet, and transportation services. Three government centres – Whitehorse, Yellowknife, and Iqaluit – have strong, middle-class economies sustained by well-paid public sector workers. In Yukon, for instance, in 2018 there were 9,300 public sector employees compared with only 8,600 employees in the private sector (Yukon Bureau of Statistics 2020). The divide between those in secure, well-paid government jobs and those reliant on the resources and private sector services economy is pronounced, particularly as many of those in the best positions are from, as Yukoners say, "the Outside." The resources economy increasingly relies on a fly-in, fly-out workforce, rooted in the South and heading north for short stints of work. Substantial numbers of the highly skilled technical workers in

Table 15.1. Key Socio-economic and Structural Factors, Canada's Territories

Factor	Yukon[a]	Northwest Territories[b]	Nunavut[c]
Land mass (square km)	482,443	1,143,79	1,994,000[d]
Population (2018)	40,483	44,956	38,780
Aboriginal population (% 2016)[e]	23	51	86
Median age (2018)[f]	38.9	34.8	26.1
Unemployment rate (% 2018)	2.7	7.4	14.6
Average income ($ 2017)	56,751	62,049	51,195[g]
GDP per capita ($ 2018)[h]	64,056	104,911	76,691
Average growth rate (% 2014–18)[i]	1.0	0.8	6.0
Government spending ($ millions fiscal year 2019/20)	1,504	1,873	1,913

[a] Yukon Bureau of Statistics (2020) unless otherwise noted; [b] NWT Bureau of Statistics (2019b) unless otherwise noted; [c] Nunavut Bureau of Statistics (2019) unless otherwise noted; [d] Canada (2017); [e] Anora (2018); [f] Statista (2019); [g] Statistics Canada (2017); [h] authors' calculations based on population figures and GDP at basic prices (Statistics Canada 2020); [i] authors' calculations based on GDP at basic prices, 2014–18; averages obscure significant variability over this period (Statistics Canada 2020).

the region likewise are based in southern cities and come in as needed. For example, in 2015, there were 2,155 non-Yukon residents employed in Yukon, and these workers received $68 million in income (Yukon Bureau of Statistics 2019a). In contrast to the three government centres, most of the other communities are smaller and more isolated, and characterized by extreme poverty and, often, the near-absence of market-based, private sector employment. Although generally spoken about collectively, significant differences among the three territories exist, and they are not strongly linked to one another. Air North provides the only flight between Whitehorse and Yellowknife, and road access between these two communities requires travelling south into British Columbia and Alberta. The Dempster Highway, Canada's only all-season public road that crosses the Arctic Circle, connects Inuvik and Tuktoyaktuk, NWT, to Yukon. Iqaluit in Nunavut is more strongly connected to Ottawa than the other two territories.

In Indigenous-dominated areas, the expansion of Indigenous governments through modern treaties and self-government agreements is adding to the growth of the professional Indigenous class. In Yukon in 2018, 51.4 per cent of the 3,500 employed Indigenous people were public sector employees (Yukon Bureau of Statistics 2019b). Because few Canadians venture into the North, the Indigenous achievements of recent decades are generally underappreciated (Gilmore 2016). These accomplishments include the emergence of a number of successful Indigenous economic development corporations and the growing strength of Nunavut's mining sector. One external indicator is that the Canadian Federation of Independent Business ranked Whitehorse as the top entrepreneurial city in Canada in 2018 (Mallett and Bourgeois 2019). While these distinctions are sometimes superficial and temporary, they often signal underlying factors that are otherwise hard to measure.

In general, Canadian policy makers and the general public assign the North to the periphery of their thinking. Long understood as "Canada's colonies," the territorial North has been viewed, somewhat inappropriately, as substantially irrelevant to the nation's economic planning. This is particularly the case with innovation studies, which in Canada focus almost exclusively on southern and urban settings, particularly those with large research-intensive universities and institutes. Waterloo, Toronto, Ottawa, Montreal, and Vancouver get a great deal of attention among those developing innovation models and programs that seldom connect with the needs of communities such as Inuvik, Pangnirtung, or Dawson City.

The lack of attention to the North is significant given that governments so firmly believe that innovation is key to twenty-first-century prosperity. The North actually represents more than 90 per cent of Canada's landmass (much of it in the near northern areas of the provinces), and none of it seems to fit with the conversations about the handful of city-states that currently drive the Canadian economy. The provincial North, running from northern Ontario through to northern British Columbia, and including the Far North regions of Northern Quebec and Labrador, parallels the territorial North, but with some key differences. These areas have uneven, occasionally robust, but always cyclical resources economies, sizeable non-Indigenous communities, a large number of isolated Indigenous villages, systemic Indigenous poverty, and substantial welfare dependency.

One major limitation throughout the North is the lack of regional governments and modern treaties, save for the Nisga'a Final Agreement in northern British Columbia (British Columbia n.d.), and the powerful combination of modern treaties and increasingly effective subprovincial administrations in northern Quebec and now Labrador. Global demand for resources supports strong economic activity in parts of each region, sustained at times by forestry, mining, oil and gas, and hydro developments. The paid workforce is dominated by resource workers and those in the knowledge-intensive support and services sectors. In the provincial North, such major communities as Fort McMurray, Grande Prairie, Prince George, Thunder Bay, Prince Albert, and Thompson outstrip the territorial North in total population and economic engagement and are important regional government centres. These areas could benefit greatly from innovation lessons learned in the territorial North.

Northern regions in the provinces attract limited government attention. The federal government's transfer to the government of Yukon, for example, amounted to $1.058 billion in fiscal year 2019/20 (Yukon 2019), compared with a tiny federal allocation for northern Saskatchewan, which has a similar population and area. Federal funding is, however, largely devoted to basic services (roads, airfields, schools, and hospitals) and transfers to individuals, with little left for innovation and new economy developments. Prosperity is unevenly distributed, based on a combination of natural resources development and government spending, and is under considerable threat. Global competition is attracting exploration and production investment away from the Canadian North, where the costs and logistical challenges are high. The uncertainties associated with Canadian regulations, heightened by the Trudeau government's Impact Assessment Act on environmental and social assessment (styled Bill C-69 during its parliamentary review), have raised questions about the sustainability of international interest in northern development. Intervention by southern-based environmental groups in regulatory processes, often but not always with local Indigenous support, is adding to project complexity. It is understandable, therefore, that the governments of Yukon and the Northwest Territories, in particular, are eager to broaden the economic base in the North.

Charting a competitive and economically sustainable alternative to resource development is complicated by a real innovation divide. Canada faces a clear and important contradiction in this regard. Those areas in greatest need of improvements to economic development and quality of life, including northern and remote regions, have the least access to innovation as a driver of economic growth. The country's greatest investments in scalable innovation are based in southern and urban settings. Small towns, rural areas, and northern regions generally urgently require innovative approaches to everything from communications to food production, job creation, and health. The North has to cope with many of the destructive elements of technological change, such as the introduction of e-commerce, autonomous machines, and remotely controlled mine operations, but attracts few of the jobs, new businesses, and new economic sectors associated with contemporary innovation.

To put it simply, the North needs Canada to "invert innovation." Inverting innovation means reorienting aspects of the innovation enterprise to better serve remote and northern regions. The current models focus innovation investments in southern major cities and at large universities, with the assumption that new developments will disseminate across the country through commercial mechanisms. This leaves remote areas behind in terms of benefiting from new developments and on the wrong side of the innovation divide. Inverting innovation includes shifting the focus from major investments in bench science and university/academic research towards solving local economic and social problems, an approach favoured in Japan (Fujisawa et al. 2015). Inverting innovation calls for more research and development to focus on remote and northern regions, and is based primarily on adapting existing technologies for specialized regional purposes rather than searching for new technologies. Such an approach requires, in turn, the infrastructure and social preconditions of new-economy engagement, from a highly educated workforce to high-quality internet service. Entrepreneurs seek to develop products for circumpolar and other remote regions, but they require the basic infrastructure to do so. Northern entrepreneurs and creators are currently unable to capitalize on global opportunities due to low speed, expensive, and unreliable internet service (CRTC 2019). If these foundational constraints can be addressed, the North would be able to begin the search for solutions to its basic challenges, including alternative energy, less expensive housing, better K–12 and advanced education, improved health care, accessible government services, more effective wildlife and wildfire management, and real-time monitoring of natural resources developments.

The North has potential advantages in terms of regional innovation. The territories, following devolution, now possess powers similar to those of provinces. Perhaps most important, the territories have developed innovative institutional structures in adapting to land claims and Indigenous self-government (Sabin 2017). The centrality of government in the regional economies means that the territorial authorities can and do play a vital role as first purchasers. For example, in 2016, Nunavut updated its Nunavummi Nangminiqaqtunik Ikajuuti policy, which provides advantages in government procurement for Inuit-owned businesses and sets minimum levels for Inuit labour in projects (Nunavut 2016). The Yukon and NWT governments, in particular, are well connected to local innovators. The small size of the population means creators and entrepreneurs have ready access to government officials and politicians. As occurred with efforts to bring food factories into the region, they have triggered rapid legislative changes and project approvals. Further, the status of the territorial North as "favoured colonies" provides remarkable access to funding sources from both the philanthropic sector (as with the annual multi-million-dollar Arctic Inspiration Prize) and territorial and federal governments. In contrast, the provincial Norths get comparatively little support from provincial authorities and even less from the Arctic-focused federal government, but have more engagement with the private sector.

The North does not yet have an effective innovation model, policies, or ecosystem. If the territorial governments engage in the field, however, they could become a prototype of what we think of as inverted innovation. Currently, investments in innovation are differentially directed to post-secondary education, curiosity-driven research, and traditional technology-push commercialization. An inverted system would instead focus on applied technology, the adaptation of existing solutions to northern conditions, and on a problem-solving approach to investments, research, and commercialization. A northern innovation model, developed and tested in the territorial North, could be of national significance, potentially applicable across the provincial North and in other rural, remote, and Indigenous regions.

The Innovation Architecture

The need for a truly northern-centred approach to innovation becomes evident when one considers the current state of the innovation architecture in the North. Except for the southern Yukon, which is comparatively well served, northern communities struggle with poor basic infrastructure (Orser and Riding 2016). Electrical systems in smaller communities, with some exceptions, are often fuelled by diesel generators and are far from perfectly reliable or environmentally sustainable. Yellowknife, the NWT capital, experiences dozens of power outages a year – a memorable headline from summer 2019, "Yellowknife, where power outages now outnumber food trucks," followed the third power outage in a week (Williams 2019). Iqaluit has challenges with its water supply. Inuvik, sitting in a region with large oil and gas supplies, relies on liquefied natural gas imported from the South. Across the territorial North, internet service is expensive, unreliable, and distressingly slow (CRTC 2019). Although efforts are under way in Yukon to build a redundant fibre optic line that will reach more than 90 per cent of the territorial population within the next few years, the emerging tech sector has complained about being held back from growth because of frequent service outages (Oudshoorn 2016). The North also stands to benefit from investments in low-earth-orbit satellite internet once it is

Table 15.2. Gross Expenditure on Research and Development by Performing Sector, average $ millions, Canada's Territories, 2013–17

		Performers					
		Government		Territorial Research	Business	Higher	Private Non-
Funders	Total	Federal	Territorial	Organizations	Enterprise	Education	profit
Total sectors	14.4	3.8	–	5.0	5.6	–	–
Federal government	4.6	3.6	–	1.0	–	–	–
Territorial government	1.7	–	–	1.4	0.3	–	–
Business enterprise	7.4	–	–	2.2	5.2	–	–
Higher education	–	–	–	–	–	–	–
Private non-profit	0.3	–	–	0.3	–	–	–
Foreign	0.3	–	–	–	0.3	–	–

Note: Columns and rows may not sum due to rounding.

Source: Statistics Canada 2015.

commercialized. In the smaller communities – many of the villages in NWT and all Nunavut settlements are fly-in only – the shortcomings of electrical power and internet connectivity are exacerbated by serious overcrowding in homes (Canada 2018).

Deficiencies in the innovation system are commonplace, and the North has little research capacity beyond the natural resources sector (Table 15.2). The existing research institutes – the Yukon Research Centre, the Aurora Research Institute, and the Nunavut Research Institute – punch well above their weight primarily by facilitating research by southern and international scholars. However, little of this work focuses specifically on the commercialization of science and technology for regional development or regional problems. The Cold Climate Innovation initiatives started by Yukon College are a notable territorial exception, as is the mining innovation centre at Laurentian University in Sudbury, Ontario (Hall 2017).

The territorial North has poor educational outcomes, with high school graduation and post-secondary participation rates well below the national average. These differences are especially pronounced between Indigenous and non-Indigenous populations. For example, in the NWT in 2019, 33.9 per cent of non-Indigenous people ages fifteen and over had a university degree, compared with 6.7 per cent of Indigenous people in the same age group (NWT Bureau of Statistics 2019a). There are particular shortcomings in scientific and technological fields: northern students have to head south for most advanced technical diplomas and degrees, although this is beginning to change as educational opportunities in the North expand.

For generations, territorial businesses have suffered from limited access to investment capital. In earliest times, international investments in the White Pass and Yukon Route Railway and the mechanized development of the Klondike gold fields sustained Yukon's economy for years; that was followed by a few discrete mining and resource developments by multinational firms. More recently, the settlement of Indigenous land claims has given the region access to substantial locally controlled investment pools for the first time, but that money is being mobilized primarily for infrastructure projects and equity positions in regional "old-economy" businesses.

Given the small scale of the population and the domination of southern-based resource companies, it is not surprising that the territorial North has a small commercial sector (Orser and Riding 2016). Most of the territories' businesses serve either the resources sector or government. Only a small number of northern companies are technology based (other than those serving the resources sector) or attempt to penetrate external markets. Businesses speak frankly, as well, about the regulatory and administrative burdens of working and innovating in the North (Morrill 2018), a comment on both the dominance of government in the region and the fact that officials in small territorial administrations are stretched as they manage multiple portfolios, which makes it especially difficult for territorial rules and regulations to keep up with market needs (Yukon Chamber of Commerce 2020). Much of the current legislation comes from pre-devolution decades and is not drafted to modern standards, making it inflexible and difficult to adapt to changing conditions. Although efforts are under way to professionalize the public service, and Yukon has announced a focus on reducing red tape (Silver 2019b), collectively the territories are not entrepreneur friendly.

The Policy Efforts

The existence of innovation challenges, mirrored across much of non-metropolitan Canada, does not mean the absence of significant initiatives. In general, Yukon has made a more comprehensive effort than NWT and Nunavut to develop an innovation sector, with support for both northern-related innovation research and formal incubation facilities. It should be noted that, although Yukon has a partisan government, the legislatures and executives of NWT and Nunavut are consensus based and do not have political parties.

In Yukon, the current Liberal government of Premier Sandy Silver recently committed to an innovation strategy and five-year plan for funding innovation in the technology sector (Silver 2019a). Yukon's extensive innovation commitments include the YukonU Research Centre, Innovation & Entrepreneurship (formerly the Cold Climate Innovation Centre), NorthLight Innovation (a Whitehorse-based incubator), and the Centre for Northern Innovation in Mining. The government has also sponsored specific COVID-response programs in connection with Yukon University, launching a Pivot program for local businesses and an Elevate initiative to support territorial tourism with input from the Tourist Industry Association. As these are all small units, focusing more on partnership development and support for Yukon entrepreneurs, they lack the economies of scale that are characteristic of the more successful innovation centres across the nation.

The NWT and Nunavut innovation commitments are less substantial. Both jurisdictions focus intensely on crisis-type challenges, particularly related to housing, regional infrastructure, and social issues. The forward-looking commercialization of science and technology is a luxury for which there is not much in the way of local human resources, money, or business commitment. The largest initiative is the Canadian High Arctic Research Station (CHARS) based in Cambridge Bay, Nunavut. CHARS is not designed as an innovation research facility; it focuses primarily on natural science research with only occasional connections to commercialization. The facility lacks the intentional economic impact of, for example, the University Centre in Svalbard, which has found interesting ways to commercialize localized scientific knowledge, particularly through ecotourism (Viken 2011). The Svalbard model is followed on a smaller scale by the Nunavut Research Institute, associated with Arctic College, and the Aurora Research Institute in the Northwest Territories, which emphasizes academic research partnerships with southern institutions, the promotion of Nunavut-focused research, and the training of local residents as field researchers.

Like many jurisdictions around the world, the territorial governments have invested heavily in post-secondary education and institutional reform, recognizing that the economy requires an increasingly well-educated workforce. The challenges of advanced training are complicated by the aforementioned shortcomings in K–12 educational outcomes, particularly in smaller and isolated communities. Consequently, northern post-secondary institutions are forced to invest heavily in remedial and career-entry programming. Nunavut, having flirted with the idea of creating its own university, has partnered with Memorial University of Newfoundland to expand its university-level offerings. The territory's most successful program is probably its environmental monitoring and field-research-training program run by the Nunavut Research Institute. Yukon has, once again, taken the most significant steps, expanding the research capacity of Yukon College, which transitioned in mid-2020 to Yukon University, the first university north of the sixtieth parallel in Canada. Yukon College had robust research capacity, especially in the natural sciences (Association of Canadian Universities for Northern Studies 2017). Since research is a central element in the plan for Yukon University, the institution is likely to assume an expanded role in the northern innovation landscape.

The territorial governments have made substantial commitments to scientific research, including generating northern commercial benefits of such activities. Nunavut Research Institute facilitates southern and international scholarly research and has built a significant research presence in its field. In Yukon, the Office of the Science Advisor helps coordinate scientific research across the territory. The Yukon government financially supports commercial research in the mining sector, which remains central to regional economic plans. The Aurora Research Institute, based in Inuvik, is the one obvious entity supporting and attracting research funding to the NWT, including a massive and now-completed multiyear research program, financed by Japan, on methane gas production in the Arctic. For the most part, territorial scientific research is focused on natural and environmental projects, which is likely to expand with the Arctic's particular need to adapt to climate change.

Although there are deficits and challenges in northern innovation more broadly, territorial innovation achievements are more significant than generally appreciated. Northern companies, especially Arctic UAV in Iqaluit and Ryanwood Explorations in Whitehorse, have made impressive strides in commercializing drone technologies, which have widespread applications in the near and far North. The mining and construction industries across the North have delivered new ways of working in Arctic and permafrost conditions. In some specialized fields, including northern transportation and placer mining, Yukon companies are globally competitive. Meanwhile, the imperative of providing health care across vast distances has spurred innovation in medical care delivery and preventative health care, including in tele-health, tele-psychiatry, and remote diagnostics. The challenge is that none of these has spurred commercialization of new northern-created products or services; they are adaptations and applications of technologies from elsewhere.

While few northern innovations have resulted in substantial commercial activity or employment in the North, the seeds of commercialization are being sown across the region. The creation of TechYukon, an organization of Yukon-based firms interested in the commercialization of science and technology, has contributed to the formation of a northern ecosystem. One early success is the Whitehorse-based start-up Proof, which won Startup Canada's National Innovator of the Year Award in 2019 (Hong 2019). The region's two greatest assets – smallness that makes cross-sectoral collaboration comparatively easy and the scale and openness of government – could, if effectively mobilized, provide a foundation for a more substantial and sustainable technology sector. For generations, the small size of the territorial business community was a major liability, but in a world of technological transformation the potential exists to take advantage of this space for more cross-pollination and problem-based, integrated innovation. The current model, however, is based on the adaptation of "outside" technologies for northern purpose and less on original research. Reorienting government spending and the building on pan-Northern collaboration could capitalize on government procurement and develop a level of government-scientific-business collaboration that has been largely absent across Canada.

Compared to the provinces, the territorial North lacks the population, research capacity, investment capital, and consistent commercial interest needed to create and sustain an innovation ecosystem. Meanwhile, the need for practical, region-specific solutions to pressing quality-of-life issues is substantial. The North certainly provides an important illustration of where scientific and technological innovations can be mobilized to the betterment of society. Creating an effective innovation environment, however, requires systematic attention to underlying challenges, the mobilization of partnerships with southern institutions and businesses, and a future-orientation that, to date, has eluded a region understandably focused on the formidable existing challenges facing the people and governments of the territorial North.

What would be needed to create a Canadian northern innovation system? First, there must be a clear government commitment to northern innovation, at the territorial or pan-territorial level. This is underway in Yukon, where the territorial government has made mandate commitments to innovation, but is still nascent in NWT and Nunavut. Following this, the North needs to identify northern technological needs and opportunities clearly, which requires a shared understanding of current and emerging technologies in the world. Infrastructure deficiencies, often related to transportation, water supply, electricity, and internet access, are significant challenges across the North. These problems can be addressed through the innovative application of technologies from elsewhere, provided they are adapted to the unique northern context, rather than simply transplanted. To support these efforts, a clear national commitment to rural/northern innovation is needed. Importantly, this national commitment should focus on the North, but not only on the territories, as is often the case – the provincial North must be included as well. This will require the inversion of a portion of our current innovation investments and program priorities.

One way to start would be with a national circumpolar/remote regions strategy for the commercialization of northern innovation. This strategy could emphasize development opportunities for many remote and harsh-climate technologies, such as drones, gold-mining systems, remote airport/road construction, housing construction, and remote delivery of health, education, and government services. To be effective, such a strategy needs a sharpened focus on the central realities of life in the North, including cold, darkness, snow, ice and permafrost, isolation, and vast distances, which are important challenges and potentially valuable opportunities that, to date, have been largely unexplored. If successful, these initiatives could make the territorial North a showpiece for circumpolar and remote region innovation.

Recognizing government procurement as a key element in practical innovation initiatives, targeted government spending dominates the territorial economies and is the only real and substantial source of forward-looking investment capital and purchasing. Innovative procurement policies by territorial governments could also encourage participation from Indigenous-owned businesses and non-Indigenous businesses with substantial Aboriginal presence in their workforce or supply chains (Canadian Council for Aboriginal Business 2017), promoting economic reconciliation with Indigenous people. Although there are constraints on procurement policy changes related to the free trade agreement with the United States and Mexico, the Yukon government is working on reforming procurement policy to maximize the territory's economic benefit and improve opportunities for local businesses and First Nations within the bounds of those constraints (Yukon 2018). Further, integrating Indigenous communities, governments, and economic development corporations as a centrepiece of innovation efforts has the potential to mobilize several billion dollars of investable assets into the innovation system. While most of these corporations have focused on traditional commercial developments, several have explored more creative business operations, such as Na-Cho Nyäk Dun's collaboration with Yukon-based Coldacre's hyper-local food factory. These funds could help commercialize new products and services specifically designed for the North. Northern governments should also focus more on the "lone eagles" – individual specialists with globally competitive skills or professional services – since attracting and retaining these externally marketable professionals could contribute to economic growth and improving the innovation environment. Northern living, particularly in the larger, more cosmopolitan centres of Whitehorse, Yellowknife, and Iqaluit, appeals to many, and should be marketed to professionals who could be successful anywhere but could make a significant difference in small northern economies.

We noted above that part of inverting innovation is shifting the focus of major investments away from bench science and university/academic research towards solving social problems. Some means of accomplishing this could include research partnerships with southern researchers, educational institutions, and companies, with the territories controlling the funding envelopes. While a lot of research is conducted in the North, research questions and methods are generally determined in the South, often without a lot of consultation or engagement with northern communities. Shifting the funding control to the territories would allow them to control the agenda, and would open the opportunity for extensive and sustained engagement among universities, polytechnics, and companies on northern needs. Building these relationships could encourage further collaborations with and among colleges, polytechnics, and universities to train workers and entrepreneurs for the northern innovation economy.

This envisaged future is the antithesis of the present situation, where deficiencies and gaps attract more attention than achievements and opportunities. Such an expansive and positive approach would go a long way to counter prevailing negative images of the North held across the country and in corporate offices more broadly (Kassam 2001), and would demonstrate the transformative potential of new and emerging technologies for a much broader range of citizens, both in the North and in other rural and remote parts of Canada.

Conclusions and Lessons

By most aggregate measures, Yukon, Northwest Territories, and Nunavut face major socio-economic challenges, particularly in their rural Indigenous communities. If, as so many governments assume, successful innovation is the key to long-term growth and sustainability, the current policy will simply ensure that the North falls further behind the rest of the country. Although the northern territories have been described as "favoured colonies" in terms of financial support from the federal government, this support has not effectively assisted innovation. We argue that inverting innovation by reprioritizing research and development on northern needs is essential to ensure the North is not left behind. This focus on addressing northern problems is crucial. Innovating for innovation's sake will not help address the very real problems affecting northern economies.

Furthermore, the standard approach to commercial innovation, which emphasizes the interaction of ideas, institutions, and interests, does not capture the unique circumstances of the territorial North. In the territories, the small scale of the commercial sector, most of which is owned and controlled externally, and the comparatively large scale of government in their economies, create stable but far from innovative business and research sectors (save in the natural sciences). With little local risk capital, limited regional research capacity, and a heavy reliance on government spending and natural resources development, the territorial North is a comparatively passive recipient of southern and international innovation.

Emerging institutions, particularly those controlled by Indigenous organizations, could be key to long-term innovation efforts. Indigenous economic development corporations and Indigenous-owned companies speak of taking the long-term view of economic transition that is important to many forms of innovation, Several larger organization, including the Denedeh Development Corporation, the Nunavut Development Corporation, the Sahtu Renewable Resources Board, and the Nunavut Development Corporation, have the combination of substantial financial resources, keen interest in local/regional economic prosperity, and steadily improving commercial operations needed to sustain longer-term investments in innovative products and services.

While developments in the North lag well behind southern activities, conditions in the three territories are more favourable than those in the provincial Norths. Save for major resource development projects such as the Alberta oil sands, the Voisey's Bay mine in Labrador, and the northern British Columbia natural gas sector, the northern areas of the provinces generally lack large-scale government support and active innovation centres. The larger resource firms, in addition, centralize their research and development operations in urban centres, often far away from the development sites. Innovation, in these contexts, sustains and supports resource extraction, but with limited spin-offs to other sectors in the local economy.

The missed innovation opportunities are significant. The territorial economies share many characteristics with other parts of Canada, including accelerated climate change, cold-weather climates, vast distances and small populations, vulnerability to external markets, and boom-and-bust resources economies. Territorial innovations, in many aspects, could be applied in many other parts of Canada and internationally. Some regional innovations – placer gold recovery systems, drones for commercial and search-and-rescue purposes, high-elevation airfield construction, permafrost-related construction challenges, and the like – have much broader business potential.

The region, therefore, has potential to do much more, capitalizing on the natural assets and funds available to industry, governments, and Indigenous communities to exploit the opportunities for collaboration and integration presented by the small size of the population and the concentration of activity in the three territorial capitals, along with access to natural resources. The provincial Norths and the territories are vastly underdeveloped, with approximately 5 per cent of Canada's population living in 78 per cent of the country's landmass (Hall 2017). The territories, almost uniquely in the world, could place Indigenous peoples and communities at the centre of the innovation agenda. Although some might argue that persistent infrastructure deficits can be solved through classical technologies that were deployed in the south in the nineteenth and twentieth centuries, this brings to mind the importance of context. Such technologies have not fixed the North's problems. Instead, the key to improving quality of life in the North is focusing on innovative applications of existing and emerging technologies adapted to the northern realities of extreme darkness and cold, permafrost, and remote locations separated by vast distances.

At present, the national and international innovation world is bringing greater disruption than positive benefits to the territories. Transformative technologies from the automation of resources extraction to e-commerce have eroded northern employment, undercut territorial businesses, and created technological unease across the North. The innovation experiences of the territorial North illustrate the dangers of the digital and innovation divides. Yukon, Nunavut, and the Northwest

Territories, like much of the provincial North and most rural areas in Canada, have largely been left out of the twenty-first-century economy and the transformation towards a high-technology workforce. Given the vagaries of the private sector, without additional and targeted policy initiatives, the North will face more dislocation and disruption than growth and prosperity. The choice is stark. Left to drift along, the North could become a symbol of the hollowing-out effect of innovation and its ability to undermine already vulnerable economies. With carefully developed territorial innovation policies, the territories could exemplify the potential of creative scientific and technological change to secure a positive future.

References

Anora, A. 2018. "Yukon: Beautiful, Complex, and Changing." *Talking Stats: A Discussion Series with Statistics Canada*. Ottawa: Statistics Canada. Online at https://www150.statcan.gc.ca/n1/pub/11-631-x/11-631-x2018006-eng.htm.

Association of Canadian Universities for Northern Studies. 2017. "Research Excellence in Yukon: Increasing Capacity and Benefits to Yukoners in the Social Sciences, Humanities and Health Sciences." Ottawa. Online at https://acuns.ca/wp-content/uploads/2013/09/YUKON-ENGLISH -WEB.pdf.

British Columbia. n.d. *First Nations in Treaty Process*. Online at https://www2 .gov.bc.ca/gov/content/environment/natural-resource-stewardship /consulting-with-first-nations/first-nations-negotiations/first-nations-in -treaty-process, accessed 20 April 2020.

Canada. 2019. *Federal Support to Provinces and Territories*. Ottawa, 2 February. Online at https://www.canada.ca/en/department-finance/programs /federal-transfers.html, accessed 22 September 2021.

Canada. 2018. "Northern Housing Policy Recommendations." *Canada.Ca*, 6 December. Online at https://www.canada.ca/en/polar-knowledge /northern-housing-forum-knowledge-products/policy-recommendations .html.

Canadian Council for Aboriginal Business. 2017. *Partnerships in Procurement: Understanding Aboriginal Business Engagement in the Marine and Aerospace Industries in BC*. Toronto. Online at https://www.ccab.com/wp-content /uploads/2017/12/CCAB-MarineAerospace-Report-1.pdf, accessed 20 April 2020.

CRTC (Canadian Radio-television and Telecommunications Commission). 2019. *Communications Monitoring Report 2018–2017 Communications Services Pricing in Canada*. Ottawa. Online at https://crtc.gc.ca/eng/publications /reports/policymonitoring/2018/cmr2.htm, accessed 20 April 2020.

Fujisawa, Y., Y. Ishida, S. Nagatomi, and K. Iwasaki. 2015. "A Study of Social Innovation Concepts: A Japanese Perspective." *Japan Social Innovation Journal* 5 (1): 1–13. https://doi.org/10.12668/jsij.5.1.

Gilmore, S. 2016. "The North and the Great Canadian Lie." *Maclean's,* 11 September. Online at https://www.macleans.ca/politics/the-north -and-the-great-canadian-lie/, accessed 20 April 2020.

Hall, H. 2017. "Exploring Innovation in Northern Canada with Insights from the Mining Innovation System in Greater Sudbury, Ontario." *Northern Review* 45: 33–56. https://doi.org/10.22584/nr45.2017.003.

Hong, J. 2019. "Whitehorse startup proof wins second national competition this year." *Yukon News,* 31 October. Online at https://www.yukon -news.com/business/whitehorse-startup-proof-wins-second-national -competition-this-year/, accessed 20 April 2020.

Kassam, K.-A. 2001. "North of 60: Homeland or Frontier?" In *A Passion for Identity: Canadian Studies for the 21st Century,* ed. D. Taras and B. Rasporich, 433–55. Toronto: Nelson Thomson Learning.

Mallett, T., and A. Bourgeois. 2019. "Entrepreneurial Communities." Toronto: Canadian Federation of Independent Business. Online at https://www.cfib-fcei.ca/sites/default/files/2019-04/Entrepreneurial -Communities-2018.pdf, accessed 20 April 2020.

Morrill, G.E. 2018. "Paving the Way: An Evaluation of Small Business Support Programs in the Kivalliq Region of Nunavut." MA thesis, University of Alaska Fairbanks. Online at https://scholarworks.alaska.edu/bitstream /handle/11122/10329/Morrill_G_2018.pdf?sequence=1.

Nunavut. 2016. *Nunavummi Nangminiqaqtunik Ikajuuti (NNI) Policy.* Online at https://assembly.nu.ca/library/GNedocs/2016/002712-e.pdf, accessed 20 April 2020.

Nunavut Bureau of Statistics. 2019. "Nunavut Bureau of Statistics Home." Online at http://stats.gov.nu.ca/en/home.aspx, accessed 20 April 2020.

NWT (Northwest Territories) Bureau of Statistics. 2019a. "Education - Highest Level of Schooling." Online at https://www.statsnwt.ca/education /highest-level/, accessed 20 April 2020.

NWT (Northwest Territories) Bureau of Statistics. 2019b. "NWT Bureau of Statistics Home." Online at https://www.statsnwt.ca/a, accessed 20 April 2020.

OECD (Organisation for Economic Co-operation and Development). 2004. "New Economy Definition." *OECD Glossary of Statistical Terms,* 26 August. Online at https://stats.oecd.org/glossary/detail.asp?ID=6267.

Orser, B., and A. Riding. 2016. "Women Entrepreneurs in Northern Canada: Contexts and Challenges." *International Journal of Entrepreneurship and Small Business* 27 (2-3): 366–83. https://doi.org/10.1504/IJESB.2016.073984.

Oudshoorn, K. 2016. "Yukon's IT crowd: Territory's tech sector is growing." *CBC News*, 14 September. Online at https://www.cbc.ca/news/canada /north/yukon-information-technology-sector-growing-1.3758982, accessed 20 April 2020.

Sabin, J. 2017. "A Federation within a Federation? Devolution and Indigenous Government in the Northwest Territories." *IRPP Study* 66. Montreal: Institute for Research on Public Policy. Online at http://irpp.org/research -studies/study-no66/, accessed 20 April 2020.

Silver, S. 2019a. "Mandate Letter to Ranj Pillai." Online at https://yukon.ca /sites/yukon.ca/files/eco-mandate-ranj-pillai.pdf, accessed 20 April 2020.

Silver, S. 2019b. "Mandate Letter to Richard Mostyn." Online at https:// yukon.ca/sites/yukon.ca/files/eco/eco-mandate-richard-mostyn_0.pdf, accessed 20 April 2020.

Statista. 2019. "Canada – Median Age of Population by Province 2018." Online at https://www.statista.com/statistics/444816/canada-median-age-of -resident-population-by-province/, accessed 20 April 2020.

Statistics Canada. 2015. "Provincial and territorial gross domestic expenditures on research and development, in the total sciences – Yukon, Northwest Territories and Nunavut." Table 4–11. Ottawa.

Statistics Canada. 2017. *Nunavut and Canada. Census Profile. 2016 Census.* Cat. no. 98–316-X2016001. Ottawa. Online at https:// www12.statcan.gc.ca/census-recensement/2016/dp-pd/prof/index .cfm?Lang=E, accessed 20 April 2020.

Statistics Canada. 2020. "Gross domestic product (GDP) at basic prices, by industry, provinces and territories (X1,000,000)." Table 36-10-0402-01 . Ottawa. Online at https://doi.org/10.25318/3610040201-eng.

Viken, A. 2011. "Tourism, Research, and Governance on Svalbard: A Symbiotic Relationship." *Polar Record* 47 (4): 335–47. https://doi.org/doi:10.1017 /S0032247410000604.

Williams, O. 2019. "Yellowknife, where power outages now outnumber food trucks." *Cabin Radio*, 22 June. Online at https://cabinradio.ca/17053/news /yellowknife/yellowknife-where-power-outages-now-outnumber-food -trucks/, accessed 20 April 2020.

Yukon. 2018. *Procurement Improvement Framework.* Whitehorse: Government of Yukon. Online at https://yukon.ca/sites/yukon.ca/files /hpw/hpw-procurement-improvement-framework.pdf.

Yukon. 2019. *2019–20 Interim Fiscal and Economic Update.* Whitehorse: Government of Yukon. Online at https://yukon.ca/sites/yukon.ca/files/fin /fin-budget-2019-20-interim-fiscal-economic-update.pdf, accessed 20 April 2020.

Yukon Bureau of Statistics. 2019a. "Inter-Jurisdictional Employees." Whitehorse: Government of Yukon. Online at https://yukon.ca/sites

/yukon.ca/files/ybs/fin-inter-jurisdictional-employees-2015.pdf, accessed 22 September 21.

Yukon Bureau of Statistics. 2019b. *Yukon Employment Annual Review 2018*. Information Sheet 80. Whitehorse: Government of Yukon. Online at https://yukon.ca/en/yukon-employment-annual-review-2018, accessed 22 September 2021.

Yukon Bureau of Statistics. 2020. "Yukon Fact Sheet." Whitehorse: Government of Yukon. Online at https://yukon.ca/en/statistics-and-data /yukon-bureau-statistics/yukon-fact-sheet, accessed 22 September 2021.

Yukon Chamber of Commerce. 2020. "The Yukon Chamber of Commerce proposes five new year's resolutions for the Yukon Government to adopt." 6 January. Online at https://www.yukonchamber.com/post/2020/01/06 /the-yukon-chamber-of-commerce-proposes-five-new-year-s-resolutions -for-the-yukon-governme.

PART III

Lessons Learned

16 Conclusions and Lessons Learned

DAVID CASTLE AND PETER W.B. PHILLIPS

A "trifecta" is a bet placed in horse racing that predicts the first three finishers in the correct order. The bet goes by other names depending on where you are. In the United Kingdom, it is a "tricast"; in Canada, it is called a "triactor"; and in the United States, a "triple." The temptation to place a bet with such low odds of success is the potential for an enormous payout. Carrying the idea of a "trifecta" over to the context of science, technology, and innovation (STI) policy, the metaphor has "legs" in the sense that innovation is sometimes likened to placing bets (see, for example, Schilling 2017). Bets on new products and services, whether technologically or socially innovative, rely on risk capital to support new ventures to success or failure. Sometimes bets on these entrepreneurial horses really do pay off – some become "unicorns" that exit with a market capitalization over $1 billion. A "trifecta" also gestures towards the role of system coordination so ably captured in the triple-helix model of entwinements of government, industry, and universities, both the system architecture and the actions in each and interactions among the three strands (Etzkowitz 2008).

In this book, we have argued that innovation policy can be motivated, described, or justified in terms of three factors: ideas, institutions, and interests. Individually or jointly, these factors are core parts of any causal story about how innovation policy arises, leads to action, or is explained publicly. The description and analysis of innovation policy can be guided by reflection on these three factors and their interaction. Ideally for a province or territory, ideas, institutions, and interests would align around STI policy. This ideal case is the innovation "trifecta." Less than a prescriptive formula, this trifecta is an alignment of the major contextual preconditions that enable innovation. Landing all three at once creates a low-transaction-cost environment as governments, industry, and universities navigate their environments.

Furthermore, alignment prepares the way for capitalizing on innovation capabilities and tapping into receptor capacity, often demonstrated regionally and described as "smart specialization" (Rosiello et al. 2015). As the preceding chapters have shown, the perennial policy challenge is that goals of the innovation horse race are easily identifiable – new technologies, social systems, wealth, or prosperity – but no single race plan reliably produces these outputs and outcomes.

Instead, some rough rules exist about desirable conditions for innovation. We note three common framings. First, throughout this and other studies, one can see sets of ideas that motivate and sustain a strong science and technology base to create commercializable inventions, institutional linkages designed to improve knowledge flows between higher education and the private sector, and interests that motivate firms and governments to engage in wealth creation either for its own value or to support desirable social outcomes. Across Canada, these and other rough rules guide policy and program development, providing a foreground for some of the innovation policy in the provinces and territories. Second, the background to this policy effort is embodied in the broader Canadian system of institutions – a system known to induce stability – consisting of factors such as Confederation, division of powers under the Constitution, a common currency, institutional continuity, uniform standards in the higher education sector, and a host of other federal or multilevel governance efforts to advance the economy. Third, by most measures, Canada's governance system excels. By the six governance indicators – voice and accountability, political stability and absence of violence/terrorism, government effectiveness, regulatory quality, rule of law, and control of corruption – measured by the Worldwide Governance Indicators project, Canada generally performs well into the mid-ninetieth-percentile rank on all indicators (World Bank 2020).

The prevailing conundrum is why – with such broad socio-economic advantages and a whole host of other factors such as multiculturalism, a merit-based immigration system, broad social safety nets, and good social mobility – Canada is not generating better innovation performance? As the most recent of the periodic Council of Canadian Academies' studies of Canadian innovation performance concludes, firms are underperforming research and development (R&D), companies are not scaling, entrepreneurs seek to work in other jurisdictions, and those who stay struggle to reach international markets (CCA 2018). Canada's significant socio-economic advantages mean that major obstacles that could lie in the path to better innovation performance have been cleared away – obstacles that continue to beset, for example, the resurgent economies of former Eastern Bloc countries, many of which now seek to plan and implement innovation strategies similar to ours (see Mastroeni and Rosiello 2013). For Canada, the perennial question is how to disrupt the status quo bias in our industry and our society in order to optimize opportunity, perform better, keep system constraints and transactions costs low, and compete against comparator nations. One alluring approach to short circuit innovation underperformance would be to import into Canada those approaches that have worked well elsewhere. For example, the 2014 federal science strategy recommended that the National Research Council emulate Germany's Fraunhofer or the United Kingdom's Catapults approach to industry engagement and regional impact (Canada 2014). In recent years, joint provincial-federal delegations have toured both countries, and have had reciprocal engagements with Technion in Israel, all in an effort to shore up Canada's innovation performance and improve business competitiveness. Perhaps somewhat ironically, Technion recognized that it could reverse the model, and drew on Canadian talent for Israel's benefit by creating Technion Canada, a registered Canadian charity. Enthusiasm for adopting other countries' approaches wanes quickly once it is realized innovation policy and related strategies are highly context dependent and generally perform poorly when grafted onto other countries. For example, even if a country has a comparatively centrist approach to STI policy, it is the aggregations of local interactions that make for success. As Canada is a relatively decentralized federation, its provinces and territories are quite free to adopt or ignore imported innovation strategies. The federal government might try to call the tune, but not all of the provincial and territorial players join, at the same time, or in the same key and tempo.

The approach taken in this book contextualizes subnational policy efforts in light of national and international activity, but in full awareness that provincial and territorial jurisdictions have powers over, and proximity to, many of the main drivers of innovation. We have described the idiosyncratic trajectories in provincial and territorial innovation policy as natural experiments. One purpose of this book is to document the recent history of what happened, what worked, and what failed along the way to developing and implementing innovation policy in this multilevel, pan-continental system. Another purpose is to consider how the Canadian system could be optimized to improve innovation performance through more strategic approaches to subnational STI policy.

We now take up the challenge of surveying the provinces and territories to explore the ideas, institutions, and interests that might have contributed to STI policy itself or to demonstrably positive innovation performance. Along the way, we also consider the lacunae in policy and performance, using our diagnostic framework, to make it more open to remedy. We begin by unpacking the subthemes associated with ideas, institutions, and interests, and then scan across the chapters on the provinces and territories to identify situations where the thematic applied – or did not – for interesting or less salubrious reasons. It is fascinating to see that, where some of the rough rules of innovation policy were consistently applied in different regions, divergent outcomes sometimes arose. Conversely, where divergent approaches to innovation policy were taken, convergence on outcomes sometimes occured.

Ideas

The nature of political discourse – that is, the style of the discourse shaped by political leanings and prioritization of topics – generates most of the important ideas that influence innovation policy. Politics shapes what people know and care about, and it is the source of the willpower that stimulates action and creates opportunity. The provincial and territorial narratives show that the political differences and dynamics across the country shape the many different ways of approaching innovation policy: innovation policy in some provinces and at various times is more an after-the-fact explanation than a driver of innovation; clusters are fundamental to innovation policy in most provinces; federal government innovation policy often leads, and regions follow; and the skills agenda is salient, but often not well developed in provinces and territories. Although it is increasingly common for national governments to have innovation policies, it is less common for subnational jurisdictions to have them. Since the locus of many of the key drivers of innovation are at the local or regional level, accounts of success are often highly localized and do not reflect precisely the policy stance of a national government in which innovation is the driving idea in the policy agenda. This perhaps explains why policy support for innovation in the provinces and territories, whether it is more implied than explicit, nevertheless generally has an aura of being reactive, opportunistic, and a post facto rationalization for the successes, rather than a driver of policies that create, sustain, and explain why the successes materialized according to planning and strategy.

The Atlantic provinces represent this duality of approaches. Newfoundland and Labrador, with the exploitation of natural resources, particularly offshore oil, created an innovation technocracy. No particular innovation policy by government explains the multidecade rise in innovation in the sector, although the McKinsey-supported *2019 Economic Growth Strategy for Newfoundland and Labrador* can be viewed as an effort to make this more explicit. New Brunswick similarly has operated with a general view that funding scientific research can lead to innovation in natural resources and digital sectors, and Throne Speeches have for decades referenced the importance of R&D and technology. But government policy specifically was an "artefact," not an input, until the Liberal Gallant government in 2014 formally shifted the focus towards the service economy, and then created an *Innovation Agenda* in 2018. These provinces contrast with Prince Edward Island (PEI) and Nova Scotia, which have undertaken more explicit innovation policy development. For PEI, this reaches back as far as the 1969 *Prince Edward Island Comprehensive Development Plan*, which paved the way for higher education institution building, and subsequently to established technology transfer organizations. At times, Nova Scotia has had an explicit strategy – for example, during the mid-1990s under Premier Hamm and with the 2003 *Innovative Nova Scotia*.

Quebec is an important outlier, as it has created an innovation architecture as a deliberate part of nation building. This approach started in the 1960s with the Conseil de recherches médicales, followed in 1969 with technological assistance for small and medium-sized firms through the Centre de recherche industriel du Québec. The contemporary period for Quebec starts with the creation of the Fonds de recherche en santé du Québec in 2001, which consolidated a number of earlier organizations. Quebec's systematic approach was not replicated in Ontario, as provincial supports to innovation have more often been moulded by macro fiscal policy considerations than by explicit innovation concerns. The Liberal government of David Peterson is widely viewed as having succeeded in setting the conditions for innovation, but Bob Rae's New Democratic Party (NDP) government changed tack considerably by bringing organized labour to what were recast as more diffuse policy tables. The Harris and Eaves governments were fiscally conservative, mostly focused on tax and program cutting to balance budgets, albeit selectively using challenge funds to bring private sector interests and culture to post-secondary institutions. The McGuinty government might have done the most to try to create an innovation system architecture in Ontario that would compare with Quebec's, but even then, the strategy was more additive in its approach to institutions than rationalizing and streamlining. The contrasting narratives are striking.

The situation westward is similarly heterogeneous. Manitoba has not advocated much for innovation in the province over recent decades – to some extent, innovation policy has not even emerged as an after-the-fact justification. By contrast, Saskatchewan has been much more deliberate, particularly in the agri-food and resources sectors. Alberta likewise has tended to be very sector specific its efforts to shape innovation, placing large bets on the future demand for fossil fuels and developing new technologies to cope with extraction challenges and costs. The energy sector's relevance to the overall prosperity of Alberta (and the rest of Canada) continues to dominate the discourse in the province, but, curiously, innovation in the sector, and innovation to diversify the economy, includes a greater share of renewable energy. British Columbia is now quite straightforwardly pro-innovation through explicit policy, an important advancement from previous decades during which innovation policy was a side issue to serving traditional sectors of the economy. This is where the territories find themselves at the moment, but with the caveat that landing the trifecta of coordinated ideas, institutions, and interests is a slim prospect. The more immediate challenge for the territories is to broaden their economic base of resources industries in the face of volatile global commodity markets and increasingly difficult domestic environmental approval processes and regulation.

Absolute clarity about whether a province or territory has an explicit or implicit innovation policy is hard to reach. STI policy, as with many policy files, is not always articulated in accessible and forward-looking written strategies. Policy statements about innovation are more often retrospective acknowledgments of decisions and actions that had some measurable effect. This is particularly true of the influence of Porter's ideas about clusters on innovation policy across Canada (Porter 1990). Every province has invested in clusters at some point, or invoked cluster thinking to develop bespoke assemblages of R&D capabilities. Canada's Cluster Map, which illustrates the geographically concentrated clusters of sectoral activity in the provinces and territories since 2006, visually corroborates much of what the chapters in this book show – namely, that most Canadian clusters have grown around extractive industries and associated specialized services industries. This is true of agricultural services and transportation in the Prairies, forestry, marine services related to shipping and fisheries on all coasts and in the Great Lakes, oil and gas exploration in Alberta, Saskatchewan, and Newfoundland and Labrador, and mining and power generation across the provinces. Few industrial clusters outside metropolitan Toronto, Montreal, Vancouver, and maybe Ottawa host any activities distinct from their resources endowments, a fact which suggests that Canada has a bifurcated innovation policy environment that gets reinforced by the unaligned actions of different levels of government: one for the big cities and one for the regions.

From a policy point of view, Porter's cluster model and its variants can be found in most provinces. Quebec was an early and aggressive adopter of the cluster paradigm to organize its nation-building efforts. About the same time, Ontario adopted the cluster model to complement and differentiate provincial economic activity from the dominant federal system. At times this has been technology specific (for example, biomedical and aerospace) and at times focused on cities' natural capacity to cluster (as in Toronto's fashion district). In the early 1990s, the Saskatchewan government promoted clusters through the Partnership for Renewal strategy, under which triple-helix-style partnerships have grown. Newfoundland and Labrador and Nova Scotia have both undertaken to develop marine science and technology–focused clusters, and New Brunswick and British Columbia have both placed bets on digital technology clusters. British Columbia is perhaps the most cluster-focused province at the moment, as the first innovation commissioner, Alan Winter, used his two-year mandate to identify nascent clusters for provincial investment. The federal Innovation Supercluster Initiative has re-energized interest in the cluster model, as it encouraged more than fifty communities to pitch for a supercluster based on their local capabilities and assets. The five successful regionally based superclusters – in Atlantic Canada, Montreal, Toronto, the Prairies, and Vancouver – are a sort of $950 million stimulus package of business expenditure on R&D, designed to leverage greater private sector investment and participation in R&D and to coalesce and spur the growth of firms to scales where they can access international markets. From an innovation policy perspective, it remains an open question about the potential for the liberation of a "cluster" from geographical constraints to create "superclusters" that are regionally based, nationally relevant, and explicitly tie together innovation, economic growth, and export strategy.

Every touchpoint between the federal, provincial, and territorial governments generates new, multilevel governance – trade, environmental protection, resources development, health, education, and, of course, innovation policy. Since the advent of Industry Canada in 1990, innovation performance has been an explicit federal policy focus; as it morphed into Innovation, Science and Economic Development (ISED) over the past few years, innovation policy has now been baked into more than thirty of the department's programs and initiatives. With such a strong policy push for innovation from the federal government, one might expect that federal framing of innovation systems and policy design would dominate, with provinces forced to conform to incentives and engage in policy alignment.

The Innovation Superclusters Initiative is an example of this style of leadership, and reflects the willingness of regions to adapt to the federal priorities. But other, more systematic, longer-term approaches to regional economic development suggest there are dynamics other than simple call-and-response as a driver for new policy initiatives. For example, the Atlantic Canada Opportunities Agency (ACOA), the Atlantic Investment Partnership, and the Atlantic Innovation Fund have created regional opportunities for provinces to build capacity in partnership with the federal government, rather than simply in response to federal direction. Similarly, the Prairie provinces have relied on investments from Western Economic Diversification Canada (WD), to advance their priorities in the agri-food and energy sectors. Sector-specific alignments between the federal government and Quebec and Ontario, with major industries such as the aerospace and automotive sectors, have likewise created enduring partnerships. Wherever federal laboratories exist, there also tends to be alignment with provincial capabilities, rather than provincial conformity with federal interests. The Federal Science and Technology Infrastructure Initiative (now relaunched as the Laboratories Canada Initiative) might further entrench this type of partnership. These types of investment allow the federal government to extend its long reach into provinces and territories to influence innovation policy. Provinces and territories accept these arrangements, knowing that in areas they are most concerned about – for example, education, health, and trade – the provinces have the constitutional jurisdiction to articulate programs and initiatives as they see fit.

The knowledge-based economy is a dominant idea in innovation policy discussions that harkens back to the 1980s and 1990s. The central notion of the knowledge-based economy is that economies of the future would be dominated by services and intangibles, rather than by tangible assets (Bell 1976; Romer 1990), and countries needed to take steps to prepare their future workforce for "new" knowledge-based economies, with a technology-enabled orientation towards services (OECD 2004). Despite having a highly educated workforce, Canada has taken a softer approach to the skills agenda than have countries such as the United Kingdom and Germany. While education is a provincial or territorial matter, the federal government, as part of its 2017 budget, launched a government-wide Innovation and Skills Plan, signalling that Canada had work to do to remain globally competitive and prosperous. The federal initiative was building on antecedents at the regional level, including, for example, PEI's 2008 *Island Prosperity Strategy*, Nova Scotia's *We*

Choose Now – A Playbook for Nova Scotians, and the 2017 Quebec Strategy for Research and Innovation, each of which focused on talent growth and innovation. But in other provinces and territories, the skills agenda has been more often about skilled workers in pre-existing extractive industries, rather than in sectors associated with the knowledge-based economy. One of the more puzzling patterns identified in the regional chapters in this book is that provincial governments, perhaps with the exception of Quebec, struggle to define for themselves a skills agenda that effectively tracks both the priorities for innovation from the federal government's perspective and the localized needs of the province or territory.

Institutions

The institutional composition of a province or territory refers to the funders and performers of R&D, the scale and scope of those investments, and mechanisms by which innovation policy is developed and implemented by elected and unelected officials. As revealed in the provincial and territorial chapters, the key subthemes associated with institutions include: the provincial decision-making machinery; the uniqueness of Quebec among the rest of the subnational governments; the status of the provincial research organization model; reliance on advisory councils; attempts to use arm's-length agencies to develop and drive innovation; the special role of universities; the level of private sector engagement; the uneven presence of foreign companies or investors; and the limited contribution of the not-for-profit sector.

In Part I of this book, we described how provinces and territories have direct oversight of many of the key organizations, institutions, and regulations underpinning the capacity to innovate. Over time, these have not changed much; post-secondary institutions are stable, labour and industry organizations evolve slowly, financial and trade institutions vary moderately over time, and very little that is invented, bought, or sold is not captured by the fine mesh of Canadian regulatory systems. Against this stable backdrop, the critical variable in the provinces and territories is how changing political perspectives affect the operation of the system, often with little change in the architecture. Left-right political cycles tend to shift between expansionary social program spending and fiscal constraint, leaving much of the innovation architecture unaffected. Since the 1990s, both Ontario and British Columbia have had fairly hard political lurches compared with many other provinces, but both still advanced their innovation agenda. Political stability in other provinces has not necessarily yielded better results – the most obvious case is Alberta, where stable governments have ridden the boom-and-bust cycles in the oil patch, often creating greater entrenchment in resources, rather than much success in diversifying the economy or making it more resilient. In contrast, fiscal stability in Manitoba has not yielded dramatically better results. Generally. provincial and territorial governments need to see innovation as a solution to political and financial challenges before they will make strategic choices and invest in post-secondary institutions, technology transfer, growth and challenge funds, and other programs and initiatives. At least in theory, regions with science advisors (Quebec and Yukon) or an innovation commissioner (British Columbia) should be better innovation performers because of an overt commitment to think about the role of science and technology in government decision making (science-for-policy) and how to foster innovation through investments in R&D (policy-for-science) (Gluckman 2014, 2016).

We suggested above that, for decades, the federal government has set the agenda and pace of innovation policy in Canada, and that the provinces and territories selectively respond to Ottawa's programs and initiatives. Not much gets done in Canada without two or three levels of government finding a consensus position on priorities and the way forward. Given the nested hierarchy of municipalities, provinces and territories, and the federal government, the system rewards alignment and cooperation. Disputes about jurisdiction are rarely litigated. Within this system, provinces have more in their control, and have more latitude, to develop their own innovation-focused programs and initiatives than they currently employ. The major outlier is Quebec, which for cultural and political reasons not only professes to be a nation state, but builds institutions in precisely this vein. While separatist ambitions appear to have waned as a newer generation of Quebecers finds its special status within the Confederation advantageous, the unique innovation architecture in the province remains steady. Recently, British Columbia has become more vocal about its regional innovation position in Cascadia, but that initiative is less about dissatisfaction with its place in Canada and more a matter of a recognizing British Columbia's potential beneficial linkages from its geographical proximity to Washington, Oregon, and California. Other provinces and territories generally do not channel their position in Confederation in any particular direction with respect to innovation policy. Most provinces in fact are happy to work with or leverage federal efforts for their own interests.

Provincial research organizations (PROs) are a type of institution over which provinces (and territories) can exert control and align with innovation policy. All provinces, with the exception of PEI, maintain

PROs; Alberta was first, with the Alberta Research Council, in 1921, and Newfoundland and Labrador is the latest, with the creation in 2009 of the Newfoundland and Labrador Research and Development Council. There is no consistent model across Canada. Some PROs, such as the New Brunswick Research Productivity Council, the Saskatchewan Research Council, and the Centre de recherche industriel du Québec, are consistent performers of research with a mix of technical services. Others, such as the Manitoba Research Council (now amalgamated into Research Manitoba), match funding of research with technical services. Still others, such as Research Nova Scotia and Innovate BC, are essentially funders of entrepreneurs, with a secondary role of informing provincial research and innovation policy. Complicating the landscape further is that some provinces' historical PROs are responsible for health research, but only among other things, while other provinces have special-purpose health-oriented research organizations that are aligned with the province's conception of its obligations to deliver health services (NAPHRO 2020).

Some provinces have opted to make use of special arm's-length agencies to obtain advice about innovation or to lead investments. A good example in the Atlantic region is Nova Scotia's Innovacorp, which, like many of these types of agencies, acts an incubator and provides services for start-ups. The three Prairie provinces all tried but abandoned industry-led development agencies, and others have made efforts to generate more industrial and regional input into policy and administration, but no single model stands out as offering much in the way of better results. Regional agencies also exist. Springboard, for example, sustained by ACOA, provides a network of commercialization services for regional post-secondary institutions and their partners in Atlantic Canada; Quebec's Sociétés de valorisation de la recherche universitaire offers similar services.

Post-secondary institutions, particularly research-intensive universities, are among the most important institutions engaged in innovation. Provinces and territories have enabling acts that set out the governance framework for universities, and ministries that oversee the accreditation and regulation of post-secondary institutions. The focus of these ministries, however, tends to be on teaching rather than on research, since most of the research funds and programs spring from federal initiatives that work to bring provinces and territories in as partners. Across Canada, universities are differentially important and successful, sometimes rising to become dominant regional innovation champions. In Atlantic Canada, each province has one main research-intensive university among smaller universities and colleges that undertake research less comprehensively and intensively. Each anchor Atlantic university is capable of creating and sustaining research programs that draw in federal funds from the Canada Foundation for Innovation and the Tri-Council funding agencies, and to lead the development of regional consortia, such as the Ocean Supercluster, which involves three of the region's main universities. In recent years, Atlantic universities have had provincial support to expand their reach by developing extensive R&D networks with private sector partners and to create incubators and accelerators.

In Quebec, there are the large, research-intensive universities of McGill, the Université de Montréal, and the ten-member, regionally based Université du Québec system. One might say the Quebec system has both intensive research enterprise and extensive reach around the province. Provincial confidence in the university system is generally strong, and seems able to withstand day-to-day politics. For example, the centre-right Coalition Avenir Québec party, upon election, supported the 16 per cent research fund increase for 2018–22 initiated by the former Liberal government. The same cannot be said of Ontario, where the centre-right Progressive Conservative leadership, upon election in 2018, immediately sought to cut back provincial funding for universities. Provincial funding in Ontario long ago slipped below 40 per cent of the base budget for universities, making it the lowest contributor among the provinces. Nevertheless, irrespective of political stripe, Ontario governments have pushed universities to partner and co-develop R&D platforms with the private sector and to commercialize their research.

West of Ontario, each of the provinces has only one or two major cities, each with a large, research-intensive university and other post-secondary institutions. Many of these universities have built up enviable research programs and associated large-scale research infrastructure, much of which is in the service of national and international research interests in areas such as agriculture, vaccines and infectious diseases, nanotechnology, high-energy physics, and ocean science. There is always a question about whether and how these research facilities should be supported by provincial governments that are otherwise struggling to fund primary and secondary education, the health system, and provincial infrastructure. Western universities tend to follow a common pattern of building out knowledge parks for partnered R&D collaborations, creating often highly visible incubator spaces, and partnering with local colleges and technical institutes to develop pathway programs and blended accredited offerings. These go some way to building diversity and robustness into the local innovation systems and to fending off criticisms about universities' relevance to local and political interests. The Universities of Saskatchewan and Manitoba, in particular, play an oversized role in anchoring the regionally strong agri-food innovation system; the other research-intensive universities are important players, but not so obviously centres of innovative efforts in the larger and more diversified economies of Alberta and British Columbia. The need to balance aspirations of research excellence with local relevance certainly is a challenge in Yukon, which in 2020 created Canada's first university "north of 60."

Over the past two decades, research funders have increasingly required matching funds from partners, which typically are expected to be in the private sector (Doern, Phillips, and Castle 2016). There are two dimensions to this demand. First, the ability to create a partnership is a kind of validation of the proposed project, in that another intended user of new knowledge or technology is built into the research design from the outset. Second, the requirement can lead to some interesting partnerships. Canada's private sector consists mostly of small and medium-sized enterprises (SMEs), a handful of large firms, and a small number of multinational subsidiaries. Consequently, leveraged R&D activity is dominated by local SMEs, some of which might be newly established under previous R&D projects. This explains why Canadian innovation success stories often resemble those of PEI firms such as Standard Aero, PEI Mussel King, discoverygarden, and Diagnostic Chemicals, while accounts of innovation in Ontario's branch-plant auto industry are seldom heard. The challenge is that, by and large, domestic and international industry in Canada is a low performer of its own R&D, and while every university can expound on the number and significance of its industry-university partnerships, the overall performance of Canada's innovation system is not obviously enhanced significantly by their efforts. It would, one might hazard, be much worse without them.

Few provinces have made explicit efforts to make big bets on innovation. Most prefer to join or lead larger teams of public and private actors. In some ways, the exception that makes the rule is Alberta, which invested heavily and for an extended period in the Alberta Oil Sands Technology and Research Authority to undertake research to resolve barriers to oil sands development, and consequently built a world-scale industry that has had a material impact on the national macroeconomy. No other provincial government can identify such a sustained and significant effort to develop science, technology, and innovation.

Interests

The discrete and sometimes overlapping interests of individuals and institutions ultimately motivate the development, implementation, and use of innovation policy and programming. The provincial and territorial narratives in this book identify a number of key subthemes, including: how wide and varied interests can be; relationships where the federal government is not only important but dominant; the extent to which a province or territory is motivated to drive its own innovation agenda; and the preferences exhibited in the choices about which mechanisms are used to drive innovation.

The unique geographical, cultural, and political circumstances of each province and territory make regional interests predictably wide and varied. Reliance on good economic winds from a few extractive industries is part of the history of all provinces and territories. What differentiates them now is how they develop and implement policies, some of which rely on innovation-driven growth. Most have attempted to make primary industries more efficient or to find niche products that earn more. For example, Newfoundland and Labrador was dependent on fisheries for many decades, and subsequently on oil and gas. The need to diversify is recognized, but it is a need that appears to be less than fully embraced by Alberta, as that province continues to focus on sustaining and growing its oil and gas sector. In many instances, there is only tacit recognition that economic diversification might mean relying less on old economic sectors and embracing new ones. When this recognition is made explicit, there is usually a rapid surge of interest in the services economy, new economic sectors, and redevelopment through a skills agenda. Self-aware use of innovation language by politicians is now common across Canada; everyone understands that good socio-economic conditions will remain or improve only if things do not stay the same. The variable success across provinces and territories in translating the rhetoric into action, and in generating the envisioned successes, indicates there is much more systematic work to be done.

One way to read these changes in subnational innovation policy is that the federal government has raised the need for improved innovation performance and business competitiveness, and the provinces and territories have responded. This federalist account would appeal to those from Industry Canada, now ISED, and it has some truth to it. After all, the federal government is responsible for many programs and initiatives that have fuelled significant socio-economic improvements, including regional economic development agencies such as ACOA and WD, the development of local R&D capabilities by locating federal labs across the country, and the delivery of infrastructure programs such as the Knowledge Infrastructure Program in 2012 and the Strategic Innovation and Smart Cities Challenge Funds in 2017. As noted, little gets done in Canada without the coordination of multiple levels of government, making the success of these federal ventures dependent on the engagement of provinces, territories, and some municipalities. Provinces perhaps initially started down the innovation road because of federal incentives, but in many ways they are now taking ownership of their efforts. The large number of digital economy initiatives, far in excess of any federal design, illustrates how provinces are beginning to assert leadership in their local innovation systems. Recent federal programming, such as the Innovation Supercluster Initiative, takes advantage of local initiatives by offering opportunities for innovative sectors and communities to self-define and self-select their own targets and preferred mechanisms.

While provinces and territories realize the need to be more innovative and to create the conditions that enable innovation-led economic growth, their ability to implement policies and programs effectively and efficiently has been more challenging. The interest is there, but experience with mechanisms that work *in situ* is often underdeveloped. Various natural experiments have been undertaken, many of which appear to have paid off, but few blockbusters such as AbCellera or Verafin have been driven forward. There is a sense that provincial and territorial governments hesitate to be too visibly selective in policy choices that might preferentially reward one part of the economy over another – for example, information and communications technology instead of cleantech. Instead, these subnational governments fall back to offering general support to whichever firms or sectors can organize and access their programming. This leads to efforts that are more incremental than potentially transformative – and incrementalism tends to lead to the accretion of programming and institutions: a 2017 review of federal programs that support business innovation identified ninety program streams across twenty different federal organizations (Canada 2019). The narratives in this book illustrate that, for each federal program, there is probably a provincial analogue. In short, the system architecture is complicated and difficult to navigate.

Somewhat tellingly, none of the provincial or territorial accounts in previous chapters identifies any substantive assessments of programs or other incentives to support innovation. While each province can point to undeniable successes, it is hard to attribute these, and arising benefits, to any specific policy or program. This absence of evidence is both puzzling and troubling. Given the obvious concern among policy makers to design more effective policies, it is surprising that none of the reviews of the major programming does much more than tote up the outlays and tell just-so stories about their effects on firms and sectors. There are few, if any, counterfactuals that could validate the actual contributions of any of the measures. Given the large number of programs and relatively small number of firms, one would think that more could be done. The troubling part of this is that, in the absence of evidence, any idea that sounds new and flashy has a chance to be considered and taken up. Consequently, provinces are far from being able to land a trifecta of ideas, institutions, and interests if an appetite to assess the appropriate mix of measures is missing. One effect of this is that, at times, the wrong models and mechanism to match geography, capacity, or culture are selected – the successful agro-sciences cluster model in Saskatoon seems, on the face of it, to be a good idea that might have greater application, but does that imply that the agricultural research stations linked to the University of Guelph in southwest Ontario should be resurrected? Or does the Saskatchewan experience provide insights about how Nova Scotia might calibrate agricultural research in Truro? Good ideas need to be adapted to local conditions, but that requires better understanding of the preconditions for success and the local pathways to impact.

Forward Thinking

We introduced the metaphor of landing a trifecta to provide an idealized vision of how the alignment of ideas, institutions, and interests could generate better science, technology, and innovation policy in the provinces and territories, and how this in turn could generate better socio-economic outcomes for Canada. This is not simply a call for the Confederation to be better coordinated across the country, since the autonomy of provinces and territories is protected by the Constitution, and the regional identities and differences that define Canada's culture and identity transcend individual provinces and territories. Undoubtedly, the federal government works to bring greater unity to the country with its policies, but that works better when the initiatives are more squarely under federal jurisdiction (such as refugee settlement in immigration policy) than in areas of mixed responsibility (such as climate change mitigation). Given these realities, it would be better if each province and territory sought its own trifecta to help create the environment of low transaction costs and high returns on investment we envision. So, how should they begin to go down this path?

We can start with some thoughts about the ideas that dominate and their sources. Perhaps because of Canada's proximity to and relationship with the United States, there is a strong bias towards technological innovation. This focus is reflected in investments such as the Innovation Supercluster Initiative at the federal level and at the provincial level the standard model, with post-secondary institutions as local drivers of innovation through investments in upstream research and as downstream partners with the private sector. The evidence that a science-and-technology-focused research funding strategy will generate innovation in a predictable fashion is, however, slim to none (Usher 2020). Even if there were good evidence for this approach, a different dynamic is lost when research funding is deemed necessary to generate science and technology precursors to innovation.

This dynamic has a strong technological and urban focus. Regarding the former, much of Canada's economy continues to be resource based. Many of the contributions of innovation to economic growth in the recent past have occurred because of investments in becoming better resource extractors, whether in agriculture, mining, forestry, or fisheries. Although science and technology are undoubtedly drivers, the uptake and use of innovations by Canada's resources industries have generated most of the returns. Moreover, few of these innovations have been generated solely in urban contexts, and none is uniquely or even mostly applied in cities. Many were not created in Canada, but just put to good use here. A complicating factor is that many federal programs and initiatives with a technology focus are primarily designed to advance sectors in the major cities: Vancouver, Toronto, Ottawa, and Montreal. When provinces and territories respond to programs and initiatives likewise focused on major municipalities, support for innovation in resources sectors in rural areas attracts less attention.

If the ideas that dominate thinking about science, technology, and innovation policy are technology focused and target specific sectors, there is a risk that supply-side thinking will create blind spots about which global markets are shrinking, expanding, or changing. An alternative approach would be to reposition from "what can we sell" to "what the world is buying." Canada's approach of producing what it can sell arguably has generated locked-in, path-dependent thinking about innovation strategy. We see this in Ontario's commitment, which became Canada's commitment, to being a branch-plant manufacturer for US and Japanese vehicles, with little or no domestic leadership to accelerate greenfield opportunities in electric and hybrid vehicles. Much in the same vein, hardly an eyebrow was raised at the apparent contradiction in terms when Bombardier divested its railway holdings while discussions about the fabled highspeed link between Toronto and Montreal continued.

A different issue arises when we consider the strong focus on science and technology as the most important – or only – drivers of innovation. In the case of the territories, the ideas, institutions, and interests that motivate science-and-technology-focused innovation policy are ill-suited to regional needs. The ideas that drive innovation in the provinces and allow for federal-provincial collaboration have little relevance for the immediate needs of the North. Again, this might be a function of urban-rural dynamics and the large metropolitan provenance of the most-prized innovative activity in digital technologies such as quantum computing, digital twinning, and artificial intelligence, but it does isolate 98 per cent of Canada's geography and more than 40 per cent of its people. As a result, not only does social innovation's actual and potential contribution become downplayed, but all of the social capital that lies outside high-technology sectors has low visibility and is only loosely engaged in mainstream discussions about innovation. The contribution of the voluntary, cultural, and creative sectors, for example, have measurable impact on processes, organizations, and markets, but does not receive much attention compared to technology products and services. Social, or socio-technological, innovation might figure more prominently in innovation policy were it more widely known that the non-profit sector generated $169.2 billion in 2017, representing 8.5 per cent of Canada's gross domestic product (Statistics Canada 2019).

Each of the provincial and territorial chapters alludes to the fact that the institutional layer that would support innovation policy tends to be fairly thin, perhaps with the exception of Quebec, where there has been a concerted effort to replicate and align provincial and federal institutions. Our authors note that support for innovation policy is relatively new, often offered as a post facto account of success, and is not systematically part of the policy agenda. It should come as no surprise, therefore, that measurement and evaluation of provincial and territorial efforts is difficult, if not impossible. Even factors thought to be critical in the dominant innovation narrative are poorly measured – for example, the size, utilization rate, and economic contribution of university-generated intellectual property are poorly understood. It is worth pointing out, further, that universities, touted as a significant wellspring of ideas that lead to commercialization, are not evaluated provincially or federally in a way that would account for their net economic contribution. Universities Canada (n.d.) estimates that approximately $13 billion is required to sustain the research functions in Canada's universities, but among the best-documented indicators is that they generate less than

$75 million annually in commercial technology transfer activity (AUTM 2016). Unlike the European Union, which has a system of regional innovation scorecards, however imperfect they might be, Canada and its provinces and territories have a very weak evidence base for assessing options, setting directions, measuring impact, and evaluating programs and initiatives.

With respect to interests, the evidence arising from the provinces and territories is that, when good ideas and institutional supports align and there is an interest in pushing an agenda forward, good results can be achieved. This is true, for example, in the way Atlantic Canada, with the support of ACOA, has made use of the Atlantic Opportunity and Atlantic Innovation Funds; as well, sector development, aligned with effecting clustering, has had good, if transient, effects in high-tech sectors in both Ottawa and Waterloo. The lesson is that, although it is an attractive option to focus on specific technologies and charismatic entrepreneurs with high-growth but small-tech start-ups, the enduring impact on the Canadian economy arises from incremental innovation in sectors that are not trendy or urban (or urbane) but that most often contribute to more basic drivers of economic activity: agriculture, forestry, fisheries, and mining. The potential for incentives to stimulate innovation in these sectors, especially with respect to climate change mitigation and adaptation, is enormous. Yet the interests that prevail in policy discussions about science, technology, and innovation policy skew the conversation away from these possibilities.

Final Thoughts

This study of the state of subnational innovation policy in Canada has used the framework of ideas, institutions, and interests to describe provincial and territorial innovation architecture and to evaluate the state of the policy effort. In this final chapter, we have posited the ideal state of a trifecta that would lead to better policy coordination for science, technology, and innovation. We recognize that, for Canada, any account of innovation policy will be difficult to reconcile with the actual macro-complexity: a colonial history, persistence of a symbolic monarch in a parliamentary democracy, a slowly emerging Confederation, vast geography, cultural diversity, and an economy deeply integrated with that of the United States. We also appreciate that innovation systems are incredibly intricate and that strong causal relationships are hard to generalize, so the microcomplexity of all the interactions that aggregate into an innovation system is impossible to capture in a single account. With nearly 100 universities, a workforce of nearly 20 million (Statistics Canada 2020), interactions of four orders of government, and more than 1.1 million firms, the permutations and combinations of activity are virtually infinite.

Each of the provincial and territorial chapters was written by individuals or small teams working in those regions with our framework in mind. In this concluding chapter, we have used the framework to round up some of the consistent themes and discontinuities that appear in the accounts of innovation policy in each province or territory. A few themes, however, are not captured in our framework or in the provincial and territorial chapters, and deserve further comment, as they are important to mention for future scholarship. This is especially the case because we think that science, technology, and innovation policy in Canada, both federal and in the provinces and territories, faces some difficult challenges in the coming years. Historical legacies (Canada's continuing dependence on commodity trade), institutional gaps (the lack of robust "innovation intermediaries"), domestic challenges (First Nations, rural and northern development) and global disruption (post–COVID-19 recovery, the zero-carbon future, and the rise of China and other developing regions) are talked about in the provinces and territories, but have yet to spur new innovation goals or strategies.

These challenges focus attention on the relationship between innovation policy and the broader economic policy environment for each province or territory, and where they stand in the context of Canadian economic policy. Canada was founded on territorial expansionist ambitions, strongly motivated by access and control of natural resources. To this day, much of the Canadian economy is based on extractive and primary industries: oil and gas, mining, agriculture, forestry, and fisheries. While the federal government is preoccupied with innovation as a country-versus-country competition on the global stage, the survey of subnational science, technology, and innovation policy in this book suggests that much of the regional policy effort is directed at lowering exposure to volatility in commodity-based economies. This involves making higher-value products and services out of our commodities and diversifying local economies. The challenge is that, in many provinces, the "staples trap" has made it difficult to find the right mix of old and new economic sectors. Some of these sectors have led to greater volumes of exports without improving Canadian competitiveness, suggesting that Canada might have a chronic problem of immiserizing growth (Bhagwati 1958).

Local economies structured around highly cyclical commodity production face the so-called Dutch disease, where, in periods of high commodity prices, all the effort revolves around exploiting valuable commodity opportunities, so that all other sectors have difficulty competing for resources (Beine, Bos, and Coulombe 2012). Overexploitation of the commodity sector leads to excess capacity locally and globally, which then creates commodity price collapses. While commodity-based firms release resources in this period, there is often no locally available capital to use effectively in new sectors, so highly skilled workers and footloose firms simply migrate to where they can get better wages or returns. Among the provinces, Alberta, Saskatchewan, and Newfoundland and Labrador are most affected by this problem, but the rest of Canada is also affected as the exchange rate follows the commodity cycle, so that everyone shares in the pleasure and pain of Canada's commodity dependence. Federal, provincial, and territorial policies need to come to grips with this enduring threat to the country's economic future. They might begin with a concentrated analysis of the impact on innovation by examining how the Dutch disease torques R&D opportunities and creates a difficult climate for investors.

Since the mid-1960s, the foil for primary industries has been the knowledge economy, where knowledge work contrasts with manual labour (Drucker 1969). While all economic activity depends on some knowledge base, the knowledge economy concept is motivated by the recognition that intangible assets (knowledge, intellectual property) can be more valuable than tangible assets (raw materials, value-added commodities, infrastructure, real property). Across Canada, diversification into knowledge-based activity has involved expanding higher-value services to resource sectors, professional and technical services, telecommunications and other digital technologies, and, most recently, financial technology or "fintech." Most provinces have recognized the need to find avenues into these parts of the knowledge economy, but few have directed post-secondary institutions to drive the skills agenda forward. Instead, the private sector has the perception that post-secondary institutions are not in tune with labour market needs, while post-secondary institutions are generally sceptical about the transitory nature of some knowledge economy labour needs. This complicates any federal effort to orchestrate a national strategy with provinces and territories as partners.

Most provinces have had success in developing some new aspect of the overall innovation architecture – technology parks and innovation incubators and accelerators are favourite investments. Technology parks have developed in a variety of ways, sometimes via co-location of facilities with federal and provincial labs and other times on or adjacent to university campuses. Some technology parks are, from the university's standpoint, merely a real estate investment, but most are meaningfully connected to R&D that the university wishes to advance. Many technology parks are consequences of adopting clustering strategies in response to federal incentives and funding requirements to realize better commercialization outcomes. The more recent variants of the technology park – incubators and accelerators – are truly built for the knowledge economy. These are arising in a range of ways, including in response to federal programs such as the National Research Council's Canadian Accelerators and Incubators Program, which distributed $86 million to sixteen entities over the 2013–18 period (Robbins and Crelinsten 2018). Others are the result of universities and municipalities working together to develop talent pools, support commercialization pipelines, and create venues to attract investors. At the top end of the technology-transfer pipeline are campus-based incubators that focus on ideation and pitch-it mentoring to generate commercially viable businesses to attract early, often angel, investors. Still other incubators and accelerators offer a broad array of programs and supports for later-stage developments.

In addition to technology parks, incubators, and accelerators, innovation and entrepreneurship programs are offered by universities, colleges, and technical institutes across Canada. Of particular notice are those programs that are specifically targeted towards First Nations. The Truth and Reconciliation Commission's recommendations for post-secondary institutions to do more for Indigenous peoples have generated responses ranging from ecological restoration work to language revitalization. They have also fostered an interest in Indigenous innovation and entrepreneurship to address economic disparities, mobilize potentially valuable innovations generated by and for marginalized people, and encourage innovation and entrepreneurship that will contribute to the self-determination that is essential to Indigenous nationhood. Inspired by the Commission's recommendations, there are now many centres and programs for Indigenous innovation and entrepreneurship across Canada; in the next few years, an account of subnational innovation policy in Canada will surely have more to report on the contributions of these programs to the innovation landscape nationwide. Significant change in the socio-economic standing of First Nations, Métis, and Inuit is likely as they establish how they wish to realize rights of self-determination, coupled with restorative justice, and provide new opportunities to shape their communities.

Another gap that deserves further consideration in future scholarship is "impact": the other book end of our focus on the "policy effort." To the extent that provinces and territories develop and implement innovation policies, it is important to know how well they have performed.

Because so few provinces have overt innovation policies, and most have introduced measures only recently, the little evaluation there is has not itself been programmatic. Instead, many provinces use fairly basic measures as evidence of innovation – for example, many efforts to create clusters or improve technology transfer have used metrics such as numbers of patents filed or firms created as evidence of innovation. Evidence that is harder to access, such as patent use or gross returns for new businesses, is not generally reported. At an admittedly high level, the federal government has undertaken more evaluation associated with the Innovation and Skills Plan (Canada 2020), but this is at least partly to promote current programs and initiatives. As provinces and territories become more systematic about innovation policies and programming, evaluations should follow. If not undertaken by government itself, management consultancies, independent research institutes, and academics likely will do the research.

By any objective measure, Canada has some obvious institutional gaps that impair the national ability to deliver sustainable, inclusive growth that allows for the greatest possible participation of all Canadians. The gaps cannot be filled by federal action alone. The provinces and territories, First Nations, and all the other local resources need to be engaged. In the first instance, there is a need to raise Canada's research and development effort. This requires both more resources and better institutions. Some actors, such as provincial and territorial governments, many industries, business consultancies, and the not-for-profit sector should be encouraged to invest and engage more in economic and social innovation. Those sectors where Canada leads or wants to lead the world – including agri-food, energy, mining, advanced manufacturing, and higher-order exportable services – must meet or exceed the global averages of R&D. Too often, Canadians are happy with just being in the pack. Universities are reasonably well capitalized, but continue to have difficulty moving their results into the hands of users; more effective and more strategic technology parks and technology transfer offices are undoubtedly part of the solution. While more resources are necessary, they will not be sufficient. At the moment, innovation policy is more in the limelight than is industrial or manufacturing policy, but some greater coordination is needed to make a difference in the outcome. Canada is commonly singled out among member countries of the Organisation for Economic Co-operation and Development (OECD) as offering the least direction to innovation. One compelling message from the provincial and territorial accounts in this book is that motivated and sustained efforts can, and often do, change outcomes. Ocean industries in the Atlantic region, digital industries in New Brunswick and PEI, aerospace and transportation in Quebec, agri-food in Manitoba and Saskatchewan, and the oil sands in Alberta are all examples where long-term, sustained partnerships among industry, government, and local communities generated innovation and growth. Coordinating and directing some of the expanded effort through the provinces and territories to large, strategic plays could yield higher returns than simply doing more of the same. ACOA and, to a lesser extent, Western Economic Diversification (subdivided in 2021 into Pacific and Prairies Economic Development Canada agencies) have engaged in this approach, but the next step is to expand it to all the regional agencies and to more aggressive targets, particularly if diversification and firm growth are desired.

Canada is inextricably linked globally – for example, as a large exporter and importer of goods and services, as a source of, and destination for, skilled talent, and as a leading nation globally in the OECD, the Group of Seven, at the United Nations, and in the Five Eyes intelligence alliance. Canadians cannot ignore global pressures, such as the current trading environment, which is complicated by disputes between the United States and China and the transition to a post-Brexit Europe; to deal with the latter, Canada will need to make a trade agreement with the United Kingdom that works in parallel with the 2016 Canada-European Union Comprehensive Economic and Trade Agreement. Canada, like any other nation, must also fend off predatory trade measures in many of its major markets, which will require remaining competitive to sustain its market positions. Disruptions raise fears of conflict, which will require rebuilding the country's defence capabilities despite a long history of procurement challenges, a virtually non-existent domestic defence industry, and general unease about Canada's role in armed conflict that does not square with lingering self-conceptions of a 1950s-era, peace-keeping, blue-helmeted force. Threat identification and hazard mitigation domestically can give rise to R&D and innovations that are dual-use for civilian security and protection and defence applications, supported by the Department of National Defence's Innovation for Defence Excellence and Security program. This program creates some intriguing opportunities to build internationally competitive niche applications through a judicious application of subsidy and procurement.

An arguably unavoidable source of innovation policy in Canada, now and for the foreseeable future, will be in response to climate change. Canada is a signatory to the 2015 Paris Agreement within the United Nations Framework Convention on Climate Change, which commits the federal government to find climate change mitigation strategies that will help, in proportion with its greenhouse gas emissions, to keep the average global temperature to less than 2°C above pre-industrial levels.

Realizing that a carbon-neutral global economy entails bold action, while it has one of the world's most carbon-intensive economies, means that the Canadian economy will require relatively greater adjustment to comply with emerging global norms. During the first Justin Trudeau government, the Pan-Canadian Framework on Clean Growth and Climate Change (Canada 2016) was released, offering a central (and contested) conception of a Liberal government that was pursuing mutually supporting economic growth and climate measures. Following the themes we have been describing, there is already selective uptake of aspects of federal climate change policy – even the energy-rich and politically conservative provinces that have resisted the imposition of carbon taxes embrace technology and job-creation schemes for climate change mitigation and adaptation. Despite a tremendous R&D effort and the introduction of innovative products and services to markets, however, we anticipate that the provincial and territorial responses to federal policies and initiatives will not produce a single voice for Canada on the international stage. In contrast, countries such as Denmark and New Zealand have made clear proclamations about their divestment and reinvestment strategies. It is unclear if Canada's relatively decentralized capacity and effort will impair its ability to meet the Paris Agreement targets, generate large transaction costs, or, perhaps somewhat counterintuitively, lead to a host of experiments that will identify more efficient and effective pathways to a low-carbon economy.

Our original schedule for completing this book was in the first quarter of 2020. As that hopeful target was slipping by, one of us was on sabbatical in Sydney and the other travelling for a double bill of conferences in Melbourne, and we planned to meet and finish off the manuscript – in March that year. On 11 March, the World Health Organization declared the COVID-19 pandemic, leading to a quickly cancelled itinerary and a retreat from the Antipodes. Like much of the rest of the disrupted world, we carried on virtually with our colleagues to finish the manuscript. As we now complete this work, we have been reflecting on the implications of COVID-19 for science, technology, and innovation policy. We did not, however, want to revisit the manuscript with an appliqué of COVID-related themes on all of the chapters. This would have constituted an afterthought to the original purposes of the book, and there was no anticipating where we would land along the continuum between doing violence to original authorial intention and making the work "contemporary." Besides, as we finish our work in late 2021, death tolls continue to mount, COVID vaccinations are slowing in OECD countries and lagging in the rest of the world, and the medium- and long-term socioeconomic consequences of the pandemic are mostly guesswork.

For what it is worth, here is our prediction, and we hope that we are only half-right. The part we hope will materialize is that COVID provides a systemwide impetus to be more coordinated in Canada and globally. The global response to COVID has included many Canadian contributions, providing indisputable evidence that it is possible to create, share, and deploy knowledge and technology to control the pandemic. In May 2020, *Science* reported that 23,000 COVID-19–focused papers had been published since January, doubling every twenty days (Brainard 2020). Naturally, this raises questions about effective quality control of fast-tracked research, access conditions, and management of enormous and growing repositories of knowledge (Crow and Tananbaum 2020). Canada has been an active contributor to national and international efforts, including the Office of the Chief Science Advisor's CanCOVID initiative to share research findings and data across Canada, Genome Canada's CanCOGeN sequencing network and significant contributions to the global Research Data Alliance's *COVID-19 Recommendations and Guidelines for Data Sharing* (Walker 2020). In Canada, as elsewhere around the world, there has been a tremendous effort on the part of researchers, the private sector, health care workers, and others to learn about, adapt to, and address the pandemic with tremendous vigour. In one respect, the response shows what is possible when a serious threat compels the alignment of ideas, institutions, and interests. It will take years to sort out what worked and why, and how to generate and perpetuate this kind of focus and effort where and when it is needed.

We hope Canada becomes imprinted with this level of focus and effort, because there is much at stake. COVID-19 has illustrated Canada's vulnerabilities and lack of resilience, as it has in other countries, revealing persistent obstacles in the innovation system that are now expressed and felt more acutely. For example, there has been discussion about the role of intellectual property protection in innovation that cuts both ways (de Beer and Gold 2020). Some see this as a chance to reset Canada's priorities to fit in the future world, and science, technology, and innovation policy as determining how effectively we manage this process. The rallying cry is to "build back better." While there is some merit in using the COVID-19 interregnum to trigger a rethink of priorities, we need to do this thoughtfully.

Around the world, the digital revolution has transformed sectors and created new ones. Canada is not currently home to any of the major disrupting enterprises, and there is evidence that, for twenty-five years, Canada has lagged behind other countries' efforts to adapt and adopt some of this digitization. The Public Policy Forum's *A Challenge-Driven*

Industrial Strategy for Canada (Asselin, Speer, and Mendes 2020) raises concerns that Canada has not attended to its "intangibles" economy – that is, one based on digital technology, digital services, progressive approaches to intellectual property, and data regimes – and needs to focus on the entire innovation continuum, leverage its strength in human resources, and implement a multifaceted R&D and commercialization strategy. Digitization has been described as an "absolute imperative" by former Bank of Canada governor David Dodge (2020), and digital infrastructure investments have been recommended by the Royal Society of Canada (McCabe et al 2020) as part of the post-pandemic recovery strategy. In the same vein, the federal Industry Strategy Council's report, *Restart, Recover, and Reimagine Prosperity for All Canadians*, stresses the need for a "digital and data-driven economy" through "purposeful R&D and connectivity investments" in order to create local digital companies, transform existing sectors, and prepare talent for the future (ISC 2020). If the pandemic were to provide the impetus to tackle this chronic and acute challenge, some enduring good could come of it for Canada.

What we hope will not materialize is the loss of the sense of urgency, direction, and purposefulness characteristic of recovery strategies and planning as COVID-19 eventually disappears from bodies and minds. There is some evidence that humans are programmed as individuals to forget and move on from hardship (Crosby 2003), but given the ubiquity of the global digital record of the pandemic, it is doubtful that our era will recreate the collective amnesia about the Spanish flu and the ushering in of the Roaring Twenties. Our concern, rather, is that, whether COVID-19 is vanquished or becomes endemic, the post-pandemic future could look very much like the past if Canada fails to seize the opportunity to "build back better." Given the three-decade historical record of inconsistent alignment of ideas, institutions, and interests, none of our provinces or territories seems individually well positioned to land innovation trifectas at the best of times. The track record for collective success orchestrated between the federal government and the provinces and territories is generally unimpressive. Although there is evidence about how much can be achieved when ideas, institutions, and interests are aligned and governments at different levels work to common goals, such outcomes are far from the norm. Our concern is that, while post-pandemic recovery plans might generate an appetite to achieve better coordination, the initiatives might turn out to be fleeting.

This book provides a cautionary tale about the potential consequences of misalignments in science, technology, and innovation policy, revealed through the analysis of federal, provincial, and territorial approaches to ideas, institutions, and interests relating to such policy. One could think of this book's central contribution to the literature as a *diagnostique* of the policy challenges. It is not intended as a prospective framework for assembling compelling responses to many of the grand challenges facing Canada, as a nation or globally, in which Canadian research and ingenuity could contribute significantly. What we have learned is that innovation policy misalignments frequently generate idiosyncratic policy development in different jurisdictions, which tends to produce localized outcomes. At other times, divergent approaches to innovation have led to policy incoherence and gaps that generate nearly systemwide stasis.

Perhaps the most troubling of these misalignments is Canada's approach to energy and climate. On the one hand, we have developed nuclear, hydro-electric, and fossil technologies that lead to technology and resource exports. At the same time, east-west energy corridors struggle on the policy agenda, and regional electrical grid integration is far from a priority. In this respect, science and technology investments have created energy sector innovation, but the policy environment is stranding assets and stifling further innovation in that sector. On the other hand, Canada has yet to engage fully with the science, technology, and innovation effort that will be required to meet its Paris Agreement targets, let alone Canada's loftier ambition about becoming a net-zero economy. The efforts required to mitigate and adapt to climate change are unlikely to leave any part of the economy untouched. The level of effort needed to discover and apply innovative solutions is daunting. As a consequence, Canada finds itself in the paradoxical situation of being a hampered energy producer/exporter while struggling to raise the capital to pay for the science, technology, and innovation that will enable the transition to new energy sources and the decarbonization of the economy.

References

Asselin, R., S. Speer, and R. Mendes. 2020. *New North Star II: A Challenge-Driven Industrial Strategy for the Age of Intangibles.* Ottawa: Public Policy Forum. Online at https://ppforum.ca/publications/new-north-star-ii/.
AUTM. 2016. "Canadian Licensing Activity Survey, FY 2016." Online at https://autm.net/AUTM/media/SurveyReportsPDF/FY16_Canadian_Licensing_Survey_no_Appendix_New_Logo.pdf.

Beine, M., C. Bos, and S. Coulombe. 2012. "Does the Canadian Economy Suffer from Dutch Disease?" *Resource and Energy Economics* 34 (4): 468–92. https://doi.org/10.1016/j.reseneeco.2012.05.002.

Bell, D. 1976. *The Coming of Post-Industrial Society: A Venture in Social Forecasting.* New York: Basic Books.

Bhagwati, J. 1958. "Immiserizing Growth: A Geometrical Note." *Review of Economic Studies* 25 (3): 201–5. https://doi.org/10.2307/2295990.

Brainard, J. 2020. "Scientists are drowning in COVID-19 papers. Can new tools keep them afloat?" *Science*, 13 May. Online at https://www.science.org/news/2020/05/scientists-are-drowning-covid-19-papers-can-new-tools-keep-them-afloat.

Canada. 2014. *Seizing Canada's Moment: Moving Forward in Science, Technology and Innovation 2014.* Ottawa: Industry Canada. Online at https://www.ic.gc.ca/eic/site/113.nsf/vwapj/Seizing_Moment_ST_I-Report-2014-eng.pdf/$file/Seizing_Moment_ST_I-Report-2014-eng.pdf.

Canada. 2016. *Pan Canadian Framework on Clean Growth and Climate Change.* Ottawa. Online at http://publications.gc.ca/collections/collection_2017/eccc/En4-294-2016-eng.pdf.

Canada. 2019. "Inventory of Federal Business Innovation and Clean Technology Programs." Ottawa: Treasury Board Secretariat. Online at https://www.canada.ca/en/treasury-board-secretariat/corporate/reports/inventory-federal-business-innovation-clean-technology-programs.html#toc1.

Canada. 2020. *Tracking Progress and Results: The Innovation and Skills Plan.* Ottawa: Innovation, Science and Economic Development. Online at https://www.ic.gc.ca/eic/site/062.nsf/eng/h_00083.html.

CCA (Council of Canadian Academies). 2018. *Competing in a Global Innovation Economy: The Current State of R&D in Canada.* Ottawa: Council of Canadian Academies.

Crosby, A.W. 2003. *America's Forgotten Pandemic: The Influenza of 1918.* Cambridge: Cambridge University Press.

Crow, M., and G. Tananbaum. 2020. "We Must Tear Down the Barriers That Impede Scientific Progress." *Scientific American*, 18 December. Online at https://www.scientificamerican.com/article/we-must-tear-down-the-barriers-that-impede-scientific-progress/.

De Beer, J., and R. Gold. 2020. "International Trade, Intellectual Property, and Innovation Policy: Long-Term Lessons from the COVID-19 Crisis." In *Vulnerable: The Policy, Law and Ethics of COVID-19*, ed. C.M. Flood, V. MacDonnell, J. Philpott, S. Thériault, and S. Venkapuram, 579–90. Ottawa: University of Ottawa Press.

Dodge, D. 2020. *Two Mountains to Climb: Canada's Twin Deficits and How to Scale Them.* Ottawa: Public Policy Forum. Online at https://ppforum.ca/publications/two-mountains-to-climb-canadas-twin-deficits-and-how-to-scale-them/.

Doern, B., P.W.B. Phillips, and D. Castle. 2016. *Canadian Science, Technology, and Innovation Policy: The Innovation Economy and Society Nexus.* Montreal; Kingston, ON: McGill-Queen's University Press.

Drucker, P. 1969. *The Age of Discontinuity: Guidelines to Our Changing Society.* New York: Harper and Row.

Etzkowitz, H. 2008. *The Triple Helix: University-Industry-Government Innovation in Action.* Milton Park, UK: Routledge.

Gluckman, P. 2014. "Policy: The Art of Science Advice to Government." *Nature News* 507: 7491.

Gluckman, P. 2016. "The Science–Policy Interface." *Science* 353: 6303.

ISC (Industry Strategy Council). 2020. *Restart, Recover, and Reimagine Prosperity for All Canadians.* Online at https://www.ic.gc.ca/eic/site/062.nsf/eng/00118.html.

Mastroeni, M., and A. Rosiello. 2013. "Pursuing a Biotechnology System of Innovation in Lithuania: A Conceptual Framework for Effective Policy Intervention." *Technology Analysis & Strategic Management* 2 (7): 817–33. http://doi.org/10.1080/09537325.2013.815711.

McCabe, C., R. Boadway, F. Lange, E.R. Gold, C. Cotton, W. Adamowicz, D. Breznitz, et al. 2020. *Renewing the Social Contract: Economic Recovery in Canada from COVID-19.* Ottawa: Royal Society of Canada. Online at https://rsc-src.ca/sites/default/files/Econ%20PB_EN_3.pdf.

NAPHRO (National Alliance of Provincial Health Research Organizations). 2020. "Who We Are." Online at https://www.naphro.ca/about.

OECD (Organisation for Economic Co-operation and Development). 2004. "New Economy Definition." *OECD Glossary of Statistical Terms.* 26 August. Online at https://stats.oecd.org/glossary/detail.asp?ID=6267.

Porter, M.E. 1990. *The Competitive Advantage of Nations.* New York: Free Press.

Robbins, M., and J. Crelinsten. 2018. "Accelerating Growth: Canadian Funding Policy for Innovation Intermediaries." Online at https://munkschool.utoronto.ca/ipl/files/2018/08/Accelerating-Growth_-Canadian-Funding-Policy-for-Innovation-Intermediaries-AU2018.pdf.

Romer, P. 1990. "Endogenous Technological Change." *Journal of Political Economy* 98 (5 (2): S71–S102. http://doi.org/10.1086/261725.

Rosiello, R., M. Mastroeni, D. Castle, and P.W.B. Phillips. 2015. "Clusters, Technological Districts and Smart Specialisation: An Empirical Analysis of Policy Implementation Challenges." *International Journal of Entrepreneurship and Innovation Management* 19 (5-6): 304–26. http://dx.doi.org/10.1504/IJEIM.2015.073220.

Schilling, M.A. 2017. "What's your best innovation bet?" *Harvard Business Review,* July-August. Online at https://hbr.org/2017/07/whats-your-best-innovation-bet.

Statistics Canada. 2019. *Non-profit institutions and volunteering: Economic contribution, 2007 to 2017.* Ottawa. Online at https://www150.statcan .gc.ca/n1/daily-quotidien/190305/dq190305a-eng.htm.

Statistics Canada. 2020. "Labour force characteristics by province, monthly, seasonally adjusted." Ottawa. Online at https://www150.statcan.gc.ca/t1 /tbl1/en/tv.action?pid=1410028703.

Universities Canada. n.d. "Facts and Figures." Online at https://www .univcan.ca/universities/facts-and-stats/.

Usher, A. 2020. *When Science Outruns Business.* Higher Education Strategy Associates, 8 December. Online at https://higheredstrategy.com/when -science-outruns-business/.

Walker, B. 2020. "Recommendations and Guidelines for Data Sharing." Research Data Alliance. Online at https://www.rd-alliance.org/group /rda-covid19-rda-covid19-omics-rda-covid-19-epidemiology-rda-covid19 -clinical-rda-covid19-0.

World Bank. 2020. "World Governance Indicators." Washington, DC. Online at https://info.worldbank.org/governance/wgi/Home/Reports.

Contributors

Anne Ballantyne, Corporate Strategy Advisor with the Sylvia Fedoruk Canadian Centre for Nuclear Innovation at the University of Saskatchewan, was previously director of the Technology Cluster Secretariat with the National Research Council of Canada, Strategic Projects Manager with the Industrial Research Assistance Program, managed a consulting company, and was a science policy advisor with the government of Saskatchewan. Anne contributed to the development of the Canadian Light Source Synchrotron and a number of other major infrastructure and development projects in Manitoba and Saskatchewan.

Derek Brewin, Professor and Head of Agribusiness and Agricultural Economics at the University of Manitoba, undertakes research on grain and oilseed markets as well as innovation in food processing and plant breeding. Derek is a past president of the Canadian Agricultural Economics Society, served as a senator at the University of Manitoba, and prior to his academic career worked with the Canadian Wheat Board, Agriculture and Agri-Food Canada, and Farm Credit Canada.

Ken Carter, Director, Grenfell Office of Engagement, Memorial University of Newfoundland, previously worked for fifteen years with the government of Newfoundland and Labrador in rural social and economic development and rural policy, as director of research and analysis with the Office of Public Engagement. Ken works with territorial innovation models and their application to rural areas of Newfoundland and Labrador.

David Castle is Professor in the School of Public Administration and Gustavson School of Business, and former vice-president research, University of Victoria. Previously he held the Chair of Innovation in the Life Sciences, was director of Innogen Institute at the University of Edinburgh, and Canada Research Chair in Science and Society at the University of Ottawa. He has published on the social dimensions of science, technology, and innovation, holds major research awards, and has considerable experience leading strategic research initiatives and research project management.

Ken Coates is Canada Research Chair in Regional Innovation at the Johnson Shoyama Graduate School of Public Policy at the University of Saskatchewan. Ken was previously dean of Arts, University of Waterloo. Ken was raised in Yukon, and his research focuses on scientific and technological innovation in northern and remote regions. He has worked extensively on innovation in Japan and the global digital economy.

David Foord is Assistant Professor of Management at the University of New Brunswick. He conducts research in science and technology studies, the history of science and technology, and management of technology and innovation. He is the author of works on the history of powered prosthetics, energy innovation, and science, technology, and innovation policy. He has over twenty-five years of professional experience in technology and innovation management.

Yves Gingras is scientific director of the Observatoire des sciences et des technologies, professor in the Department of History, and member of the Centre interuniversitaire de recherche sur la science et la technologie (CIRST) at the Université du Québec à Montréal (UQAM). He previously held a Canada Research Chair in History and Sociology of Science at UQAM, and was for a time director of CIRST.

Rob Greenwood is Associate Vice President (public engagement and external relations) at Memorial University of Newfoundland, and Director of the Leslie Harris Centre of Regional Policy and Development. He has operated his own consulting business and served as a director and assistant deputy minister of policy in economic development departments in Newfoundland and Labrador and in Saskatchewan. He was vice president, corporate development, at the Information Services Corporation of Saskatchewan, and founding director of the Sustainable Communities Initiative, a partnership of the University of Regina, the City of Regina, and the National Research Council of Canada.

Heather M. Hall is Assistant Professor and Director of the Economic Development and Innovation program at the University of Waterloo. Prior to joining Waterloo, she worked at the University of Saskatchewan and Memorial University of Newfoundland. She is a leading scholar on innovation and economic development in rural and northern regions in Canada. Her research focuses on the impacts of new technologies in the mining sector, the community impacts of large-scale resource development projects, and innovation and economic development policy, planning, and practice.

Richard Hawkins is Professor in the Department of Communication, Media and Film at the University of Calgary. Previously he held a Canada Research Chair in the Social Context of Technology, was senior scientist at the Netherlands Organization for Applied Scientific Research, and senior fellow in the Science Policy Research Unit at the University of Sussex. He has consulted widely in Canada and abroad on science, technology, and innovation policy.

Richard Isnor is Associate Vice President, Research and Graduate Studies at St. Francis Xavier University. He is a director and past chair of the Offshore Energy Research Association, as well as a board member of the Atlantic Computational Excellence Network and Springboard Atlantic. Prior to joining St. Francis Xavier in 2015, he held positions with the Natural Sciences and Engineering Research Council, the International Development Research Centre, the National Research Council, Environment Canada, Natural Resources Canada, the Privy Council Office, and Nunavut Research Institute.

Peter Josty is Executive Director of THECIS, a not-for-profit research company that specializes in innovation research. Earlier, Peter had a diversified career in the chemical industry in Canada, holding positions as research chemist, market development specialist, technical manager, new products application manager, business development manager, and head of strategy and planning. In these roles, he was a practitioner of innovation, and led numerous new product introductions to North American markets.

Gregory S. Kealey, CM, FRSC, is Professor Emeritus of History at the University of New Brunswick, and served as vice president research there from 2001 to 2012 and provost from 2008 to 2012. He is the founding editor of the journal *Labour/Le Travail* and author of *Spying* *on Canadians* (2017) and *Secret Service: Political Policing in Canada from the Fenians to Fortress America* (2012), with Reg Whitaker and Andrew Parnaby.

Mark Leggott is Executive Director, Research Data Canada and Director of CANARIE's RDM Funding Program. He was formerly the university librarian at the University of Prince Edward Island and president/ CEO of discoverygarden Inc. He was also university librarian, associate dean of education, and a founding director of the Global College at the University of Winnipeg. Mark is the founder of the Islandora project, an open-source digital asset management system, and is a proponent of open science and data.

H. Wade MacLauchlan is President Emeritus of the University of Prince Edward Island (UPEI), and served as thirty-second premier of PEI, president of UPEI, and dean of law at the University of New Brunswick. With a scholarly focus on public and administrative law and active interest in innovation and economic and regional development, he has been a board member of CANARIE, Public Policy Forum, the Atlantic Provinces Economic Council, and several public and private companies.

Michele Mastroeni is Associate Professor, Faculty of Design, OCAD University, Toronto, working on Strategic Foresight and Innovation. Michele pursues a research agenda exploring innovation systems and innovation policy. Before OCAD, he worked in the Ontario ministries of Research and Innovation and Economic Development and Growth, at the Conference Board of Canada, with RAND Europe, and universities in the United Kingdom.

John McLaughlin, President Emeritus at the University of New Brunswick, is currently Scholar in Residence at the Centre for Technology, Management and Entrepreneurship. With an academic background in engineering and institutional economics, he has worked in more than forty countries on property reform and land administration, and co-founded two companies. A former president of the Canadian Academy of Engineering and director of the Council of Canadian Academies, Dr McLaughlin has received both the Order of Canada and the Order of New Brunswick.

Sara McPhee-Knowles is an instructor at Yukon University in the School of Business and Leadership. Previously, she was the policy manager for the Government of Yukon's Department of Highways and Public Works. Born and raised in Regina, she completed her PhD at the Johnson Shoyama Graduate School of Public Policy at the University of Saskatchewan. Her research focuses on innovation in policy systems, consumer behaviour, and decision making.

Peter W.B. Phillips is Distinguished Professor of Policy and Founding Director of the Centre for the Study of Science and Innovation Policy at the University of Saskatchewan. Previously, he worked in industry and was assistant deputy minister (policy) for Saskatchewan Economic Development. He created and held a Natural Sciences and Engineering Research Council of Canada-Social Sciences and Humanities Research Council of Canada Chair in Managing Technological Change, served as chair of the board of Ag-West Bio, and was an advisor to the teams developing the Global Institute for Food Security and Protein Industries Canada.

Index

advanced manufacturing, 85, 375; in Alberta, 289; in New Brunswick, 189, 190; in Nova Scotia, 171, 177; in Prince Edward Island, 145, 148, 150, 155; in Quebec, 209

aerospace, 99; in Manitoba, 248, 254, 261, 262; 359, 360, 376; in New Brunswick, 190; in Newfoundland and Labrador, 123, 125; in Nova Scotia, 169; in Prince Edward Island, 142–5, 149–51; in Quebec, 212, 214, 216

agriculture, 34, 42, 49, 50, 83, 103, 107; in British Columbia, 310, 316, 364, 369, 371, 372; in Manitoba, 247, 248, 249, 250, 251, 253–4, 258, 262; in Newfoundland and Labrador, 119, 125; in Nova Scotia, 159, 160, 163, 171, 185–6; in Ontario, 236; in Prince Edward Island, 143–4, 151; in Quebec, 216; in Saskatchewan, 270, 272–4, 280, 281–2, 283, 284

Agriculture and Agri–Food Canada (AAFC), 89, 90, 166, 252, 257, 258, 262, 270

Ag-West Bio Inc., 274, 276

Alberta, 9, 36, 43, 44, 45–6, 47, 50, 53, 63, 64, 68, 74, 78, 80, 83, 85, 87, 96, 99, 106, 107, 118, 135, 187, 247, 248, 249, 250, 252, 258, 259, 276, 280, 308, 315, 332, 345, 358, 362, 363, 365, 366; federal involvement in, 292, 298; industry, 292–3; policy efforts, 293, 294–302; post-secondary education in, 292–3, 298,

301; provincial funding, 292, 296, 300

Alberta Informatics Circle of Research Excellence (iCORE), 296–7

Alberta Innovates, 295, 298, 299–300, 301

Alberta Machine Intelligence Institute, 298

Alberta Oil Sands Technology and Research Authority (AOSTRA), 295, 296, 365

Alberta Research and Innovation Framework, 300

Alberta Research Council, 288, 363,

Alberta Science and Research Authority (ASRA), 296

aluminum, 33; in Quebec, 216

Alward, David, 190, 197

Arctic, 125, 135, 251–2, 313, 337, 341

Arctic College, 340

Arctic Science Partnership, 252

ArcticNet Networks of Centres of Excellence, 251

artificial intelligence (AI), 215, 235, 291

Association canadienne-française pour l'avancement des sciences (Acfas), 208–9, 211

Atlantic Accord, 126, 127, 128, 132

Atlantic Canada Opportunities Agency (ACOA), 120, 122, 134, 152, 166, 167, 184, 188, 193, 194, 199, 360, 363, 366, 371, 376

Atlantic Growth Strategy, 121

Printed and bound by CPI Group (UK) Ltd, Croydon, CR0 4YY

09/06/2025

14685785-0005